THE WARS OF NAPOLEON

MODERN WARS IN PERSPECTIVE

General Editors: *B.W. Collins and H.M. Scott*

This ambitious new series offers wide-ranging studies of specific wars, and distinct phases of warfare, from the close of the Middle Ages to the present day. It aims to advance the current integration of military history into the academic mainstream. To that end, the books are not merely traditional campaign narratives, but examine the causes, course and consequences of major conflicts, in their full international political, diplomatic, social and ideological contexts.

ALREADY PUBLISHED

Mexico and the Spanish Conquest
Ross Hassig

The War of the Austrian Succession, 1740–1748
M.S. Anderson

The Wars of Napoleon
Charles J. Esdaile

The Wars of French Decolonization
Anthony Clayton

The Spanish–American War: Conflict in the Caribbean and the Pacific 1895–1902
Joseph Smith

China at War, 1901–1949
Edward L. Dreyer

THE WARS OF NAPOLEON

Charles J. Esdaile

LONGMAN
London and New York

Longman Group Limited,
Longman House, Burnt Mill,
Harlow, Essex CM20 2JE, England
and Associated Companies throughout the world

*Published in the United States of America
by Longman Publishing, New York*

First published 1995

ISBN 0 582 05954 2 CSD
ISBN 0 582 05955 0 PPR

British Library Cataloguing-in-Publication Data

A catalogue record for this book is
available from the British Library

Library of Congress Cataloging-in-Publication Data

Esdaile, Charles J.
  The Wars of Napoleon / Charles J. Esdaile.
    p. cm. -- (Modern wars in perspective)
  Includes bibliographical references and index.
  ISBN 0-582-05954-2. -- ISBN 0-582-05955-0 (pbk.)
  1. Napoleon I, Emperor of the French, 1769–1821--Military
leadership--Juvenile literature. 2. Napoleonic Wars, 1800–1815-
-Juvenile literature. I. Title. II. Series.
  DC151.E7 1995
  940.2'7--dc20   94-44377
                                                                CIP
                                                                AC

Set by 7B in 10/12 Sabon
Produced by Longman Singapore Publishers (Pte) Ltd.
Printed in Singapore

CONTENTS

LIST OF MAPS

PREFACE

So, why yet another book on the Napoleonic Wars? After all, it is hardly as if we are in unknown territory, the series of conflicts that devastated Europe between 1800 and 1815 having given birth to a bibliography that in the mid-1980s was calculated by one authority to have grown to at least 220,000 volumes. Ten more years, of course, have done nothing to reduce that total, the general public continuing to display an appetite for bygone martial glory that is all but insatiable. Therein, however, is the rub. If the bibliography of Napoleonic Europe is extensive, it is also extremely uneven. Whilst there is a plethora of material on certain of its aspects, on others there is little or nothing. Biographies and narratives – especially campaign narratives – abound and continue to pile up remorselessly, whilst broader works of analysis are relatively few and far between. Let us take, for example, the subject of Napoleon's marshals. A quick check suggests that thus far in the course of the twentieth century, these twenty-six commanders have been the subject of ten general studies of one sort or another, and at least thirty-five individual biographies. All this work – much of it highly scholarly – has revealed a great deal about the detail of Napoleon's campaigns (themselves recounted in prolix detail elsewhere), the internal workings of the French army, the relationship between the various French commanders, and, of course, the personalities of the marshals themselves, but it has told us little about such wider questions as the nature of the Napoleonic Wars or their impact on European society and, in general, tends to portray the period in terms of a narrow élite.

None of this is to suggest that there is not a place for biography or campaign history. However, fine though the quality of much of what has been produced in this area has been, even in terms of its *forte*, the English-language bibliography, at least, is highly uneven. Taking biography first of all, whilst the coverage of Napoleon and his marshals is quite relentless, studies of the statesmen and administrators who implemented imperial policy in the *grand empire* or otherwise collaborated with the French, such as Melzi, Zurlo, Gogel and Montgelas, are all but non-existent. Furthermore, if we turn to the numerous biographies of such figures as Joseph Bonaparte and Eugene de Beauharnais, we discover that they are woefully inadequate with regard to such matters as the governance and administration of the satellite states, preferring instead a less challeging diet of Venus and Mars. As for battle history, meanwhile, the campaigns of Wellington and Napoleon have been fought and refought *ad infinitum*, and yet the conflicts in the Balkans and Scandinavia remain all but unknown, whilst even well- rehearsed subjects are inclined to be viewed through an overly simplistic prism (thus the Peninsular War and the Waterloo campaign – note the name – tend to be recounted very much in terms of the doings of the Duke of Wellington).

Intermixed with this is a further problem in that the 'new' history that has arrived on the scene from the late 1950s onwards has rather tended to pass the Napoleonic era by. Thus, whilst the French Revolution has attracted the attention of myriads of political, social and economic historians who are well versed in modern methods and techniques, such scholars have been far less active in the Napoleonic period, with the result that the extraordinary torrent of material on the domestic history of the Revolution is simply not replicated with regard to that of the empire (by contrast, the military history of Napoleonic France has been 'done to death' and that of the Revolution neglected), the reason being almost certainly that the appeal of the period has been dimmed by its association with an approach that is seen as narrow and even *jejune*.

With regard to European history as a whole, the neglect of the Napoleonic era can only be regarded as most unfortunate. Thus, notwithstanding its enormous long-term significance, the French Revolution in its own era essentially remained just that – a *French* revolution. Though not without significant echoes outside France, the Revolution actually brought about only limited changes beyond her borders, its adherents remaining relatively isolated and, for the most part, few in numbers, and the various satellite republics wholly ephemeral except to the extent that they were upheld by French bayonets. At the same time, whilst certain European governments embarked on a process of military and administrative reform that was designed to meet the French challenge, generally speaking, their efforts proved as limited as they were halting and abortive. How different, however, is the picture when we come to the Napoleonic period. Not only was more of Europe physically occupied by the French armies, formed into satellite states or annexed to France, and thus subjected to wholesale reform, but political turmoil far exceeded the levels of the 1790s with dramatic changes taking place in the situation of Prussia, Spain, Sicily and Sweden, and the whole of European society being deeply affected. For all the thousands of books that have been generated by the Napoleonic era, then, there is most certainly room for one more, and it is the most earnest hope of the author that it will do something to break down the walls of the ghetto in which the Napoleonic Wars have in large part tended to repose.

ACKNOWLEDGEMENTS

There is perhaps only one moment in the whole process of writing a book that can be described as being entirely pleasant, and that is the point at which the author comes to record the encouragement, advice and guidance that have been offered him over the years. In the present case, I have indeed received much kindness. Taking first of all the editors of the series, Bruce Collins at the University of Buckingham and Andrew Maclennan at Longman have from the start provided me with much practical assistance and responded to my ideas with sympathy and understanding, whilst yet endeavouring to keep my slightly errant feet firmly upon the straight and narrow. At Longman, too, Stephanie Cooke handled matters technical with skill and common sense. Meanwhile, successive superiors at the University of Liverpool – Professors Alan Harding, Peter Hennock and Christopher Allmand – have all done what they could to further progress with the manuscript; at the same time, too, they, and, indeed, my other colleagues, have been most understanding in tolerating the vagaries induced by a frenetic writing schedule. Also of great help has been the assistance with conference attendance regularly received from the University of Liverpool and the British Academy. Nor could this work have been written without the patience and diligence displayed by the staff of the university's Sydney Jones Library, particularly in the departments of acquisitions and inter-library loans.

With regard to the manuscript itself, the comments of Andrew Maclennan and Bruce Collins have already been noted. In addition, however, I owe an immense debt of gratitude to Rory Muir and Irene Collins, who have both read every word of the successive drafts of this work, and have proved unstintingly generous in the time that they have given me and the trouble that they have taken to point me in the direction of, or even to supply me with, fresh material. Very significant portions of the manuscript, meanwhile, were also read by Jon Lawrence, John Belchem, Phillip Bell, Clive Emsley, Alan Forrest, Mike Broers and Neville Thompson, all of whom were more than happy to share their specialist knowledge with me. Also important here have been those of my students, including Claire Lindsay, Lis Butler, David Claridge, Kay Smith, Clare Williamson and Lisa Cam, who have provided me with a most useful 'worm's eye view': as with all the students who have ever grappled with 'War, nationalism and society in Europe, 1792–1815', I am sure that I have gained far more from them than they have ever gained from me. Finally, Pam Thompson made a quick and efficient job of retyping part of the original manuscript. Needless to say, colleague, friend, student and typist alike bear no responsibility for such errors as might be found within these covers.

With regard to the sources on which this book is based, considerations of space have inclined me to keep the number of footnotes to a bare minimum, though I hope that the inclusion of a substantial bibliographical essay will do something to make good the lack. In the absence of numerous footnotes, however, I should like to take this opportunity to thank the many historians of the current era who have, my remarks above notwithstanding, done so much to advance our knowledge and understanding of the Napoleonic age and whose work is the real basis for this book. In this respect a special mention is due to the many scholars who regularly attend the annual Consortium on Revolutionary Europe (and, by extension, to Donald Horward of Florida State University, whose energy and enthusiasm is the Consortium's mainstay), the numerous discussions that I have had in their company having been as valuable as they have been enjoyable.

Finally, I come to my family, without whose love this book could never have been written and to whom it is dedicated. As ever, Alison has remained most patient and tolerant with regard to the rather irregular habits of a husband and father who is all too inclined to be thinking of Napoleonic Europe when he ought to be listening to her, whilst our two children have already made me far prouder of them than this book can possibly ever make them of me. To you, especially, greetings, love and many thanks.

Charles Esdaile, Liverpool, 29 July 1994

For Alison, Andrew and Helen, in the hope that they will never know another Bonaparte.

I THE NATURE OF THE NAPOLEONIC WARS

THE WHEAT AND THE CHAFF

> The first fifteen years of the nineteenth century present the spectacle of an extraordinary movement of millions of men. Men leave their habitual pursuits; rush from one side of Europe to another; plunder, slaughter one another, triumph and despair; and the whole current of life is transformed . . . . What was the cause of that activity, or from what laws did it arise?[1]

What indeed? Were the Napoleonic Wars the fruit of the boundless ambition of a single man, or of a determination on the part of the powers of Europe to bring about his overthrow? Alternatively, were they the continuation of an ideological struggle between the French Revolution and the *ancien régime*? Yet again, were they the result of a struggle for economic supremacy between Britain and France? Contradictory as these explanations are, the first task of any survey of the Napoleonic Wars must be to address this debate.

Though each of these theories appears to have some merit, several of them may in fact be dismissed with relative ease. Let us take, for example, the claim that Napoleon was at heart a man of peace whose noble desires were constantly frustrated by the unremitting hostility of his opponents to the principles of the French Revolution. In this argument, of course, the claims of the emperor himself were crucial, his central complaint being that 'Europe never ceased warring against France, against French principles and against me'.[2] However, perpetuated though such arguments have been by a veritable *grande armée* of apologists, in reality none of this holds good.[3] If Europe was indeed plunged into an ideological war in

---

1 L. Tolstoy, *War and Peace* (BCA edition, London, 1971), p. 888.
2 P. Geyl, *Napoleon: For and Against* (London, 1965), pp. 228–30.
3 For some modern examples, cf. A. J. P. Taylor, *How Wars Begin* (London, 1979), pp. 35–7; F. Markham, *Napoleon* (London, 1963), p. 100; V. Cronin, *Napoleon* (London, 1971), p. 291.

1792–93, many states either quickly forgot their aversion to the Revolution or only entered the war when their traditional interests were threatened. Thus, Russia remained primarily concerned with the partition of Poland, only becoming involved in the fighting when France impinged on the Balkans and the Levant; Prussia kept the bulk of her troops in the east so as to maximise her gains in Poland, and eventually came to an early settlement with France in 1795; and Spain not only made peace with France in 1795, but the following year joined her in an alliance against Britain. Finally, even Britain and Austria, the two powers most committed to resisting France, were not wholly eager to restore the Bourbons and never ruled out the possibility of a compromise peace.

With France also moving away from the militant evangelism of 1792–93, there seems no reason to suppose that she could not have enjoyed a settled peace at any time. To attempt to explain the Napoleonic Wars in terms of a clash of ideologies is therefore futile, this being equally the case with the idea that they stemmed primarily from Anglo-French economic and commercial rivalry. Unlike the ideological explanation for the wars, such an argument does at least rest on plausible foundations. Napoleon's most consistent opponent, Britain was a prime mover in many of the coalitions that were formed against him; during the Revolutionary and the Napoleonic Wars, Britain expended considerable energy on occupying the colonies of France and her allies, greatly extended her Indian empire, drove all her rivals from the seas, and proved utterly ruthless in her drive for fresh markets, even going so far as effectively to foster the revolutions that broke out in Latin-American possessions of her Spanish ally in 1810. Yet here again there are problems. If Britain was France's most consistent opponent, an equally plausible explanation can be found in her desire for security in Europe, to which object she was in fact willing to make substantial colonial concessions. Meanwhile, to attribute all the conflicts of the Napoleonic period to her hostility is ridiculous. Far from being some sort of pan-European puppet master, Britain was actually widely distrusted, many countries having good reason to fear and resent her pretensions at least as much as they did those of France. With her naval strength securing both colonial expansion and commercial supremacy, her blockade wreaking havoc with the European economy, and her armies, at least until 1812, playing little discernible role in the Continental struggle, suspicions grew that Britain's war was being fought for the beggary of every other power. Such fears were naturally fanned by French propaganda, whilst matters were not improved by Britain's inability to satisfy the financial demands of her potential allies and by the inadequacy of her diplomacy, which all too often was arrogant and sanctimonious. Britain's actions, too, were utterly unscrupulous, as witness the surprise attacks she launched against Spain in 1804 and Denmark in 1807. If British enmity really had been the sole motor of the war, in short, then Britain would probably have fought alone. And, as for her colonial offensives and naval blockade, they were entirely consonant with a situation in which she had few other means of striking directly at France, offensives in the colonies in fact tending only to occur when opportunities for British intervention on the Continent were limited. In any case, not only did captured French colonies make excellent bargaining counters, but their seizure was necessary for defensive purposes given their potential as bases from which British colonies could be attacked and trade disrupted. And, if their acquisition benefited British trade, this can be argued to have been vital to the prosecution of the war.

To argue, then, that the Napoleonic Wars were primarily an economic conflict between Britain and France makes no more sense than to argue that they were an ideological conflict between France and the *ancien régime*. This is not to say that without Napoleon the first fifteen years of the nineteenth century would have been a period of profound peace. France had emerged from the revolutionary decade with her territory greatly expanded by the annexation of Belgium, the left bank of the Rhine, Savoy and Nice, with a considerable degree of influence beyond even her new borders, with an army swollen by conscription and precluded from demobilisation by an extremely parlous economic situation, and with a régime whose increasingly narrow base at home made external belligerence the keystone of its revolutionary legitimacy. Concealed within her, meanwhile, was a powerful constituency whose interests had become bound up with war, this being centred upon a clique of young and ambitious generals for whom continued conflict offered virtually unlimited personal advantage and to whom the weakness of the Directory had given unwonted influence in Paris. War, then, was always very likely, but, even so, there can be no denying the enormous impact of the politics and personality of Napoleon Bonaparte.

THE FIRST CONSUL

Born in Corsica to a family of the petty nobility on 15 August 1769, the then Nabuleone Buonaparte had first come to France as an

3

officer cadet. Poor, intense, physically unprepossessing, and fiercely Corsican, he was a classic outsider for whom struggle was a psychological necessity – hence the personal ambition, love of martial glory, political radicalism, and self-conscious Romanticism that characterise his early writings. Whether it was the neglected child born to a mother who had suffered a difficult pregnancy, the scion of a family of inveterate social climbers, the second son engaged in endless rivalry with his elder brother, Joseph, the despised outsider at Brienne, or the penniless young artillery officer teased by girls as 'Puss-in-Boots', a whole succession of Nabuleones combined to produce a Napoleon whose first instinct it was to see any and every situation as an opportunity to impose himself upon his fellows and establish his own superiority by every means available.

Such was the young man who in 1789 found himself witnessing the turmoil of the Revolution. In these events he at first took little part, but, realising the direction that events were likely to take, the young officer quickly aligned himself with the Jacobins, and, in between brief spells of service with his regiment, busied himself with fomenting radicalism in Corsica. At first he remained a Corsican patriot, but the association did not last: increasingly discontented with Republican rule, in 1793 Corsica rose in revolt, the Bonapartes being driven into exile. If there was any doubt in Napoleon's mind that his future lay with France it was now dispelled. Caught up in the so-called 'revolt of the provinces' in the Midi in 1793, he published a denunciation of the rebels and played a prominent role in the reduction of Toulon. Surviving the sucessive upheavals that followed, by 1795 he had acquired both a considerable reputation as a staff officer and a number of useful political connections, the latter being reinforced by his suppression of the Vendémiaire rising in Paris in 1795 (by means of the famous 'whiff of grapeshot'), and his subsequent marriage to Josephine de Beauharnais, the erstwhile mistress of the important politician, Paul de Barras.

At length these connections brought Napoleon the command of the Army of Italy, the result being that he suddenly soared to fame. Adopting an offensive strategy in the wake of the withdrawal of Prussia and Spain from the First Coalition in 1795, the Directory had intended to strike its main blows against Britain and Austria by means of a major invasion of Ireland and an offensive in southern Germany, but the first was turned back by a 'Protestant wind' and the second defeated by the Austrians. In Italy, however, matters were very different: striking across the frontier from its base at Nice in April 1796, within a few short months Napoleon's ragged little army had forced Piedmont and the Papal States to make peace, over-run northern Italy, and beaten a succession of Austrian armies, the following spring threatening Vienna itself with occupation. Badly shaken, the Austrians asked for an armistice, an initial peace settlement being signed on 18 April 1797. By this time, however, Napoleon had become much more than a simple general. Very early on in the campaign, success in battle, the devotion of his troops, and a growing sense of his own power convinced him that he was 'a man called upon to influence the destiny of the people'.[4] At the same time, French failures elsewhere, to which his own victories provided a vivid contrast, reinforced his importance to the Directory, and thus his political independence. Stimulated by the need to provide his small army with a secure base for its operations, Napoleon therefore deliberately encouraged republican feeling, the result being the formation of the Milan-based Cisalpine Republic in June 1797. With the initiative firmly in his hands, Napoleon was also effectively left to offer the Austrians peace terms of his own making, these finally being agreed in the treaty of Campo Formio of 17 October 1797.

Yet, though Austria did remarkably well out of it, gaining large parts of the old Venetian Republic, which was partitioned between her, the Cisalpine Republic, and France (who took the Ionian Islands), this settlement achieved nothing. As de facto ruler of the Cisalpine Republic Napoleon had acquired a taste for political power, remarking, 'I have tasted supremacy and I can no longer renounce it.'[5] Giving himself the airs of a hereditary prince, he allowed himself to indulge in flights of fancy that were ever more unbridled. Thus:

> What I have done so far is nothing. I am only at the beginning of the course that I must run. Do you think that I am triumphing in Italy merely to . . . found a republic?[6]

By the end of 1797, in fact, Napoleon was already thinking of seizing control of the French government: he openly spoke of not wanting to leave Italy unless it was to play 'a role in France resembling the one I have here', and further remarked:

4   Cit. J. Tulard, *Napoleon: the Myth of the Saviour* (London, 1984), p. 58.

5   Cit. H. Parker, 'The formation of Napoleon's personality: an exploratory essay', *French Historical Studies*, VII, No. 1 (Spring, 1971), 22.

6   Cit. A. Castelot, *Napoleon* (New York, 1971), pp. 90–1.

The Parisian lawyers who have been put in charge of the Directory understand nothing of government. They are mean-minded men . . . I very much doubt that we can remain in agreement much longer.[7]

For this, however, he admitted that the time was not yet ripe, the inference being that he must embark on a search for still more glory. Action, in fact, was essential: when he did return to France late in 1797 he commented, 'In Paris nothing is remembered for long. If I remain doing nothing . . . I am lost.'[8] To suggest that this restless energy and ambition now became the only factor in the determination of French policy would be incorrect – not only did expansion offer the same benefits as before, but the Cisalpine Republic had now to be protected, a task which presupposed the occupation of Switzerland, whilst all over Italy patriots were in a state of ferment – but, even so, it is clear that Napoleon gave it renewed impetus. Within a few months republics had been established in Genoa and Rome, Switzerland had been invaded, and, fired by dreams of an eastern empire, Napoleon himself had sailed for Egypt, thereby embroiling France in a war with the Ottomans. Thus provoked, Naples, Austria and Russia all went to war, initially obtaining a series of dramatic victories and driving the French from most of Italy. In the midst of the War of the Second Coalition, however, matters were transformed by the coup of 18 Brumaire 1799. Escaping from Egypt, where his army had been trapped by the destruction of the French fleet at the battle of Abukir, Napoleon returned to a France assailed by political disintegration, internal unrest and economic crisis, and joined hands with an assortment of disaffected politicians to bring down the Directory. Skilfully exploiting the situation to his own advantage, Napoleon emerged from the turmoil as de facto ruler of France, his official title being first consul.

Ironically, Napoleon came to power as a peacemaker. Virtually all shades of French opinion were heartily sick of war by 1799, the new first consul's great advantage being that he seemed to be able to combine peace with the protection of the Revolutionary settlement. As he rode into Paris immediately following the coup, his way was therefore lined by cheering crowds, his response being to proclaim, 'Frenchmen! You want peace; your government wants it

---

7   *Cit.* Parker, 'Formation of Napoleon's personality', p. 22; Tulard, *Napoleon*, p. 64.

8   *Cit.* Markham, *Napoleon*, p. 58.

even more than you!'[9] Virtually the first action of consular diplomacy was the dispatch of appeals to both George III of England and
Francis II of Austria for an end to the war (strictly speaking, Francis
was at this time Francis II of the Holy Roman Empire; however,
when this collapsed, he took the title 'emperor of Austria', becoming
Francis I). These, however, were hardly serious. Whilst, as Talleyrand
wrote, they 'had a happy effect upon the internal peace of the
country',[10] as Napoleon well knew, the Second Coalition was hardly
likely to accept them, at this time still having strong hopes of
victory: an Anglo-Russian invasion of Holland had failed and Russia
had withdrawn from the war, but the Bourbons had been restored
to the throne of Naples, powerful Austrian forces had occupied the
Cisalpine Republic, Piedmont, and southern Germany, and Britain
was supreme at sea and had isolated the army left behind by
Napoleon in Egypt. Not surprisingly, the response was fiercely
hostile, but this was almost certainly exactly what the first consul
wanted, for, having thrown the responsibility for continuing the war
upon his enemies, he could now seek further victories that would
augment his glory and allow him to dictate peace on his own terms.

There followed the campaign of 1800. Seizing the initiative, the
Austrians attacked in Italy with 97,000 men, drove back the outnumbered French and besieged the French in Genoa, which,
defended with great courage by Massena, held out till 4 June.
Despite the fact that he had been taken by surprise, Napoleon's
response was dramatic: whilst Moreau crossed the Rhine and
defeated the Austrians at Stockach on 3 May, the first consul led the
newly-created Army of Reserve across the Alps and descended on
the Austrian rear, winning a very narrow victory at Marengo on
14 June. Although the campaign was badly bungled by Napoleon's
standards, sufficient damage had been done to the Austrians to force
them to evacuate their Italian conquests, whilst Francis II now
succumbed to the renewed appeal for a peace settlement which
Napoleon dispatched to him from the battlefield of Marengo.
Protracted peace negotiations followed at Lunéville, but in the event
the Austrians stood firm and hostilities were resumed, whereupon
Moreau defeated the Austrians again at Hohenlinden on
3 December. Demoralised and exhausted, Vienna sued for peace, the
result being the treaty of Lunéville, by which Austria was forced to
accept France's annexation of Belgium and the left bank of the

---

9 *Cit.* Cronin, *Napoleon*, p. 278.
10 *Cit.* J. F. Bernard, *Talleyrand: a Biography* (London, 1973), p. 229.

Rhine, to recognise the independence of the various satellite states, and to give up the Habsburg-ruled duchies of Modena and Tuscany, together with some of the territory she had acquired from Venice in 1797 (of these territories, Modena and Venetia went to the Cisalpine Republic, whilst, in a gesture intended to conciliate Spain, Tuscany was given to the son of the duke of Parma – a son-in-law of Charles IV – as the Kingdom of Etruria).

With Austria completely humbled, there yet remained the Ottoman Empire, Naples and Britain. Of these, however, preoccupied with a series of internal disorders, the Turks took no further part in the war after the elimination of the French presence in Egypt in August 1801. Meanwhile, a Neapolitan foray into Tuscany was defeated at Siena on 14 January 1801, Ferdinand IV then being forced to sue for peace. And, at the same time, even British commitment to the war was rapidly beginning to fall away. Left to herself, her military prospects were limited, her helplessness being underlined by her inability to prevent Portugal from being coerced into closing her ports to her commerce by a Spanish invasion force. As for her seapower, though still able to bring significant returns – Malta was seized from the French, the Spaniards defeated in a number of skirmishes, the Danes beaten at Copenhagen, and the French army in Egypt forced to surrender – it could not reverse French dominance and was powerless to prevent the French from closing more and more ports to British trade. Meanwhile, at home there was a growing economic crisis, this producing widespread popular unrest. Despite the defeat of the rising of 1798, Ireland, too, remained restive, Pitt's attempts to conciliate her through Catholic emancipation leading only to a political crisis that culminated in his replacement by the far weaker Addington. Unbeaten but nonetheless unable to secure final victory, the new cabinet therefore announced that it was ready to come to terms.

In keeping with his image of the reluctant warrior, Napoleon was content to entertain these overtures. With the French garrison on the verge of surrender, a peace treaty was the only means of salvaging anything from the Egyptian fiasco. Meanwhile, Napoleon had also recently suffered a severe blow in the diplomatic field. At the end of 1799, as we have seen, Russia had withdrawn her troops from operations against the French following differences with Britain and Austria, the first consul being quick to take advantage of the breach in the hope of further disconcerting his remaining opponents. Paul I – in theory, a ferocious opponent of the

Revolution – was therefore wooed with promises of the return of the 7,000 prisoners then in French hands, and of the cession of Malta, which was at this point still held by the French. Much impressed with this generosity, Paul allowed himself to be persuaded that an alliance with France was in the Russian interest, and by the autumn of 1800 he was mobilising an army on the Austrian frontier and organising an alliance of the Baltic states – Russia, Sweden, Prussia and Denmark – to put pressure on Britain through the so-called League of Armed Neutrality. For Napoleon these events were highly promising, but on 23 March 1801 Paul was murdered in a palace coup, whilst on 2 April came the victory of Copenhagen. With all hope of striking against the British gone, there was simply no point in taking hostilities any further, especially as France remained as war-weary as ever, whilst the British seemed likely to accept whatever terms they were offered. At the same time, peace offered further advantages, for the French navy could be rebuilt and Germany brought more under France's sway. In short, it was very much in France's interests to offer terms, the result being the treaty of Amiens of 25 March 1802.

THE PEACE OF AMIENS

The treaty of Amiens was never likely to lead to a lasting peace. Britain and France were prepared to come to terms, but neither had relinquished its essential war aims. Thus, whilst Britain still desired security in Europe, Napoleon was equally concerned to preserve French hegemony, the two goals soon proving to be incompatible. Nor were matters helped by the fact that the settle- ment was essentially an unequal one. In order to obtain peace, Britain had been prepared to offer conditions that were extremely generous. France's natural frontiers were recognised, along with the various satellite republics, and her colonial losses restored, together with the Dutch possessions of the Cape, Surinam, Curaçao, Malacca and the Spice islands, Britain retaining only Spanish Trinidad and Dutch Ceylon. At the same time, Menorca was to be returned to Spain and Malta to the Knights of Saint John, France reciprocating by agreeing to withdraw all her forces from her satellites, which were henceforth to be treated as independent states. Britain, in short, had gained almost nothing, and the treaty was greeted with alarm and disquiet.

For peace to last, therefore, much would depend upon Napoleon. At the very least, the first consul would have to withdraw his troops from Holland – especially – Switzerland and Italy, respect the integrity and independence of the Cisalpine, Ligurian, Helvetic and Batavian Republics, and generally restrain his actions on the continent of Europe. A liberal policy towards British trade would have been advisable, not to mention progress towards the trade agreement called for – though not stipulated – by the treaty, whilst it was imperative that the French curb their activities in the wider world. Given Napoleon's character, ambition and ever more inflated view of his own abilities, however, all this was most unlikely.

If Napoleon was the key, of what did his foreign policy consist? Though few questions are more elusive, the main influences that shaped it are very clear. First and foremost, Napoleon, as we have seen, was obsessed with the concept of power. As Count Molé put it, 'The more I saw of him, the greater was my conviction that he . . . thought only of satisfying his own desires and adding incessantly to his own . . . greatness.'[11] And, if the goal was power, war was the means – at times the only means – by which it could be attained and safeguarded, Napoleon always realising that this was inseparably bound up with his political survival, just as war had been inseparably linked with his rise to prominence. Innumerable quotations may be cited in support of such a thesis. To take just three examples from various stages of his career, in 1803 he commented, 'The First Consul does not resemble those kings by the grace of God who consider their states as a heritage. He needs brilliant actions and therefore war'; in 1804, 'Death is nothing, but to live defeated and inglorious is to die daily'; and in June 1813, 'I would die before I ceded one inch of territory. Your sovereigns born on the throne can be beaten twenty times and still return to their capitals. I cannot do that because I am an upstart soldier. My domination will not be able to survive from the day I cease . . . to be feared.'[12]

Nor was the question purely a matter of guaranteeing Napoleon's personal prestige in the eyes of his fellow rulers or of stamping his authority upon the continent of Europe. Fearing the mob as he did, he seems also to have regarded war as a means of disciplining his subjects and curbing French volatility. At the same time, although the French ruler was in no sense its prisoner, there

11 Marquis de Noailles (ed.), *The Life and Memoirs of Count Molé (1781–1855)* (London, 1923), I, pp. 148–9.
12 *Cit.* Tulard, *Napoleon*, 134, 307; Markham, *Napoleon*, p. 41.

was also the question of the army. Exactly as had been the case under the Republic, the sheer size of the French military establishment could sometimes be a spur to a forward policy: the occupation of Hanover in 1803, for example, was at least in part occasioned by the desire to quarter a substantial body of French troops on German soil. Economics aside, moreover, Napoleon had also to ensure that its aspirations were met, and all the more so given its rapid evolution from the Jacobin 'army of virtue' to the 'army of honour' that it had now become. Significant too was the tendency of many senior commanders to become 'over-mighty subjects', Napoleon being threatened both by die-hard Republicans such as Bernadotte (king of Sweden though he was one day to be, at this point the Gascon soldier was a convinced Jacobin), and ambitious rivals such as Moreau. Whether to retain the affections of the army as a whole or to keep the generals out of mischief, it could be argued that continuous warfare was essential. Meanwhile, much the same was true of civilian society: though he had come to power ostensibly offering France peace, he also wished to offer her prosperity, and this, too, seemed to demand the continuation of a belligerent foreign policy that would offer *la grande nation* resources and markets that she could not otherwise command.

It will be objected here that Napoleon also saw himself as a great law-giver, and that the peace that he had now obtained had given him the opportunity to pursue this ambition unimpeded. As first consul he ostentatiously abandoned his general's uniform for civilian dress and spent the bulk of his time immersed in questions of civil government, whilst numerous quotations may be found from this period that can be used to suggest that his inclinations were essentially pacific, as, for example, the moment just after the treaty of Amiens when he told one of his Councillors of State that his intention was 'to multiply the works of peace'.[13] Yet such an impression is misleading. In the very same conversation Napoleon also expressed his doubts whether France was 'sufficiently settled to dispense with more victories' and remarked that 'in our position I look upon peace as a short remedy only'.[14] At the same time, too, Napoleon the law-giver was by no means separate from Napoleon the man of war, the first consul's classical studies having left him with the firm belief that the greatest figures of antiquity had been leaders who had excelled in both fields, such as the Spartan hero,

13 Cit. A. C. Thibaudeau, *Bonaparte and the Consulate* (London, 1908), p. 120.
14 Cit. ibid., pp. 119, 121.

Lycurgus. Thus, much though Napoleon may have claimed to have distrusted the other powers' willingness to live at peace with him, it is impossible to believe that he could ever have remained content with the settlement that he had now obtained, or, indeed, that a lasting peace was compatible with his aims.

What, however, were these aims? Any answer to this question must clearly be prefaced with the statement, first, that Napoleon never had a settled plan of aggression, many of his later annexations being quite clearly the fruit of circumstance, and, second, that he was above all an opportunist who was prepared to set aside general principles of policy when they clashed with the needs of the moment. Yet certain general objectives may still be established, the first of these being Napoleon's vision of himself as a new Charlemagne – a supreme temporal ruler to whom all the other monarchs of Europe would owe allegiance. France, meanwhile, would truly be *la grande nation*, greatly increased in size and enjoying a position of political and cultural dominance that would be cemented by the consolidation of the sphere of influence constituted by her satellite states, who would be bound to France through common principles of law and government. As these principles were essentially those of the French Revolution, it is possible to argue that in this programme there lurked a trace of the political radicalism of Napoleon's early years, and all the more so given his notorious hatred for the surviving Bourbon monarchies. However, such reforms were as much a tool of imperial policy as they were one of its goals, whilst in both Naples and Spain the Bourbons would have been left alone had not other circumstances intervened. In any case, inextricably linked with this expansionism was the question of the Bonaparte family. As its de facto head, Napoleon the Corsican was determined to secure the personal interests of his numerous brothers and sisters, just as Napoleon the statesman was determined to use them to further his aims – in this case to consolidate his empire, reinforce his status in the eyes of the other monarchs of Europe, and attract the services of the old nobility. The French ruler was never able to forget that he was, above all, a *parvenu*, the insecurity of his early life and personality thereby being transferred to his foreign policy. As for the other powers of Europe, they could either accept the new dispensation, in which case, of course, they would have to accept perpetual inferiority – the only basis on which Napoleon was prepared to accept the general peace which his apologists argue that he desired – or they could face war. Compromise was impossible: convinced of the superiority of his armies, the invincibility of his generalship, and the primacy of his interests, he would not accept either that there were limits to what he could achieve, or sensibilities that he must consider, seeing every partnership as a tool of exploitation and every peace settlement as an exercise in humiliation.

Continued war, then, was very likely, for co-existence with Napoleon was in the last resort impossible. As for the peace of Amiens, the first consul certainly did nothing to protect it, virtually his every action provoking grave disquiet in London. As Talleyrand later admitted:

> Hardly was the peace of Amiens concluded when moderation commenced to abandon Bonaparte; this peace had not yet received its complete execution before he was sowing the seeds of new wars . . . [15]

Thus, in the first place, far from living quietly within the borders allotted to him at Amiens, Napoleon continued actively to intervene in the affairs of the areas bordering upon them: though Naples and Switzerland were evacuated, French troops continued to occupy Holland throughout, whilst in January 1803 Switzerland was reoccupied, given a new constitution – the so-called Act of Mediation – and stripped of the Valais; the Cisalpine Republic – now renamed the Italian Republic – was reordered along the lines of consular France, Napoleon becoming its president; Piedmont and Elba were annexed; and in Germany the Holy Roman Empire was effectively dismantled. So important was this last development that it must be looked at in some detail. Essentially a heterogeneous collection of independent kingdoms, principalities of all shapes and sizes, bishoprics, abbeys, free cities and feudal fiefs united only by the theoretical allegiance of their rulers to the house of Habsburg, the Empire was a major bastion of Austrian influence in Germany, and as such had become the object of Napoleon's ire. At the same time, however, it was also threatened with destabilisation from within, for many of the rulers of the larger states were increasingly determined to absorb the free cities, the territories of the Church and the host of petty principalities and baronial estates. Such a policy could not but prove disastrous for Austria, whose strongest supporters in the Empire had traditionally been the bishops, abbots

---

15 *Cit.* H. Deutsch, *The Genesis of Napoleonic Imperialism* (Philadelphia, 1975), p. 77.

and imperial knights, but the problem of finding some compensation for the evicted Italian Habsburgs was now attracting even Francis II to the process. Having occupied and annexed the Rhineland, the French had suggested that the German rulers affected should be compensated by the acquisition of fresh territory in Germany. Needless to say, however, the result was deadlock, and in the end it was effectively left to Napoleon to arrange a settlement. Whilst Prussia and Austria were bought off with substantial territorial gains in Westphalia and the South Tyrol, and, in the latter case, the gift of Salzburg to the duke of Tuscany, middling states such as Bavaria, Baden and Würtemberg were allowed to make huge gains. At a stroke Germany was transformed. The Holy Roman Empire survived, but the virtual annihilation of the free cities, the imperial knights and the princes of the Church had reduced its component territories from some 365 to approximately forty, and completely broken Austria's predominance, this now to some extent being supplanted by that of France: though much expanded in size, the southern states, in particular, remained terrified of Austria, and therefore looked to Napoleon to protection, in effect now joining the ranks of France's satellites.

Needless to say, none of this activity was to Britain's taste, her sense of unease being heightened by the actions of Napoleon in other areas. In the realm of commerce, British trade continued to be discriminated against, in both France and her satellites. Meanwhile, French activity in the wider world showed no signs of abating. Having already dispatched an expedition to Australia, acquired Louisiana from Spain and restored slavery in the French colonies, the first consul now extended French hegemony in the Mediterranean by means of agreements with the rulers of Tunis and Algiers, openly examined the possibility of a fresh expedition to Egypt, attempted to restore French influence in India, dispatched a large force to reconquer Saint Domingue from the victorious slave revolt of Toussaint L'Ouverture, and commenced a large programme of naval construction. In short, the British could be justified in feeling that their interests were being challenged not just in Europe, but in every quarter of the globe.

As such, few of Napoleon's actions actually infringed the letter of the treaty of Amiens. Nevertheless, they certainly infringed what the British regarded as its spirit, and gave them reason to suspect that the first consul would soon dispense with the agreement itself. When repeated protests failed to produce any result – for Napoleon insisted that he would make no concessions beyond what had been agreed at Amiens, was not prepared to tolerate any let or hindrance to his aspirations, and was genuinely incensed with the increasingly scurrilous attitude adopted towards him by the British press – the Addington administration resolved to resist France over the question of the vital strategic base of Malta, which Britain was supposed to give up under the terms of the treaty but in fact still held. As a result Napoleon was faced with demands that he should evacuate Holland and Switzerland, respect the political independence of the satellite states, and sanction British occupation of Malta for ten years. Realising, perhaps that he had overplayed his hand – for France's programme of naval construction was at yet in the earliest of stages, a resumption of hostilities therefore threatening renewed colonial and commercial disaster – Napoleon attempted to draw back, but in the last resort his pride would not let him agree to the sort of curbs on his freedom of action which the British were demanding. With neither Britain nor France prepared to make fundamental concessions, on 18 May 1803 the former declared war, thereby opening the Napoleonic Wars.

THE NAPOLEONIC WARS

In going to war in 1803, it can be categorically stated that Britain was driven by neither ideological nor economic motives. Political change in France per se was not one of her primary objectives – the cause of royalist counter-revolution was rapidly abandoned and the question of a restoration left open – whilst the economic and colonial warfare which she now resumed was clearly a means of striking at France rather than an object in itself. What concerned Britain was the question of her security in Europe and the wider world, the Addington administration being convinced that war was the only means by which this could be secured. To achieve her aims, however, Britain needed the support of Continental partners, and this for the time being she could not obtain, the other powers as yet remaining convinced that they could co-exist with Napoleon. In the first place, there was no enthusiasm for an ideological crusade à la 1793, for, far from provoking widespread terror, the first consul's restoration of a recognisably monarchical form of government and generally conciliatory domestic policies made him positively reassuring as a political figure, whilst, as Paul Schroeder has rightly suggested, his diplomacy made him appear 'a normal, calculable statesman . . . who could play the game by the known rules, even if more ruthlessly and successfully than most'.[16] In the second place, meanwhile, there was little sympathy for Britain: not only was the *casus belli* for which she was ostensibly fighting – the retention of Malta – regarded as typically self-serving, but, by means of his last-minute display of conciliation, Napoleon had made her appear the aggressor. Thirdly, in 1803 the intentions of all the great powers were essentially pacific, none of them wanting war – and particularly not with Napoleon – or seeing it as necessary to their interests.

At least in so far as the third point is concerned, much of this was to change (it should be noted that the overthrow of Napoleon was not agreed upon as an objective until the very end of the war, and that, as late as the Waterloo campaign of 1815, bitter distrust of the British continued to be rampant amongst Prussia's generals). However, before we look at the process by which the war became general, we must look at the state of Europe in 1803. Taking Napoleon and his allies first of all, France had emerged from the Revolution immensely strengthened. With over 29,000,000 inhabitants, she was second only to Russia in terms of population, and by far the most advanced state in Continental Europe. Though political paralysis and widespread unrest had done much to nullify these advantages under the Directory, Napoleon had, as we shall see, put an end to these disorders and was now in an excellent position to capitalise upon the very considerable financial and demographic resources at his disposal. Meanwhile, making full use of the military advances of the *ancien régime* and Revolution, he was in the process of building an army that in size and quality was to have few equals: indeed, even as it was, it consisted of 265 infantry battalions, 322 cavalry squadrons and 202 batteries, the whole amounting to perhaps 300,000 men.[17] At the same time, in contrast to the situation elsewhere, replacements and reinforcements were little

16 P. W. Schroeder, 'Napoleon's foreign policy: a criminal enterprise', *Consortium on Revolutionary Europe Proceedings,* 1989 (Bicentennial Consortium), p. 110.

17 These figures for the size of the French army, and all those which follow, should be regarded as approximate as organisation was often in a state of flux, whilst it should also be noted that in all cases second-line and technical units have been omitted; however, in so far as possible, they represent the military forces available to the powers at the moment when they entered the conflict. At the same time, the figures quoted take no account of different types of infantry and cavalry and other such variations. A further problem is that battalions, squadrons and batteries varied in size from army to army, and even within each army: thus a battalion of infantry might number anything between 600 and 1000 men, a squadron of cavalry 120–150 riders, and a battery six–twelve cannon or howitzers.

problem, for the entire male population was theoretically eligible for military service. Finally, even at sea, if France's immediate position was very weak – in 1803 Napoleon had only twenty-three battle-ships ready for service – her shipbuilding potential easily equalled that of Britain whilst the design of her vessels was actually more advanced. In short, having already embarked upon a large-scale programme of naval construction, Napoleon could in the long term entertain serious hopes of naval supremacy.

Nor, of course, did France stand on her own. Holland and the Italian and Ligurian Republics were all quickly forced to enter the war against Britain, and to place their armed forces at France's disposal (the most important element here was the Dutch fleet which in 1801 had fifteen battleships), whilst at the same time contributing very substantially to her war effort in financial terms. Permitted to remain neutral, Switzerland was nevertheless in 1804 forced to agree to maintain the various Swiss regiments in the French army at a strength of 16,000 men. Yet even this did not exhaust the list of support for France beyond her borders. Eager to stay out of the war, Spain secured this privilege at a cost of a monthly subsidy of 6,000,000 francs, a lump sum of another 16,000,000 being paid over by Portugal, whom Britain was at this stage powerless to protect. If she was forced to enter the war, however, Spain could in theory call upon an army of 130,000 men (153 infantry battalions, ninety-three cavalry squadrons, forty artillery batteries), a navy of thirty-two ships-of-the-line, and all the resources of her Latin-American empire. And, last but not least, with the exception of Portugal, all of these states were forced to close their ports and frontiers to British goods, Napoleon's grand design for a Conti-nental blockade already being well under way. As yet unaffected by the trade embargo, there were also the middling states of southern Germany. For the most part in the process of a notable programme of state-building which brought with it a notable increase in their efficiency – a development which also affected France's formal satellites – all these states could be expected to lend France considerable military support in the event of a Continental war.

Supreme at sea though she was, Britain's chances of making head against such an array on her own were very limited, at least in the short term. In Germany, George III was elector of Hanover, but such benefit as might have accrued from this was nullified by Hanover's military weakness and strategic vulnerability. Though unrivalled in its training, seamanship and morale, the Royal Navy had been greatly reduced in size since 1801 (only thirty-four battleships were actually in service, although a further seventy-seven were in reserve), whilst the British army, at some 130,000 men (115 battalions, 140 cavalry squadrons, forty batteries) was under-strength, overstretched and notoriously inefficient and poorly-officered. Needless to say, of course, with her rapidly growing population and immense financial, commercial and industrial resources, Britain could in theory expect to raise a much larger army, whilst the first years of the nineteenth century saw a dramatic improvement in its quality. Nevertheless, with most of the German states whose troops had traditionally been hired to augment her forces now aligned with France, conscription a political impossibility, home defence a major priority, and transporting large numbers of troops to the Continent a serious problem in logistical terms, Britain could not but look to Continental allies.

In military terms, the only possible counter to French preponderance were the large professional armies of Austria, Prussia and Russia. At full strength these were impressive indeed. Thus, assuming that all her formations were complete, Austria could supposedly field over 300,000 men – 255 infantry battalions, 322 cavalry squadrons, and over 1000 guns (Austrian artillery had not yet been organised into permanent batteries, but the number of pieces was sufficient to equip at least 125). For Russia the figures were even greater, amounting to perhaps 400,000 men if her swarms of cossacks – irregular horsemen recruited from the settler communities of the southern and eastern frontiers who paid for their land and personal freedom by means of military service – are included, first-line regular units numbering 359 infantry battalions, 341 cavalry squadrons, and 229 batteries. Alone amongst the eastern powers, meanwhile, Russia was also a major naval power with fleets in the Baltic and the Black Sea that in 1805 amounted to forty-four ships of the line. These forces allowed her to overcome some of the limitations of her geographical isolation – in 1799 Russian troops had served in both Italy and Holland (needless to say, they also made a Russian alliance particularly attractive to Napoleon). As for Prussia, its 175 battalions, 156 squadrons and fifty batteries amounted to some 254,000 men. If Prussia came into the fray, moreover, there was a strong possibility that she would be assisted by the forces of a number of minor states such as Brunswick and Saxony whom geography placed in her sphere of influence rather than that of France.

Of course, mere numbers were not everything: for a variety of reasons, as we shall see, the armies of the eastern powers were militarily inferior to the forces of Napoleon. At the same time, setting aside the very real problems posed by mobilisation, they would by no means necessarily all be available for service against France. Austria, Russia and Prussia alike might all be diverted by other opponents, and it is therefore necessary for us to turn briefly to the latters' forces. Thus, in the south of Europe we have the Ottoman Empire. Engaged since he had come to the throne in 1789 in a desperate struggle for reform against a variety of overmighty subjects, Sultan Selim III had effected considerable improvements in his empire's fighting power. Already in possession of a powerful and up-to-date western-style battle fleet of twenty-two ships-of-the-line, with the aid of French experts he modernised the artillery and built up a new regular army. Organised and trained on western lines, by 1806 this Nizam-i-Cedid had reached a strength of 24,000 men. However, effective though this force was, it was but a small component of an Ottoman array that was as enormous as it was ineffective. Thus, the heart of the regular army still consisted of the 196 2–3,000-strong regiments of Janissaries, this force having long since become notoriously ill-trained, undisciplined and unfit for war. Backing up these regular infantrymen were hordes of light cavalry, many of whom were effectively feudal lords who held their estates in exchange for military service, mercenary irregulars, and poorly trained peasant levies. A large part of these forces had fallen under the control of a variety of local satraps who might or might not be prepared to rally to Constantinople's call. Generally described as an ungovernable mob, as Napoleon had already proved, Ottoman armies were no match for western-style forces, but the empire's amorphous political organisation and sprawling nature made it a difficult foe to defeat, the result being that it remained an important factor in diplomatic calculations. At the other extreme of the Continent, meanwhile, there were the Danes and the Swedes. Negligible as a land power – the Danish army had a mere thirty infantry battalions and thirty-six cavalry squadrons – even after the defeat of Copenhagen of 1801 Denmark retained a powerful fleet of twenty ships-of-the-line. As for Sweden, with between seventy and eighty infantry battalions, sixty-six cavalry squadrons and seventy artillery batteries, she could put a significant force into the field, her geographical remoteness meanwhile being countered by her powerful navy – twelve ships-of-the-line together with a large number of heavily-armed galleys that had been specially designed for amphibious operations in the shallow waters of the Baltic – and her possession of the important bridgehead of Swedish Pomerania.

Setting aside the question of these other forces, there was in any case little reason to believe that any power was eager for war with France in 1803. Taking Austria first of all, following the treaty of Lunéville Francis II found himself at the head of a country that was not only exhausted and bankrupt but helpless to prevent Napoleon from presiding over a reorganisation of Germany that threatened to be catastrophic to her interests. Meanwhile, Hungary, which had been embroiled in a series of disputes with the Habsburg monarchy since the 1780s, was restive, whilst Francis' brother, the Archduke Charles, had just persuaded him of the necessity of embarking upon a major programme of administrative and military reform. With Charles himself vehemently opposed to any renewal of hostilities with France, deeply suspicious of Russia, and inclined to a policy of expansion in the Balkans, the naturally cautious and pacific Francis was most unwilling to risk a further conflict, whilst in any case being in private an admirer of Napoleon. As a result, far from courting a new war, he aspired to a deal with France in the hope that this might act as a counterbalance to Russia and Prussia. With Britain much disliked in Vienna on account of differences that had arisen in the course of the War of the Second Coalition, there was therefore no chance of her obtaining Francis' aid, Austria instead remaining firmly neutral.

For Russia, too, the Napoleonic period opened with an attempted *rapprochement* with Napoleon. Alexander I had been angered by Britain's destruction of the League of Armed Neutrality, harboured a certain admiration for Napoleon, and wished to apply himself to domestic reform, also being eager to co-operate with the French in the reorganisation of Germany. By 1803 this initial warmth had cooled, much alarm having been caused by the evident desire of Napoleon not only to dominate completely the whole of western Europe, but also to partition the Ottoman Empire (during the peace of Amiens Saint Petersburg had received repeated communications from Paris suggesting some 'arrangement' in the Balkans). Greatly angered by Napoleon's pretension in having himself declared first consul for life, Alexander had come to the conclusion that the French ruler was 'one of the most notorious tyrants that history has ever produced'.[18] For all that, however, he showed no sign of springing to arms, and instead attempted to

18 *Cit.* W. Zawadzki, 'Prince Adam Czartorysky and Napoleonic France, 1801–1805: a study in political attitudes', *Historical Journal*, XVIII, No. 2 (June, 1975), 248.

mediate by offering terms that would have deprived Britain of Malta and guaranteed France's current borders and spheres of influence in Europe in exchange for French recognition of the status quo elsewhere, particularly with regard to Naples and the Ottoman Empire. As we shall see, even as this offer was being made, Alexander was being driven into a more hostile position, but, if his policy became more and more anti-French, it yet remained complicated by other factors. Under the influence of his close adviser and personal friend, Prince Adam Czartorysky, who became deputy foreign minister in September 1802, he became increasingly persuaded that the best means of checking French expansion was by establishing Russian hegemony in eastern Europe, whether through direct annexation or through the establishment of subordinate satellite states of his own (Czartorysky was, for example, an enthusiastic devotee of a reborn Poland). Yet such a scheme was clearly counterproductive, for it was certain to embroil Russia with Sweden, Prussia, Austria and Turkey, each of these powers in turn being given a powerful motive to turn to France (indeed, in 1803 Gustav IV of Sweden was already considering the possibility of an alliance with Napoleon). Join the fray though Russia might, the effect might be to win France fresh allies.

Let us now turn to Prussia. In 1803, of all the European capitals, Berlin was the least hostile to Napoleon. Frederick William III detested the Bourbons and had been entirely content to see Napoleon made first consul. At the same time, too, he was a man of a pacific disposition, his chief happiness consisting, in the words of one British diplomat, of 'the absence of all trouble'.[19] Thus inclined, he naturally chose as his advisers men who believed that Prussia should maintain the neutrality that had characterised her policy since 1795, the desirability of such a course being reinforced by financial weakness and traditional suspicions of Austria and Russia. This, of course, did not mean that Prussia would necessarily remain inert, territorial gain being attractive even to Frederick William, but the sort of gains to which she might aspire – Hanover and Swedish Pomerania – were by no means incompatible with continued friendship with France whilst being as likely as the plans of Czartorysky to foment enmities elsewhere.

In brief, then, the conflict between Britain and France need not on its own have produced a general war, the fact that it had done so being wholly the fault of Napoleon. In this respect, much weight is

19 *Cit.* Deutsch, *Napoleonic Imperialism*, p. 165.

often given to the so-called 'tragedy of Vincennes' in which the Duc d'Enghien, a distant connection of the French royal family, was kidnapped from his exile in Baden and executed on suspicion of involvement in a royalist conspiracy. However, although the response was one of general horror, only in Sweden did the affair have any real effect on foreign policy, the news of D'Enghien's death causing the rather unbalanced Gustav IV to abandon all plan of an alliance with France and champion the idea of a crusade against her. In this idea he remained entirely isolated, however: though Alexander I also broke off relations with Napoleon at this time, it is clear that what motivated him was the threat France posed to the balance of power, the question of a Bourbon restoration being firmly excluded from the war aims of what in 1805 became the Third Coalition.

To understand the origins of the Third Coalition we must therefore turn once again to the growth of French power. Thus, war against England produced an immediate expansion of French influence on the Continent. On the one hand, Napoleon was determined to do as much as he could to exclude British trade from its remaining outlets on the Continent, whilst on the other he needed some compensation for the disaster that the war represented to his aims in the wider world (having already been forced to sell Louisiana to the United States in January 1803, Napoleon now faced the loss of Saint Domingue as well). In consequence, whilst concentrating the bulk of his forces for a cross-Channel invasion, Napoleon occupied Hanover, the Hanseatic dependencies of Cuxhaven and Ritzbüttel – thereby sealing off the Elbe, and with it access to Hamburg, Saxony and even Bohemia – and the Neapolitan ports of Taranto, Otranto and Brindisi. For all the eastern powers these moves were most alarming and, indeed, injurious: thus, Austria feared for her trade, whilst being deeply concerned about the growth of French preponderance in Germany and Italy; Prussia found herself with a French army placed in the very midst of her dominions and cheated of a prize which had always been one of the major goals of her foreign policy; and Russia objected to a move that presaged renewed French interest in the Levant, as well as a destabilisation of the German settlement. However, for the time being both Austria and Prussia remained quiescent: as reluctant as ever to go to war, Austria was intent on making use of French preoccupation with the war against Britain to secure territorial concessions from Bavaria, whilst Prussia was mollified by a vigorous 'peace offensive'. Had Napoleon been more placatory with regard to

Russia, even she might have been conciliated, but here the first consul's conduct displayed a complete want of moderation. Russia's proposals for mediation were rejected out of hand when they might have been accepted without any loss of face, Britain having made it quite clear that they were entirely unacceptable; the Russian ambassador to Paris was subjected to a tirade of abuse at a state dinner; and the French once again began to show a disturbing interest in the Ionian islands – granted their independence at Amiens as the Republic of the Seven Islands – and mainland Greece. As a result, Russia now adopted a position of open hostility, augmenting conscription, sending an army to the Ionian islands, and giving the British government to understand that she was prepared to negotiate a defensive alliance against Napoleon. Then, on 18 May 1804, there came the declaration that France was to become a hereditary empire. With French power as unrivalled as it was, this was not to be endured, for, by enabling to Napoleon to lay claim to the mantle of Charlemagne, it opened the way for him formally to supplant the Holy Roman emperor as overlord of Germany. Dragging in his wake a rather less enthusiastic Alexander, Czartorysky now in consequence began to work for a new coalition that would drive Napoleon back at least to the limits he had agreed upon at Lunéville and Amiens, obtaining for this purpose the promise of substantial British subsidies. Meanwhile an ultimatum was sent to Napoleon demanding that he evacuate Hanover and Naples, the French ruler's predictable refusal to comply leading Russia to break off diplomatic relations in September 1804.

With a Franco-Russian rupture now a fact, it would appear that a wider conflict was inevitable. However, even now there were considerable problems, suspicion of Britain being rife in Russia. In October 1804 Britain had shocked European opinion by launching a surprise attack on Spain so as to force her openly to enter the war. At the same time, there were persistent fears that Britain was not acting in good faith: as late as January 1805 Czartorysky was reported to believe that her intention was to embroil the other powers of Europe in the war so as to allow her to scale down her commitment to the struggle. With other problems occurring over the question of Malta, which Alexander was determined to claim for himself, having previously been ceded its sovereignty by the Knights of Saint John, by mid-1804 an Anglo-Russian alliance seemed to have become quite impossible. Even had these problems not intervened, however, the chances for a broad coalition still appeared minimal. Though Austria had been browbeaten by Napoleon into renewed quiescence in Germany and was faced with clear evidence that Napoleon was planning the formation of a new German confederation that would finally overthrow the Holy Roman Empire, she was still unwilling to go to war, the most that she would agree to being a defensive alliance with Russia that would come into action in the case of further French aggression in Italy or Germany. In the hope that this might further deter Napoleon, at the same time troops began to be mobilised and sent to the western frontiers. As for Prussia, fears that Napoleon might launch a surprise attack upon her were countered by suspicions of Russia and Sweden, Frederick William's response being to attempt to conciliate the French ruler by assuring him of his friendship and neutrality. Indeed, as 1804 wore on, he even began to explore the possibility of an alliance with France, all possibility of a general alliance against Napoleon being rejected early in 1805.

At the beginning of 1805, then, the Third Coalition was really no closer than before. Yet again, however, what changed the situation was the behaviour of Napoleon. Early in 1805 he announced that he was to take the title of king of Italy, the *ci-devant* Italian Republic now being restyled as a kingdom with Napoleon's stepson, Eugene de Beauharnais, as its viceroy. Nor was Napoleon finished: formally placing the new crown on his own head in Milan on 26 May, in early June he announced the annexation of Genoa – the erstwhile Ligurian Republic – and appropriated the duchy of Lucca as a principality for his younger sister, Elise. Such actions could not fail to make war inevitable, and as early as 11 April Britain and Russia signed a treaty of alliance that committed the latter to war unless Napoleon agreed to conform to the terms of the treaties of Amiens and Lunéville. In Austria, meanwhile, although Francis himself remained opposed to war, a more belligerent faction had begun to emerge which believed that war was inevitable, its influence being greatly strengthened by Francis' personal dislike of the Archduke Charles, whom he regarded, as we shall see, as a dangerous threat to his authority. As yet matters hung in the balance, but the dramatic developments of the first half of 1805 now pushed Austria over the brink. In themselves a major blow to Habsburg prestige, since the Holy Roman emperor traditionally also laid claim to the throne of Italy, Napoleon's actions seemed to presage the annexation of the entire peninsula, threatening noises now beginning to be heard with regard to Rome, Naples and Venetia. With Russia now committed to war, Vienna had to follow suit. Either Austria renounced all thought of recovering her influence in Italy (for Napoleon was clearly not going to abandon his gains there voluntarily) and deserted her only ally in the hope of maintaining a peace that might prove all too illusory, it being increasingly feared that Napoleon would eventually attack her anyway, or she took up arms. Faced with the choice of war now in the company of powerful allies, or war alone later, on 9 August 1805 Austria formally joined the Third Coalition, this soon being further swelled by Sweden, and, after some hesitation, Naples, which the French had hastily evacuated.

With Austrian forces moving into Bavaria and the Italian Republic, a Russo-Swedish army concentrating at Stralsund, British troops preparing to invade Hanover, an Anglo-Russian force landing at Naples, and 95,000 more Russians marching for the Danube, the coalition desired by the British since 1803 was now a *fait accompli*. Only the Prussians remained aloof, kept neutral by their distrust of Austria and Russia, guarantees that their neutrality would be respected, and hopes of obtaining Hanover and an alliance with France. For so general an alliance Napoleon had only himself to blame. Unwilling to moderate his conduct or to make even the cheapest gesture of good will, he had driven Austria and Russia into the arms of Britain. This was not a situation that he particularly wanted – he had had no especial desire for a breach with Russia and, once this had occurred, was downright unwilling to go to war against Austria – but so great was his concern for his prestige that he simply could not take the sort of steps that would have been necessary to avoid conflict. Once war had begun, moreover, he did not even take care to respect the sensibilities of the few friends he had left: in order to hasten the march across Germany to which it was now committed, the *grande armée* violated the neutrality of the Prussian territory of Ansbach in flagrant violation of the promises that had just been made to Berlin. In response a furious Frederick William now occupied Hanover (which the French had temporarily evacuated) and mobilised for war in his turn.

The events of the campaign of 1805 need not detain us here – in brief, the Austrians were crushed at Ulm, Vienna occupied, and the Russians defeated at Austerlitz (Slavkov). For good measure, Naples was invaded, Ferdinand and Maria Carolina forced to flee to Sicily, and Joseph Bonaparte placed upon the throne. As it happened, these crushing blows, for which the British naval victory at Trafalgar was little or no compensation, did not bring peace, but for some months it appeared that they might do so. Forced to surrender, Austria was subjected to a peace settlement so humiliating and injurious that it could not but create a powerful war party in the Habsburg court. Thus, by the treaty of Pressburg (Bratislava) Austria was forced to cede Venetia, Dalmatia and Istria to the Kingdom of Italy, Vorarlberg and the Tyrol, including the newly acquired Trentino, to Bavaria, and the isolated pockets of territory still held by Austria in the area of the Black Forest and the upper Rhine to Baden and Würtemberg. In addition, Napoleon had to be accepted as king of Italy, and Bavaria, Würtemberg and Baden recognised as independent states, whilst Austria also had to pay an indemnity of 40,000,000 francs. For all this, the only compensation was that Austria was allowed to annexe Salzburg, the Habsburg duke of Tuscany, to whom it had been given in 1803, receiving in exchange the Grand Duchy of Wurzburg. Although Austria was now in an even worse military and financial position than before, the demands of those eager for revenge – the displaced Italian Habsburgs, the new chancellor, Stadion, and the young and idealistic Archduke John – were being countered by other views which the naturally pacific Francis found far more congenial. Thus, on the one hand, the Archduke Charles, who had now been restored to favour, wanted a programme of military reform that would facilitate a process of expansion to the east and south at the expense of the Ottoman Empire, the corollary being the abandonment of Germany and Italy and peaceful co-existence with Napoleon, whilst, on the other, the Archdukes Rainer and Joseph argued for demobilisation, disengagement, and a revival of the Josephinian reformism of the 1780s. For the time being, then, Napoleon, had nothing to fear from the Austrians, Russia and Britain, too, being inclined to a settlement. Badly shaken by the traumatic experience of Austerlitz, unable to strike directly at Napoleon except in the Adriatic, where the Russians had seized Cattaro (Kotor) and were impeding the annexation of Dalmatia, dispirited by the predictably hasty retreat now beaten by Frederick William, and mistrustful of Britain, Alexander now opened peace negotiations. As for Britain, the belligerent William Pitt had died at the beginning of 1806, his administration being replaced by a new one – the so-called 'Ministry of All the Talents' – composed of his opponents and dominated by leading proponents of the idea that a compromise peace could be negotiated with France. Whilst keeping in touch with Russia, Britain therefore joined her in sending emissaries to Paris. Last but not least, we come to Prussia. On the brink of going to war with France at the time of Austerlitz, she had quickly drawn back, on 15 December signing a treaty of alliance. Later modified in further negotiations in Paris, this agreement committed Prussia to closing to British trade her own ports, together with the rivers Elbe, Weser and Ems, which gave access to Hamburg, Bremen and Emden; to ceding Cleves-Berg and Neuchâtel to France and Ansbach to Bavaria; and to guaranteeing the integrity of France, the German states, Napoleon's Italian satellites, and the Ottoman Empire, in exchange for all of which Prussia was allowed to annexe Hanover.

Once again, then, Europe seemed to be on the threshold of a general peace, but in the event nothing of the sort transpired. In so far as Britain and Russia were concerned, Napoleon would make none of the concessions that were necessary to secure a peace settlement. Far from offering to withdraw from any part of his sphere of influence as he had originally intimated that he might, Napoleon demanded that Britain surrender Sicily, the most that he would offer in exchange being the return of Hanover. As for Russia, the Russian plenipotentiary, D'Oubril, was prevailed upon to sign a treaty whereby, in exchange for recognising the independence of the petty states of Ragusa (Dubrovnik) and the Ionian Islands, France was to be confirmed in all her gains, but this proved unacceptable to Saint Petersburg, and negotiations therefore lapsed, the war in any case now being revived in dramatic fashion by the Prussians. Thus, in the wake of his treaty with Napoleon, Frederick William had suddenly discovered the limitations of the emperor's friendship. With Prussia's trade badly hit by the blockade that Britain had promptly imposed on her ports, she now experienced a period of unparallelled humiliation, for Napoleon, whilst certainly not desirous of a war with her, was not prepared to treat her with even a modicum of respect. Thus, in July 1806 Napoleon organised his new Confederation of the Rhine – initially a league of fourteen of the minor states of central and southern Germany – without any reference to Prussia. To sweeten the pill, it was suggested that Frederick William form a Prussian-dominated confederation in northern Germany, but, when the minor states concerned were approached, it was discovered that the French had persuaded them to reject the whole idea. Still worse, it then transpired that in the course of the abortive peace negotiations opened with him by the Talents, Napoleon had offered to return Hanover to Britain. An influential party deeply concerned at the manner in which the prestige of the state and army was being undermined having already formed in the Prussian court, Frederick William was finally, and most unwillingly, forced into a declaration of war.

Fighting all but alone when a year before she might have done so in the company of both Austria and Russia, Prussia was now crushed: with her army broken at the double disaster of the battles of Jena and Auerstädt, most of the country was occupied, and Frederick William forced to flee to Königsberg (Kaliningrad). Joined in East Prussia by large Russian forces, the Prussians fought on, and on 7–8 February 1807 the French were held to an extremely bloody draw at the battle of Eylau (Bagrationovsk). However, on 14 June the Russians were overwhelmed at Friedland (Pravdinsk) and Alexander was now persuaded not only to sue for peace, but to seek an alliance with Napoleon. In doing so, his reasons were manifold. War had broken out between Russia and Turkey in October 1806, the Russian army was exhausted, Prussia was clearly enfeebled beyond hope of recovery, and distrust was growing of Britain, which was felt to have done too little to help the Russians and to be far too preoccupied with selfish commercial concerns. Meanwhile, Napoleon, who for various reasons of his own also wanted a deal, for once did not resort to the diplomacy of *diktat* and made use of his considerable personal charm to win over the tsar, the result being the Treaty of Tilsit (Sovetsk). Securing peace through the relatively modest concessions of the evacuation of Cattaro (Kotor) and the Ionian islands and the recognition of the Napoleonic settlement of Italy, Germany and Poland, Alexander obtained in exchange a substantial portion of Prussian Poland. Meanwhile, Russia was to offer to mediate between Britain and France, and to join with Napoleon, should these offers be rejected, in the process pressurising Denmark, Sweden, Portugal and Austria to do likewise. As for Turkey, France would put pressure upon her to make peace, declaring war upon her if her terms were not accepted. If Russia had escaped relatively lightly, however, the Prussians fared disastrously. Completely abandoned, they were forced to pay a heavy indemnity, to reduce their forces to a tiny rump of 42,000 men, to maintain a large French garrison, and to accept the loss of half their territory, their western territories and the bulk of Prussian Poland being seized to form the new states of Berg, Westphalia and the Grand Duchy of Warsaw.

Harsh though these terms were, Frederick William was for some years loath to challenge them: indeed, far from heeding the demands of the powerful reformist party that emerged in Prussia after 1807 that he should go to war when opportunities offered in 1809 and again early in 1811, he backed down when a full-blown crisis occurred in Franco-Prussian relations in the autumn of 1811 and repeatedly mooted the idea of an alliance with France, such an agreement finally being signed early in 1812. As a result, if one disregards a weak and isolated Sweden, Napoleon once again seemed to have secured a general peace. However, within two years he was again at war with Austria, and within two more on the brink of renewed conflict with Russia. In part, of course, this was the result of the continued conflict with Britain, for, having formally initiated a total exclusion of British trade from the Continent – the so-called Continental System – by means of the decree of Berlin of 21 November 1806, Napoleon was to find himself under the necessity of extending his direct rule ever further, or, at least, of fighting any power that refused to close its ports to British ships. Moreover, locked in a titanic struggle with Britain as he was, it became ever more important to him that his allies and satellites should function in an efficient and reliable manner. As had been the case at an earlier stage in Napoleon's career, it can therefore be argued that French aggression was in part the result of circumstance, and, further, that, rather than willing such a policy, the emperor was impelled into yet more acts of conquest. However, arguments of this nature ignore the fact that, at bottom, the war with Britain was the fruit of Napoleon's own obstinacy, whilst it is also impossible to deny that many of his actions continued to be provocative in the extreme. If the wars continued, in short, the fault remained none but his.

With regard to Napoleon's reckless disregard for international sensibilities, we can find no better example than the events which now transpired in Spain and Portugal. A French ally since 1804, Spain had long since agreed to close her ports to British ships and had sent a division of troops to take part in the attack on Swedish Pomerania that Napoleon had launched following the Treaty of Tilsit. However, Portugal, though neutral, remained an outpost of British trade, with the result that she now came under Napoleon's eye. With the agreement of Spain, which expected to secure part of Portugal's territory, a French army was soon heading for her frontier, and in November 1807 she was completely occupied, the Portuguese royal family fleeing to Brazil. At this point, however, signs emerged of serious dissension in the Spanish court and Napoleon now came to a fatal conclusion. Already angered by the chronic weakness of his ally, not to mention the somewhat inept attempts of the royal favourite, Manuel de Godoy, to escape the French alliance, the emperor now determined upon the overthrow of the Bourbon dynasty and the modernisation of Spain. Suddenly seizing the Spanish border fortresses, the large numbers of troops sent into northern Spain so as, ostensibly at least, to secure communications with Portugal, therefore began to bear down on Madrid. So complicated was the political situation in the Spanish capital at this point that it defies description here, but, in brief, the result of the French move was a military coup that toppled not only Godoy but Charles IV and established a new régime under the heir-apparent who now became Ferdinand VII. With Ferdinand desperate to ingratiate himself with Napoleon and the French alliance suddenly wildly popular – for Godoy had been generally hated – the emperor need have gone no further. However, blind to anything other than his desire to advance his own family and his distrust of Bourbon monarchies, in circumstances of the utmost bad faith Napoleon now effectively kidnapped the entire royal family and forced both Charles and Ferdinand to abdicate, Joseph Bonaparte being declared king in their stead.

With Joseph on the throne, the way seemed open for Spain's enforced regeneration, but in fact the entire country rose in revolt, Portugal following suit a few days later. Thus began the so-called 'Peninsular War'. Raging unchecked till 1814, this ensured that warfare henceforth never vanished from the Continent, whilst acting as a serious drain on imperial resources, morale and prestige, and providing Britain with a permanent base on the European mainland. At the same time, however, the overthrow of the Bourbons also seriously destabilised the situation elsewhere – as the then Austrian ambassador to Paris, Clemens von Metternich, observed: 'The noise made by the fall of a throne is formidable and echoes round the world, though in principle it is no worse than the passage of a detachment to carry off a wretched Bourbon from sanctuary, and have him shot at Vincennes.'[20] Thus, though not much impressed by the Spanish revolt, and still less by the somewhat hysterical reaction of those of his advisers who feared, like Czartorysky, that Napoleon might act in a similar manner in Russia, Alexander was irritated by the emperor's failure to consult him with regard to the dethronement of the Bourbons and encouraged to become more intractable. More importantly, in Austria the news caused genuine panic, Francis, Charles, Rainer and Joseph all now concluding, firstly, that Napoleon's ambition was insatiable, and, secondly, that even the most abject appeasement could not save them. Seizing their advantage, the war party in the court now pressed their views upon Francis, pointing out that Austria had to be Napoleon's next target

20 *Cit.* J. M. Thompson, *Napoleon Bonaparte* (Oxford, 1952), p. 295.

and that, with the French tied down in Spain, no moment could be more propitious for a pre-emptive strike. As in Prussia in 1806, meanwhile, public opinion, at least amongst the Austrian Germans, was vigorously whipped up in favour of war to such an extent that it began to appear folly to resist it and on 23 December 1808 it was therefore agreed that Austria should go to war in the spring, albeit with aims that were limited to the restoration of the Lunéville settlement and the Holy Roman Empire.

There followed the campaign of 1809. After failing to obtain support from either Russia or Prussia, Austria was forced to fight alone other than with somewhat grudging British offers of military and financial assistance that failed to materialise until too late. Nor was the situation in Spain as much of a help as it might have been since Napoleon had launched a devastating counterattack in the late autumn of 1808 that had forced the evacuation of the British army from La Coruña, temporarily shattered the Spanish forces, and left the emperor himself free to campaign elsewhere (it is true, however, that the continuing war in the Peninsula left the French dangerously short of veteran troops for use elsewhere, the army that was now flung together to face the Austrians being of noticeably poorer quality than its predecessors of 1805–7). Assisted only by a popular revolt in the Tyrol, in April the Austrian armies struck simultaneously into Bavaria, Italy, Dalmatia and the Grand Duchy of Warsaw. However, little was achieved on any of these fronts, and in Bavaria Charles was badly defeated at Abensburg and Eggmühl, thereafter being forced to retreat on Vienna, which was abandoned to the French without a fight on 13 May. On 21–22 May a dramatic counterattack caught Napoleon in an unfavourable position in a bridgehead across the Danube at Aspern-Essling and forced him to withdraw to the south bank with considerable losses, but, embarrassing though this reverse was, on 5–6 July Napoleon crossed the Danube once again and inflicted a hard-fought but heavy defeat on Charles at Wagram. Battered, dispirited and facing a renewed French attack at Znaim (Znojmo), Charles called for an armistice a week later, this eventually resulting in the Peace of Schonbrunn of 14 October 1809.

Already badly hit in 1805, Austria was now punished still further. Carinthia, Carniola and that part of Croatia south of the river Sava were annexed and joined with the territories lost in Istria and Dalmatia in 1805, and the city-state of Ragusa (Dubrovnik), which had been occupied by the French in 1807, to form the French-ruled Illyrian Provinces; Western Galicia – the portion of central Poland seized by Austria in 1795 – was divided between Russia and the Grand Duchy of Warsaw; and Salzburg and Berchtesgaden, together with a small area on the right bank of the river Inn around the town of Ried, were ceded to Bavaria. Meanwhile, Austria had to pay an indemnity of 85,000,000 francs, reduce the size of her army to 150,000 men, and agree to join the Continental System. Under the leadership of Metternich, who had now become chancellor, salvation was now sought in a détente with France, for the prospects of resistance seemed worse than ever: Austria's financial position was catastrophic, the army in disarray, and Hungary restive and unco-operative; as for allies, meanwhile, a British expedition to Holland had petered out in delay, fever and fiasco on the island of Walcheren; Prussia was helpless; and Russia not yet to be relied upon, despite the evidence of her growing differences with France. Whilst not ruling out the possibility of revenge at some point in the future, Metternich therefore for the time being confined Austrian policy to what he called 'tacking, turning and flattering'.[21] Thus, Austria co-operated in the implementation of the Continental System and later provided a strong force of troops for the attack on Russia; the Archduchess Marie Louise was, at the direct instigation of Metternich, married to Napoleon; and the chancellor himself spent ten months in Paris in an attempt to insinuate himself into the emperor's good graces.

With both Prussia and Austria reduced to a state of abject servility, there remained only Russia as a potential focus for hostility, though it had in fact at first seemed that a war with her was most unlikely. Charmed by Napoleon as he was, the tsar had been perfectly sincere at Tilsit, believing that Russia had emerged remarkably well from the war, and that a deal with France was not only beneficial to Russia's interests but the only way to ensure peace in Europe. At the same time, already mistrustful of the British, he was infuriated by the attack launched on Copenhagen in September 1807. Determined to make the alliance work, he appointed Count Nicolai Rumyantsev, a fierce long-term opponent both of involvement in the French wars and of British commercial influence, as foreign minister, Rumyantsev also being an enthusiastic slavophile who was eager for the partition of the Ottoman Empire. In taking such a position, moreover, the tsar was flying in the face of virtually the entire court and nobility, amongst whom hatred for Napoleon

---

21 Metternich to Francis I, 10 August 1809, *cit*. R. Metternich (ed.), *Memoirs of Prince Metternich, 1773–1815* (London, 1880), II, p. 364.

was matched only by fear for the immense profits that accrued to them from the export of grain, timber, flax and hemp to Britain, and thus risking the same fate as his assasinated father.

In Russia, then, Napoleon had the makings of a genuine ally, but, being Napoleon, he was incapable of capitalising on this situation: within a year Alexander had come to the conclusion that another war was only a matter of time. In the first place, the alliance with Napoleon brought few benefits. As expected, Russian trade with Britain collapsed, seaborne exports being slashed by two thirds. However, France could not make up the deficit, for, though as eager for naval materials of all sorts as Britain, transporting such materials by land across Europe simply was not feasible (not, in fact, that Napoleon did much to help: though exports to France did increase, by 1810 even Rumyantsev was complaining of Napoleon's tariff policy). Modern research has suggested that the damage to trade was not as great as has been suggested, and that the removal of British competition stimulated some modest economic growth, but what is undeniable is that Tilsit did lead to a financial crisis with customs revenue falling dramatically and the paper currency, on which the régime was increasingly forced to rely, depreciating by a factor of perhaps one half. Meanwhile, persuaded to go to war against Sweden (which had evacuated its Pomeranian outpost the previous year, but which remained at war with Napoleon), Alexander found that he received little support from Napoleon; it took a palace revolution in Stockholm finally to assure him of the annexation of Finland. Finally, in the Balkans, Napoleon, who, it will be recalled, was supposed to mediate between Russia and Turkey, and, in the event of the latter proving obdurate, go to war against her, first proposed unacceptably lenient peace terms, then put forward a grandiose plan for the partition of the Balkan peninsula (whose details, incidentally, were wholly unacceptable) as the preliminary step in a march on India, and, finally, distracted by the outbreak of the Peninsular War, ended up by giving Alexander no support at all.

If the French alliance was proving unsatisfactory, in other respects matters were becoming distinctly alarming. At home it was discovered that French agents were active in White Russia, this giving rise to fears that Napoleon intended to transform the region into an independent principality. Linked with this issue was the question of the extensive territories seized from Poland during the partitions, for, having created the Grand Duchy of Warsaw, Napoleon was courting the violently nationalistic Polish gentry.

Abroad, meanwhile, in the last resort both Prussia and Austria were essential to Alexander as a means of maintaining the balance of power, but the former seemed to be in danger of still further territorial losses and the latter in growing danger of attack. And, finally, further afield, Napoleon was proceeding with the same lack of moderation that had so dismayed Alexander before 1805: thus, setting aside the question of Spain and Portugal, in Italy Rome was occupied and the short-lived kingdom of Etruria annexed to France.

In view of all of this activity, Napoleon's attempts to embroil Alexander in a partition of the Ottoman empire and an invasion of India, and encouragement of his attack on Sweden could not but appear in a most sinister light. Never as ambitious with regard to the Balkans as either Czartorysky or Rumyantsev, Alexander abandoned all thought of driving the Ottomans from Europe, and, whilst rejecting the pleas of the Prussian leader, Stein, that he unite with Austria in a common front against Napoleon, he nevertheless decided to become far more obdurate, and, in particular, to secure some lessening of the pressure on Austria and Prussia. Meeting the French ruler at Erfurt in September 1808, he was further encouraged in his resistance by the French foreign minister, Talleyrand, who, much concerned by the ever more alarming behaviour of his master, spent much time secretly trying to persuade Alexander to resist him. Whilst still maintaining a show of friendship for Napoleon, Alexander in fact became determined to do no more, his resolution being hardened by the treatment meted out to Austria the following year. Needing Russia's support for the war against Britain, Napoleon now at last tried a policy of conciliation, reining in Polish ambitions and opening negotiations for a marriage with the tsar's younger sister. Yet the emperor would not go so far as to completely to rule out a restoration of the kingdom of Poland, and outraged Alexander by switching his attentions to the rival bride offered by Austria. By now the breach between the two rulers was virtually open, the year 1810 seeing Alexander hinting at the incorporation of the Grand Duchy of Warsaw into a Russian-dominated greater Poland and imposing an anti-French tariff, and Napoleon pursuing his crusade against British trade by means of annexing not only the Hanseatic states, but also the Duchy of Oldenburg, whose ruler happened to be Alexander's brother-in-law. So angry was the tsar at these actions that he now began to undertake serious preparations for war by increasing the size of the army and putting out feelers for a *rapprochement* with Sweden and Turkey, eventually securing a treaty of alliance with the former and a peace settlement with the latter. As to Alexander's precise intentions, for some time early in 1811 he seriously considered taking the offensive against Napoleon, believing that he could persuade Austria, Prussia and Denmark to join him, together with the Poles (who would be offered a restored kingdom of Poland under Russian rule), but, when Vienna and Berlin proved unenthusiastic, the tsar had no option but to confine himself to an attitude that was entirely defensive. Knowing this, Napoleon nevertheless resolved that he must be overborne, and in the winter of 1811–12 he began to mass the largest army that Europe had ever seen in East Prussia and the Grand Duchy of Warsaw. Mere threats proving useless, on 24 May 1812 Napoleon finally resolved on invasion.

AN APTLY-NAMED CONFLICT

The dramatic events of the campaign of 1812 and its aftermath are dealt with at a later point. Suffice to say that Napoleon again refused chance after chance of a general peace. In so far as this chapter in particular is concerned, we may conclude with the simple observation that the Napoleonic Wars are amongst the most aptly named of all conflicts. Having achieved what could have been a lasting European settlement in 1801, the then first consul threw all chance of peace away through a policy of brinkmanship that forced Britain back into the war in May 1803. Thereby began the first of three inter-linked long-term struggles from which Napoleon was never able to disentangle himself (the other two were those that broke out with Sicily in 1806 and Spain and Portugal in 1808). Not content with fighting Britain and her *protégés,* the French ruler drove first Russia, then Austria, and then Prussia into war against him in their turn, provoked a further desperate outburst on the part of Austria, and finally induced such a mood of determination and obduracy in Alexander that invasion became the only means by which he could be cowed. Although Austria was not finally to concede the point until 1813, as ruler after ruler learned, there was no hope of co-operation with Napoleon upon an equal basis, his personality simply being impossible to accommodate within any normal framework of international relations.

In this sense, then, the wars of the period 1803–15 were very much 'Napoleonic', without the emperor it being very unlikely that there would have been so lengthy and generalised a conflict. This is not to say that, had an Austrian cannon ball carried off General

Bonaparte on, say, the bridge of Lodi, there would have been no war. With France committed to the natural frontiers and the creation of a sphere of influence stretching from Holland to northern Italy, serious differences separated her from the other powers, whilst it can at the same time be recognised that in France war had acquired a momentum of its own. Yet Europe had nonetheless come to terms with the Revolution, whilst even Britain's economic ambitions – supposedly the motor of her hostility to France, and, by extension, of the entire conflict – were clearly subordinate to other ends. In short, a compromise peace of the sort arranged at Lunéville and Amiens should never have been an impossibility, the unique contribution of Napoleon being to ensure that it could not last. To conclude, Napoleon may not have wanted to conquer the world, but he could not live with it on equal terms, responsibility for the endless conflict therefore being his and his alone.

2 THE TRIUMPH OF THE FRENCH

A NATION-IN-ARMS?

> During the wars of liberty, each soldier considered himself an
> important person . . . rather than regarding himself as only a cog in a
> military machine entrusted to the supreme direction of a master . . ..
> Thus, it is not entirely inexact to say that the incredible French victories
> were due to 'intelligent bayonets'.[1]

With these words, the French writer and philosopher Georges Sorel
encapsulates what has become a standard explanation for the
dramatic series of victories that between 1805 and 1809 made
Napoleon Bonaparte de facto master of Europe. In essence, this
explanation is social and political rather than military, it being
argued that the changes in French society brought about by the
Revolution produced a new style of warfare based upon the Nation-
in-Arms that overwhelmed France's more conventional opponents.
Sanctified by Carl von Clausewitz in *On War*, the idea that the
French Revolution brought about a transformation of warfare has
almost attained the status of holy writ. Thus:

> Whilst, according to the usual way of seeing things, all hopes were
> placed on a very limited military force in 1793, such a force as no-one
> had any conception of made its appearance. War had again suddenly
> become an affair of the people, and that of a people numbering thirty
> millions, every one of whom regarded himself as a citizen of the state
> . . .. By this participation in the war . . . a whole nation . . . came
> into the scale. Henceforward, the means available . . . had no longer
> any definite limits . . . and consequently the danger for the adversary
> had risen to the extreme.[2]

---

1   G. Sorel, 'Reflections on violence', *cit*. J. Stanley (ed.), *From Georges Sorel:
Essays in Socialism and Philosophy* (Oxford, 1986), pp. 219–20.
2   C. von Clausewitz, *On War*, ed. A. Rapoport (London, 1968), pp. 384–5.

For Clausewitz, too, it was axiomatic that the armies of Napoleon were synonymous with the armies of the Revolution: in his own words, 'perfected by the hand of Bonaparte', the strength of the whole French nation 'marched over Europe, smashing everything in pieces so surely and certainly, that, where it only encountered the old-fashioned armies, the result was not doubtful for a moment'.[3]

Powerful though such arguments are, however, they can yet be seen to be flawed. Whilst no-one would deny that the Revolution did indeed bring a dramatic increase in France's military strength, on close examination it becomes apparent that many of these advantages had been dissipated by 1799, that the armies of Napoleon were not synonymous with those of the Revolution, and that, above all, Napoleonic France was the very antithesis of a Nation-in-Arms. Whilst Napoleon undoubtedly benefited from the Revolution and its legacy, the full explanation for his success must therefore be sought elsewhere.

Before entering further into this controversy, however, it might first be advisable briefly to summarise the campaigns on which it is based, beginning, of course, with that of Austerlitz. Thus, in the autumn of 1805 Austria and Russia declared war on France, an army of 72,000 Austrians invading Bavaria under Mack whilst 95,000 Russians set out westwards across the Habsburg empire in support (though substantial Russian and Austrian forces were also deployed in Italy, these figures bear witness to the difficulty which all the great powers encountered in mobilising all their forces). Hastily switching the 210,000 men of his *grande armée* from their encampments on the Channel coast to the Rhine, Napoleon then advanced southeastwards towards the Danube, picking up 25,000 Bavarians en route, and cut Mack's line of retreat. Realising the danger, Mack tried repeatedly to break out, but his every effort was defeated and on 20 October 1805 he capitulated, total Austrian casualties amounting to over 50,000 men. Within three weeks the French were in Vienna and were preparing to deal with the Russians, who, with a small force of Austrians, were concentrating their forces at Olmütz (Olomouc) under Kutuzov. Enticing the 86,000 Allied troops into an offensive, Napoleon then caught them at Austerlitz (Slavkov) on 2 December with 73,000 men, launching a devastating attack from concealed positions as they marched across his front and inflicting some 25,000 casualties.

Following the campaign of Austerlitz, there followed a lull in

3 Clausewitz, *On War.*, p. 385.

the fighting before Napoleon was presented with fresh opponents in the form of the Prussians. Provoked beyond endurance by French arrogance, Frederick William III concentrated 170,000 troops, including 20,000 Saxons, in Saxony and Thuringia prior to an attack on the *grande armée*, which was currently quartered along the river Main. Once again, however, Napoleon was too fast for his opponents. Striking northwards into Saxony with 180,000 men, he succeeded in outflanking the Prussians, and then attacked them from the east at the neighbouring towns of Jena and Auerstädt. Thrown into complete confusion, the Prussians were badly beaten with the loss of over 40,000 men, their resistance now collapsing as the French fanned out northwards in a great offensive that by the end of November had taken them to the shores of the Baltic. However, rather than giving up, Frederick William fell back with the remnants of his army to Danzig (Gdansk) and Königsberg (Kaliningrad) where they were joined by 90,000 Russians under Bennigsen. Forced to advance into the difficult and inhospitable region of East Prussia in the depths of winter, the *grande armée* collided with Bennigsen at Eylau (Bagrationovsk) on 7 February 1807, and, in an appalling struggle fought in the midst of severe blizzards, was able to secure no more than a draw. With the forces of both sides totally exhausted – the French had lost perhaps 25,000 men, and the Russians 15,000 – there followed a pause in operations, which Napoleon made use of to besiege the isolated Prussian outpost of Danzig (Gdansk). When this fell on 27 May, Napoleon then moved against Königsberg (Kaliningrad), only for his right flank to be threatened by a Russian counteroffensive. In the event, however, this ended in disaster: Bennigsen was caught in an exposed position with his back to the river Alle (Lyna) at Friedland (Pravdinsk), and on 14 June his army was split in two and decisively beaten with the loss of 20,000 men, the result being the peace of Tilsit (Sovetsk).

With Austria, Prussia and Russia all now forced to make peace, the focus of military events shifted to the Iberian peninsula. French intervention in Spain and Portugal had in the course of the early summer of 1808 led to a series of popular uprisings against the French. With their forces scattered in a series of isolated pockets, the French were soon in difficulties: attempts to capture the weakly garrisoned cities of Gerona, Valencia and Zaragoza were beaten off; an army of 20,000 men was forced to surrender to General Castaños at Bailén; and the garrison of Portugal capitulated to the British after the defeat of its main body by a British expeditionary force at Vimeiro. Much enraged at the consequences – the reduction

of his hold on the Peninsula to the area north of the river Ebro –
Napoleon now transferred the *grande armée* to Spain – the bulk of
the forces that had previously been employed there had been
composed of second-line forces of a distinctly dubious character –
and at the end of October launched a massive counter offensive
with 230,000 men. Bedevilled by poor organisation and political
paralysis, the 150,000 troops whom the Spaniards had managed to
send to the front suffered a series of crushing defeats at Gamonal,
Espinosa de los Monteros, Tudela and Somosierra, Napoleon
securing the surrender of Madrid on 4 December.

For reasons that need not detain us here, these successes settled
nothing (though it should be noted that they were sufficient to place
the initiative in the Peninsula firmly in French hands until 1812),
but Napoleon nevertheless now left Spain in the belief that all that
remained of the campaign was a few mopping-up operations.
Within a few months, however, he was again at war in central
Europe, where, as we have seen, the Austrians succeeded in
obtaining a surprise victory at Aspern-Essling on 21–22 May. Yet
recovery was swift in coming, Napoleon recrossing the Danube with
188,000 men and on 5–6 July obtaining a decisive victory over the
Archduke Charles' 155,000 Austrians at Wagram.

These, then, were the victories that consolidated the French hold
upon Continental Europe, and which provided the foundation for
the legend both of Napoleon and of his *grande armée*. Merely to list
them, however, is not enough, our chief task being to establish the
methods by which they were fought, and the reasons for which they
were won.

THE CONTOURS OF NAPOLEONIC WARFARE

In examining Napoleonic warfare, the first feature to strike the
observer is the very great increase which occurred in the size of the
contending armies. Traditionally, it is the French Revolution that is
supposed to have injected a new element of mass into European
conflict, but, whilst the *levée en masse* of 1793 did have some effect
in this respect, the figures suggest that this was rather more limited
than might be expected. Indeed, if we compare the totals of
combatants in the twelve battles fought by Frederick the Great in
the Seven Years' War with those for the six greatest battles fought
in the period 1793–94, we find that the average actually fell from
92,500 to 87,500. However, similar calculations for the battles of
Austerlitz, Jena, Eylau, Friedland, Tudela, Aspern-Essling and

Wagram reveal that French armies now averaged some 81,000 men (as opposed to 49,000 under the Jacobins) and their opponents 84,000. In short, for reasons that we shall examine below, Napoleon succeeded in raising armies of a size that was almost unprecedented, his opponents being forced willy-nilly to follow suit (significantly, the only comparable example from earlier periods was Louis XIV who in wartime managed to maintain an army of between 360,000 and 390,000 men).

From this growth in the size of armies, there followed a number of consequences. In the first place, efficient staff work became imperative if armies were not to break down in complete disorder, the staff officer being transformed in the course of the wars from an aristocratic hanger-on to a skilled professional; hence, too, the emergence in most armies of a permanent general staff. In the second, armies could no longer be a mere collection of individual battalions and regiments. As the French had already shown during the Revolutionary Wars, armies had to develop a system of permanent higher formations that would allow them to disperse whilst they were on the march, thereby easing a wide range of logistical problems. Whilst all armies retained the infantry battalion and the cavalry regiment as the basic formation, these were therefore grouped into larger units known as brigades, divisions and corps, the smallest formation that could be used on its own being the division. As initially established in the French army in the 1790s, this had consisted of a force of all arms – infantry, cavalry and artillery – the theory being that each division should be able to operate on its own until relieved by friendly forces. However, whilst this pattern persisted for some time in the armies of some of Napoleon's opponents, in the French army a division came to consist of infantry or cavalry alone (together with a single battery of foot or horse artillery as appropriate), the basic unit of manoeuvre now becoming the *corps d'armée* of several divisions.

Thus organised, at the outset of a campaign armies would be deployed in an area that could often measure many hundreds of square miles (at the start of the campaign of 1806, for example, the *grande armée* was deployed in a band of territory some 160 miles long and thirty miles wide stretching from Frankfurt in the west to Amberg in the east; the Prussians, meanwhile were arrayed on a roughly parallel 175–mile front between Göttingen and Dresden). Arrayed in this fashion, they could draw supplies from a wide area of territory (in this respect the idea that French armies lived off the country, whilst their opponents relied on supply trains and magazines, is largely a myth, the latter being physically impossible for logistical reasons: whether before or after 1792 all armies relied on buying or seizing the bulk of their day-to-day needs from the local populace). At the same time, the French were both faster and more flexible: being able to advance along a number of different axes of movement simultaneously, they did not clog Europe's rather primitive roads; meanwhile, deployed over a wide area, they could respond to threats from a variety of different directions.

Having mobilised his forces, whether, as was generally the case with France's opponents, this involved assembling them in their home depots and bringing them up to the front, or simply activating them in their cantonments in the field, a general had then to decide what to do with them. If he was lucky, this task might be left to him and him alone, but, if he was not, he would find himself having to deal with monarchs, statesmen and administrations who were more or less interfering and obstructive. In many armies, too, the high command was rent with competing factions, this making life still more difficult for the unfortunate commander-in-chief. Thus impeded, he had also to deal with the fact that the art of war now stood at a genuine crossroads. In the eighteenth century, because they had been relatively few in number and, of necessity, highly trained (for the infantryman, especially, was expected to operate in formations that were notoriously cumbersome, and to fight in a manner that required an almost superhuman degree of commitment and concentration), soldiers had been regarded as a valuable commodity that had to be husbanded at all costs. Given the enormous casualties that could result from a major action and the intrinsic uncertainty of the result, war came to be based on manoeuvre rather than battle (the contrary example of Frederick the Great might be cited here, but he fought as many battles as he did not because he wanted to but because he had to). Rather than destroying the enemy army, commanders concentrated on preserving their own forces by adopting a position in which they could not be attacked and on forcing their opponents to withdraw by cutting their communications or depriving them of supplies. As for battles, whilst they continued to be fought, they became very much a last resort, the tactical and organisational limitations of eighteenth-century armies in any case ensuring that both sides remained bloodied but more or less intact. With the French Revolution, however, the situation changed dramatically. With an endless supply of fresh soldiers assured by the *levée en masse* and the need for intensive training reduced by the introduction of simpler tactics based on shock action, French generals could fight battles more frequently, whilst at the same time having a far greater chance of securing the complete destruction of the enemy (whilst the divisional system made it far easier to envelop an opponent, the columnar tactics favoured by the French made attacks on the actual battlefield far more effective). Thus it was that first the Revolutionary generals and then Napoleon were able to adopt a strategy which made the chief object of a campaign the destruction of the enemy army. For those who fought the French, however, the result was that all the known rules of warfare had been torn up, this making the task of the commander still more problematic.

Once the commander had settled on his plan of operations on the basis of such intelligence as he had been able to gather of the enemy's whereabouts and dispositions, his various subordinates would be issued with orders instructing them to hold their positions, retire, or move in the general direction of the enemy, preparatory to an attack. Assuming that this last was the course adopted, the army's columns would be preceded by a cloud of light cavalry who would have the dual tasks of reconnaissance and security. In theory, the movement of the different parts of the army would also be closely co-ordinated with one another, its various components gradually drawing closer as they drew nearer the enemy. As the offensive progressed, of course, so the defenders would also be gathering their forces together, and, in theory at least, both sides would end up confronting one another upon a single battlefield measuring only a few miles across, if they were not already doing so, those troops not present being hastily summoned to march to the sound of the guns.

Of course, matters rarely worked out so neatly. Even in the French army, commanders misunderstood their orders or disobeyed them altogether, whilst formations might be delayed by bad weather or poor roads. Alternatively, incompetent commanders might be surprised, or spread their troops over so wide an area that they could not be concentrated in time, or issue contradictory or misleading orders, whilst even good ones might be misled or be bluffed into guarding against threats that did not exist (at Waterloo, in the entirely unfounded belief that Napoleon intended to turn his right flank, Wellington deliberately deprived himself of some 17,000 much-needed men who sat the day out eight miles away at Halles). Some armies, too, might not even have any means of co-ordinating their operations upon a single point – the heterogeneous Spanish forces that faced the French on the Ebro in October 1808 are a good example, the provisional government formed in Spain in the wake of the national uprising having failed to appoint a commander-in-chief. Last but not least, even forces which found themselves in the vicinity of the main confrontation might fail to come up in support, or might arrive too late to be of assistance.

All these factors notwithstanding, a reasonably competent commander could expect to face his opponent with at least the bulk of his forces. In doing so, moreover, he could anticipate one of two roles, for, almost without exception, all Napoleonic battles were ones of attack and defence – in other words, one army adopted a position that was then assaulted by the other. There were, of course, variations upon the theme – thus, at Marengo, Auerstädt, Friedland and Aspern-Essling, armies that were on the offensive in strategic terms suddenly found themselves the object of attack, whilst at Austerlitz, Eylau, Salamanca and Waterloo armies that were being attacked turned the tables upon their assailants by launching devastating counterattacks – but only at Wagram can a case be found where both sides attacked one another simultaneously.

Almost invariably, then, the problem set for one commander would be to attack his opponent, just as the problem for the other would be to hold his ground. Coming upon his opponent's position, the attacking general would have first to assess the enemy positions (a task which might not be easy if the defenders had been hidden behind, say, the crest of a convenient ridge) and then deploy his leading troops into combat formation. Generally speaking, this would be just out of the range of the enemy's artillery (if he came any closer he might run the risk of his formations being smashed to pieces by the opposing guns or even of the defenders launching a sudden sally that might catch his own troops at a disadvantage as they deployed). Well behind the front line, meanwhile, a powerful reserve would be left in such a position and formation that it might be sent into action at any point where the course of events made it seem necessary. On the 'other side of the hill', meanwhile, a similar process would also have been carried out, with part of the forces available assigned to defend the front line, and part held well back in reserve so that they could shore up any breach that might appear or launch a local counter-attack. Last but not least, on both sides care would be taken to ensure that no formation had all its troops in the front line, each division or corps holding at least some of its men back as a local reserve so as to allow its commander to be able to plug gaps or exploit successes himself rather than having to send for help from elsewhere.

On both sides, all this – usually quite a lengthy process given the amount of time it took to change troops from their marching formations into combat ones – required much skill and judgement, for the fact was that, once an army's initial positions had been taken up, they were almost impossible to change in the presence of the enemy. For the defender, then, it was essential that troops were not heavily committed to sectors the enemy was unlikely to attack, that it was possible to switch reserves from one flank to the other, that it was possible to retreat in good order should the day go badly, and that the army could not easily be split into isolated fragments by reason of the terrain (as, for example, happened to the Russians at Friedland). Equally, for the attacker, it was axiomatic that he could physically get at the defenders, and that he, too, could move reserves around to reinforce success or meet a sudden danger.

With these preliminaries over, the battle could begin. Normally, for the assailant the first step would be an artillery bombardment designed to disrupt the enemy's front-line formations and undermine their morale, for which purpose it was increasingly the practice for 'grand batteries' of as many as 100 guns to be massed so as to deliver concentrated fire. After a certain time, the first of the assault formations would then move forward, these almost always being composed of infantry. Essentially, two formations were available for this manoeuvre. Until 1792 it had been the practice for all European armies to fight in linear formation with each infantry battalion deployed in a three-deep line so as to maximise its fire effect. For most of France's opponents, this tactical system remained the norm until defeat at the hands of the French forced a reappraisal, but under the Revolution in the French army it had become the practice to form each battalion in column – i.e. a solid block of men perhaps fifty wide and twelve deep. Thus arrayed, the troops could move faster, it being notoriously difficult to manoeuvre in line, whilst training in musketry became less important, for only the troops in the front ranks could use their weapons. In theory, the drill adopted by the French allowed columns to switch rapidly back into line so that they could engage in a fire-fight if engaged by enemy infantry, but in practice this was never the intention: not only were battalion columns frequently crammed in so close together that it would have been impossible for them to deploy into line, but experience had shown that, once troops in line had stopped to open fire, it became virtually impossible to get them on the move again, the combat degenerating into an indecisive exchange of musketry. In short, the column was a weapon designed for shock action that was meant to intimidate through sheer size and weight of numbers, another of its advantages, of course, being that it allowed the concentration of much larger numbers of troops in a much smaller space than did the line. Imposing though a divisional column was as a psychological weapon, however, particularly when its appearance of mass was reinforced with repeated cheering and the rhythmic drumbeat of the *pas de charge*, its success required other factors, the first of which was a successful bombardment of the defenders. Extremely vulnerable to artillery and musketry, it had also to be protected by a heavy screen of skirmishers – troops who fought in open order as individuals – whose task it was to advance ahead of the columns unsettling the opposition by picking off officers and NCOs (as skirmishers were sometimes – but not always – better trained, able to take their time loading and firing and to make use of such cover as was available, less blinded by smoke, and free of the encumbrance of being jostled by close-packed neighbours, they were invariably more accurate than close-order troops).

Whether arrayed in line or column, then, the front-line infantry would advance, their opponents usually waiting for them in line, this remaining the standard defensive formation in all armies. As they did so, the attackers' artillery necessarily fell silent, leaving that of the defenders free to ply them first with shot and then, as they got closer, with the deadly antipersonnel weapon known as canister (or, more popularly, grapeshot). So severe could this fire be that it might on its own be sufficient to turn back an assault, but as a rule the advance would continue until the attacking infantry came to within 150 yards – musket range – of their opponents. If formed in line, they would then open fire, their officers endeavouring to ensure that they continued to advance after each volley, but, if formed in column, they would simply keep going, if possible at a still faster tempo (a variation here was that columns might halt at a distance and wait for their skirmishers to soften up the defenders, only charging forward when it was clear that the latter were wavering). Meanwhile, the defenders would generally open fire in their turn, clashes between two forces formed in line now degenerating into an extended exchange of fire which one side or the other would eventually be too exhausted and depleted to continue. Where the attackers were in column and chose to charge home, however, one of two things would happen. Either the attackers would be brought to a halt as the front ranks of each battalion disintegrated into what rapidly became a wall of dead and and wounded men, or the defenders would break and run. Assuming that they fled, this would be the moment to bring up fresh formations to widen the breach in the enemy line or to launch a dramatic cavalry charge that would sweep away wavering units and convert retreat into a frantic, panic-stricken *sauve qui peut*. However, if the defenders stood, the result would be an exchange of fire at close range which they would generally win, the attackers eventually tumbling back in disorder to their original positions (a highly successful alternative much favoured by the British was to deliver a single volley and follow it up with a bayonet charge).

This combat between infantry and infantry was the heart of the Napoleonic battle, cavalry generally playing a subsidiary role. Thus, on their own, cavalry could almost never break steady infantry. Although a massive charge might scatter entire armies of poor-quality troops in a matter of minutes (as at Ocaña on 19 November 1809), an oncoming wall of horsemen being an even more terrifying sight than an infantry column, experienced soldiers knew that cavalry could not touch them so long as they held their ground. Attacked from the front, even a line could turn back a mounted attack, but, as lines were extremely vulnerable if cavalry could get round their flanks, wise commanders would form their men into battalion 'squares' (crudely speaking, a line bent back upon itself to form a hollow box). In this formation, infantry were absolutely safe, the unfortunate horsemen being left to gallop aimlessly about until they were chased away by mounting casualties or a counter-charge by other cavalry.

On their own, then, cavalry were of little use in a direct attack upon enemy infantry so long as the latter were not caught by surprise, though they might achieve a little more if accompanied by batteries of horse artillery, half a dozen guns being able to destroy in a few minutes the closely packed target presented by a square. However, in other ways they could be a most valuable asset. Through the simple threat of a charge, a few regiments of cavalry could pin down entire enemy divisions and thus prevent them from intervening elsewhere, whilst, as part of a combined attack, cavalry could be deadly. For example, attached to attacking infantry, cavalry could force the defenders into a square, thereby severely impeding their ability to defend themselves against infantry; alter-natively, at a decisive moment they could launch a sudden charge that might cause already shaken defenders to turn and run. Where the target was enemy cavalry, however, the classic charge would really come into its own, for, with the defenders driven away, the victorious horsemen could wheel to right or left and attack the next enemy formation in flank or rear, this tactic particularly successful if that force was already engaged. And, finally, once an enemy had been broken, it was the task of the cavalry to harry his retreating formations, hunt down fugitives, and generally ensure that all chances of organised resistance were at an end. Meanwhile, on the defensive, cavalry could be used to break up an assault that had begun to falter, or, in really desperate situations, to launch suicidal charges against attacking infantry that might buy a little time for help to be brought up or the defenders disengaged.

Whilst there were an almost infinite number of variations upon the theme, the sort of actions that we have been describing constituted the main outlines of the Napoleonic battle. Attack would succeed attack, and, sooner or later, one side or the other would be overborne, in that, with all its formations either neutralised, defeated or committed to the fighting, it would have nothing left either, in the case of the attacker, to continue the struggle, or, in the case of the defender, to counter a fresh move on the part of his assailant. Occasionally, of course, this point might never be reached, the battle being curtailed by, say, the coming of night and the result becoming a draw or, at best, a tactical victory. Otherwise, however, a competent general would now exploit the decisive moment by one last stroke, the defeated army giving way altogether and being hurried on its way by an energetic pursuit. Indeed, as such hollow victories as Borodino and Bautzen show, such a pursuit was the key to decisive strategic success, the losses to the beaten army in men, morale and general cohesion often being far more serious than those inflicted on the battlefield itself (taking the campaign of 1806 as the most obvious example, the Prussians lost at least three times as many casualties during the great pursuit that followed their defeat as they did at Jena and Auerstädt).

In some of Napoleon's campaigns a single victory of this type sufficed to bring an enemy to the peace table. More commonly, though, campaigns consisted of a series of actions, each of which followed naturally from the one that preceded it. Just as in a field battle, the fortunes of war might swing violently from one side to the other, but, so long as mutual exhaustion did not set in or political considerations lead to a compromise peace, sooner or later one of the belligerents would establish a preponderance over the other, the campaign thereafter proceeding inevitably to the dictation of peace.

NAPOLEON AND FRANCE

These, then, were the main characteristics of warfare in the Napoleonic era. To understand the reasons for France's dramatic successes in the period 1805–9, however, we must first consider the policies pursued by Napoleon Bonaparte when he took power in France in 1799. Given her population of 29,000,000, it might be thought that all that France had to do to acquire a mass army was to introduce a law establishing the principle of universal military service. Needless to say, however, matters were not nearly so straightforward, an effective system of conscription being contingent upon the process of political and administrative reform to which we must now turn.

France had in fact possessed a system of universal conscription since 1798, the so-called Loi Jourdan introduced in that year decreeing all unmarried men to become liable for military service at the age of twenty according to a quota based on the population of each department and commune. Thus, the government would announce the conscription of so many thousand men, its representatives in the provinces then compiling lists of all those liable to the call-up, after first excluding the various exempt categories (other than the physically unfit, these included sole bread-winners, government officials, priests and students). A comparison of the two figures having established the number of recruits each area was expected to produce, a ballot would be held in each commune to determine who should actually serve. However, although it was essentially to be the basis for conscription to the French army throughout the Napoleonic period, at the time of its introduction the Loi Jourdan was little more than a dead letter. From the time of the first introduction of compulsory service on an ad hoc basis in the emergency of 1793, this had been hated by the peasantry who constituted the bulk of the population. Service in the army meant loss of home and family, not to mention the security of familiar surroundings, and brought with it privation, danger and death; soldiers were notoriously brutal and licentious; and finally conscription deprived peasant communities of much-needed labour, whilst being rightly perceived as being socially unjust (for, in general, the towns and the bourgeoisie suffered less than the countryside and the peasantry). Nor did large sections of the peasantry think the Revolution was worth fighting for: in many parts of the country the financial burdens under which they had laboured had actually worsened since 1789; they had benefited little from the sale of the lands of the Church and the *émigrés*; they had periodically been subject to ruthless requisitioning by the representatives of the hated *bourgs*; and they had seen their religion – the centre of their cultural and emotional life – subjected to wave upon wave of ever more virulent anticlericalism. Across large parts of France, peasant unrest in consequence reached massive proportions and the problem of public order was worsened still further by the growing incidence of desertion, many of those who fled the ranks turning to brigandage as the only means by which they could support themselves. By 1798, in fact, so serious had the problem become that the Directory was quite incapable of enforcing its authority, local government, and with it the power to enforce taxation and levy troops, having fallen into a state of complete collapse. With its problems augmented by the military disasters of 1799, the Directory turned in desperation to a revival of the Jacobinism of 1793, but in doing so it only deepened the crisis. Much alarmed by what they saw as a further threat to property and order, and financially very badly hit by economic depression and the Directory's attempts to stabilise the financial situation by slashing payments on the national debt and re-organising the fiscal system, the *notables* – the men of property, much of it obtained in the course of the Revolution, who formed the bedrock of French local government – also withdrew their support from Paris. Sabotaged by popular resistance and propertied non-co-operation alike, the Loi Jourdan therefore initially proved a complete failure, only 131,000 of the first 400,000 men men called up ever reaching their units.

When Napoleon came to power, then, France essentially had the makings of a large-scale war effort, but not the ability to capitalise upon them. Within a very short space of time, however, the first consul had changed all that, in the first place by reinforcing the structures of government. At the very apex of the system, a council of state was established to help draft legislation and provide Napoleon with expert advice, whilst the various ministries were reorganised and various measures introduced to co-ordinate their work, the bureaucracy, the fiscal system, the judiciary, and the very law itself (through the promulgation of the famous *Code Napoléon* of 1804) being rationalised and reordered. At the same time, in February 1800 the whole system of local government was transformed. Whereas the ideal since the Revolution had been that the law should be implemented by elected local councils, authority was now placed in the hands of officials appointed by Paris, the administration of each department now being headed by an all-powerful prefect (to fill this new position in the future a trained corps of senior bureaucrats was created through the appointment of *auditeurs* – young men attached to the council of state to observe the workings of government before being sent out into the administration). Assisting the prefect, meanwhile, was a network of subordinate subprefects, one of whom was appointed to each of the *arrondissements* into which the departments were henceforth divided, the communes that formed the lowest tier of the system in turn having a mayor, who again was appointed from above. Department, *arrondissement*, and commune alike all had a council, but this was now co-opted from lists of local *notables*, the elective principle virtually disappearing. In theory, at least, highly efficient – on 16 February Napoleon boasted to the legislature that in future 'the orders of the government will be transmitted to the uttermost limits of the body politic with the swiftness of an electric current'[4] – the system ensured that the men in charge of local affairs were now entirely dependent upon Paris for their survival. Highly paid and very often hailing from other parts of France than the areas in which they served, the prefects, in theory at least, were also immune to bribery and the pressures of local interests (at the level of the *mairie*, in particular, problems continued to be experienced in this respect, but in so far as possible these were short-circuited by transferring many responsibilities to the more reliable *arrondissement*).

Whilst these measures did achieve some success – by 1801, for example, the military authorities were at last beginning to receive reliable information on draft evasion – the mere reform of local government was not enough. Backing up the prefects were military resources that were both more powerful and more reliable: efforts were made to rotate National Guard battalions so that they served outside their own locality; the Gendarmerie Nationale was purged, rebuilt with reliable veteran soldiers, placed under an Inspector General, and greatly increased in size; Paris and other large cities were permitted to form municipal guards; and in 1805 each prefect was given a company of reservists as an immediate source of military support. More immediately, the lull in hostilities following the battle of Marengo also allowed the dispatch of large numbers of troops into the interior to suppress brigands and round up deserters, their activities being strengthened by the introduction of special judicial measures that effectively authorised summary execution.

4 *Cit.* M. J. Sydenham, *The First French Republic, 1792–1804* (London, 1974), p. 240.

Thanks to the régime's greater ability to turn to repression, the inhabitants of Napoleonic France knew that open opposition would be likely to have unpleasant consequences. However, the political settlement that followed 18 Brumaire was characterised as much by the carrot as it was by the stick. Whilst Napoleon was certainly concerned above all to boost the power of the state – whose interests, of course, he had come to identify with his own person – he was well aware that his rule could not be consolidated unless, as he put it, 'we can plant on the soil of France some masses of granite'.[5] In effective terms, what this meant was that the new régime should seek to conciliate key elements of society. The peasantry, for example, were bought off by the abandonment of Revolutionary dechristianisation, the concordat of 1801 restoring freedom of worship to the Catholic Church. Also helpful here was a reduction in conscription, between 1800 and 1805 the number of men taken by the army amounting to a mere 78,000 per annum. Most importantly, however, the propertied classes in general received especially favourable treatment. Thus, the *notables* were guaranteed in the possession of the land they had obtained from the Church and the nobility since the Revolution, whilst both *ci-devants* and *notables* were given a very high degree of representation in the political and administrative structures created by the régime. This brought with it generous salaries and other emoluments, not to mention considerable social status (those nobles who had emigrated were also encouraged to return, being welcomed into the army and bureaucracy with open arms). At the same time, too, with most secondary school places still fee-paying, they had a monopoly of higher education; they could escape the worst rigours of conscription, and came to dominate the officer corps; they were favoured heavily by Napoleon's fiscal policy, which relied heavily on direct taxation; and they could rely on the régime to protect their economic interests through such measures as restrictive labour legislation or, for that matter, many of the provisions of the *Code Napoléon*.

In addition to the conciliation of certain sectors of society, Napoleon also made great efforts to persuade public opinion as a whole that his policies were in the national interest, propaganda becoming a vital part of his régime. For example, if the *ci-devants* and the *notables* were co-opted into the régime, it was in part so that, as leaders of local society, they could become ambassadors

5   *Cit.* A. C. Thibaudeau, *Bonaparte and the Consulate*, ed. G. Fortescue (London, 1908), pp. 266–7.

amongst the people. Equally, if an emasculated legislature continued to meet in Paris, it was in part because it acted as a forum in which Napoleon could justify his policies and extol his successes. In this respect, moreover, every aspect of cultural life was pressed into service as a mouthpiece of the government. With regard to the press, for example, Napoleon on the one hand imposed rigid censorship, and on the other ensured that his message reached the widest possible audience by having papers produced in cheap editions and read aloud in public places. Amongst the intelligentsia, meanwhile, writers who supported the régime were patronised and encouraged, whilst those who did not were harassed, imprisoned or forced into exile. And in education, teachers fell increasingly under the control of the state, whilst *lycée* students were made to wear uniform, do drill, and study a national curriculum that combined utility with propaganda. Granted freedom of worship, the Church, too, found that the price was the use of religion to underpin the régime – a convenient Saint Napoleon was even discovered – and the conversion of the pulpit into an instrument of political indoctrination. Finally, even the arts – painting, music and architecture – were appropriated to glorify Napoleonic rule, the result being the so-called 'empire style'.

Through a combination of factors, then, Napoleon restored order to France, and thereby made it possible for her considerable resources to be converted into actual military power. Having said this, it should be stressed that the transformation was not as absolute as the French ruler's many hagiographers have made out, brigandage proving slow to die down, many mayors continuing to connive at draft evasion, and resistance to conscription remaining an extremely serious problem for many years. However, enough had been done to end the utter disorder of the Directory, Napoleon henceforward being backed by a system of government that would, so long as too much was not required of it, provide him with adequate supplies of men and money. This situation, moreover, should be compared with that of his opponents who everywhere remained tied to the limitations of the *ancien régime*, and, above all, its defence of corporate privilege. With the Church, the nobility and many towns and cities protected from more than the barest minimum of taxation, with systems of conscription that affected only a limited section of the population thanks to a variety of social, occupational and geographical exemptions, and with administrative systems that were notorious for their confusion and lack of logic, none of the Continental powers could hope to equal France in terms of resources or efficiency.

THE *GRANDE ARMÉE*

On the basis of the armies of the Revolution and of the political and administrative reforms that we have just examined, Napoleon created a superlative fighting force whose qualities have continued to fascinate military historians even to this day. *Pace* Sorel and Clausewitz, however, he did not in any sense preside over a Nation-in-Arms, it being clear that, had he attempted to rely on this principle, his whole political system would have collapsed, which is precisely what occurred in 1814. On the contrary, raised by mass conscription though it largely was, his military machine was wholly professional, this greatly accentuating its undoubted technical merits.

Surprising though the claim that France was not a Nation-in-Arms might seem, it is in fact easy to substantiate, the army inherited by Napoleon having been radically transformed from that of the heroic days of 1793. Thus, whereas it can be argued that the armies of 1793–94 had fought out of a spirit of civic and patriotic duty, by 1799 France's soldiers were driven by *esprit de corps* and self-interest, the reason being that the fall of the Jacobins had been followed by the collapse of all such links as had existed between the army and the nation. With conscription abandoned, the bulk of the troops now permanently stationed outside France, and the army increasingly bitter at the incompetence and corruption associated with the Directory, the military became more and more alienated from society. Meanwhile, eager for advancement and glory, all too many of its generals were determined to throw off civilian tutelage and eradicate all traces of egalitarianism from the military estate. As a result, a new spirit began to emerge in its ranks. Henceforward soldiers were encouraged to identify, not with the nation, but with each other, with their regiments, which now once again began to acquire individual distinctions and traditions, and with their generals. With the rank and file increasingly composed of hardened veterans, the limited numbers of new recruits who did reach the army were simply swamped by the new mentality, the squad of approximately a dozen men to which each rookie was assigned as he arrived acting as an important means of socialisation. Eventually, so far was the army removed from the spirit of 1793 that, in striking contrast to the young volunteer of that era who said that he was so anxious not to be considered as a soldier that 'I consistently refused to receive either pay or rations and provided my own arms and equipment', in 1807 a group of mutineers could state, 'The emperor should not go to war if he has not enough money to pay soldiers. We do not want to get ourselves killed for nothing.'[6]

As we shall see, far from being reversed with the advent of Napoleon, this tendency towards professionalisation was if anything intensified. Even had this not been the case, however, the manner in which he conducted France's war effort was hardly conducive to the survival of the principle of the Nation-in-Arms in so far as this implies the total mobilisation of the nation's resources on the basis of equality of sacrifice. In so far as was possible, in fact, Napoleon arranged matters so that France was asked to sacrifice comparatively little. With regard to the economic resources required by his wars, for example, harsh peace settlements, extortion and outright plunder continued to bring in much of what was required. Meanwhile, with regard to the army, the French were spared a great deal, conscription at first remaining at a relatively low level. In the first place France included a growing amount of non-French territory that could be raided for manpower in a manner that would have been totally unacceptable in the metropolitan heartland, one estimate putting the number of men gained from such sources at as many as half all those who served in the army as a whole. This is, perhaps, excessive, but it is known that, between 1798 and 1809 alone, Belgium provided over 90,000 men, that at least thirty of the line infantry regiments in existence in 1805 drew a part of their manpower from Italy, and that most of the many new regiments formed after that date were wholly foreign (the 111^e Ligne, for example, was Piedmontese, the 112^e Belgian, the 113^e Tuscan, the 123^e, 124^e, 125^e and 126^e Dutch, and the 127^e, 128^e and 129^e German). At the same time, the army also came to include a varying number of specifically foreign units composed of deserters, refugees and adventurers of all sorts, the total for 1805 including four Italian, four Swiss, three German, two Polish, one Negro and one Irish infantry regiment. After 1805, moreover, the variety grew still greater, the army also coming to include Croat, Albanian, Greek, Portuguese, Spanish, Lithuanian and Dutch units.

Although the burden represented by military service was at first relatively light in overall terms, it did not weigh equally upon all sections of society and parts of the country, all conscripts in the first

6 *Cit.* G. Pernoud and S. Flaissier, *The French Revolution* (London, 1961), p. 282; J. Tulard, *Napoleon: the Myth of the Saviour* (London, 1984), p. 275; for a discussion of the army's professionalisation, cf. J. Lynn, 'Toward an army of honour: the moral evolution of the French army, 1789–1815', *French Historical Studies* (hereafter *FHS*), XVI, No. 1 (Spring, 1989), 159–61.

place being allowed to send substitutes to serve in their place. Such men (usually the desperate) were secured for cash, and, as their price rose dramatically – from 300 francs in 1800 to 6500 in 1811 and even more thereafter – the concession favoured only a small minority, no more than ten per cent of those called up being able to avail themselves of it. For those with money, however, substitution was not the only escape: officials and doctors might be bribed, and posts obtained for young men of wealth and education in the civil or military administration. Alternatively, men who could pay for their own uniform and equipment could enlist in one of the many companies of ceremonial *gardes d'honneur* that were formed throughout the empire in the almost certain knowledge that they would never have to ride out against an enemy. At the same time many exemptions, especially those depending on a measure of higher education, were a near-monopoly of the propertied classes in the first place. Added to all this, meanwhile, was a measure of geographical inequality, Napoleon regarding it as politic to treat some areas far more lightly than others: in 1801 Haut Rhin, a frontier area with a long tradition of military service, was levied at a rate of one man in 860, whereas the rate in Finistère, an area much affected by peasant resistance to the Revolution, was only one in 4930.

In other areas, too, both opportunities and sacrifices were wholly unequal, the propertied classes dominating the officer corps to an extent that belies the common myth that every French drummer boy had a marshal's baton in his knapsack. Promotion from the ranks continued to be important, and, indeed, was almost certainly much higher than in any other army, but it could only be obtained through long years of service and was unlikely to lead to fame and fortune. As officers were expected to command social respect, a certain degree of culture and education was important, men who had risen from the ranks rarely possessing either; as a result, of 2248 Revolutionary and Napoleonic generals, only 177 were the sons of labourers, domestic servants or poor peasants, whilst, as for the twenty-six marshals themselves, only three had actually started their career as private soldiers. If serious progress was to be made, it was necessary to enter the officer corps directly as a cadet, and the various means of doing this, such as a course in one of the various military academies established by Napoleon, or service in the *gardes d'honneur* or one of the cadet battalions attached to the Imperial Guard between 1804 and 1806, all required considerable financial resources. If the propertied classes could not escape the wars altogether – it was not unknown for young men of good family who had failed to enlist voluntarily in the officer corps to find themselves more or less conscripted into its ranks – they were therefore assured that they would not be required to serve as common soldiers, and, further, that the potential rewards would be considerable. Thus, at least fifty-three prefects out of 306 came from a military background, as did ninety-five per cent of the members of the Legion of Honour and fifty-nine per cent of the imperial nobility, rather more than half the thirty million francs disbursed by Napoleon in the form of endowed income every year also going to army officers (in this respect the marshalate did particularly well, being rewarded with immense estates that in some cases conveyed incomes of over one million francs).

With a quasi-professional army raised by blatantly inegalitarian means and a war effort geared to saving the human and material resources of the metropolis by every means available, Napoleonic France hardly constitutes a Nation-in-Arms. To understand the reasons for the triumph of the French, we must therefore move away from Clausewitzian generalisations in favour of a detailed assessment of the Napoleonic army. In so far as this is concerned, it must first be understood that Napoleon inherited a number of valuable advantages from the armies of the Revolution in terms of tactics, organisation and personnel. Taking the issue of tactics first of all, the French infantry, in particular, had what was by far the most flexible and efficient system of tactics in the whole of Continental Europe. Whereas other armies at the time of the outbreak of war remained wedded to the cumbersome close-order line, as a result of prolonged debate in the latter years of the *ancien régime* in 1791 the French army had introduced new tactical regulations of which the basic formation for manoeuvre was the battalion column, the numerous advantages of this formation in terms of flexibility and speed of movement having already been discussed. At the same time, whereas in other armies only a relatively small number of specialist troops were trained as skirmishers, these generally being formed into separate regiments, which, of necessity, could not be omnipresent, all French infantrymen, whatever their precise designation, could fight in open order on account of their very high level of individual motivation. As a result, every attack could be covered by a thick skirmish screen, which if necessary could be more and more heavily reinforced until entire battalions were deployed in this fashion, the defenders then being overcome through musketry alone. In the absence of sufficient numbers of skirmishers – which, as the British became the first to understand, were the only counter to such tactics – an assault delivered in this fashion could be devastating. At the battle of Jena in 1806, Von Gräwert's division was virtually shot to pieces by French skirmishers hidden around the village of Vierzehnheiligen (although the Prussian army possessed twenty-seven light-infantry battalions and was further supposed to deploy the third rank of each line-infantry battalion as skirmishers, a mixture of conservatism and incompetence seems to have prevented it from deriving much benefit from these features of its organisation). Equally, on the second day of the battle of Espinosa de los Monteros (10–11 November 1808), the Asturian division of General Acevedo was routed when its commander and a large number of other officers were shot down by a strong force of French troops who had approached its position in open order, the Spaniards being so ill-trained that they could not send out an adequate number of skirmishers of their own. In the face of such threats, troops formed in close order could make no effective reply, for skirmishers were effectively immune to volley fire, whilst advancing against them with the bayonet was at best a temporary expedient and could also prove highly dangerous: at Waterloo a unit of the King's German Legion was destroyed when it was charged in the flank by French cavalry whilst advancing against some skirmishers near La Haye Sainte. Only skirmishers, in short, could counter other skirmishers, but in most Continental armies there was so rooted a prejudice against such troops – on the grounds that open-order tactics were prejudicial to discipline and an invitation to desertion – that even those units trained to fight in such a fashion were rarely properly used. Nor was the superiority of their infantry tactics the only tactical advantage enjoyed by the French. Extremely mobile, light and well-constructed, France's guns and howitzers were superior to those of almost every other army with regard to manoeuvrability and weight of fire, whilst also being available in very large numbers and commanded by officers who understood the need to concentrate them in grand batteries. Whether they were attacking or defending, French armies could therefore count on powerful support.

In organisational terms, meanwhile, the army inherited by Napoleon was strengthened by the fact that it had been formed in permanent divisions for some years, the inherent advantages of this form of structure having already been discussed. Less obviously, its introduction had also improved the quality of the army's generals. In some respects this was already very high, the Revolution having produced a crop of new commanders who would almost certainly have achieved little recognition before 1789. Napoleon himself, of course, is the prime example, but there were many others, including at least eighteen of his marshals, and, at a slightly less exalted level, such noted middle-ranking figures as Friant, Vandamme, Montbrun, Junot and Delaborde. Counting those officers whose family backgrounds were such that they would probably have made field rank anyway, perhaps half the generals serving in the army in 1805 had been commissioned since 1789. Some, of course, were found to have been promoted beyond their talents, but on the whole they were young, dynamic, ambitious and in a hurry, their boldness and aggression naturally having a great impact on French operations. Thanks to the divisional system, moreover, they were also used to handling independent bodies of troops, which on the whole their opponents were not whilst also being hindered by a series of other disadvantages. Whilst the generals of *ancien-régime* Europe have been much maligned, it has to be said that, with the exception of a few inexperienced aristocrats who owed their appointment solely to their status – the Archduke John was a mere eighteen when he was defeated by Moreau at Hohenlinden in 1800 – they were much older than their French counterparts: in the Austrian army their average age was sixty-three, whilst, in that of Prussia, out of 142 generals in 1806, seventy-nine were over sixty and only thirteen under fifty. Nurtured in an earlier age of warfare, they were unaccustomed to thinking in terms of the destruction of the enemy army being the main object of operations, and therefore found it very difficult to compete with their French counterparts (not, however, that this dissuaded them from an inclination to disparage French prowess, in 1806 the Prussian Von Rüchel even going so far as to say that Frederick William possessed 'several generals equal to M. de Bonaparte'[7]).

In terms of their personnel, too, the French armies were far superior to those of their opponents. Whereas the French junior officer of 1805 tended to be relatively young and to owe his advancement wholly to merit, his counterpart elsewhere too often tended either to be an ageing veteran who had clawed his way up from the ranks (by no means an uncommon phenomenon) and now found himself to be an 'eternal subaltern' sunk in routine, poverty and lack of education, or, alternatively, an inexperienced young nobleman given over to hunting, gaming and womanising. As for

7   *Cit.* J. R. Seeley, *The Life and Times of Stein* (Cambridge, 1878), I, p. 248.

the rank and file, perhaps fifty per cent of French soldiers had been serving in the army since 1799 or before, whilst no more than 60,000 had seen less than one year's service. Tough and experienced, they were therefore well able to withstand the rigours of campaigning, and, furthermore, to fend for themselves in the field, being particularly renowned for their ability to live off the country. In the words of one Spanish observer:

> The soldier who goes for supplies never returns with empty hands. If oxen or cattle are lacking, he brings back calves, pigs or lambs. He wages a cruel war on hens, and despises neither bread nor vegetables. The . . . country must be very poor for them not to find something more palatable than their rations.[8]

Here, too, can be seen the impact of the new style of discipline and training that had been introduced in the French army since the Revolution: no longer beaten, flogged and reduced to dehumanised automata, French soldiers were encouraged to show initiative and to retain their self-respect. At the same time, of course, they were supremely self-confident. Whatever the political changes that had taken place since 1792, and, more importantly, since 1799, for many soldiers the army's goals remained, as Charles Parquin put it, 'the great ideals of the French Revolution – the ideals of liberty, of unity, and of the future – which, as everyone instinctively knows, the Emperor Napoleon personified'.[9] With the evidence of the Revolution constantly there to remind them that Frenchmen belonged to a higher species of humanity than that of the rest of Europe, they were also fortified by an unparalleled record of success, Marengo and Hohenlinden having amply compensated for the disasters of 1799. And, last but not least, each and every man had something to fight for, for, setting aside the stimulus that might or might not have been provided by the fact that they were all free citizens with an interest in the fortunes of *la patrie*, they knew that courage and long service could bring substantial rewards. Of course, the impact of such factors should not be exaggerated, for all the evidence suggests that there were considerable limitations on the degree of loyalty and commitment which they achieved, desertion remaining a serious problem throughout the Napoleonic era. Yet,

8 F. X. Cabanes, *Ensayo acerca del sistema militar de Bonaparte* (Isla de León, 1811), p. 20.
9 B. T. Jones (ed.), *Napoleon's Army: the Military Memoirs of Charles Parquin* (London, 1987), p. 185.

for all that, the army inherited by Napoleon was better endowed with sources of positive motivation and *esprit de corps* than that of any of his opponents. In almost every other army in Europe, the soldier, who was often a foreigner and invariably recruited from the most wretched classes of society, was generally despised, lived in appalling conditions, could expect few rewards and was subject to the most savage discipline, whilst being trained in a fashion designed to eradicate all traces of initiative and personality. Nor was he even especially well-prepared: for reasons of economy many armies maintained their armies at a reduced level in peacetime or sent most of their soldiers home for much of the year, whilst in others the men were allowed to work as artisans or manual labourers. Far from being composed of hardened veterans, the armies that faced the French in the period 1805–7 therefore tended to be deficient in training and unused to life in the field, the *grande armée*, by contrast, having been permanently under arms since 1803.

In a variety of ways, then, the French army inherited a number of advantages from the Revolutionary period that were inclined to make it superior to its opponents when it came to the actual business of fighting. However, all of these were greatly enhanced by Napoleon. Taking the organisation of the army first of all, under the Republic the highest formation available to the army had been the division. From 1800, however, Napoleon introduced a new level of organisation in the form of the *corps d'armée*, this being composed of a number of divisions. However, whereas the latter had been forces of all arms, they were now essentially composed of infantry and cavalry alone. Thus, in 1805, aside from the Imperial Guard, which at this point consisted of three infantry and two cavalry regiments, the French army in Germany consisted of a cavalry reserve of eight divisions, an artillery reserve containing perhaps twenty-five per cent of all the army's guns, and seven infantry corps, each composed of two to four infantry divisions, a division of light cavalry and a number of batteries of heavy artillery. Both strategically and tactically, the advantages conferred by this organisation were enormous. With the immense French field armies – 210,000 men in 1805, 180,000 men in 1806 and 160,000 men in 1807 – broken down into manageable units, communications within the army were greatly simplified whilst the emperor was afforded unrivalled strategic flexibility. On the advance, for example, the corps could be dispersed in a lozenge formation – the *bataillon carré* – that could without delay switch the axis of its advance in any direction. Enabled to spread out over a front that was much broader than before (for each corps was now effectively an army in miniature that could, in an emergency, fight a battle entirely on its own), the French were sometimes able to envelop entire enemy forces, as was done at Ulm in 1805, and in general to disguise their real objectives. Thus inveigled, nervous commanders might be tempted to spread their forces out so as to protect every conceivable line of advance, thereby merely increasing their own vulnerability. Alternatively, they might, as at Friedland, be deceived into attacking a corps that was apparently isolated, only to find that they were confronted by the entire *grande armée*. Last but not least, the increased dispersal permitted by the corps system further intensified the logistical advantages already observable under the old divisional system. Not only was the pressure on supplies thereby lessened, but wings were lent to the army's feet – hence the emperor's ability to make use of strategic manoeuvres whose success depended above all on speed: the *manœuvre sur les derrières*, whereby the enemy would be outflanked and attacked from the rear; the strategy of the central position, whereby the French would insinuate themselves between two enemy armies and defeat each in turn; and the strategy of deep penetration, whereby an enemy would be forced to accept battle by a French thrust deep into his territory. In every case the aim was to bring the enemy to battle on unfavourable terms, and thus to achieve the destruction of his army.

Once battle had been joined, moreover, the principles by which the *grande armée* was organised were again conducive to success. In the first place its general striking power was greatly increased by the concentration of the cavalry into independent divisions (and later corps) of its own, this process being taken still further by Napoleon's formation of an élite force of twelve – later sixteen – regiments of armoured cavalry. Meanwhile, much the same was true of the artillery in that the concentration of so much of it at corps and army level facilitated the formation of the 'grand batteries' necessary for the delivery of effective bombardments (also worthy of note here are Napoleon's abolition of the light battery that used to accompany each infantry regiment, substitution for the standard four-pounders by heavier six-pounders at divisional level, introduction of a higher proportion of eight- and twelve-pounders, and establishment of a fully militarised corps of drivers in place of the undisciplined and unreliable civilians who had, except in the horse artillery, driven the gun teams hitherto). However, not only did the *grande armée* now pack a heavier punch, but it could deliver it in a more flexible manner. Thanks to the corps system, Napoleon could use a part of his army to tie down much larger enemy forces, whilst he achieved local superiority in another part of the field: thus, at Austerlitz a single division of the IV Corps at one point held the French right against 40,000 enemy troops, whilst I Corps, the rest of IV Corps and the Guard prepared a devastating blow against the Allied centre. Alternatively, whilst one or more corps occupied the attention of the enemy army, the remainder of the French forces would be sent on a flanking march that would culminate in a massive attack from an entirely unexpected direction at a critical moment of the struggle. Finally, even when such sweeping man-œuvres were not attempted – as at Borodino and Waterloo – the corps system ensured that it was possible to launch attacks without committing the entire army, to reinforce success when it was achieved, and quickly to react to unexpected dangers. When we remember that in the period 1805–7 France's opponents had barely embarked upon the introduction of separate divisions, let alone corps, and that, where they had, the change had often been effected in the clumsiest of manners – Russian divisions, for example, had no sub-units and were cumbersome affairs the size of a French corps, whilst their Prussian equivalent had too little artillery – it will be understood that the advantage enjoyed by France was very great.

Whilst addressing the army's technical quality, Napoleon also paid much attention to its morale. In the first place, every effort was made to stimulate self-interest in the service of the régime, a wide variety of new incentives being introduced to spur on the soldiery to even greater efforts. Thus, in addition to promotion to the officer corps, soldiers could aspire to a transfer to one of the élite companies of their battalion or regiment (each infantry battalion had a light company and a grenadier company, and every hussar, chasseur and dragoon regiment an élite company, these units all having special uniforms and higher pay), or alternatively to the highly privileged Imperial Guard – the body of veteran troops formed by Napoleon in 1804 to act as a personal bodyguard, battlefield reserve, and pattern for the rest of the army. In 1802, moreover, Napoleon established the Legion of Honour, a decoration open to all ranks of the army that was coveted all the more because of the substantial personal pension which accompanied it (still, to be congratulated by the First Consul himself in the presence of the entire regiment, mobbed by beautiful women, saluted by sentries, flattered by senior officers, and stood free drinks by obsequious café proprietors was doubtless extremely agreeable to all concerned). Secondly, the French ruler encouraged the army to develop a common identification and to take pride in its achievements, through such measures as constant parades and reviews, good examples being the ceremonies attached to the mass presentation of the Legion of Honour to its first recipients (at one such event in Paris no fewer than 1800 were distributed). Also important here were uniforms, the dress of the Napoleonic armies achieving a level of sartorial splendour that completely eclipsed the functionalism of the 1790s. As Jean-Roch Coignet wrote in his memoirs:

> Nothing could be handsomer than [my] uniform. When we were on dress parade we wore a blue coat with white lapels sloped low down on the breast, a white dimity waistcoat, gaiters of the same, short breeches, silver buckles on the shoes and breeches, a double cravat, white underneath and black on the outside, with a narrow edge of white showing at the top . . .. In addition to all this we wore our hair brushed out in front like pigeons' wings, and powdered, and a queue six inches long, cut off at the end like a brush and tied with a black worsted ribbon, with ends exactly two inches long. Add to this the bearskin cap and its long plume, and you have the summer uniform of the Imperial Guard.[10]

However, uniforms were also important in another sense in that they marked one regiment – and, indeed, one soldier – out from another. Napoleon may have encouraged the army to see itself as a band of brothers, but it was a band of brothers that was in a state of constant competition. Thus, already reviving under the Directory, regimental *esprit de corps* was inflamed to the highest possible degree. Different regiments were encouraged to develop their own traditions, and constantly to emulate one another, the result being acts of remarkable courage on the battlefield, and constant duelling and brawling off it. Only in this manner, too, can the extraordinary multiplicity of troop types that marked the French army be explained: though one heavy cavalryman fought much like any other heavy cavalryman, one light cavalryman much like any other light cavalryman, and one infantryman much like any other infantryman, not counting the differences between guard and line, we find no fewer than four different species of the first, five of the second, and thirteen of the third, the point being that each of these different categories could be given its own uniform distinctions and allowed to develop its own traditions (in the hussars, for example, it was the fashion to wear long moustaches and braided pigtails).

10 J. Fortescue (ed.), *The Notebooks of Captain Coignet, Soldier of the Empire, 1799–1816* (London, 1928), pp. 104–5.

Whilst appealing to the army's baser instincts in this manner, Napoleon was also careful to encourage loyalty to his own person, the soldiers being instilled with the concept that their own personal interests were indistinguishable from those of Napoleon and, indeed, France. It was not simply that all honours and rewards ultimately stemmed from the French ruler, although there can be no doubt that he dispensed them with consummate skill. The soldiers were also made to feel that Napoleon was one of them and one with them – hence the sedulous promotions of such nicknames as *le petit caporal*, and his constant appearances among his men, even in the worst conditions. Hence, too, the exaggerated concern which Napoleon affected for their welfare and his habit of singling out old soldiers whom he recognised from past campaigns to greet them and ask after their welfare.

Qualify the situation though we must – and it should be remembered that at least 800 men were deserting the army every month in the period 1804–6 – there seems no doubt that all this had some effect. By the time that land conflict resumed in Europe in 1805 the French army had developed a unique ethos. Once a soldier had served in its ranks for even the shortest period, the chances were that he stayed in them and fought in them – based as it is on desertion in metropolitan France, it is noteworthy that the bulk of such evidence as we have seems to relate primarily to men who had just been inducted into the army[11] – and there is little doubt that morale was very high. As one soldier wrote in his journal in 1805:

> We left Paris quite content to go campaigning . . .. I was especially so, for war was the one thing I wanted. I was young, full of health and courage, and I thought one could wish for nothing better than to fight against all possible odds; moreover, I was broken to marching; everything conspired to make me regard a campaign as a pleasant excursion, on which, even if one lost one's head, arms or legs, one should at least find some diversion.[12]

THE IMPACT OF GENIUS

As remodelled by Napoleon, then, the French army was a powerful instrument that could not but outclass the forces that it faced in the

---

11 Cf. E. Arnold, 'Some observations on the French opposition to Napoleonic conscription, 1804–1806', *FHS*, IV, No. 4 (Autumn, 1966), 452–61.

12 M. Barrès (ed.), *Memoirs of a French Napoleonic Officer: Jean Baptiste Barrès, Chasseur of the Imperial Guard* (London, 1925), p. 55.

period 1805–7. That said, however, it was far from perfect, its cavalry, in particular, remaining poorly mounted and much inferior to its counterparts in other armies (well-trained, well-mounted and composed of a far higher standard of recruit than was the norm in the infantry, the cavalry of the *ancien régime* was excellent); indeed, so short of horses was the army that an entire division of dragoons had to fight on foot, horses not being found for them until after the battle of Austerlitz. Staffwork, too, was frequently mediocre, whilst many even of the marshals proved capable of extraordinary acts of folly and disobedience. Nor was the *grande armée* overwhelmingly superior in numbers to its opponents – at Austerlitz 73,000 French faced 85,000 Austrians and Russians; at Jena and Auerstädt 123,000 French faced 116,000 Prussians; and at Eylau 75,000 French faced 76,000 Prussians and Russians – the latter also frequently putting up a furious resistance on the battlefield. Though their other advantages must not be ignored, it is therefore safe to say that that one of the most important reasons for French success was the irreplaceable genius of Napoleon himself, the duke of Wellington once remarking that 'his presence on the field made a difference of 40,000 men'.[13]

Unlike Wellington, who was notorious for braving enemy fire and commanding in the very midst of the front line, after the 1790s Napoleon rarely led his men into battle himself. Instead, his contribution was exerted entirely from well behind the front, the first of his secrets being that his headquarters became the centre of the whole French war effort. In the case of other powers, the conduct of war was often extremely diffuse. If we take the example of the campaign of 1805, for example, the titular Austrian commander-in-chief was the Archduke Charles, but he was distrusted by his brother and packed off to the minor Italian front, the command in Germany going to his bitter enemy, General Mack. With Mack secretly authorised to ignore Charles, still further confusion was caused by the fact that Francis began to interfere in operations through the medium of the Hofskriegsrat, or Palace War Council, an amorphous body with a range of functions ranging from general administration to the elaboration of plans of campaign. Nor did the arrival of the Russians help matters: theoretically commanded by Kutuzov, the preponderant influence was actually wielded by the tsar, who had travelled west with the army, and, encouraged by his

---

13 *Cit.* Earl of Stanhope, *Notes of Conversations with the Duke of Wellington, 1831–1851* (London, 1888), p. 9.

sycophantic suite, thought of himself as a great military commander. Somewhat similar difficulties also emerged in Prussia in 1806. Unlike the unfortunate Austrians, the Prussians at least had a proper commander-in-chief in the person of the duke of Brunswick, but Brunswick was old and weak, whilst his authority was further reduced by the decision of Frederick William to accompany the army. As a result, Prussian strategic planning disintegrated in a welter of intrigue and disagreement as rival advisers struggled to gain the ear of their superiors, whilst Brunswick's orders were flouted, sabotaged or simply disregarded. In consequence, the army's movements were uncertain and disjointed, the climactic confrontation at Jena and Auerstädt finding its forces spread out across many miles of countryside and being fought in a notably piecemeal fashion.

In the French army, by contrast, all authority was vested in Napoleon who was both head of state and commander-in-chief. As such he was able in the first place to prepare the way for his armies by means of diplomacy, the classic example being his reorganisation of the Holy Roman Empire in such a manner as to give France both a group of loyal and effective allies in southern Germany and a springboard for operations against Austria and Prussia. Also noteworthy here is his persuasion of the Persians to declare war on Russia in 1807, and his attempt to sabotage the Russo-Turkish peace settlement of 1812 by promising the restoration of Moldavia, Wallachia and the Crimea to the Ottomans if they would resume hostilities with Moscow. Once preparations for war were complete, moreover, all military planning for the campaign was carried out by Napoleon himself, it being essentially the case that, notwithstanding the titular appointment of Marshal Berthier to this position, he functioned as his own chief-of-staff.

With Napoleon in complete control, it followed that the *grande armée*'s operations were generally better synchronised than those of its opponents. Even more importantly, however, they were also marked by a far greater clarity of aim. Owen Connelly has recently advanced the thesis that the emperor 'blundered to glory' – that, in short, 'his genius lay in scrambling, not in carrying out a preconceived plan'.[14] To the extent that Napoleon sometimes made mistakes and, further, that events frequently did not turn out in the manner that he expected, this is undoubtedly fair enough, but in arguing thus Connelly misses the point that, if France's victories

14 O. Connelly, *Blundering to Glory: Napoleon's Military Campaigns* (Wilmington, Delaware, 1987), p. 222.

were not always the product of a preconceived plan, the French ruler did possess a single unwavering purpose in the form of the destruction of the enemy's means and will to resist through the medium of a decisive battle. And, 'scrambler' or not, Napoleon was a commander of extraordinary capacities, being a master of detail, calculation, deception, celerity, concentration and morale. Aided by boundless energy and a capacious memory, the emperor was able to assimilate and make use of immense quantities of information, much of it ever-changing. On this basis he was able, *pace* Connelly, to calculate the most likely situation of the enemy, to plan for every contingency that might arise, to foresee the effects of chance and misfortune, and to establish both the risks and the potential consequences of every course of action. Having once settled on a plan – a decision that was not necessarily objectively 'right', and was always susceptible to modification (hence the *bataillon carré*) – he sought by every means available to mislead the enemy: at Austerlitz, for example, Alexander was enticed to give battle by being fed the impression that the French were vulnerable and exhausted. At this point, too, speed was of the essence, and, whether it was through adopting an organisation that facilitated manoeuvre, driving his soldiers to the limits of their endurance, or selecting the approach that led most directly to the objective, Napoleon never lost sight of its importance. Just as vital was concentration: whether in terms of strategy or tactics, all Napoleon's efforts, at least in the period 1805–7, were directed to the application of the whole of his resources towards a single end, and, ultimately, upon a single point, so as to gain local superiority. And, finally, Napoleon was a master of morale – hence his predilection for the enveloping *manœuvre sur les derrières*: used no fewer than thirty times between 1796 and 1815, its effect was both to place the enemy army at a tactical disadvantage and to overawe and confuse its unfortunate commanders. Hence, too, the importance in his grand tactics of overwhelming artillery bombardments and of assaults launched by masses of infantry and cavalry that were seemingly as unstoppable as they were imposing. Taking all this together, we may therefore state that the secret of Napoleon's generalship lay in the first place in a commitment at all times and in all situations to the offensive, and in the second in an almost unparalleled ability to ensure that this was achieved in conditions of superiority. With no enemy commander able to match such dynamism, his dominance was virtually guaranteed.

A VICTORIOUS SYNTHESIS

To conclude, it is quite clear that France did not triumph because, to paraphrase Clausewitz, the strength of the whole French nation marched over Europe.[15] In no sense a Nation-in-Arms, the Napoleonic empire was in fact organised in such a way as to keep the sacrifices required of France to a minimum. Whilst not decrying the contribution of the Revolution, which had facilitated the adoption of new tactics and organisation, tapped fresh reservoirs of military talent, and provided the troops with positive stimuli that survived into the Napoleonic period, we must look to other explanations for the French triumph. To Napoleon himself France owed, first, the restoration of order in the state; second, the perfection of the army as a fighting force of unrivalled power and flexibility; and, third, a talent for command that at its best has rarely been equalled. Probably just as important, however, was the army's professionalisation in a process that, whilst certainly encouraged by Napoleon, had been in train ever since the downfall of the Jacobin dictatorship in 1794. As Clausewitz himself had recognised, whatever might be done to 'combine the soldier and the citizen in one and the same individual', war is 'different and separate from the other pursuits which occupy the life of man', the consequence being that 'those who belong to it . . . will always look upon themselves as a kind of guild'.[16] Instead of contests between entire societies, then, wars – or, at least, the battles by which wars were decided – remained contests between restricted military castes, the determining factor, everything else being equal, being their professional *esprit de corps*. As to how this was defined, Clausewitz had no doubt:

> An army which preserves its usual formations under the heaviest fire, which is never shaken by imaginary fears, and, in the face of real danger, disputes the ground inch by inch, which, proud in the feeling of its victories, never loses its . . . confidence in its leaders, even under the depressing effects of defeat; an army . . . inured to privations and fatigue . . . which looks upon its toils as the means to victory, not as a curse which hovers over its standards, and which is always reminded of its duties and virtues by the short catechism of the honour of its arms; such an army is imbued with the true military spirit.[17]

15 Clausewitz, *On War*, p. 385.
16 *Ibid.*, pp. 254–5.
17 *Ibid.*, p. 255.

There is nothing here to bring to mind either the French Revolution or the Nation-in-Arms, but a great deal that is redolent of the army of Napoleon. Moreover, the prowess of the *grande armée* certainly cannot wholly be explained by reference to the developments in French society that may or may not have led France into the path of total war in the period 1793–94, to do so being highly ahistorical – as John Lynn has written, 'The regulars and volunteers who defended France under the Terror were driven by a set of factors peculiar to the height of revolutionary fervour . . . Napoleon's army fought in a very different political and emotional environment.'[18]

18 Lynn, 'Towards an army of honour', p. 157.

3 THE EMPIRE OF THE FRENCH

THE IMAGE OF REFORM

> The invasion of the Peninsula by the French army had, from a combination of circumstances, been the means of introducing extraordinary changes in the situation of Aragón . . .[1]

With these words, Louis Suchet, who commanded the French forces in Aragón from 1809 to 1813, epitomises a key element of the Napoleonic legend, namely Napoleon's association with a dramatic process of political, social and economic reform that consummated the French Revolution. Feudalism was abolished, aristocratic privileges curtailed, administration rationalised, restrictions on trade and industry reduced, and the power of the Church undermined. All over Europe, meanwhile, the bourgeoisie sprang forth to a position of ever greater social and economic importance. Such developments are very much in accordance with the manner in which Napoleon would have chosen to be remembered. Until the end of his life, the French ruler identified himself with the ideals of the Revolution. During the consulate and empire this theme was integral to French propaganda. Thus, Austria, Prussia, Russia and Britain were all portrayed as being hostile to France on ideological grounds; meanwhile, their rulers were irredeemably corrupt, their political systems archaic and inequitable, and their inhabitants miserably oppressed – hence the constant triumph of French arms, which in turn brought economic progress, religious toleration, the abolition of feudalism, and administrative and judicial reform. During Napoleon's exile in Saint Helena, moreover, the campaign increased in intensity, with the erstwhile emperor embarking on an elaborate campaign of self-justification that portrayed himself as the champion of liberty and progress. Needless to say, this legend of the 'liberal

---

1 L.G. Suchet, *Memoirs of the War in Spain from 1808 to 1814* (London, 1829), p. 310.

empire' was seized upon by the emperor's apologists and its traces have survived into the modern period. One is hardly surprised to find such Napoleonists as Cronin stating: 'Napoleon brought to every corner of Europe equality and justice as embodied in the civil code. He wished to free the peoples of Europe and train them towards self-government.'[2] But for Hobsbawm, too, 'The French soldiers who campaigned from Andalusia to Moscow, from the Baltic to Syria . . . pushed the universality of their revolution home more effectively than anything else could have done.'[3]

There was, however, a darker reality. Napoleon did strive to remodel Europe, but he did not do so through any sense of altruism. On the contrary, if the empire experienced reform, it was so that it could serve him all the better. Hand in hand with integration with the French model went the most ruthless exploitation, and in practice this displaced all else, the exigencies of conquest taking priority over, or at least impeding, the cause of reform.

THE TERRITORIES OF EMPIRE

Before examining imperial policy, we must first establish what we mean by the empire. Strictly speaking, this only consisted of metropolitan France and the territories that were directly annexed to her. When the Napoleonic Wars began in 1803, in addition to the territory which she had possessed in 1789, France comprised Belgium, the left bank of the Rhine, Savoy and Nice and Piedmont. To these were added Genoa in 1805, Parma, Piacenza, Guastalla, and Tuscany – the short-lived Kingdom of Etruria – in 1808, Rome in 1809, Holland, the Valais, parts of Hanover and Westphalia, the Hanseatic towns – Hamburg, Bremen and Lübeck – and Oldenburg in 1810, and Catalonia in 1812. As a result, the 108 departments and thirty-three million people of 1803 had risen to the 130 departments and forty-four million people of 1811. However, Napoleon's influence was not restricted even to these swollen frontiers. In the first place, a number of areas – Portugal, the Ionian islands, Slovenia, Dalmatia, and various parts of Croatia and Germany – at one time or another were occupied militarily or brought under direct rule without being formally annexed to France. In the second place, several states were ruled by other members of the Bonaparte family or its adherents. Starting with the least

2 V. Cronin, *Napoleon* (London, 1971), p. 320.
3 E. Hobsbawm, *The Age of Revolution, 1789–1848* (London, 1977), p. 117.

important, the tiny Swiss territory of Neuchâtel was given to Napoleon's chief-of-staff, Marshal Berthier, in 1806, while Elise Bonaparte was settled in the Italian states of Piombino and Lucca. Also in Italy the erstwhile Italian Republic had become the Kingdom of Italy in 1804; theoretically headed by Napoleon himself, government was actually in the hands of the emperor's stepson and viceroy, Eugene de Beauharnais. Further south, in 1806 Ferdinand IV had been driven out of Naples (though he continued with British help to defy the French from Sicily), to be replaced by Napoleon's eldest brother, Joseph. Two years later Joseph moved on to Spain, where Napoleon had just deposed the ruling Bourbons, being replaced by the emperor's brother-in-law, Joachim Murat. Murat had hitherto been ruler of the specially-created duchy of Berg in western Germany, which was thereafter ruled by an imperial commissioner for Napoleon's young nephew, Napoleon Louis. As for Spain, though Joseph was placed on the throne in 1808, her right to a place in the roll of Bonapartist satellites is actually highly dubious: beset by popular resistance, the operations of Spanish and Anglo-Portuguese regular armies, the intransigence of military commanders whom Napoleon purposely allowed to operate outside Joseph's authority, and growing bankruptcy, the administration of *el rey intruso* was reduced to impotent irrelevance. In consequence, Spain is perhaps best regarded as an occupied territory rather than a satellite. In northern Europe, meanwhile, we have the kingdoms of Westphalia and Holland. Created in 1807 from Hesse-Cassel, Brunswick and parts of Hanover and Prussia, until 1813 Westphalia was ruled by Napoleon's brother, Jerome. In Holland, by contrast, Louis Bonaparte was elevated to another newly created throne in 1806, only to be forcibly removed by Napoleon in 1810 as a result of imperial dissatisfaction.

In addition to the states that came directly under French rule, there was a further group that fell within the Napoleonic orbit to a greater or lesser extent. Most important of these were the states of the Confederation of the Rhine, the league of small and medium German states organised by Napoleon in 1806 on the wreckage of the Holy Roman Empire. At first consisting of Westphalia and Berg, together with those states that had thrown in their lot with Napoleon, such as Bavaria, Würtemberg and Baden, it eventually came to include all the German states except Prussia and Austria. It is important to note here, however, that there were important limits to French influence in the confederation. Except for Westphalia and Berg, and a few other territories that had French clients imposed upon them (the best examples here are the Grand Duchies of Würzburg and Frankfurt, which were new creations awarded to the Habsburg duke of Tuscany and the erstwhile archbishop of Mainz, Carl von Dalberg), they were ruled by legitimist princes who possessed widely differing views on reform, and were determined to safeguard their own prerogatives. In theory, therefore, Napoleon could only recommend, though in practice his influence was considerable, the German princes having far too much at stake to incur his wrath. Other areas that could be considered as belonging to this sphere of influence are Switzerland and the Grand Duchy of Warsaw. The latter – the Polish buffer state created in 1807 from the Polish territories Prussia had lost at Tilsit – was in theory ruled by the king of Saxony as grand duke. In fact, however, Frederick Augustus never visited Warsaw, and the duchy was in practice a French protectorate, its independent government having to share power with a powerful French governor-general. As for Switzerland, she was in theory neutral, but in 1803 Napoleon had renamed her the Helvetic Confederation and given her a new constitution in the form of the so-called Act of Mediation with the result that she, too, was no more than nominally independent.

PRESSURES FOR INTEGRATION

This, then, was the *grand empire*, a somewhat heterogeneous collection of territories that had been annexed to France, given to French rulers or clients, occupied by French armies, or penetrated by French ideas. As far as the emperor was concerned, however, it could not remain heterogeneous for long, a number of factors impelling him in the direction of integration. First place here must perhaps be accorded to the tradition of cultural and intellectual dominance that France had enjoyed in Europe since the days of Louis XIV, as a result of which France could regard herself as the spearhead of European progress even before 1789. With the Revolution, of course, such feelings of superiority could only be reinforced: having thrown off her own chains, France was seemingly uniquely equipped to lead the rest of the continent to higher levels of progress. France thus acquired a civilising mission that survived even when all thought of the export of revolution per se had been abandoned and this role was inevitably assumed by Napoleon. In part this was wholly cynical, as we shall see, and yet, much influenced by the model of ancient Rome, the emperor was also genuinely possessed by the notion of French excellence: just as Rome had brought peace, order and civilisation to the western world in antiquity, so France would perform a similar office in the nineteenth century. In this respect, of course, particular importance was attached to the *Code Napoléon*, which, as Lefebvre writes, the emperor saw as 'the framework for a European civilization which would consolidate the Continent's political unity and be in harmony with it'.[4]

Convinced though Napoleon was of the superiority of French models, there were also other influences at work here. Deeply influenced by the Enlightenment, he was in no doubt that, just as Newton had discovered a series of immutable laws that governed the physical universe, so it was possible to elaborate a similar code that governed its human counterpart, what had been proved to be good for France therefore being universally applicable. To argue otherwise, and, in particular, to suggest that local customs and traditions should be at least taken into account, if not respected, was anathema. This, however, was not just because such a policy contradicted notions of order and system, but also because it implied paying heed to the views of a populace whom Napoleon regarded as ignorant and primitive. As he wrote to Jerome, 'I think it is ridiculous for you to tell me that the people of Westphalia do not agree . . .. If the people refuse what makes for their own welfare they are guilty of anarchism, and the first duty of the prince is to punish them.'[5] Nevertheless, integration was at least as much pragmatic as it was doctrinaire. At the beginning of the consulate, Napoleon boasted of his flexibility, telling Roederer, 'It is by turning Catholic that I finished the war in the Vendée; by turning Muslim that I established myself in Egypt; by turning ultramontane that I won the Italian mind.'[6] Yet the flexibility of 1800 was more and more undermined by the war (it is interesting in this respect that, as the years went by, the emperor became ever more demanding with regard to the pace of reform; furthermore, the relatively small number of non-Frenchmen known to have become prefects – thirty-two out of 306 – seem rarely to have served in their own areas). Increasingly, if Napoleon had one abiding diplomatic and

4 G. Lefebvre, *Napoleon: from Tilsit to Waterloo, 1807–1815* (New York, 1969), p. 215.

5 *Cit. ibid.*, pp. 215–16.

6 *Cit.* H.A.L. Fisher, 'The French dependencies and Switzerland', in A. Ward *et al.* (eds.), *Cambridge Modern History, IX: Napoleon* (Cambridge, 1934), p. 390.

strategic aim, it was to unite the entire Continent against the British, this in turn suggesting a measure of social and political integration on the French model. As he told Louis Bonaparte in November 1807:

> The Romans gave their laws to their allies: why cannot France have hers adopted in Holland? It is also necessary that you adopt the French monetary system . . ... Having the same civil laws and coinage tightens the bonds of nations.[7]

Reform thus became an instrument of strategy, this being most clearly seen in a famous letter written to Jerome on his accession to the throne of Westphalia. Thus:

> It is necessary that your people should enjoy a liberty . . . unheard of amongst the inhabitants of Germany . . ... Such a style of government will be a stronger barrier against Prussia than . . . even the protection of France. What people would wish to return to the arbitrary administration of Prussia when it could enjoy the benefits of a wise and liberal government?[8]

Whilst consolidating the hold of intruders such as Louis and Jerome upon their new domains, reform would also increase the power and efficiency of the state and win the support of educated opinion – much influenced by the support of the bourgeoisie and intelligentsia for the republics he had established in northern Italy in 1796 and 1797, Napoleon seems genuinely to have been convinced that, in his own words, 'The peoples of Germany, France, Italy [and] Spain desire equality and [the introduction of] liberal ideas.'[9] Here again one comes across the dictates of pragmatism, this also being visible with regard to the emperor's attitudes to the wider empire. The more powerful and efficient the state, the greater its revenue, its armed forces, and its ability to serve Napoleon, and, by extension, its chances of survival. Having proved themselves effective allies, Bavaria and Würtemberg were left alone; with her finances in chaos, her court divided and corrupt, her army a ragged skeleton, and her navy a liability, Spain, by contrast, found herself being forcibly regenerated.

---

7 Napoleon to Louis Bonaparte, 13 November 1807, *Correspondance de Napoléon 1er* (Paris, 1858–1870; hereafter CN), XVI, p. 161.
8 Napoleon to Jerome Bonaparte, 15 November 1807, *ibid.*, p. 166.
9 *Ibid.*

Here, perhaps, we come to the heart of the matter. For Napoleon, reform was always a weapon of exploitation whose employment was necessitated by the demands of his perpetual wars. As he told his brother, Louis, 'Don't forget that you are first and foremost a French prince. I put you on the throne of Holland solely to serve the interests of France and help me in all I am doing for her.'[10] Such is the conclusion that must certainly be reached when the pattern of Napoleonic reform is considered in detail. Where the emperor wanted to win the support of traditional élites, as in Poland, the reform of feudalism was muted by pragmatism; when the emperor wanted to reward his followers through the creation of new fiefs, the interests of his satellites were set aside; and, when, as in *josefino* Spain, the cause of reform clashed with military exigencies, it was the latter that emerged as the undoubted victor.

THE IMPLEMENTATION OF REFORM

It was, then, axiomatic that the French imperium should be accompanied by a dynamic that was pronouncedly reformist. However, the degree to which this was effective varied dramatically. At its most dramatic in those areas actually annexed by France, its influence could be considerably moderated in the satellite states, and varied from the extensive to the almost non-existent amongst Napoleon's various allies. For all the emperor's dreams of homogenisation, then, reform came in different ways and meant different things in different parts of the empire.

In those areas actually annexed to France, of course, the means was simply administrative fiat, law, society and the machinery of government all being recast in the French mould. To take just one example, in Rome annexation was followed by the dissolution of no fewer than 519 religious houses. Nevertheless, variations remained common. In practice, whatever Paris might lay down, given the all-embracing character of the prefecturate's functions – it was expected to implement imperial legislation, maintain law and order, enforce conscription, keep a check on political dissidence, oversee relations with the religious authorities and the workings of municipal government and the fiscal system, encourage support for the empire and participation in its structures, foment industry and

10 *Cit.* Marquis de Noailles (ed.), *The Life and Memoirs of Count Molé (1781–1855)* (London, 1923), p. 145.

agriculture, ensure food supplies and poor relief, undertake public works of all sorts, and supply the capital with an endless flow of information and statistics – the key figure was the prefect (in recognition of this fact, prefects appointed to the new departments enjoyed far greater security of tenure than those employed in metropolitan France). When they exerted themselves, such men could be particularly active agents of reform, as witness the Rhenish departments of Rhin-et-Moselle and Mont Tonnerre, where Paul de Lézay-Marnesia and Jean Bon St André made great efforts to improve agricultural techniques, introduce new crops, improve the quality of livestock, reclaim marshes and wastes, and curb seasonal flooding. Equally, in Rome the Comte de Tournon sponsored a wide range of improvements that included the establishment of a cotton industry, the reform of prisons and hospitals and the reclamation of part of the Pontine marshes. Yet even the most energetic prefects could not always prevail over the obstacles which opposed them-selves to them. In Belgium, for example, which was, after all, the earliest of France's conquests, whilst we learn that the bourgeoisie and the nobility rapidly adopted French as the language of education and polite society, we also discover that they on the whole remained reluctant to participate in the structures of the empire and indifferent to its politics. With the Church not only unresponsive but openly hostile, the result was that the influence of French rule was largely superficial. Equally, as certainly occurred in the Rhenish department of the Roer, collaboration in the adminis-tration might actually represent a protective camouflage for the defence of local institutions, customs or traditions. Nor were French officials necessarily much more reliable. Constantly urged by the metropolis to conduct detailed investigations into their dominions and to intermingle with the local élites, they became increasingly aware of the difficulty of imposing the French model on their charges lock, stock and barrel, with the result that they often did what they could to urge restraint or to soften the impact of change – in Catalonia, for example, the many clauses of the *Code Napoléon* that offended Spanish religious sensibilities were never enforced. Indeed, when Holland was annexed to the empire in 1810, for all Napoleon's previous fulminations, change was in fact quite limited: most of the personnel of Louis' régime were retained in office, a variety of means were found to conciliate the *notables*, and the new governor-general, Lebrun, made great efforts not to alienate local opinion. In Holland and elsewhere, time was in any case limited, in the most extreme cases literally to a matter of months, whilst in

Catalonia anything more than nominal change was stifled by continued popular resistance. Even within the frontiers of *la grande France*, in short, change was frequently slow and never uniform.

If this was true of the so-called *pays réunis*, how much more so was it the case with the other parts of the empire? Lacking the advantage of direct rule from Paris, Napoleon had here to resort to other means. By far the most important of these was, of course, the establishment of the 'family courts' of Joseph, Louis, Murat and the rest. In addition, military commanders such as Suchet in Aragón, Davout in Poland, and Marmont in Illyria were frequently de facto viceroys. Alternatively, French generals might serve as war ministers in the satellite governments, good examples here being Dumas in Naples and D'Eblé in Westphalia. And even when French commanders had no specifically political role, their presence could be instrumental in enforcing political change: in Holland, for example, Augereau took a leading role in the coup that ushered in the authoritarian constitution of 1801. Moving away from the realm of military force, the family courts were often bolstered by French officials – Roederer in Naples, Beugnot in Berg, Siméon in Westphalia. Last but not least, in nominally independent states such as those of the Confederation of the Rhine the French ambassador played a vital role, whether it was Hédouville in Frankfurt, Bourgoing in Dresden, or Bignon in Warsaw, though the Saxon staff officer, Ferdinand von Funck, was undoubtedly going too far when he referred to Bourgoing as 'the dictator of Saxony'.[11]

Even discounting the important factor of local participation, then, Napoleon was far from bereft of the instruments necessary for change. All the same, even under Joseph, Louis, Jerome, Eugene and Murat, progress was no more uniform in the *pays conquis* than the *pays réunis*. In their role of Napoleonic proconsuls, such monarchs were viewed as agents of modernisation. To take the example of the advice given by the emperor to Jerome when the latter became king of Westphalia in 1807, we read:

> What the peoples of Germany impatiently desire is that individuals who are not noble and have talent should have an equal right to your . . . employment; that all forms of serfdom . . . should be wholly abolished. The benefits of the Napoleonic code . . . will be so many

11 O. Williams (ed.), *In the Wake of Napoleon: being the Memoirs of Ferdinand von Funck, Lieutenant-General in the Saxon Army and Adjutant-General to the King of Saxony* (London, 1931), p. 158.

distinctive characteristics of your monarchy . . .. Be a constitutional king . . .[12]

Not content with mere counsel, Napoleon reinforced the point by effectively dictating the new Westphalian constitution. In this particular case, of course, such measures were especially understandable given that the emperor regarded Westphalia as a model that might be followed by all the other states of the Confederation of the Rhine, but the experience was by no means confined to Jerome. As Eugene had been when he was posted to Milan as viceroy in 1805, Joseph was bombarded with letters advising him how to run his new dominions when he arrived in Naples in 1806; for example:

> Make changes if you must, but bring the Code into force nevertheless: it will consolidate your power, and, once in force, all . . . entails will vanish, with the result that there will be no powerful families except for those whom you choose to create as your vassals. That is why I have myself always . . . gone to such lengths to see that it is carried out.[13]

On being transferred to Spain in 1808, moreover, Joseph was provided with a new constitution drafted by the French foreign ministry.

Needless to say, Napoleon's tutelage did not come to an end with the mere installation of his satellites. On the contrary, the emperor was not prepared to allow the family monarchies much independence even in terms of day-to-day administration. Enjoined to do nothing without first consulting Paris and in some cases to write to Napoleon every day, they were the recipients of an endless stream of orders, advice and harangues of all sorts that constantly reinforced their subordinate status – to quote one such missive received by Eugene, 'If Milan were on fire, you should do nothing and wait for instructions.'[14] Last but not least, as occurred when Napoleon reoccupied Madrid in December 1808, the emperor was quite capable of sudden and dramatic personal intervention in order to speed up the pace of reform.

Thus circumscribed, the Bonaparte rulers became the spearhead

12 Napoleon to Jerome, 15 November 1807, *CN*, XVI, pp. 166–7.

13 *Cit.* J. A. Davis, 'The impact of French rule on the Kingdom of Naples (1806–1815)', *Ricerche Storiche*, XX, No. 3 (December, 1990), 377.

14. *Cit.* M. Lyons, *Napoleon Bonaparte and the Legacy of the French Revolution* (London, 1994), p. 245.

of what was on the surface a dramatic period of change in their respective domains, this also being reflected in such areas as the Grand Duchy of Warsaw and the Illyrian provinces. With regard to the governance of the state, councils of state appeared everywhere, most of the satellite states also receiving some form of assembly. Looking at Spain first of all, following the overthrow of the Bourbons, ninety-one prominent Spaniards met at Bayonne to elaborate a new constitution (whose form had, as we have seen, already been decided upon in Paris). According to the document they sanctioned, Spain was given a twenty-four member senate appointed by the king, and in addition a triannual *cortes* consisting of eighty deputies appointed by the king from the ranks of the bishops, the grandees, industry, commerce and the arts, sixty-two deputies chosen by indirect election to represent the common people, and thirty deputies elected by the town councils. In Italy, meanwhile, a very similar constitution was decreed for the Kingdom of Naples in the same year, whilst a French-style statute had been already been imposed upon the Italian Republic in 1802. In Holland the exceptionally democratic constitution that had been promulgated in 1798 was regarded with disgust and suspicion by Napoleon, and was not much better liked by many of the propertied classes. Encouraged by Napoleon's representatives, in 1801 a faction therefore hatched a plot to reverse the decisions of 1798. When this met resistance, assistance was sought from the French garrison, the resultant coup giving Holland a statute that was devoid of any genuine electoral content. Moreover, whilst the constitution of 1801 had at least restored the traditional federal structure of the Dutch republic, in 1805 this too was swept away: with the collaboration of Dutch reformers who dreamed of a powerful unitary state capable of forcing through radical modernisation, Napoleon imposed a new structure that in theory preserved the federal model, but in practice established Holland as a dictatorship under a 'grand pensionary', this in turn serving as the basis for the monarchy of Louis Bonaparte. In Poland, in July 1807 the Grand Duchy of Warsaw was given a council of state, and a bicameral legislative composed of a senate of bishops and noblemen appointed by the grand duke, and a lower house composed in part of representatives elected by the nobility and in part of deputies elected by communal assemblies. Lastly, in November 1807 Westphalia was given a constitution which provided for a council of state and a legislative of one hundred members, of whom seventy were to be landowners, fifteen manufacturers or merchants, and fifteen men of letters. Election of these deputies was to be by departmental electoral colleges appointed by the king from lists of *notables*.

If the keystone of constitutionalism is representative government, all this had little meaning, for the assemblies thus created were limited in power and elected – if at all – on a narrow franchise. In Spain and Naples the assemblies never came into existence at all, whilst in the Kingdom of Italy the legislature was suppressed at the first sign of criticism and replaced by a senate that was entirely controlled by the government. In Holland, Poland and Westphalia, by contrast, the assemblies were at least allowed to function, the sessions sometimes even being marked by genuine debate. But even in these cases the powers of the executive were so extensive that the survival of legislative assemblies meant little – as the Westphalian Minister of Finance remarked, 'The *reichstag* is only a comedy.'[15]

However limited the political powers of these assemblies, they nevertheless served the chief purpose for which they were designed, for, exactly as was the case with the *corps législatif* in France, they served to keep the satellite régimes in touch with *notable* opinion and to win the support of local élites by offering them patronage, integration and status. Whilst attempting to bind the *notables* to the régime, the satellite governments were mirroring another aspect of the French pattern of local government. Thus, in each of the satellite states we see the appearance of the department and the prefect. Although the terminology varied from place to place, Westphalia was divided into eight departments, Spain into thirty-eight, Berg into four, the Kingdom of Italy into twenty-four, Holland into seven, the Grand Duchy of Warsaw into ten, Naples into fourteen, and the Illyrian provinces into six. At a lower level, meanwhile, municipal administration and the judiciary were also reformed, a good example here coming from Holland where laws of 1805 and 1807 divided each department into French-style sub-districts and completely subordinated the local administration to the centre. Where possible, some sort of continuity with the *ancien régime* would be retained – in the Spanish province of Aragón, for example, sub-prefects were known as *corregidores*; in Holland the major towns were allowed to retain the councils of aldermen by which they had hitherto been governed; and in Naples the departments coincided with the old provinces – but such concessions were purely

---

15 *Cit.* H. A. L. Fisher, *Studies in Napoleonic Statesmanship: Germany* (Oxford, 1903), p. 294.

cosmetic: hitherto hereditary and sovereign, for example, Holland's aldermen were henceforward to be reduced to the position of humble servants of the state. Very often, moreover, they were not made at all: amongst the many cases of historic privileges being swept away altogether, we can cite the disappearance of the three Basque *señorios*.

Hand in hand with these changes went a major reform of taxation and finance, the need for such a change being reinforced by the exigencies of Napoleon's wars: with government expenditure and the demands of the emperor soaring, France's satellites were all faced with the need to stave off bankruptcy and make the fullest possible use of their resources. In Naples, for example, a central bank was established, taxes were rationalised, tax farming abolished, and various measures taken to reduce the national debt. In Westphalia a uniform system of taxes was introduced based on a series of levies on necessities, a salt monopoly, a land tax, and a household tax (later replaced by a poll tax and a graduated income tax). In Spain similar reforms were planned by Joseph Bonaparte but were never put into effect, though some changes were carried out in Aragón and Valencia by Suchet. Whatever the details of the system actually introduced, moreover, the changes were everywhere accompanied by new land registers. By 1814, in short, the French model had in principle been adopted throughout the *grand empire*. Only in Holland were matters significantly different. Here much the same processes had gone on as elsewhere, in that the traditional system of public finance, resting as it did on loans, lotteries and a multiplicity of local taxes collected by a bewildering array of different offices, had by 1805 been found to be completely inadequate to meet the demands of the state. In consequence, a new property survey was completed in 1807, the entire country subjected to a single, and much simpler, system of taxation, and the cost of collection greatly reduced through such measures as a reduction of the number of tax officials from 60,000 to perhaps one sixth of that figure. However, whereas the general tendency of Napoleonic fiscal policy was to favour the propertied classes, leaving the bulk of the burden to be borne by the poor, in Holland the minister of finance, Isaac Gogel, was determined to spread the burden more equally. Exceptionally, then, the chief emphasis was for a time placed on direct taxation, but such was the reaction of the propertied classes, whose support, like every other Bonaparte, Louis was desperate to court, that the king ordered a revision of the system, the result being that Gogel resigned in May 1809.

As we have already seen in Holland, changes also occurred in the bureaucracy. Under the *ancien régime* the administration of many states had at worst been characterised by the sale of offices, by clientage and nepotism, and at best by the existence of swarms of officials whose functions were indistinct and often in conflict with one another. Side by side with the state's functionaries, moreover, there existed the personnel of the manorial and ecclesiastical courts. Here, too, rationalisation was widespread with the creation of new professional bureaucracies that were in theory recruited by merit, and whose responsibilities were clearly defined. Closely linked with this development was the highly interventionist character of government. With the prefecture, in particular, accorded a competence that was virtually unlimited, for the first time the need emerged for a genuine technocracy. To take just one example, in Holland, the period after 1800 was marked by the emergence of a new breed of highly specialised official whose competence covered fields as diverse as hydraulic engineering, education, land reclamation and agriculture. In some cases, schools of public administration were established to train suitable officials, the process of forging a new class of state servant being facilitated by the political purges that were sometimes carried out amongst the existing bureaucracy – on the establishment of the Italian republic in 1802, its new minister of finance is reputed to have dismissed 133 officials in one day.

Implicit in most of these reforms is the assault upon the old order, and in particular the privileged corporations, that is the most commonly noted feature of the Napoleonic empire. In theory very great changes took place in this respect. The *Code Napoléon*, for example, with its provisions for equality before the law, freedom of occupation, freedom of property and freedom of conscience, was the death knell of all forms of social and institutional privilege, including that of the nobility, the guilds and the Church. Mandatory within the ever-spreading limits of France herself, under great pressure from Napoleon it was duly introduced in Berg, Westphalia, the Kingdom of Italy, Naples, the Illyrian provinces, the Grand Duchy of Warsaw and *josefino* Spain. A similar programme of legal reform took place in Holland, where Louis Bonaparte took a particular interest in the completion of the new penal code that had been under discussion since 1798. With the introduction of the new codes, feudalism and the guilds alike were doomed, but separate legislation was also introduced for their abolition. In the Grand Duchy of Warsaw feudalism was ended on 21 December 1807; in Westphalia the corresponding date was 23 January 1808; and in

Holland the guilds were swept away on 20 August 1806. Meanwhile, the Church also came under heavy pressure, secularisation and religious tolerance being further characteristics of the empire. In Spain, for example, Napoleon accompanied his occupation of Madrid in December 1808 with decrees curtailing the number of religious orders by two thirds, expropriating their property and revenues, and abolishing the Inquisition; meanwhile, the constitution of Bayonne had already put an end to the ecclesiastical courts. In August 1809, moreover, Joseph decreed the dissolution of the rest of the orders as well. In Naples between 1806 and 1808 Joseph suppressed the Jesuits, the Benedictines and thirty-three other male religious orders, as well as all the female ones (a few male ones, such as the Franciscans, being at first retained), taking all their property – thirty million ducats worth – for the state. In the Kingdom of Italy, a French-style concordat signed in 1803 was inherited from the Italian republic, whilst much of the Church's wealth had already been expropriated and its orders dissolved in the 1790s. In Westphalia admission to cathedral chapters and religious orders was opened to all classes of society where they had hitherto been a noble preserve, many of the functions given to Napoleon by the concordat were assumed by Jerome, and in 1809 there began the usual wave of dissolutions and confiscations, palliated only by the exception of a few orders that were deemed to be of service in the field of education.

With the coming of equality before the law and the attack on the Church, it followed that a further *leitmotiv* of the *grand empire* should be religious freedom. In this respect, Christian minorities did well enough: in Westphalia, for example, Catholics and Lutherans were emancipated in Hesse, and Lutherans and Calvinists in Fulda. For the Jews, success was rather more mixed if only because Napoleon, who was markedly anti-Semitic, had already shown that he was not prepared to tolerate the complete equality that they had obtained in France in the course of the Revolution. At a 'grand sanhedrin' of Jewish leaders in April 1807, the emperor had reimposed a variety of discriminatory measures upon them; with these extended, not only to *la grande France*, but also to such areas as the Kingdom of Italy and, eventually, Holland, the result was that the cause of emancipation suffered a serious setback. Nevertheless, some advances were made. In Westphalia, where Jerome was markedly sympathetic, the Jews were admitted to full civic rights on 27 January 1808; in Berg, although they were not emancipated per se, most penalties against them were lifted; and in the Illyrian provinces, however regressive in relation to what had been achieved in France, Holland and Italy in the 1790s, Napoleon's measures were still an advance on what had gone on before.

Implicit in the assault upon the old order was the creation of a new meritocracy from which the bourgeoisie could not but benefit. Such an idea can certainly be attributed to Napoleon – as he told Jerome:

> I except some places at court, to which . . . you must summon the greatest names. But in your ministries, your councils, if possible in your law courts . . . let the greater part of the persons employed be non-nobles . . . .. The declared principle is to choose talents wherever they can be found.[16]

As was the case in France and the annexed territories, immense lists were therefore compiled of men who could be considered suitable for employment by the state, and these, whilst based on social privilege – above all, landed property – took no account of traditional status. Yet, whether it was in Westphalia or the Kingdom of Italy most of the prefects came from the nobility, whilst one of Louis' first actions on arriving in Amsterdam was to host a reception for fifty of Holland's barons. To quote one official instruction, 'For reasons of social order . . . it is of interest to identify all the rich families without exception.'[17]

Also of considerable importance with regard to the encouragement of a non-noble élite were the educational advances associated with the empire, the unprecedented need for officials, technicians and army officers generating a widespread interest in an expansion of the school system, which was reflected even in such relatively backward parts of the empire as Illyria. Here Marshal Marmont ordered the establishment of a new and unified school system, whose aims, according to his decree of 4 July 1810, would be to provide the citizen with 'the necessary knowledge to perform his civic and moral duties', educate the propertied classes in French and Italian, and 'form students capable of being useful to society and . . . employed by the government in public administration, the courts, the army, the hospitals, the navy and the Corps of Public Works'.[18] In theory, Illyria was given a pyramidal system of primary

16 Napoleon to Jerome Bonaparte, 15 November 1807, *CN*, XVI, p. 173.
17 *Cit.* S. Woolf, *Napoleon's Integration of Europe* (London, 1991), p. 108.
18 *Cit.* L. Plut Pregelj, 'The Illyrian provinces and the French Revolution', *Consortium on Revolutionary Europe Proceedings,* 1989 (Bicentennial Consortium), 603–04.

schools (established at a rate of one to every commune), twenty-five junior and nine senior high schools, and two *écoles centrales*, which approximated to university colleges. With the exception of a few scholarships, all places were fee-paying, and instruction at the lower levels was given in the native tongue, principally Slovene. In the Grand Duchy of Warsaw, too, by 1814 the number of primary schools had been increased to approximately 1,200, a high school set up in every department, and a number of technical colleges and institutions of higher education established. In Holland the School Law of 1806 built on earlier edicts of 1801 and 1803 to provide free education for all children between six and twelve, the result being that by 1811 the country possessed 4,551 primary schools. And in Naples, Joseph planned that each commune should have a primary school, and each province a secondary college, though only three-fifths of the former and one-third of the latter actually came into existence.

Clearly, then, the satellite administrations were strongly reformist in their outlook, but that does not mean to say that they were mere catspaws of Paris. To one extent or another all the Bonaparte family resented the predominance of Napoleon and were eager to assert their independence. Meanwhile, in exactly the same fashion as the prefects dispatched to the *pays réunis*, they were well aware of the problems concerned in imposing Napoleon's grand design on their dominions, whilst they also realised that, as alien intruders, it was essential that they identify themselves with their new subjects – hence the eagerness of Louis to portray himself as a Dutchman and of Joseph to pose first as a Neapolitan and then as a Spaniard, these traits being reinforced in both cases by a genuine benevolence (not for nothing did Napoleon accuse Joseph of being 'too good'[19]). When it came to the imposition of reform, then, a variety of factors conspired to produce a degree of resistance that often drove Napoleon to fury.

Setting aside the question of the degree of severity with which their domains should be exploited (and it should be noted that Louis, Joseph and Murat all in one form or another sought to reduce the burdens imposed upon their subjects or at least to safeguard the particular interests of their kingdoms), the greatest problems arose with regard to areas in which French policy clashed with powerful local interests whose support was vital if the satellite

19 Napoleon to Joseph Bonaparte, 5 July 1806, *CN*, XII, p. 515.

monarchies were to be consolidated. Taking Naples as an example, we find that Murat was extremely unwilling to impose the *Code Napoléon* on his subjects in its entirety. Traditionally it has been argued that this was because the Catholic Church and local opinion alike would have been outraged by its provisions for divorce, but John Davis has shown that the reorganisation of the judiciary which it implied was certain to alienate the judges, magistrates and other legal officials when these had been in the forefront of reformist opinion prior to 1806 and now formed an important nucleus of support. Much the same difficulties are visible in Berg, the imperial commissioner, Beugnot, constantly urging the need for caution, but, like Murat in Naples, he was eventually overruled. In Holland, meanwhile, as we have already seen, local influences were allowed a major role in the reform of taxation, whilst, realising that it struck hard at the interests of the powerful commercial classes, Louis proved no more willing to introduce an exact copy of the Civic Code than anybody else, insisting instead on the promulgation of a much amended Dutch version. Finally, in Westphalia Jerome permitted the survival of entails in the hope of conciliating the nobility, and did not enforce the principle that all a man's property should be divided amongst his heirs for fear that many peasant smallholdings would thereby become so small as to be unproductive.

Not surprisingly, in view of such intransigence, Napoleon soon became disillusioned with the concept of the family monarchies and increasingly moved against them, in 1810 not only removing Louis from the throne, but also effectively stripping Joseph of what little power he possessed, and clawing back large parts of Hanover, which had been given to Westphalia at the beginning of the year, from Jerome. Logically speaking, the emperor was in fact being forced ever more towards a policy of annexation and direct rule, but, whilst his siblings might summarily be swept away, even Napoleon could not depose all the independent rulers of the *pays alliés* that made up the third component of the French empire. With the influence of Paris limited to persuasion (albeit sometimes of a very brusque nature – in January 1808, for example, dissatisfied with the slow pace of change, Napoleon bullied Charles Frederick of Baden into dismissing his third son, Ludwig, as minister of war), the extent to which change took place was moulded by the interests and characters of the princes. This is not to say, however, that they were wholly inimical to reform. In the wake of the Napoleonic reorganisation of Germany, most of the German states were a patchwork of different territories that had somehow to be welded into a coherent whole. Meanwhile, employed for the first time by the French in the campaigns of 1805–6, the troops of the newly independent German princes showed a wide range of deficiencies ranging from outmoded tactics through defective organisation to shortage of numbers. The interlinked question of military reform therefore also assumed great importance – as Lefebvre remarks, strong armies would 'satisfy Napoleon, serve to fight against him if he were conquered, and provide defence against the victors if they looked like withdrawing the benefits he had conferred.'[20]

Of course, not all the German rulers were so far sighted. In Saxony, for example, where social and political change was non-existent, military reform very slow, and the need for both enormous, Frederick Augustus I was a complacent mediocrity who was incapable of injecting the necessary element of dynamism into the administration. At the same time, not all aspects of the French programme were equally attractive, what interested the German rulers above all being strong, centralised and efficient government and an increase in the power of the state. Thus, the representative principle made no progress. The Grand Duchy of Frankfurt received an assembly similar to that of Westphalia, but it only met for a single session, and even that lasted for a bare eleven days. In Bavaria, the constitution of 1808 included provision for a 'national representation', but this body was never summoned, and would in any case only have had consultative functions. Far from gaining new assemblies, some states – Württemberg is a good example – actually lost the estates that they had until then retained. That this should have been the case was hardly surprising, for, as a Saxon officer observed, the people were looked upon 'as something entirely automatic that, with its complete incapacity for reflection, could be moved about the board as best suited government's purpose'; consequently, when Frederick Augustus of Saxony – a relatively liberal figure who had initially sympathised with the French Revolution – determined to begin issuing proclamations expounding government policy, the results were 'orders drafted in an absurdly pedantic style that did not deign to do more than to announce the arbitrary decisions of government'.[21] Yet, for all that, constitutions clearly remained in vogue, a good example being the Bavarian statute of 1808 which abolished all the old estates, corporations, provinces and juris-dictions, established the principles of judicial and fiscal equality, and

20 Lefebvre, *Napoleon*, p. 236.
21 Funck, *Memoirs*, I, pp. 62–3.

divided Bavaria into a number of *kreise* (or departments), each of them headed by a *generalkomissar* (or prefect).

As the Bavarian model shows, the real importance of a constitution was that it provided both a framework for the conduct of government and a basis for the modernisation and unification of the state. In this respect, under the leadership of such statesmen as Maximilian von Montgelas in Bavaria, Sigismund von Reitzenstein in Baden, and Ernst Marschall von Bieberstein in Nassau, the French zone of influence was indeed remodelled. Although there were exceptions which retained the institutions of the *ancien régime* more or less in their entirety – Saxony is a good example – the great majority of France's satellites adopted variations of the departmental–prefectural system (Frankfurt was divided into four such units, Württemberg into twelve, and Baden into ten), established councils of state in place of the old *kabinett* system, set up modern ministries under responsible heads, formed professional, salaried civil services, and promulgated new tax laws. In Bavaria, Württemberg and Baden alike, meanwhile, attempts were made to build a genuine national army through such measures as the introduction of the principle of universal military service, the prohibition of the enlistment of foreigners and criminals, the amelioration of conditions of service, and the promotion of commoners to the officer corps. Meanwhile, French-style tactics were introduced almost everywhere, the number of skirmishers was increased, and the armies formed into brigades and divisions, the general result being a great increase in efficiency.

As elsewhere, meanwhile, these reforms in the pattern and tools of government were accompanied by a major programme of social, economic and legal reform designed to break the power of the various obstacles that had hitherto stood in the way of bureaucratic absolutism. A prime target here, of course, was the Catholic Church. Vast expanses of territory, not to mention large quantities of religious artefacts of all sorts, were therefore confiscated and sold for the benefit of the state, numerous religious communities were dissolved, greater religious toleration decreed for Protestants and Jews (to be fair, where Catholics were discriminated against, as in Württemberg, they, too, were emancipated), and all forms of ecclesiastical jurisdiction brought to an end. Such policies offered obvious advantages: in Bavaria, for example, the sale of the fifty-six per cent of cultivated land in monastic hands brought a twenty-five per cent increase in annual income. Moreover, some attempt was made to purify popular religion and expunge 'superstition': in Bavaria, especially, but also in Baden and Württemberg, nativity scenes, passion plays and religious processions were prohibited, and many statues, calvaries and shrines destroyed. Meanwhile, much attention was also paid to the question of feudalism, though, except in a few cases such as Nassau, it was rarely abolished altogether (in Bavaria, for example, the nobility was stripped of its patrimonial jurisdiction, but not of its seigneurial dues).

In making this qualification, we come to one of the chief limitations of the march of reform in Germany and elsewhere. As much as any of the family monarchs, the other satellite régimes were in the last resort unable to risk alienating traditional élites, if only because, as in Baden, they were desperately short of officials moulded in the new style of government. When the old nobility, for example, refused to accept the demise of its privilege lying down, there was in practice little to do but compromise, and all the more so as in one form or another Napoleon showed himself to be ready to acquiesce in its pretensions (in the agreement which set up the Confederation of the Rhine, for example, the rights of the imperial knights – the 1500 aristocrats who had owed allegiance to no other ruler than the Holy Roman Emperor – were specifically protected). In this particular case, the result was that the abolition of feudalism was much curtailed with the *Code Napoléon* only being introduced, if at all, in modified form, and the nobility securing many of its traditional rights. Similar limitations can also be seen with regard to other aspects of reform: in Bavaria, for example, the guilds defied all attempts at abolition; in the Grand Duchy of Warsaw the Jews were offered only the hope of emancipation after a long period of assimilation; and in Baden Reitzenstein's reforms in the system of central and local government were never fully implemented.

Taking the empire as a whole, then, reformist though its ethos was, it would be wrong to believe that it transformed European society root and branch. Even in the *pays réunis* progress was patchy and by no means uniform, whilst in the *pays conquis* and the *pays alliés* the difficulties were even greater. Dream though he might of integrating Europe, in practice Napoleon could not do so, his aspirations in this respect therefore providing yet one more testimony to his incipient megalomania.

THE COLLABORATORS

Considerable verisimilitude is lent to the empire's association with reform by the fact that the latter was by no means an exclusively

French enterprise. On the contrary, the French always relied on the help of local élites. Talented though men such as Beugnot and Roederer were, they were simply too few in numbers to transform Europe on their own. At the same time, too, Napoleon's linking of property and stability made it natural that an attempt should be made to forge an alliance with foreign élites, and all the more so as such men formed the only link through which government could extend its reach into local society. Nor did this policy fail to produce results, the French securing a considerable degree of collaboration. The question that we must now answer is why this should have been the case.

One of the first charges hurled against the collaborators is that they were unwilling to trust the people. However, whilst there is much truth in the allegation, for the general or bureaucrat suddenly confronted with the reality of French military power without means of regular resistance, submission was entirely logical. First of all, the chief effect of the 'age of reason' in military terms had been to civilise warfare, and, in particular, to stop civilians from taking up arms, it being argued that were they to do so the horrors of war would be redoubled. Meanwhile, for all its humanity, the Enlightenment had been a rigidly élitist movement that regarded the mass of the people as mere brutes without the capacity for either reason or understanding; whilst doing no military good, mobilising them would therefore inevitably lead to horrors such as those of the French Revolution.

Such arguments certainly served to dissuade European establishments from the desire to resort to 'people's war', and their legacy may be found in the surrender of many Prussian fortresses without a fight in 1806 and the refusal of certain Spanish generals to support the rising of 1808. Meanwhile, they also encouraged active collaboration, for the Napoleonic régime was, as we have seen, equally contemptuous of the people. At the same time, the empire represented not revolution but a return to enlightened absolutism: whether it was in its religious toleration, its attack on the Church, its redistribution of ecclesiastical property, its assault upon corporate privilege, its rationalisation of government, or its centralisation of power in the hands of the state, it was following a well-worn monarchical tradition. Hardly surprisingly, then, whilst there were exceptions, all over Europe the statesmen and officials of enlightened absolutism flocked to the satellite governments: in Spain, for example, Joseph Bonaparte could call on the services of the Conde de Cabarrús, Mariano Luis de Urquijo and Miguel José de Azanza, all three of whom had held ministerial posts in the reformist régimes of Charles III and Charles IV.

Staying with the Spanish example, by 1808 a significant section of educated opinion had been won over to the cause of political and economic liberalism, and, in particular, to such key measures as the 'nationalisation' of the Spanish Church, the liberation of thought from the shackles of the Inquisition, the abolition of all restrictions on economic activity, the creation of a free market in land, and an end to the privileges of the nobility. Under the influence of the royal favourite, Manuel de Godoy, the period 1792–1808 was marked by the pursuit of many of these same objectives, and yet such were Godoy's personal failings and the depths to which the nation's fortunes fell that the *ilustrados* became ever more disillusioned. Though many were encouraged by the rising of 1808 to believe that the way was now open for reform, others were horrified, realising, perhaps, that the uprising was a protest against Spanish enlightenment as much as against French aggression. Split down the middle, many *ilustrados* therefore turned to the French in the conviction that they were fighting in the cause of progress. Thanks to this belief, Joseph gained the support of a devoted band of ministers, officials and propagandists which, in addition to Cabarrús, Urquijo and Azanza, included General Gonzalo O'Farril, and the men of letters, Llorente, Fernández de Moratín, Marchena and Meléndez Valdés.

The problem faced by these *afrancesados* was in a sense unique, for it was only in Spain that a stark choice arose between resistance and collaboration. Elsewhere participation in the empire could be seen as part of a seamless tradition of public service and enlightenment. In Bavaria, for example, the chief minister, Maximilian von Montgelas, had been much influenced by the doctrines of cameralism (a theory of government that argued that it was the responsibility of the state to maximise both its own efficiency and the happiness of its subjects) and had been working for reform ever since he had come to power in 1799. Almost every state that fell within the Napoleonic orbit provides further examples of statesmen for whom the empire was a time of political opportunity, whether it was Gogel and Schimmelpenninck in Holland, Zurlo, Melzi and Gianni in Italy, or Müller, Bülow and Malchus in Westphalia, this élite being seconded by a host of figures of the second rank. Typical examples are the officials associated with Montgelas. For such men Germany was in desperate need of reform – feudalism, for example, was seen as the root of poverty – and Napoleon 'the tamer of revolutionary violence and the standard bearer of civilization'.[22] Bavaria, and with her Germany, could now expect great things. As one official wrote in 1810, 'Germany slept on, secured by an ancient constitution . . .. Eyes were closed as new currents rose . . .. But all this is over now and a great new age has begun.'[23] To the very end the bulk of such men remained loyal, fiercely opposing the *befreiungskrieg* of 1813.

But the empire did not just attract the support of enlightened bureaucrats. The men who had followed Montgelas were anything but nationalists – for them German nationalism was a plot to restore the aristocracy – but, for all that, nationalism still played an important role in ideological collaboration. Thus, Napoleon frequently intimated that he intended to free the oppressed peoples of Europe and establish national states. Whilst never actually espousing the restoration of Poland, in 1806 he encouraged the recruitment of large numbers of Polish volunteers with the remark, 'I shall see whether the Poles are worthy to be a nation.'[24] Similarly, with regard to Italy in September 1796 he announced that the time had come for Italy 'to take her place among the nations'.[25] And in May 1809 he invited the Magyars to secede from the Habsburg monarchy and become a free and independent nation. In the Balkans and eastern Europe, particularly, nationalists rallied to his cause. Thus Greek volunteers joined the French in Dalmatia, whilst Greek revivalists lauded Napoleon as a saviour; in Hungary intellectuals such as János Batsányi appealed to Napoleon for help; in Poland nobles such as Jozef Poniatowski fought for the French as the best means of restoring Polish liberty, whilst the Polish invasion of Galicia in 1809 precipitated a general uprising against the Austrians; and in the Danubian provinces a number of Rumanian boyars looked to the French for liberation from the Ottomans. Even in Italy, where disillusioned nationalists formed the backbone of the numerous secret societies that emerged to combat French domination, in some minds pragmatism dictated continued support for France. As one young Italian officer wrote, 'What does it matter whether one is serving the ambition of this or that man? The great

22 D. Klang, 'Bavaria and the War of Liberation, 1813–1814', *FHS*, IV, No. 1 (Spring, 1965), 35.

23 *Cit. ibid.*, 41.

24 *Cit.* W. Reddaway, J. Penson, O. Halecki, and R. Dyboski (eds.), *The Cambridge History of Poland: from Augustus II to Pilsudski* (Cambridge, 1951), p. 226.

25 *Cit.* F. Markham, *Napoleon* (London, 1963), p. 50.

aim must be to learn to make war, which is the only skill that can free us.'[26]

If nationalism formed one political motive for serving the empire, so too did jacobinism. Though Napoleon crushed the popular republicanism of the 1790s wherever he encountered it, for many of the erstwhile 'Patriots' the principles of the empire remained more attractive than the alternatives with the result that they were frequently prepared to enter its service. Regard them with distaste though they might, the French were too eager to obtain local support to exclude them, the result being that in parts of Italy in particular they acquired a position of considerable dominance.

For all this, however, collaboration was a social phenomenon rather than an ideological one. Of Spain, for example, the radical exile, José Blanco White, remarked:

> I firmly believe . . . that the new French dynasty would have obtained a considerable majority among our gentry. In the first place, two-thirds of the above description hold situations under the government which they . . . hoped to preserve by adherence to the new rulers.[27]

For the aristocracy, in particular, social pressure was of very great weight. With the family courts functioning as new pinnacles of prestige, to emigrate or withdraw into private life would have been to give way to the new nobility that the Bonapartes were only too happy to create or, indeed, to old rivals with fewer scruples. Meanwhile, Napoleon's perpetual desire for a *ralliement* with the old order, not to mention the social climbing and contempt for the mob that marked all the Bonapartes, meant that collaboration was welcomed with open arms. Far from losing their influence, nobles were found places in governments, courts and bodyguards, showered with gifts (in Westphalia, for example, the munificence of Jerome Bonaparte raised the income of the prince of Hesse-Philippsthal from 16,000 francs to 84,000), confirmed in their titles and estates, protected against peasant disturbances, and, where possible, propitiated by the appointment of officials who were likely to be congenial. Whilst there was some resistance – in the Illyrian provinces, for example, many of the gentry fled to Austria, in Rome the great families remained aloof, and in Spain several grandees participated in the uprising of May 1808 – co-operation was entirely

26 *Cit.* Woolf, *Napoleon's Integration of Europe*, p. 224.
27. J. M. Blanco White, *Letters from Spain* (London, 1808), p. 374.

logical, the result being a significant degree of participation. In Naples four of Joseph Bonaparte's thirteen ministers were aristocrats, whilst in Spain his first civil and military appointments included at least eight grandees. Lured by a military career – a traditional preserve of the nobility – the Polish, Piedmontese and Westphalian gentry flocked to arms, at least two-thirds of the Westphalian officer corps being of noble origin. Albeit somewhat less frequently, noblemen could also be found in the administration, particularly in Holland and the Rhineland. On the whole, then, as Woolf says, 'the Napoleonic wooing of the old nobility was undoubtedly successful'.[28]

Moving away from the nobility to the *notables* as a whole, for the nobility, the landowning bourgeoisie – a growing group even before the *biens nationaux* began to be sold – and successful entrepreneurs with money to invest, prefectural interventionism and opportunities for the purchase of fresh estates at knock-down prices formed a strong incentive for involvement as a means of advancing or defending family interests. For those with some technical education or experience, meanwhile, the empire was a time of opportunity: public works of all sorts flourished; bureaucracies grew dramatically; education and public health received much attention; and scientists, statisticians and economists were all in great demand. For some, too, it offered the chance of glory and adventure. Hence the many young men from families that were otherwise hostile to the empire who insisted on joining the eagles, and the willingness of officers of armies disbanded by the French to transfer into the imperial service. Last but not least, in those areas of the *grand empire* where business flourished – above all the Rhineland – the captains of industry and commerce were entirely content with Napoleonic rule because it offered them unrivalled opportunities and an administration that seemed tailor-made for their aspirations, much the same being true of wealthy Jews such as Dandalo in the Illyrian Provinces and Jacobson in Westphalia.

Finally, amongst the common people, although collaboration was rare, even here it was not unheard of. In Spain and Calabria, for example, town-dwellers and prosperous peasants were frequently eager for protection against the guerrillas and, in consequence, to enlist in the local militias raised to combat them. In Italy, in general, traditions of vendetta might lead whole families or villages into de facto collaboration. And finally, in the Illyrian provinces the

28 Woolf, *Napoleon's Integration of Europe*, p. 195.

peasant-soldiers of the old Military Frontier welcomed the coming of the French as they hoped that it would alleviate the very heavy burdens imposed by the form of military service to which they were subject.

How deep this collaboration ran, however, remained to be seen. As is suggested by a discussion of Napoleonic freemasonry, participation in the apparatus of the empire did not necessarily imply political accord. Highly popular in the army on account of its anticlericalism, masonry was given a considerable boost by the march of the French armies, new lodges being established everywhere they passed. Yet local interest was mixed. Outside Italy, where local traditions of secret association and conspiracy gave masonry much *éclat*, interest among the local population seems often to have been limited, membership for the most part being confined to French residents, soldiers or administrators. Even in Italy, moreover, at least some of the lodges seem to have been completely apolitical, resisting all attempts to transform them into vehicles of Napoleonic propaganda. Furthermore, whilst it was acceptable to buy *biens nationaux* or otherwise exploit the empire, in the *pays réunis*, at least, there seems to have been much reluctance to assume any post that required hard work or a move away from home, French officials forever bemoaning *notable* recalcitrance in this respect – hence the rather pathetic total of non-French prefects already noted. Much the same was true of fraternisation, friendship with a French officer or attendance at an official ball in themselves signifying very little, whilst the appreciation shown by the highly favoured businessmen of the Rhenish departments was mirrored by the resentment and despair of their far more unfortunate counterparts in Berg and Westphalia. Vital to the French though it was, in short, outside a relatively restricted circle of bureaucrats and intellectuals, collaboration was a relatively flimsy phenomenon that might easily evaporate.

THE RAPE OF EUROPE

Though the connection between the empire and reform is not to be decried, Napoleon also said, 'I have only conquered kingdoms . . . to serve the interests of France and help me in all I am doing for her.'[29] To the extent that the empire brought reform at all, it did not result from disinterested benevolence, but rather from a desire to

29 *Cit.* Lefebvre, *Napoleon*, p. 209.

exploit the Continent more effectively. Undermined by the crushing burden of Napoleon's wars, over and over again reform also took second place: where the emperor wanted to win the support of traditional élites, the abolition of feudalism was diluted; when he wanted to reward his followers with great estates, administrative rationalisation was set aside; and, when schools vied for revenues with armies, it was the latter which won.

Not surprisingly, Napoleon's rule saw Europe increasingly become a 'continent-in-arms' whose levies served to lessen the burden faced by the French themselves. Mention has already been made of the manner in which the manpower of the annexed territories was ruthlessly exploited, and we shall here concentrate on the heavy pressure that was exerted upon Napoleon's allies and satellite states to send regular contingents to the *grande armée*. Thus, though some of the satellite monarchs attempted to forestall its imposition – Louis, for example, tried to keep the Dutch army up to strength with foreign deserters and prisoners of war, whilst in Naples both Joseph and Murat relied heavily on convicts and even had an 'African' regiment composed of Negro colonial troops transferred from the French army – sooner or later most of the *pays conquis* were subjected to the French system of conscription. The only exceptions to this were Spain and the Illyrian provinces (in the former, the war made it out of the question, Joseph being forced to raise his army from deserters and prisoners of war; in the latter, Marmont was much impressed with the system of universal conscription in force under the regulations of the Austrian Military Frontier, and allowed it to survive untouched). At the same time, the French system was also copied in the Grand Duchy of Warsaw and some of the German states such as Bavaria, Baden and Württemberg (by the treaty which established the Confederation of the Rhine in 1806, all its constituent states were compelled to maintain a contingent for service with the French army; this was assessed in accordance with population and ranged from 30,000 in the case of Bavaria to just twenty-nine in the case of Hohengeroldseck, the numerous tiny contingents of this sort being grouped in composite regiments). Even where French methods were not introduced, traditional systems of recruitment were greatly tightened up by such means as the reduction of the number of exemptions to the old ballots, the strict restriction of the right to travel abroad and to marry, and the prohibition of foreign recruiting parties.

By such means very large forces were raised. To take some examples, in 1808 the Westphalian army consisted of sixteen infantry battalions, twelve cavalry squadrons and three artillery batteries, but by 1812 it had twenty-nine of the first, twenty-eight of the second, and six of the third, the establishment of many of the individual units also having been increased. Equally, the forces of the Grand Duchy of Warsaw grew from thirty-six battalions, twenty-six squadrons and twelve batteries in 1808 to sixty battalions, seventy squadrons and twenty batteries in 1812. Finally, in 1805 Württemberg possessed twelve infantry battalions, twelve cavalry squadrons and three batteries, the totals for 1812 being twenty, twenty-three and six respectively. In addition to these regular forces, a number of states also raised militias or national guards. Considering that these increases were achieved in addition to making up the heavy losses that were suffered in Spain and elsewhere, it can be seen that this represents a very real effort, which in numerical terms ran into many thousands. Thus, the Kingdom of Italy supplied 121,000 men, Bavaria 110,000, the Grand Duchy of Warsaw 89,000, Saxony 66,000, Westphalia 52,000, and Berg 13,200, the grand total for all the foreign contingents that at one time or another served alongside the French amounting to some 720,000 men.

The huge military effort that this represented was obviously extremely costly. Though some help was occasionally received from France – in 1808, for example, Napoleon took 8,000 Polish troops into his pay – the bulk of the expense had to be met by the states concerned. Meanwhile, they also had to find food and shelter for the large numbers of French troops that were often quartered upon them (some 35,000 in Westphalia alone in November 1811), and in some cases to pay a regular financial tribute to France as well (the Grand Duchy of Warsaw, for example, was forced to redeem Prussian debts assessed at a sum of twenty million francs). At the same time the revenue available was greatly reduced by the estates set aside for Napoleon's numerous *donataires* (see below). Nor did protests to the emperor prove of any real help: even Joseph, who was faced with a full-scale war that was ravaging his Spanish kingdom, was denied anything but the most niggardly of aid; still worse, told though he was to rely on his own resources and make the conflict pay for itself, large parts of his realm were taken out of his control and allotted to the direct support of the French commanders operating in them. The result was bankruptcy: the debt of the Kingdom of Italy rose from one to five million lire in the period 1805–11; that of Westphalia, much worsened by Jerome's personal extravagance, from sixty million francs to perhaps as much as two hundred million; and that of the Grand Duchy of Warsaw from thirty-three million zlotys to at least ninety-one million. As Joseph wrote to Berthier in 1811:

> My total income is not more than four million reals a month. My outgoings, cut to the bone, are twelve million . . .. My senior ministers have asked me for rations for their families . . .. My ambassador to Russia is bankrupt; my ambassador in Paris has died in poverty.[30]

A further source of revenue was the heavy payments imposed on independent states. Thus, in October 1803 Spain agreed to purchase her neutrality at a cost of six million francs per month, the money being raised by a loan from Paris on which the Spaniards had to pay interest as well. In the same way almost every peace settlement signed by Napoleon was accompanied by a calamitous indemnity: forty million francs was extorted from the Austrians in 1805 and another eighty-five million in 1809; in 1806 Saxony was forced to agree to reparations of 25,375,000 francs; in March 1808 the Prussian indemnity was fixed at a nominal sum of 112 million; and Portugal would have been stripped of 100 million had she not been rescued by the Peninsular War. However, the sums agreed around the peace table are only a part of the story. With the French armies living off the country, the areas that they occupied also had to meet the cost of invasion. To quote Napoleon:

> If . . . we have to go to war again, I shall . . . live on Europe . . . Italy will give us forty million francs instead of twenty . . . and Holland thirty million instead of nothing.[31]

If these sums are taken into account the contributions of Austria and Prussia to the French war effort amount to 350 million and 515 million francs respectively. Two other states that suffered particularly heavily were Hanover and Spain. By 1809 French occupation had cost the former between forty and fifty million francs, whilst in the latter eight million francs were obtained from the western half of Old Castile alone in just six months in 1810. Nor could the cost simply be counted in financial terms, for the

---

30 *Cit.* M. Glover, *Legacy of Glory: the Bonaparte Kingdom of Spain* (New York, 1971), p. 197.

31 *Cit.* A. C. Thibaudeau, *Bonaparte and the Consulate*, ed. G. Fortescue (London, 1908), p. 127.

conquered also found that they were to be stripped of their material resources as well, the campaign of 1806 costing the Prussians 40,000 horses, and the Saxons all their cannon, munitions and military stores.

By such means as these, it is reckoned, that, until the war in the Peninsula spiralled out of control, Napoleon managed to make war pay for itself. However, money was not everything. Envisaging France as the custodian of European civilisation, from the 1790s onwards her rulers had been stripping their conquests of large quantities of art treasures and historical artefacts. An enthusiastic protagonist of such policies in both Italy and Egypt, Napoleon continued the practice under the empire. Thus we see the prince-bishop of Fulda, the elector of Hesse, the duke of Brunswick, and Frederick William III of Prussia all being relieved of a wide variety of *objets d'art* after the campaign of 1806, Joseph being ordered to send off fifty masterpieces to Paris from Madrid in 1808, and at least 250 paintings being taken from Vienna in 1809. However, whilst the collections of the Louvre – now renamed the Musée Napoléon – were certainly embellished by Napoleon, it is probable that at least as much of the loot was seized for private gain or sold for the war effort, Marshal Soult acquiring paintings worth 1,500,000 francs, the emperor himself lavishing numerous *petits objets charmants* upon Josephine, and many surplus objects being sold by state auction.

Here, of course, we come to a third function of the exploitation of Europe in that the empire provided the basis of an enormous spoils system. As the *grande armée* became more and more professionalised, so its ethos changed dramatically. No longer the 'army of virtue' of the early days of the Republic, its chief motivation became 'honour' – in effect the desire for personal gain, status and advancement. Given that Napoleon was determined to preside over a civilian régime in France, this presented him with a problem to which the empire gave him a natural solution. In the first place, the empire gave rise to a plethora of governor-generalships, viceroyalties and even thrones. In the second, the campaigns of the *grande armée* provided fortunes for men such as Augereau, Soult, Massena and Victor (Augereau – the 'proud bandit' – is reputed to have once marched into an Italian pawnshop and stuffed his pockets with jewels). To much of this, Napoleon turned a blind eye. As he remarked, 'Don't talk to me about generals who love money. It was only that which allowed me to win the battle of Eylau. Ney wanted to reach Elbing (Elblag) to procure more funds.'[32] Not all French commanders were so predatory – Davout and Bessières, at least, were models of probity – but loot was not the only source of wealth. From 1806 onwards the emperor was increasingly in the practice of setting aside landed estates and other sources of income for those whom he wished to reward, and by 1814 he had made 4,994 such awards with a total annual value of some thirty million francs. Over half of these estates went to senior officers, and it is noticeable that the large majority were to be found beyond the 'natural frontiers', the generals thus being given a strong motive for winning battles. As for the resources involved, when the Kingdom of Italy gained Austrian Venetia in 1806, one-fifth of its revenues had to be reserved for Napoleon's *donataires*; in Westphalia about the same proportion of the public revenue was lost in this fashion; and in the Grand Duchy of Warsaw the various awards were valued at 26,500,000 francs.

If the empire made some of its senior commanders immensely wealthy, at a lower level it provided many of the 'baubles' with which the army as a whole was led. In theory, looting and marauding were forbidden, but in practice such activity remained a hallmark of the *grande armée*. Setting aside women – the target, as we shall see, of much attention – and food and drink, the troops stole vast sums of money and valuables. Following the French capture of Zaragoza in 1809, for example, at least three million francs are believed to have disappeared. Embarking on the long march home from Moscow, meanwhile, a sergeant examined his possessions:

> I found . . . a woman's Chinese silk dress, embroidered in gold and silver, several gold and silver ornaments . . . two silver pictures in relief, a foot long and eight inches high . . . all in the finest workmanship. I had, besides, several lockets and a . . . spittoon set with brilliants . . . a crucifix in gold and silver, and a little Chinese porcelain vase.[33]

Last, but not least, the empire also provided a sumptuous living for Napoleon's large family. Joseph and Louis were relatively modest in their personal lifestyle, but all too many of the emperor's other siblings were completely unrestrained. As king of Westphalia, Jerome was positively profligate, to Napoleon's fury outspending the

32 *Cit.* D. G. Chandler (ed.), *Napoleon's Marshals* (New York, 1987), p. xliv.
33 P. Cottin and M. Hénault (eds.), *The Memoirs of Sergeant Bourgogne, 1812–1813* (London, 1899), pp. 56–7.

civil list by two million francs a year, running up a debt to the tune of five times that sum, and earning a reputation for licentiousness that was outstanding even among a family notorious for its affairs of the heart. Similarly, at Lucca Elise Bonaparte had five palaces, showered gifts of all sorts on her courtiers to ensure that her court was duly splendid, and presided over endless festivities, whilst contriving to make a fortune from the marble industry of Carrara. Last but not least, in Naples Caroline Bonaparte and Joachim Murat were so extravagant in the alterations that they carried out in city and palace alike that the returning Bourbons were left open-mouthed with surprise.

The empire, then, was spoils system as well as war machine, but it also had a strong economic purpose. We come here to the subject of the Continental System. Supreme though she was on land, France could not strike directly at the British on account of her naval inferiority. Although he never lost hope of naval victory, building large numbers of ships and attempting unsuccessfully to appropriate the Danish, Portuguese, and Spanish navies, the emperor was left with no option but to turn to economic warfare. Setting aside the operations of the numerous French commerce raiders who were sent out to scour the oceans, this meant blockade: British goods must be excluded from the Continent in the hope that this would deprive Great Britain of capital and markets alike, and thus provoke a financial and economic crisis that would force her to cease her subsidies to foreign powers and ultimately to withdraw from the war. Following the resumption of hostilities in 1803, a variety of ad hoc measures had been introduced against British trade, and in 1806 the vision of a continental blockade was transformed into reality. By the decree of Berlin of 21 November, the British Isles were declared to be in a state of blockade. Henceforward not only was the coastline of France and her allies to be shut to British ships, but all trade in British goods was forbidden and all British goods found on the Continent made liable to confiscation. Nor was this an end to the affair: not only were even more draconian measures imposed by means of the decrees of Milan of 23 November and 17 December 1807, but henceforward the Continental System became the linchpin of French foreign policy – the price paid by Prussia and Russia for peace with France in 1807, it also constituted an additional motive for the coercion of smaller powers such as Portugal and Denmark.

Great though they were, the diplomatic consequences of the Continental System need not detain us here. Far more central at this point is the fact that Napoleon was riding roughshod over the economic interests of an entire continent. As was perfectly clear even to Napoleon – as early as December 1806 he admitted to Louis Bonaparte that it was probable that port-cities would be ruined – the economic consequences of the decrees of Berlin and Milan were certain to be traumatic. With Britain in complete control of the seas, the prohibition of British goods meant that Europe would be cut off from the colonies. On one level this meant the loss of a variety of such staples as coffee, chocolate, tobacco and sugar, but more importantly it also implied that Europe's nascent industries would be deprived of vital raw materials, such as indigo and cotton. And, of course, the trade even of neutral states would inevitably suffer (Britain's response to the decree of Berlin had been to make all ships that did not put in to British ports and pay a heavy duty on their cargo liable to seizure; as the decrees of Milan declared any ship that complied with these orders to constitute a legitimate prize, neutrals were left in an almost impossible position).

Yet Napoleon could face such problems with equanimity. Not only could France's overseas trade hardly suffer any more than it had done already, but the Continental System was from the start an integral part of an economic policy designed to harness the rest of Europe to France's economic needs. On one level designed to damage Britain, on another the Continental System was aimed at the protection of French industry – since 1802, in fact, there had been a succession of heavy increases in French tariffs, whilst in 1806 the import of some goods, notably cotton yarns and cloths, was forbidden altogether. However, it was not just the internal market that was to be protected from competition. On the contrary, once British goods had been excluded from the Continent, it was to be transformed – almost literally – into a captive market. As Napoleon told Eugene de Beauharnais on 23 August 1810:

> You must never lose sight of the fact that, if England triumphs on the seas, it is because the English are stronger there. It is reasonable, therefore, that, as France is the strongest on land, French trade should . . . triumph there.[34]

Enunciated though these words were in 1810, they formed the basis for French policy throughout. Thus, French manufacturers had been calling for assistance since at least 1804; the 1806 ban on cottons was as much directed against European competitors as it

---

34 *Cit.* E. Hecksher, *The Continental System: an Economic Interpretation* (Oxford, 1922), p. 297.

was against Britain and one of the first tasks set Champagny when he became foreign minister in 1807 was to find a way to force the German states to reduce their tariffs and facilitate the passage of French goods. Peace treaties, too, had an economic dimension: in 1809, for example, Napoleon intended that his victory over Austria should be accompanied by a reduction in her tariff. Outside France, there was a limit to what the emperor could do (though much disruption was caused by the organisation of new overland trade routes with the Levant that bypassed foreign territory). For states such as the Kingdom of Italy, however, the consequences were very serious. Thus, from 1806 onwards a series of measures were introduced that prohibited the import of all textiles except those that had come from France, discouraged domestic industry, and, especially, the production of silk, reduced tariffs on imports from France, and forbade the export of raw silk except to France (the stress on silk reflecting both the importance of Italian silk production, and the determination of the Lyons silk industry to secure a monopoly). Furthermore, when a treaty was negotiated with Bavaria that would have reduced duties on trade between the two states by fifty per cent, this was immediately annulled. Holland, too, found that exports to Belgium both of her own products and of goods which crossed her territory from Germany were cut off, that such imports as Walloon linens suddenly flooded her markets, and that water-borne trade from Germany which had once come down the Rhine or Waal was now being diverted to Antwerp. And in Germany Westphalia and Berg suffered very severely. In the former duties on imported manufactures were kept to a nominal six per cent and the export of certain items, such as beer and brandy, heavily taxed. Berg, meanwhile, had been one of the leading centres of German industry, producing textiles and metal goods and acting as the major entrepôt for the transit of manufactures from the rest of Germany to France. Now, however, Berg's industries were discriminated against, and her traditional markets closed, with the result that her exports fell steadily from sixty million francs in 1803 to a mere twelve million in 1812. Small wonder, then, that her manufacturers increasingly saw outright annexation to France as their only hope. The very prospect of such a concession terrified rivals in the French-ruled Rhineland, and it was therefore bitterly opposed. Even had it been carried into effect, however, there is no guarantee that it would have been of much help, the common experience of territories annexed to the empire being one of continued discrimination. In Piedmont, for example, the production of silk was placed under similar restrictions to those imposed in Italy, whilst both Holland and the Hanseatic towns continued to be excluded from the French tariff area. Of course, all this did not take place without resistance – the independent German states and even Murat's Naples all responded by erecting their own tariff barriers – but on the whole the degree of success achieved was considerable. The industrial development of France under Napoleon can be left to a later chapter but, as one businessman exulted in 1807:

> What prospects cannot be imagined for our trade today, now that . . . friendly relations have turned Germany, Holland, Spain and Italy into vast fairs where France will always have a certain sale for her surplus industrial products.[35]

AN IMAGE FLAWED

Beneath the surface of the image of reform with which the Napoleonic empire has traditionally been associated, there therefore lurks a murkier reality. Superficially, change was dramatic: in state after state we find the imposition of rational systems of territorial organisation, the introduction of unified codes of law patterned on those of France, the abolition of feudalism, the reform of the judiciary, the subordination of the Church to the civil power, the sale of ecclesiastical lands, the dissolution of the religious orders, the formation of modern bureaucracies, and the adoption of French models in the armed forces. Though the extent of this must be discussed in a later chapter, there was, too, a certain increase of social mobility with large numbers of the bourgeoisie buying land and penetrating the new hierarchies of the Napoleonic state. Yet, for all that, one is left with the impression that, for Napoleon, reform was only valuable to the extent that it furthered his political and strategic aims. As he told his commissioner in Berg in 1812, 'It is not a question of your duchy but of France. I know . . . it is possible that you may lose; but what matter if France obtain a profit.'[36]

Obsessed by his struggle with Britain, Napoleon wanted to weld the whole of his empire into an economic unit by whose power she would be crushed, and at the same time to enjoy the support of reliable and efficient allies and satellite states. In short, reform was

35 *Cit.* Woolf, *Napoleon's Integration of Europe*, p. 145.
36 *Cit.* Fisher, *Napoleonic Statesmanship*, p. 220.

not an end, but rather a means, and, when it conflicted with other imperatives it was in fact abandoned. Unable to govern except with the support of the local élites, for example, the French, as we shall see, emancipated the peasants in name only, leaving them burdened with most of the same dues as before and in some cases in a worse position than ever. As well as the need to conciliate the propertied classes, a further motive here was Napoleon's practice of rewarding his followers with great landed estates, this imbuing the French with an obvious interest in maximising the perquisites of land ownership. At the same time, too, no account was taken of the fact that the reserved estates militated against the supremacy and indivisibility of the state, and acted as a constant drain on its revenue. Coupled with such demands were the ever-mounting exigencies of Napoleon's wars, which rendered states such as Holland and Westphalia ever less capable of effecting educational reforms or even of satisfying Napoleon's military demands (desperate for revenue, Jerome Bonaparte even retained the numerous internal customs barriers that criss-crossed his kingdom).

None of this is to say that change did not occur. Though certainly never uniform, it was in some cases very striking, particularly in Germany, where the rulers of the middling states seized upon the unique opportunity afforded by the Napoleonic era to pursue long-cherished goals. Nevertheless, the most obvious characteristic of the empire remains the ruthless manner in which Europe was exploited in Napoleon's service. Pillaged of its manpower and treasure, the empire was transformed into not only a source of 'baubles', but also a giant market for French industry. As Napoleon told Eugene, 'Therefore, take as your motto: *la France avant tout.*'[37]

---

37 *Cit.* Hecksher, *Continental System*, p. 297.

4 RESISTANCE TO THE FRENCH

THE RISE OF PEOPLE'S WAR

> We . . . held out for half an hour, everyone firing as much as he
> could. The cannon were hauled out, but the grapeshot . . . did not
> help . . . since the enemy formed a half-moon line and only a few
> could be hit, for they lay down on the ground behind the hedges . . .
> while every shot of theirs could hit our compressed column. Finally too
> many of our men fell, and . . . this hurried our retreat into the city.[1]

The Napoleonic empire was in no sense a popular institution.
Consciously administered by and for élite groups, for the populace it
constituted a wearisome burden: taxation and conscription were
heavy, and the imperial forces for the most part rapacious and badly
behaved. At the same time, of course, it was also highly intrusive,
often being visibly alien and accompanied by changes that overturned established patterns of life and threatened age-old certainties.
Already vividly demonstrated in the Revolutionary period in the
form of large-scale peasant uprisings in France, Belgium, Luxembourg,
Switzerland, Tuscany and Calabria, the tensions that these
characteristics produced led to a further series of outbreaks in the
Napoleonic era. Most important are the revolts that broke out in
Calabria in 1806, in Spain and Portugal in 1808, and in the Tyrol in
1809, and it is with these that this chapter will chiefly be concerned.

As witness the remarks of the Württemberg veteran of the
Tyrolean campaign quoted above, the revolts often presented the
imperial forces with considerable problems: the Calabrian revolt
took five years to suppress, and that of Spain and Portugal –
Napoleon's 'Spanish ulcer' – was never overcome at all. This fact
alone would probably have been enough to encourage a view of
these risings that accorded them great importance in the defeat of

---

1 J. Walter, *The Diary of a Napoleonic Foot Soldier*, ed. M. Raeff
(Moreton-in-Marsh, 1991), pp. 24–5.

Napoleon, but all the more was this the case when the downfall of the French empire was generally attributed to the adoption of the nation-in-arms by the powers of Europe as the means of their salvation. The example of Spain has always been given much weight in this respect on the grounds that it inspired popular resistance elsewhere, especially in Germany and Russia. And, if the revolts provoked a nationalist crusade against France, it followed that they too were 'national', embodying a belief that the people had the right to determine their own future and secure their political freedom.

Nothing, however, could be further from the truth. In none of the main revolts is there any trace of modern political consciousness, whilst serious doubts can also be entertained as to their military importance. Furthermore, outright rebellion was a relatively isolated phenomenon: if Spain, the Tyrol and part of Italy rose in revolt, Germany did not, successive attempts to precipitate uprisings in 1809 proving abject failures. Obviously, then, certain preconditions had to exist for general unrest to be translated into open revolt, and in examining these we shall discover ever greater reasons for disagreeing with those observers who have attributed the rebellions to a general 'awakening of the peoples'.

THE POPULAR EXPERIENCE OF EMPIRE

Whatever the reasons that may be ascribed to it, the relative infrequency of armed revolt is superficially somewhat surprising, for it is immediately apparent that the popular experience of empire was universally negative. Let us first take the question of conscription. Though compulsory military service had existed in many of the states of eighteenth-century Europe, in practice few men had actually been taken. Not only were there numerous social, occupational and geographical exemptions, but the need for general conscription was reduced by the recruitment of native volunteers, foreigners, criminals and vagrants. Indeed, conscription might not be employed at all for long periods of time – in Spain, for example, only two levies were made between 1776 and 1808, both of them during the Revolutionary War of 1793–95. Even if a man was called up he was not necessarily called upon to leave his home – in several states in peacetime conscripts were only expected to put in a short period of training each year, otherwise remaining in their home villages to till the land. Even then military service was not popular, armies generally being seen as sinks of iniquity. The extraordinary demands of the Napoleonic empire therefore came as a great shock.

Though service with the imperial armies may have been attractive to an occasional bored ploughboy or apprentice, or, more commonly perhaps, to the unemployed and desperate, particularly in areas with a long tradition of military service, such as Hesse, volunteers do not seem to have come forward in any numbers, the result being that compulsion was inevitable. Despite attempts to palliate the situation by impressing criminals, as in Naples and Switzerland, and buying the services of mercenaries, as in Holland and some of the minor German states, the impact was still enormous. Men invariably disappeared for years at a time (though some German troops seem to have been demobilised between campaigns, the French army, at least, was kept permanently under arms), whilst a very high proportion never came home at all: of 52,000 Westphalian troops who served in the *grande armée*, only 18,000 survived, whilst for Baden the figures are 17,000 out of 29,000. Small wonder, then, that Napoleon increasingly came to be seen as a bloodthirsty ogre, that men literally had to be torn away from their families, and that conscripts were often marched away roped together and under heavy guard.

In addition to conscription, the empire also signified impoverishment. In the first place, the passage of the French armies across the continent was immensely disruptive. Despite more or less genuine efforts to maintain discipline, the soldiers supplemented their rations by living off the country, fed their campfires with furniture, window frames, doors and fencing, and added to their pay by seizing a wide variety of valuables and trinkets of all sorts. Not even friendly territory was spared, a French hussar officer speaking of the *grande armée* traversing France in 1808 'as if it had been a land newly conquered and subject to our arms'.[2] In territory clearly identified as hostile the situation was even worse, for here officers were less inclined to restrain their men, the authorities being reduced 'to such a state of terror that they . . . did a good deal more than they had in the first instance been called upon to do'.[3] In extreme cases, the result could be wholesale devastation. To quote a British eyewitness of events in Portugal in 1811:

2 A. de Rocca, *In the Peninsula with a French Hussar: Memoirs of the War of the French in Spain* (London, 1815), p. 25.

3 O. Williams (ed.), *In the Wake of Napoleon: being the Memoirs of Ferdinand von Funck, Lieutenant General in the Saxon Army and Adjutant General to the King of Saxony* (London, 1931), pp. 968.

It is beyond everything horrid the way these European savages have treated the unfortunate Portuguese . . .. I have seen such sights as have made me shudder with horror, and which I really could not have believed unless an eyewitness of them.[4]

The situation in Portugal, where French behaviour was influenced by guerrilla warfare and extreme want, may be exceptional, but there is no doubt that the wars everywhere led to real suffering. Parts of Europe – for example, Norway and the area round Madrid – experienced severe famine, whilst even relatively prosperous regions found it difficult to meet demands placed upon them. Thus, in January 1808 it was reported that the charge of quartering the Franco-Spanish army that had occupied Denmark was so heavy that many of the inhabitants had had to abandon their homes on pain of 'the most serious distress'.[5] Nor did the French simply eat up the countryside, for war frequently plunged agriculture into crisis. In Saxony, for example, the arrival of the *grande armée* in 1806 led to large stocks of wheat that had hitherto been held back by speculators being precipitately flung upon the market, the result being a sudden fall in prices that hit landed interests very hard. In Prussian Poland, too, the partitions had been followed by a wave of investment in land in which the gentry incurred heavy debts, and, when Poland was devastated by the campaigns of 1807, both they and the peasantry were in consequence ruined.

Of course, French demands were not restricted to supplies of food, the empire also being regarded as a source of finance. There is no need here to recapitulate the immense levies that were imposed upon satellite states and conquered enemies alike. Suffice it to say that everywhere taxation rose dramatically in a development that was felt all the more for being accompanied by the introduction of new land registers and more efficient fiscal mechanisms. In Holland, for example, the already crushing burden represented by ordinary taxation, extraordinary levies and forced loans was augmented in 1806 by a series of financial reforms that increased ordinary revenue from around thirty million florins in 1805 to nearly fifty in 1809, even this increase having to be joined by a further forced loan of

---

4   W. Verner (ed.), *A British Rifleman: the Journals and Correspondence of Major George Simmons, Rifle Brigade, during the Peninsular War and the Campaign of Waterloo* (London, 1899), p. 152.

5   Thornton to Canning, 15 January 1808, Public Record Office (hereafter PRO), FO.73/46, 1–3.

forty million florins in 1807. As a result, the minister of finance had to admit to King Louis that 'a burden unknown even in England is crushing your good subjects.'[6] To add insult to injury, moreover, when Napoleon finally annexed Holland in 1810, he arbitrarily liquidated two-thirds of the enormous Dutch national debt, thereby depriving the numerous landowners, merchants and businessmen who had contributed to the various forced loans of much of their income. Meanwhile, in Berg revenue more than tripled between 1808 and 1813, whilst in Naples it rose by fifty per cent in the first three years of Murat's reign alone, similar examples offering themselves *ad infinitum*. All this, of course, came at a time when the Continental System and French protectionism were together spreading bankruptcy and unemployment across large areas of Europe, matters often being made still worse by social, political and economic reform. Thus, the abolition of feudalism frequently made the position of the peasantry more burdensome than ever, whilst the suppression of the monasteries and of large numbers of petty political units deprived numerous office-holders and dependants of all sorts of their livelihood and dealt a heavy blow to the local economies which they had sustained. At the same time, too, the suppression of the religious orders stripped away much of such infrastructure as had existed for the relief of poverty. Meanwhile, conscription was in itself an economic disaster: in Germany, especially, since they had normally only served for part of the year, it was common for the troops who composed the old armies to have wives and families, and their prolonged absence frequently reduced the latter to destitution; in addition, for many families the loss of one or more sons to military service represented a catastrophic loss of labour and income. From all sides, then, there came reports of distress and misery, between one third and one quarter of the population of parts of Holland and Germany being in receipt of poor relief even before the great slump that affected Europe after 1810.

To impoverishment was added repeated humiliation. All too often the poor were criminalised, beggars being rounded up and forced into armies or workhouses. More generally, convinced of their political and cultural superiority, the French were inclined to regard Belgians, Dutchmen, Germans, Italians and Spaniards alike as backward, superstitious, priest-ridden and uncouth. Furthermore,

---

6 Cit. S. Schama, *Patriots and Liberators: Revolution in the Netherlands, 1780–1813* (London, 1977), pp. 516–17.

the troops were brutalised, long years of service away from their homes not only habituating them to violence, but making them indifferent and even hostile towards civilians. And, last but not least, with its constant stress upon emulation and competition, the Napoleonic army encouraged – indeed, expected – bullying, bluster and braggadocio. Not all imperial soldiers were brutes – indeed, Peninsular diarists somewhat ruefully remark that on the whole French officers got on better with the local population than did their British counterparts – but it is nevertheless clear that the presence of the *grande armée* was anything but pleasant. In addition to the incessant looting, the troops were all too often drunken and badly behaved: brawling and duelling were common, whilst the civilian population were treated in a manner that ranged from the merely boisterous to the downright brutal. And, of course, women were a perennial bone of contention. According to veterans of the *grande armée*, large numbers of girls and married women were all too eager to throw themselves into the arms of the first dashing soldier who came their way. Charles Parquin, for example, boasted of having affairs at Lannion, Breda, Bochenheim, Bayreuth, Salamanca, and Epernay. How much these stories owe to fabrication it is hard to say, but clearly for at least some women the coming of the *grande armée* represented a temporary respite from the drudgery and boredom of everyday life and sometimes even more, many choosing to follow the eagles for good. But even if there was a measure of romance and eager complicity, there was also a darker reality: economic hardship forced large numbers of women into prostitution, as, for example, during the French occupation of Vienna in 1809; rape was clearly common; and many girls were seduced by promises of marriage only to be left to bear the consequences. And for cuckolding a continent, the empire paid a heavy price. As one veteran observed, 'The hate which the German have for us should not be too surprising. They cannot pardon us for having for twenty years caressed their wives and daughters before their very faces.'[7]

French domination was also offensive in other respects. Despite recent challenges, the Catholic Church remained central to the lives of millions of Europeans. Whilst its teachings provided explanation and consolation for death, disease and natural disaster, its rituals, customs and festivals were integral to daily life and a symbol of

---

7 *Cit.* J. Elting, *Swords around a Throne: Napoleon's Grande Armée* (London, 1988), p. 593.

communal pride and identity, each town, village and guild having a patron saint whose feast day would be celebrated with all due ceremony. Shrines and statues, too, were deeply venerated, their presence bringing with it an added measure of protection and prestige. Interference with the Church at the official level might matter little – to the inhabitant of a small German or Spanish village the question of who should appoint his bishop was probably immaterial – but attacks on popular religion were likely to prove calamitous. Yet it was precisely such an attack that the French Revolution had unleashed – hence in part the unrest that had swept France in 1790s – and largely through the medium of the *grande armée* this was now translated to Napoleonic Europe. Whilst Napoleon himself was prepared to tolerate 'superstition' as a means of keeping the populace quiet, many of his soldiers retained a strong allegiance to the violent anticlericalism of the Republic. Some commanders tried to keep this under control – a good example is the governor of Rome, General Miollis – whilst Joseph Bonaparte, in particular, tried hard to propitiate religious sensitivities, but at a lower level disrespect for the clergy and acts of sacrilege remained common. And, if respect for the practice of religion was generally encouraged at the higher levels of French command and administration, beyond the frontiers of the empire proper there were areas, such as Bavaria, where anticlericalism remained official policy. Yet French officials were not always far behind: in Genoa, for example, the chief of police remained a staunch anticlerical, and used the provisions of the concordat with regard to the public practice of religion to interfere with Catholic customs of all sorts. Allied to the question of the Napoleonic state's relation to Catholicism was the question of the Jews. In a development that could not but compound popular religious discontent, all over Europe the empire brought a measure of emancipation. The tension that this could provoke had already been demonstrated in the Rhineland and Italy in the 1790s, when anti-French feeling had expressed itself in anti-Semitism, and, on occasion, terrible atrocities. And as the Jews – or, at least, the wealthy amongst them – often collaborated, such anger was redoubled.

Oddly enough, however, the bitterness of the Catholic peasantry was mirrored amongst the Jews themselves. Throughout Europe the vast majority of Jews were extremely poor, the wealthy élite who collaborated with the French in fact representing only a tiny handful of the community (and it should be noted that, as was the case with the Rothschilds, some even of the wealthy remained hostile). For traditionalists the sort of reforms that Napoleon was desirous of forcing upon European Jewry were anathema (following the Grand Sanhedrin of 1807, Napoleon had decreed that henceforward all Jews were to be gathered into national 'consistories' that would be subject to state control; although allowed to practise their religion under these conditions, Jews would be denied recognition as a separate 'nation', a series of measures being imposed to ensure their rapid assimilation including, for example, a demand that one-third of all marriages should be to non-Jews). Orthodox anger was further inflamed by attempts of Napoleonic administrators to purge the practice of the Jewish faith of many popular customs, but the Jews suffered very heavily in other respects too: in *la grande France* Napoleon's discriminatory legislation led to the cancellation of many of the debts owing to them; in Holland, desperate to man his army without having recourse to conscription, Louis formed a special Jewish regiment whose ranks were filled by coercing the poor and kidnapping children from Jewish orphanages; and everywhere soldiers seem to have been inclined to cheat and bully them without mercy. Indeed, taken as a whole, no other section of the population seems to have suffered quite so badly – from Italy and Holland alike we find reports suggesting that the Jews were far worse off than their struggling Christian neighbours.

The empire did not just threaten popular religion. Nationalism in the modern sense may have been of little account in most of Europe, but that did not preclude a strong sense of pride in local institutions or past glories. When the French blew up the fortifications of Vienna in 1809, for example, they were destroying the symbols of the city's heroic resistance to the Turks in 1683. Not surprisingly, the result was outrage. Similar violence was done by the French in Spain, where virtually the first act of Marshal Murat when he occupied Madrid in March 1808 was to demand the surrender of the sword taken from Francis I of France after his defeat by the Spaniards at Pavia in 1525. Equally, in Germany the self-government enjoyed by many cities under the Holy Roman Empire, and even some of the dynasties that now lost their thrones, had been the subject of much local pride. More tellingly, perhaps, the empire also represented a serious threat to popular culture. Throughout the empire, police officials saw many plebeian recreational activities as a danger to public order and a source of idleness, corruption and waste. In consequence, cafés, and bars – the haunt, of course, of prostitution, drunkenness and gambling – were regularly raided; various restrictions, generally of a socially discriminatory nature, were placed on carnivals and masked balls; and the celebration of religious holidays was discouraged. Very often, too, traditions of popular assembly were also swept away – in Naples, for example, the reform of municipal government led to the disappearance of the village *parlamenti* which had hitherto given a voice to all adult males.

Thus emerged a climate of popular hostility that was not primarily political but rather economic, social and cultural, and was aided and abetted by local élites that remained aloof from collaboration. Threatened in its very identity, the populace for the most part rejected the empire. However, rejection is not the same as revolt, and it is to the transition from one to the other that we must now turn our attention.

THE ORIGINS OF REVOLT

The whole of the Napoleonic empire suffered from the grievances that have just been outlined, resistance being widespread. As might be expected, conscription was especially opposed. Both draft evasion and desertion were frequent. With regard to the former, in Belgium, for example, over forty-two per cent of conscripts absconded in the period 1805–9 whilst the rate of absenteeism when conscription was first imposed in Rome in 1810 was one-third. As for desertion, by 1809 18,000 men, or over one-third of its current strength, had deserted from the army of the Kingdom of Italy, whilst the imperial forces suffered so many deserters in the Peninsular War that Wellington was ultimately able to maintain no fewer than ten foreign infantry battalions. Meanwhile, setting aside the complicated question of banditry, which, though widespread in large areas of Germany, Italy and the Rhineland and closely related to desertion, was also the product of social unrest, conscription gave rise to considerable popular violence. Finally imposed in Holland early in 1811, the draft led to a series of disturbances of varying degrees of seriousness that culminated in the takeover of Leiden by a mob of perhaps 1,000 peasants in April 1813. However, military affairs were not the only causes of violence: in Frankfurt in January 1807 Jews who had gathered to welcome the entry into the city of its new ruler, Prince Carl von Dalberg, were set upon as they returned to their homes; in northern Italy increases in taxation to pay for the war of 1809 led to a series of peasant risings; in Westphalia disputes over feudal dues occasioned disturbances among the peasantry and in Oldenburg fishermen rioted when the French sought to curb smuggling and register them for service at sea. Nor, indeed, was all resistance violent: 'state' Catholicism, and, indeed, Judaism, was boycotted or moderated; orders to illuminate cities in honour of French victories were defied, or houses decorated with rags instead of bunting and efforts to enforce collaboration dodged or otherwise short-circuited.

For all this unrest, however, in only three areas – Calabria, the Iberian peninsula and the Tyrol – do we see full-scale popular insurrections. Clearly, then, rebellion needed very special circumstances: even in the seemingly highly auspicious conditions of 1809, five successive attempts to raise a revolt in Westphalia (the most famous being those of Major Schill and the duke of Brunswick) were almost completely ignored by the peasantry. Essentially, these preconditions were threefold, the first being discontent with the dynasty supplanted by Napoleonic rule, the second social tension, and the third traditions of popular military activity. This is not to say that other factors – Catholicism, rugged terrain, and geographical isolation – were not of importance, but it should be pointed out that they applied to many areas which did not rise en masse in the same style. Taking each of our three preconditions in turn, we find that both Calabria and the Tyrol had been alienated by royal policy, and that in both Spain and Portugal the ruling dynasties had become utterly discredited. Immense, as we shall see, in Spain, Portugal and Calabria, even in the more homogeneous Tyrol – essentially an area of free peasant farmers – there was friction between towns such as Innsbruck, Trent (Trento) and Bozen (Bolzano) and the rural hinterland. And, above all, there was a widespread habituation to the use of arms. In Spain, Portugal and Calabria banditry and smuggling were a common feature of the rural economy, and frequently involved large-scale skirmishes with the security forces (by the same token Spain maintained a wide variety of irregular police units that provided a further source of quasi-military experience). Meanwhile, Spain, Portugal and the Tyrol all possessed traditions of popular mobilisation – as opposed to formal conscription to the regular army – that were largely absent elsewhere. Thus, in Spain the Basques and Catalans had to serve in irregular home-guards known as *miqueletes* or *somatenes*; in Portugal there survived the *ordenança*, the traditional mediaeval militia composed of every male inhabitant between sixteen and sixty; and in the Tyrol all men between eighteen and sixty were liable for service as *schützen*, or sharpshooters.

In each of the three areas under discussion, then, revolt found a ready basis. Taking Calabria first, although resistance broke out in the immediate aftermath of the French invasion of Naples early in 1806, there had been little reason to expect any great display of loyalty. If Calabria had risen against the French in 1799 under the leadership of Cardinal Ruffo, the so-called 'Army of the Holy Faith' – the original ruffians – had chiefly been encouraged by the promise of lower taxation (in the form of an end to the hated salt tax), and loot – as the commander of the Neapolitan army, Damas, sourly recollected, 'Two poor villages accused a rich one of Jacobinism, whereupon the Cardinal promised that the two should combine to pillage the third.'[8] As for attitudes to the dynasty, they could hardly have been worse. Using a terrible earthquake that had hit the province in 1783 as a pretext, the government of Ferdinand IV set about the dissolution of a number of monasteries and the distribution of their lands amongst the peasantry. In the event, however, the policy miscarried, the bulk of the land going to the aristocracy and the peasantry being left worse off than they had been before. Restored to power with the fall of the short-lived Parthenopean republic, Ferdinand IV and his queen, Maria Carolina, did little to improve matters, reneging on Ruffo's promises and initiating large-scale recruitment to the army. When British and Russian troops landed in Naples in November 1805, they therefore received at best a tepid welcome from the populace. Indifference then turned to hostility, for the large contingent of Albanian mercenaries attached to the Russian forces ravaged the countryside without mercy, one British observer writing that they did 'little harm to the French, but [were] deadly protectors to the Italians.'[9] As the Russian and Neapolitan regulars were not much better behaved, the queen's desperate efforts to whip up popular feeling came to nothing: only a few thousand men came forward, and even these dispersed without resistance when the French crossed the border. To quote the same observer as before:

> In . . . Naples there was no sort of commotion . . .. On the day . . . the functions of government were abdicated, the courts of law were open and business was carried on as though there was nothing the matter.[10]

8 J. Rambaud (ed.), *Memoirs of the Comte Roger de Damas, 1787–1806* (London, 1913), p. 401.
9 H. Bunbury, *Narratives of Some Passages in the Great War with France from 1799 to 1810* (London, 1854), p. 219.
10 *Ibid.*, pp. 216–17.

When the unpopular *émigré*, Damas, retreated into Calabria, moreover, the populace refused to provide him with supplies and even launched a series of attacks on his troops, eventually leaving him with no option but to evacuate the remnant of his forces to Sicily.

With the Bourbon monarchy and its agents so unpopular, all would probably have remained quiet had it not been for the actions of the French, who not only engaged in forced requisitioning but also began to pay court to, if not to molest, the local women (who were still kept veiled and sequestered). The response was riots in the towns of Nicastro, Soveria and Fiume Freddo, the French responding with wholesale burnings and executions. Reprisal now led to counter-reprisal, the British lending a hand as well by plying the Calabrians with arms, supplies and money and disembarking a small expeditionary force under Sir John Stuart which defeated the French at Maida on 4 July. With fewer than 10,000 troops scattered over hundreds of miles of mountain and coast, the invaders were powerless to restore order, the entire region soon getting completely out of control. Nevertheless, serious doubts exist as to the nature of the uprising. Writing after the British had once again withdrawn, Sir John Moore commented:

> The general has been much pressed to land in Calabria where as usual it is said the inhabitants will immediately join him . . .. But when Sir John Stuart landed in Calabria not a man joined him . . . until after his success at Maida, and not even after that was he joined by any man of respectability . . .. The *mafia* only rose, who are a lawless banditti, enemies to all governments whatever . . . fit to plunder and murder, but much too dastardly to face an enemy. They did not, after Reynier's defeat, harass or attack him in his retreat . . . nor have they been able to offer the smallest resistance to the French in their advance again into Calabria. It is perfectly evident that whatever is undertaken we have ourselves alone to trust to.[11]

This is, perhaps, a little unfair, but it is nevertheless quite clear that there was little sympathy for the Bourbons per se. To quote Moore again:

> We hope . . . you are better informed than to expect any assistance from the inhabitants of . . . lower Italy. It is a melancholy truth . . . that the royal cause is not the popular one in this part of the world.

11 Moore to Gordon, 11 October 1806, British Library, Additional Manuscripts (hereafter BL. Add. Mss.) 49482, 39–43.

However much the inhabitants disapprove of the French, they prefer them to their own . . . government, and, as long as . . . we support its re-establishment, the French will have more friends than us.[12]

Again, Moore is exaggerating, though it is fair enough to say that the Bourbons had not experienced any growth in their popularity – on the contrary, when royal troops launched a short-lived invasion of the mainland in May 1807, the partisans attacked them and raided their baggage. Devotion to the monarchy was hardly necessary to keep the revolt alive, however. Given the savagery of the occupying forces, itself fuelled by the torture and massacre of French prisoners, traditions of vendetta and sheer destitution would probably have been enough to do so (as the devastation mounted so more and more peasants were forced into taking up arms for want of any other means of procuring their subsistence). Equally provocative, however, were the actions of the new régime. Even before the French had arrived, Calabria had been an area of extreme social tension in which the mass of poverty-stricken tenant farmers were being brutally exploited by their feudal overlords and a rising rural bourgeoisie. Thanks to the French-inspired reforms that were now introduced – emancipation, the sale of the lands of the Church and the municipalities, the transformation of local government – the position of the peasantry now became even worse: access to grazing land and watercourses disappeared; the Church could no longer provide the charity, secure leases and cheap credit that it had traditionally provided; village democracy was broken; the local *podestà*, who acquired the bulk of the fresh land and filled the ranks of the administration, became even more powerful than before; many peasants were ultimately reduced to the status of landless labourers; and, last but not least, in 1809 Murat announced the introduction of conscription. To the extent that the insurgents had any ideological motivation at all, it was provided by the Catholic Church whose friars and parish priests frequently preached resistance and in some cases provided military leadership as well. With the insurgents taught that it was no sin to steal from either the French or their supporters, the campaign quickly became, as one French observer remarked, 'a type of *jacquerie*'.[13] Thus, the Calabrian guerrillas were in fact bandits,

12 Moore to Gordon, 31 October 1806, BL. Add. Mss. 49482, 44–6.
13 *Cit.* M. Finlay, 'The most monstrous of wars: suppression of Calabrian brigandage, 1806–1811', *Conference on Revolutionary Europe Proceedings*, 1989, II, p. 167.

much of their activity being directed towards the spoliation of the local towns, where lived the bulk of the nobility and other notables, and the slaughter of 'collaborators' – for which read the propertied. As Stuart wrote, 'It is the attack of the poor, the worthless, the needy, against the better class of society.'[14] And, as the British found in Sicily, where the stimulus of loot did not exist there was little interest in the struggle: in 1808, for example, attempts to form two volunteer battalions proved a fiasco. As the British chief-of-staff, Henry Bunbury, wrote:

> Of the Agosta battalion not a single man was produced! But at Milazzo, by crimping and all sorts of discreditable means, 380 men were brought together. Such was their voluntary ardour that the officers found it necessary to place them immediately in confinement, and, about ninety of them being locked into a house, they tore off the roof and betook themselves to the mountains.[15]

If our picture of the Calabrian revolt is a muddy one, that of events in Iberia is even muddier, Spain's resistance, in particular, being closely linked with her domestic situation. In any discussion of Revolutionary and Napoleonic Spain it is customary to begin with a description of the 'trinity upon earth' of Godoy, who was secretary of state from 1792 to 1798 and generalissimo of the armed forces from 1801 to 1808, Charles IV (1788–1808), and his queen, Marie Louise. Though much obloquy has been heaped upon all three, they have not been fairly treated by history. Charles was vapid and his wife voluptuous, but the policies that they followed were not without intelligence. They did, however, show a lack of judgement. A good example is Godoy's elevation to the premiership in November 1792. Godoy was a man of genuine ability who stood out from most of the senior ministers and officials of the previous reign and his advancement shows at least a certain acumen: fearful both of revolution and the political intrigues that had long dogged the Spanish court, the king and queen saw the value of placing at the head of affairs a man who owed everything to them. But therein lay the rub: Godoy was inexperienced (in 1792 he was only twenty-five), a scion of the petty nobility, and, above all, the queen's supposed lover. Regarded as an usurper by the great magnates, a more general feeling emerged that his only qualification for power

14 *Cit.* Bunbury, *Narratives*, p. 437.
15 *Ibid.*, p. 359.

was his prowess in the royal bed, and all the more so as he had arrived at the court as a simple trooper in the Guardias de Corps in 1787, since when he had been showered with favours of all sorts, created a grandee of the first class, and elevated to the rank of captain-general. Nor was Godoy's conduct once in power entirely wise, for he developed a well-merited reputation for ostentation, venality and licentiousness that alienated the men of talent and imagination whose support he desperately needed, and reduced his own supporters to a crowd of self-seeking sycophants. Yet Charles and Marie Louise continued to lavish honours upon him – in 1795 he was made a prince – and thereby brought the régime into ever greater discredit.

For all their numerous faults, it cannot be denied that the 'trinity upon earth' were dogged by extremely disadvantageous circumstances. In March 1793 Spain was dragged into war with France. Hopelessly unprepared – her army had been allowed to run down in favour of building a powerful navy against Britain in alliance with France – she was badly beaten and forced to sue for peace in 1795. Caught between Spain's two traditional enemies, Godoy now took the only way out, signing an alliance with France and going to war against England from 1796 to 1801, and then again from 1804 to 1808. Whilst there had been little option, the results were disastrous. Spanish naval power – the foundation of her colonial strength and, thus, of her prosperity – was shattered at Trafalgar, whilst Trinidad was lost and present-day Argentina and Uruguay only saved from British conquest by the efforts of the local inhabitants. Satisfactory thought this feat was on one level, it was yet at the same time highly alarming: cut off from Spain by British blockade, the colonies found themselves deprived of manufactured goods and in consequence grew increasingly restive, the defeat of the British greatly boosting *criollo* self-confidence. With Spain meanwhile forced to permit a measure of trade by neutral ships, the ties that bound the empire together were clearly slipping. At the same time the prosperity which she had enjoyed in the 1780s was brought to an end. Whilst government expenditure soared, revenue declined dramatically, efforts to finance the wars by issuing paper money merely increasing the chaos by fuelling Spain's already rampant inflation (taking 1780 as a base, by 1798 prices had gone up by fifty-nine per cent). Industry, meanwhile, was hard hit, the silk and cotton manufacture of Valencia and Catalonia both suffering particularly badly (whereas in 1804 105 ships weighed anchor from Catalan ports, within three years the number had dropped to just one). And all the time France's predominance seemed to grow ever greater: not only was the Spanish navy ruined, but from 1803 a heavy subsidy was being paid to Napoleon, whilst in 1807 Spain had to agree to send troops against both Sweden and Portugal.

The corollary to fiscal and economic dislocation was impoverishment. Unemployment soared and the real incomes of the labouring classes registered a serious fall, their plight being worsened by the steady growth in population that Spain experienced in the later eighteenth century. With the propertied classes themselves under pressure, meanwhile, great efforts were made to increase rents and exact more profit from feudal dues. To the impact of war was added that of natural disaster, Spain being assailed by a series of crop failures, epidemics, floods and even earthquakes. As a result, the cities became ever more thronged with beggars (whom the authorities tried to deal with by drafting them into the army) whilst bands of desperate peasants and day labourers roamed the countryside. Nor was the crisis limited to the humble, for those on fixed incomes – pensioners, widows and army officers – all found themselves facing destitution. With the régime clearly unable to cope, the climate grew steadily worse: Guadalajara, Seville, Asturias, Madrid and Valencia witnessed outbreaks of rioting, banditry increased, and the 'trinity upon earth' became ever more hated.

With frightening speed, for a number of reasons the economic unrest became politicised. As we shall see, Godoy quickly offended the Church, and, with the régime being denounced from the pulpit, the idea took root that Spain's misfortunes constituted divine punishment for his sins. These sins, moreover, were well-known. From 1800 onwards a group of disgruntled courtiers motivated by a mixture of personal jealousy and sectional discontent had coalesced around the heir to the throne, Prince Ferdinand, who was bitterly jealous of the favourite on account of the way that he had supplanted him in the affections of his parents. Determined to block any further advancement on his part, they spread subversion by mingling with the crowd and circulating a series of couplets and cartoons of the utmost scurrility (in this respect, Godoy was his own worst enemy, his fondness for women being notorious). For many Spaniards, the result was that the favourite became the epitome of evil, and Ferdinand the epitome of good.

Godoy's difficulties would not, perhaps, have been so great had he in fact been the idler of legend. A man of some vision, with the support of Charles IV he perpetuated the absolutist reformism of the preceding reign of Charles III. Thus, repeated efforts were made to extend conscription to the regions that had hitherto been exempt – above all, the Basque provinces, Catalonia and Valencia – and to lessen aristocratic privilege within the army, especially by reducing the swollen royal guard. The Basques' *fueros* were eroded; some attempt was made to tap the resources of the wealthy through new taxes on luxuries; much support was given to the promotion of education, science and industry, and of new theories of economics, to which end certain curbs were imposed upon the Inquisition. Within the Church encouragement was given to the Jansenists (a faction of the clergy which believed that the power of the papacy should be restricted in favour of that of the bishops). Heavy fees were imposed on the foundation of new *mayorazgos* (the inalienable landed estates held in perpetuity by individual families that formed the basis of the Spanish nobility's wealth); some guilds were abolished; controls on prices and rents were relaxed; and a start was made on the expropriation and sale of the commons and the estates of the Church.

The effect of these policies was simply to swell the ranks of the discontented. Substantial elements of both the Church and the nobility were alienated, as, of course, were the Basques. As for the populace as a whole, they found themselves subjected to new demands for conscription – which provoked serious risings in Valencia and Bilbao – and to irritating interferences in their cultural life (in an attempt both to discourage popular idleness and to bring the vast quantities of land employed to raise fighting bulls under cultivation, Godoy prohibited *los toros*). At the same time, social tensions increased. Much of the ecclesiastical land that was sold had been devoted to the upkeep of charitable foundations which now disappeared. Moreover, tenants on the land affected often found that their rents were increased. The result was still more antagonism towards Godoy, and yet the favourite did not gain in popularity even among the groups who had benefited from the land sales and other reforms. On the one hand, his hands were tied in that he could not go beyond the point that his far more timid royal sponsors would allow, so that in the Church the Jansenists eventually had to be sacrificed to their ultramontane opponents. On the other, the favourite's potential supporters – doctrinaire liberals and the wealthy propertied groups who had been buying the substantial amounts of land on offer – wanted still more change, and despaired of his ability to deliver it. Meanwhile, society grew ever more polarised between the beneficiaries and the victims of reform, and it is in this polarisation that much of the explanation for Spanish resistance to the French is to be found.

In fact, it was the internal situation that gave rise to Napoleon's intervention. In October 1807 a force of French troops had been dispatched across Spain to Portugal to enforce the Continental System. Aided by the Spanish army, they had quickly driven the Portuguese royal family into exile in Brazil, and placed the country under occupation. Precisely at this moment, however, matters in Spain reached boiling point. Convinced that the aging Charles IV intended to make Godoy his successor, Ferdinand had been engaging in secret negotiations with the French to secure his future by establishing himself as a loyal Napoleonic ally. In the so-called 'affair of El Escorial', however, this plot was suddenly unmasked by Godoy, who further claimed to have found papers suggesting that Ferdinand was plotting to kill his parents. A humiliating act of submission was then extracted from the prince, his accomplices being arrested and put on trial for treason. Yet Napoleon forbade any reference to himself in the proceedings, the result being that the whole affair was left to appear an underhand plot on the part of Godoy to remove the prince as a rival, and all the more so when the accused, found innocent by the court, were promptly dispatched into internal exile. Already much alarmed at the reliability of his Spanish ally – not only was Spain in a state of obvious bankruptcy, but in 1806 Godoy had treacherously planned to attack Napoleon whilst he was making war on Prussia – the emperor now resolved to regenerate Spain by force, thereby opening up for France the wealth of the Indies, and ridding himself of the last of the Bourbons. From December 1807 onwards, therefore, increasing numbers of French troops began to enter northern Spain under Marshal Murat. Suddenly seizing control of the Spanish border fortresses, by early March they were bearing down on Madrid.

Seeing that all was lost, Godoy now made a last ditch effort to organise resistance, but Ferdinand's supporters saw that this must be disastrous: believing that Napoleon intended only to remove Godoy or to replace Charles and Marie Louise with Ferdinand, they saw that war might lead to the removal of the Bourbons altogether. The favourite's orders were therefore sabotaged, and a military coup – the first in Spanish history – organised at the temporary royal residence of Aranjuez. Held as it was by the royal guard, which had hated Godoy ever since an earlier decision greatly to reduce its size, this was an easy matter: supported by a large and vengeful crowd of local residents, on 17 March the troops rose in revolt. Utterly terrified, the king and queen first dismissed the favourite and then abdicated in favour of their son, and on 24 March the prince, now King Ferdinand VII, rode into Madrid to a triumphant welcome (Godoy, meanwhile, was arrested and flung into prison). However, if Ferdinand had believed that he would be accepted as an ally by the French, he was much mistaken: despite abject attempts at conciliation, Charles and Marie Louise were encouraged to denounce him as an usurper. With matters in this state, Napoleon stepped in as mediator: assembling the entire Spanish royal family at Bayonne he bluntly informed them that Charles and Ferdinand alike must abdicate in favour of his brother, Joseph. Charles caved in immediately, and, though Ferdinand put up some resistance, on 6 May he surrendered his rights to the throne.

In deciding to overthrow the Bourbons, Napoleon had been convinced that Spain would at worst witness only sporadic disorders but in this he was seriously mistaken. At first the French troops had been welcomed as the deliverers of Ferdinand, but it was not long before their usual mode of behaviour was causing serious irritation. At the same time, there was increasing popular disquiet as to Napoleon's intentions. As a result, throughout April a series of disturbances took place in Madrid, Burgos, Toledo and Vitoria, these reaching a climax in the famous rising of the Dos de Mayo in the capital. By the end of April news was arriving of Ferdinand's predicament, and public opinion in Madrid had become extremely excited. When news spread on 2 May that the French were on the point of removing the last members of the royal family left in Madrid, a large crowd gathered before the palace and tried to prevent their departure, the French responding by opening fire. At the sound of the volleys, however, large numbers of the inhabitants poured into the streets attacking every Frenchman that they could find. For an hour or two the capital was out of control, but Murat soon had reinforcements marching in from all sides, and within a few hours all was quiet.

If this was the case with the capital, it was not so in the rest of the country. Faced by the growing disquiet, the Spanish civil and military authorities – the vast majority of them composed of men appointed by Godoy – had been doing their best to maintain order. In doing so, however, they opened the way for revolution, for their collaboration conflated resistance with the redress of domestic grievance. The coup at Aranjuez had been accompanied by numerous attacks on the favourite's partisans elsewhere, and all over Spain dissatisfied elements of all sorts now seized the chance to secure revenge or to advance themselves or their ideas. Thus, ultramontane clergymen eager to restore the property of the Church and disaffected magnates who wished to revive the power of the nobility came together with Jansenists and liberals who wanted, not to turn the clock back, but rather to sweep aside the barriers that hindered further reform. Underpinning both were groups such as the subaltern officers of the army whose lowly origins – most stemmed from the petty *hidalguía* or even the commonalty – stood in the way of their promotion, and tenant farmers, landless labourers and the urban poor, for all of whom Godoy was the incarnation of evil and Ferdinand VII their saviour. Nor was hatred of Godoy the only factor which bound the movement together. In Bourbon Spain the army had enjoyed an elevated position in society and state. Its consequent pretensions had earned it considerable jealousy among large sections of the propertied classes, and all the more so as the chances of a satisfactory career in the officer corps were small except for the upper nobility. At the same time, in line with the influence of the Enlightenment, the army was felt to be an economic burden, a danger to the health and morals of society, and a pillar of despotism. Meanwhile, the populace resented military service, forced billeting and the army's requisitioning of transport and labour. By 1808, then, antimilitarism had acquired considerable strength in Spain, and this, too, was now added to the brew.

Despite the universal cry of loyalty to Ferdinand VII, it is therefore clear that the series of uprisings that now broke out all over the unoccupied regions of Spain starting on 23 May at Cartagena and Valencia had a powerful domestic interest. Often the work of conspiratorial groups and sometimes headed by men who were declared enemies of Godoy, they swept aside the established organs of power and established new ones in their place, generally speaking in the form of provincial committees or juntas. Even where the local civil or military authorities had called for resistance they were ignored, their personnel at best being co-opted into the juntas and at worst deposed, imprisoned or murdered, in some cases after they had gone over to the insurgents. Amongst the dead were four captains-general, four military governors, the director of the artillery academy of Segovia, three *corregidores*, an intendant, a retired general killed for the sole reason that he was the brother-in-law of Godoy's mistress, and a militia officer who had been involved in the suppression of the Valencian rising of 1801. Even where partisans of Godoy survived in positions of prominence, they were often harassed for long periods thereafter – the greatest example is the victor of Bailén, General Castaños, who at the time of the uprising commanded the large force of troops blockading Gibraltar: saved by his personal popularity, he declared for the insurgents only to be removed from command at the close of the year after months of innuendo and sabotage.

Inchoate as it was, the Spanish uprising had no political unity, with each provincial administration exhibiting a different complexion. Yet common to all was hatred of Godoy and a growing determination in one way or another to reshape Spain even though there was no agreement as to how this should be done. The manner in which this question was resolved must be left to another chapter, however. What interests us here is rather what the crowd who had made the revolution thought it was fighting for. In this respect such evidence as we have is very mixed. In those parts of the country into which the French had actually penetrated – and it should be remembered that in May 1808 the French only occupied parts of Catalonia, the Basque country and Navarre, a strip of territory along the main road to Madrid, and the immediate area of the capital – popular resistance was often desperate from the beginning. Similarly, as in Aragón, Valencia and Andalucía, an offensive movement could bring the population flocking to arms in large numbers. Yet if we take the example of Galicia, which was far removed from any source of danger, enthusiasm for the war was almost non-existent. Not only did very few volunteers come forward, but many young men arranged hasty marriages, fled across the frontier into Portugal or cut off their own trigger fingers rather than submit to the levies that were now imposed by the provincial junta. Moreover, as soon as any area had been liberated, enthusiasm for the war declined dramatically. Thus, taking León as an example, temporarily relieved of all danger by the victory of Bailén, its population seemed to lose all interest in the struggle. As one British officer complained:

> It often looks as if Spain were not even willing to defend herself. In all the . . . towns the inhabitants lounge about in their hundreds, completely . . . sunk in utter idleness. Is this the daring, patriotic and impetuous race about which the press has raved so bombastically?[16]

As a result of this evident parochialism, many of the levies who had sprung to arms in May 1808 went home, whilst it proved extremely difficult to procure recruits for the regular armies sent to face the

16 A. Ludovici (ed.), *On the Road with Wellington: the Diary of a War Commissary in the Peninsular War* (New York, 1925), pp. 79–80.

French on the Ebro. The appearance of the French might galvanise ferocious outbursts of resistance, just as the long-term experience of their administration stimulated guerrilla warfare, but a general impression nevertheless persists of chronic parochialism, and, above all, resistance to regular forms of military service. In Catalonia, for example, the *somatenes* were willing enough to fight the French in their own localities, but they would not move away from them and fiercely resisted the many attempts that were made to establish a more permanent form of military organisation. And throughout Spain desertion remained a serious problem, particularly once large numbers of guerrilla bands had emerged to provide not only an obvious form of sanctuary, but an infinitely preferable form of military service – as one observer put it, in the guerrillas 'there was more freedom, whilst the advantages of better food and fewer duties flattered the soldiery'.[17] In short, it would appear that, for the Spanish peasant to take up arms, far more was needed than devotion either to Ferdinand or to traditionalist Catholicism. What was needed was above all the physical presence of the French and the experience of their rule.

The Spanish guerrillas are a highly complex issue. In so far as they were a popular phenomenon – and it should be remembered that some of them, at least, were actually regular soldiers – their motivation included devotion to Ferdinand VII, hatred of the French, religious fervour, and the desire for revenge. However, as in Calabria, the popular struggle became conflated with the economic grievances of rural society. In order to foment popular resistance in December 1808 the Junta Central – the provisional government that had eventually emerged from the chaos of the uprising – had ruled that the personal effects of the French and their collaborators were legitimate booty. With collaboration an affair of the propertied classes and the towns – the *afrancesados* had their strongest base amongst grandees, bureaucrats and *ilustrados*, whilst British observers regularly noted a discrepancy between the hatred of the countryside and the acquiescence of the towns – in the words of one French general, the struggle became 'a war of the poor against the rich'.[18] That being the case, it is hardly surprising that the Spanish

---

17 L. Picado Franco, *Historia del origen, acontecimientos y acciones de guerra de la sexta división del Segundo Ejército (o sea de Soria) durante nuestra sagrada lucha al mando del Excmo. Sr. D. José Joaquín Durán y Barázabal, Mariscal de Campo de los reales ejércitos* (Madrid, 1817), I, pp. 59–60.

18 *Cit.* R. Carr, *Spain, 1808–1975* (Oxford, 1982), p. 109.

authorities were deluged by protests and pleas for aid, or that the French were able to form a number of urban militias.

If anything, as the French slowly evacuated the Peninsula from the middle of 1812 onwards so the problem grew worse, for many of the erstwhile guerrillas, rather than following the French or joining the Spanish armies, simply settled down where they were and lived off the countryside around them (by this stage it is clear that they were more or less entirely distinct from the mass of the population, which, though 'decidedly inimical to the French', is described as murmuring 'under the oppression and tyranny which it suffers without exerting itself to remove or diminish what it complains of').[19] With the emergence of a liberal régime in Cádiz, and the passage of legislation which confirmed many of the social and political changes embarked upon by the *antiguo régimen*, the struggle acquired a new dimension. As the details of the liberal programme became known, so they were everywhere rejected – the guerrilla leader, Espoz y Mina, is even supposed to have pinned a copy of the constitution to a tree and had it executed by firing squad! – and by the summer of 1813 both Wellington and his brother, Henry, then British ambassador to Spain, were discussing the possibility of 'a civil war in our rear'.[20] The catalyst for such fears was the hostility provoked by the liberals' anticlericalism (in the Basque country their attack on the *fueros* was also a significant factor), but in fact the traditionalism that is usually seen as the hallmark of popular resistance in Spain cloaked bitter social and economic resentments. As Brian Hamnett has written:

> In a large part of eastern and southern Spain the rebels fought as much against the *señorial* nobility, secular or ecclesiastic, as against the French themselves . . .. The legitimist posture of the popular movements hid an illegitimacy of far greater import . . .. Church and king were symbols not of conformity but of resistance.[21]

Much evidence may be put forward of the importance of social and economic issues in the Spanish struggle (though it should be

---

19 Sydenham to H. Wellesley, 12 September 1812, University of Southampton, Wellington Papers (hereafter US. WP.) 1/361.

20 Wellington to H. Wellesley, 2 July 1813, US. WP.1/373; cf. also H. Wellesley to Wellington, 31 May 1813, US. WP.1/369; H. Wellesley to Castlereagh, 14 July 1813, PRO. FO.72/145, 11–13.

21 B. Hamnett, *La política española en una época revolucionaria* (Mexico City, 1985), pp. 92–3.

pointed out that popular unrest was as much directed against the *ancien régime* as it was against liberal reformism). In Galicia, where the tensions arising from the seigneurial system were very great, the outbreak of war was followed by a general refusal to pay the Church's tithes. In Asturias the mere rumour that the provincial junta, which in this case was strongly liberal, intended to rescind a law of 1785 that prohibited landowners from evicting tenants from leasehold properties provoked a peasant uprising in September 1808. And from all over Andalucía, Valencia and Murcia – from Elche, Montealegre, Rute, Grazalema, Benaocaz, Ubrique, Villaluenga – came reports of villages refusing to pay the dues owed to their *señores*, invading the land, or even rising in revolt. Murder, too, was by no means infrequent: on 2 February 1809 resentment at the growing capitalisation of the fishing, textile and ceramic industries prior to 1808 led to a serious riot in the town of Ribadeo that culminated in the murder of a leading local *entrepreneur*, Raimundo Ibañez. So alarming did the situation become that, in order to restore order, in November 1813 the *cortes* authorised the formation of a paramilitary police force – a forerunner of the brutal Civil Guard – recruited from men who could afford to equip themselves at their own cost.

Turning now to Portugal, it is clear that here, too, resistance was connected with factors other than simple loyalty to the Braganças. Governed from 1750 to 1777 by the enlightened reformer, Pombal, Portugal had experienced a period of unprecedented upheaval which had had a very serious impact on the lower classes. Huge numbers of peasants were ruined, for example, when Pombal ordered the destruction of their vines in order to concentrate production in the hands of a small group of large landowners. In the same way, the favour afforded to great merchant houses proved disastrous for many small traders. Though the monarchy got rid of Pombal in 1777, it did not reverse his policies and in fact continued to shower rewards on the wealthy bourgeoisie who had been his protégés. Growing still further in power, such families and their allies in the bureaucracy began to acquire much land, particularly amongst the large estates of the south, the peasantry in the meantime continuing to suffer the most abject poverty. Meanwhile, insult was added to injury by the events of 1808, for, by escaping to Brazil, the royal family, who were in any case less than prepossessing, were perceived to have abandoned their unfortunate subjects to the mercies of the French. With as many as 10,000 nobles, merchants, landowners and officials joining them on the high seas and the remainder for the most part collaborating wholeheartedly with the invaders, when rebellion broke out in Spain there followed an explosion of social protest which the local *notables* only succeeded in bringing under control by declaring war on Napoleon. Even then order was at best tenuous: after the French had been forced to evacuate the country following the arrival of a British army under the future duke of Wellington, there were serious disorders throughout the area between the Minho and the Tagus, these being repeated when the French launched a second invasion of Portugal in March 1809. Given that the perpetrators of these crimes, whose victims were universally drawn from the propertied classes, were often the government's own levies, the decision to request the dispatch of British officers to take command of the army therefore acquires a new social dimension.

Clearly, then, in Portugal as much as in Spain resistance to the French was accompanied by violence against the propertied classes. As a British officer serving with the Portuguese army wrote to his father in October 1809, 'You know the nature of the people, and their malicious propensities are not improved by the . . . revolutionary state in which they have latterly been.'[22] However, the breakdown in authority never went as far as it did in Spain. Beaten by Wellington at Oporto the invaders of 1809 were quickly driven back over the border, and thereafter, even during the third French offensive of 1810–11, in which a large army under the command of Marshal Massena advanced to the very gates of Lisbon, the bulk of the country remained unoccupied. Opportunity was therefore lacking for the widespread irregular struggle experienced by the Spaniards. Meanwhile, the central authorities did not attempt to emulate the ambitious reformism of the Spanish liberals. Last but not least the French themselves never had time to integrate Portugal into the Napoleonic empire in the same manner as the rest of their conquests. The disruption to social relationships was therefore never as severe as in Spain or, for that matter, Calabria, but even so endemic poverty and wartime devastation ensured that brigandage survived long after the French had been driven out.

Turning now to the Tyrol, we again see a pattern of social and political disaffection that goes back to the eighteenth century. Thus, under the Habsburgs the Tyroleans had enjoyed a highly privileged status in that they were exempt from conscription, determined their

---

22 E. Warre (ed.), *Letters from the Peninsula, 1808–1812, by Lieut. Gen. Sir William Warre, C.B., K.T.S.* (London, 1909), p. 87.

own taxation, and were represented by a provincial assembly drawn largely from the peasantry. However, like so much else in the empire, these privileges were eroded by the reforms of Joseph II (1780–90), who was determined to impose conscription, centralised government, and a uniform system of taxation upon all his domains. Applied in the Tyrol, these reforms led to uproar, whilst the province's feelings were further inflamed by Joseph's religious policy which amongst other things brought the dissolution of all lay brotherhoods, the closure of one third of the Tyrol's monasteries, the 'purification' of traditional religious practices so as to expunge superstition and fanaticism, the emancipation of Protestants and Jews, and the reorganisation of the Church's parishes and dioceses. When 1789 brought not only serious floods, but also a decree imposing retrospective restrictions on the ability to claim compensation for losses arising from the disappearance of the lay brotherhoods (which had come to function as friendly societies much patronised by the peasantry), the result was widespread rioting, encouraged by fierce protests in the Tyrolean estates. Confronted by even more tumultuous resistance elsewhere, Joseph revoked his military and administrative reforms, the Tyrol's freedoms therefore surviving into the Napoleonic age. As such, they could not but present an immediate challenge to the centralising policies of the Bavarian chief minister, Montgelas, when the Tyrol was ceded to Bavaria in 1806. The Tyrolean assembly was abolished; the province was split into three *kreise* and its very name erased; moves were made to introduce conscription and the Bavarian system of taxation; large numbers of 'foreign' officials were appointed and numerous petty steps were taken to reinforce the image of assimilation, the name of the region's characteristic fruit, for example, being changed from the 'emperor pear' to the 'king pear'. Meanwhile, of course, the Tyroleans' Catholic sensibilities were being outraged by the religious reforms that we have already described, these in fact being based on the very Josephinian model that had caused such anger twenty years before. All this was accompanied by economic decline: Bavarian protectionism and the Continental System hit such native industry as there was very badly, trade was seriously disrupted – hence, perhaps, the prominence of innkeepers in the organisation and leadership of the uprising – whilst the poor exchange rates offered for Austrian paper money led to heavy financial losses.

As a result of these factors, the Archduke John and other members of the war party which was now emerging in Vienna had no difficulty in fomenting a conspiracy in the Tyrol through a series of local notables of whom the most famous was the innkeeper, Andreas Hofer. Much encouraged by the small size of the Bavarian garrison and by the appearance of Austrian troops upon the frontiers, when Austria went back to war in April 1809 the Tyrol duly rose against its oppressors. As elsewhere, the ostensible rallying-point was loyalty to the established dynasty and the Catholic faith, but once again this legitimism was only a cloak for other interests. Many of those who had benefited from Josephinianism or Bavarian annexation were attacked, Jews were victimised, and a number of towns were pillaged, but the central focus of insurgent attention can be seen to have been the defence of Tyrol's traditional way of life. During the planning that had preceded the insurrection, Hofer – who had been a member of the rebellious diet of 1789 – had been at great pains to impress upon the Viennese authorities the need to resurrect Tyrolean privileges in full; the peasant levies who sprang to arms did so under the flag of the Tyrol rather than that of the dynasty; and relations between the Tyroleans and the representatives of Vienna soon soured on account of disputes over taxation and the limits of imperial authority, not to mention Hofer's determination to overturn the anticlerical measures implemented during the reign of Joseph II (unlike, say, the emperor's abolition of Tyrolean political liberty, these had never been cancelled). Once the Austrians had been forced to make peace following the battle of Wagram, the split became even more apparent, the fact being that the Tyrol's identity was being asserted in the face not just of Bavaria but also of Austria.

To sum up, then, most of Napoleonic Europe suffered from common grievances under the empire, but in very few areas did the resentment develop into outright revolt. Where it did, the key factors were a combination of suitable terrain, traditions of banditry or irregular warfare, and extreme socio-political tension. Often encouraged by exiled or defeated dynasties, revolt everywhere assumed a legitimist outlook (as, indeed, did lower-level disorder, with rioters wearing orange ribbons in Holland, and waving Austrian and Venetian flags in northern Italy), but this is clearly not the full story: whilst more research is needed, it seems likely that the peasant insurgents of Calabria, Spain, Portugal and the Tyrol were motivated above all by a combination of longstanding socio-economic grievances and a determination to preserve traditional society. If that is so, then it is hardly surprising that even in reformist Prussia the response of the local authorities to ostensibly anti-French peasant unrest was to call on the occupation forces for help in maintaining order. As for any sense of modern nationalism, this was non-existent. Spaniards, Portuguse, Calabrians and Tyroleans had little concept of themselves as citizens of a modern nation. To the extent that popular resistance took place, it therefore hardly marked the emergence of a new spirit in Europe.

THE EFFICACY OF RESISTANCE

The dramatic character of the Peninsular War, in particular, has led to much importance being attributed to 'people's war' in the defeat of Napoleon. However, the reality was rather different. Although they were undoubtedly in part the authors of the difficulties the French experienced in the Peninsula, not even in Spain and Portugal did the guerrillas succeed in throwing off the French yoke. As for Calabria and the Tyrol, the fact is that they were ultimately pacified. Militarily speaking, in fact, popular resistance simply lacked the potential to justify the weight it has been given.

In the first place, in those instances where the insurgents tried to emulate the tactics of their opponents, they were everywhere beaten. Crowds of ill-armed and untrained peasants commanded by improvised officers and NCOs had neither the cohesion nor the skill needed on the battlefield. Extremely vulnerable to panic, lacking in firepower and unable to manoeuvre except in the utmost disorder, they were generally swept away at the first shot. Examples of such incidents are legion. Thus, in Calabria in August 1806 the French scattered large bands of irregulars that tried to stand against them at Lauria and Cosenza with the loss of hardly a single man. In Spain and Portugal, too, the first months of the Peninsular War were littered with such defeats as the patriot authorities desperately tried to oppose the French with raw levies. A good example is the action at Cabezón on 12 June 1808 in which 2,500 Frenchmen routed 5,000 Spanish peasants for the loss of thirteen dead and thirty wounded. Only when they were protected by fortifications or difficult terrain were the levies of any use. Thus, attempts to take Gerona and Valencia by storm were driven off, and at the defile of Bruch a column was turned back and forced to retreat in disorder. Most famously, at Zaragoza the armed citizenry first beat off two full-scale French assaults and then continued fighting from house to house even after the French finally broke into the city. However, the famous Spanish victory of Bailén, in which 20,000 French troops who had become isolated deep in Andalucía were forced to surrender, was only indirectly the work of popular resistance, the Spanish forces involved being largely regular troops from the old army. As for the Tyrol, if the insurgents succeeded in winning a string of dramatic victories, it was usually because they managed to trap enemy columns in mountain gorges or to overwhelm forces that had become over-extended amidst hill and forest. Such victories were typified by the action at Mittewald and Oberau on 4–5 August 1809. Pushing up the narrow valley of the river Eisack, 8,000 German troops under General Rouyer were harassed by sniping and man-made landslides every foot of the way and finally brought to a complete halt. Unable to make further progress, and with his men exhausted, depleted and demoralised, Rouyer eventually retreated, leaving behind over 1,000 casualties.

Such actions are typical of perhaps the most effective form of popular resistance to the French, of which a good description is provided by a German veteran of the war in Aragón, Heinrich von Brandt:

> As soon as an opportunity for a capture offered itself . . . the most active and daring among the people assembled and . . . rushed with the utmost rapidity upon their booty . . .. As soon as the enterprise was completed . . . the levy, as I may call it, quietly returned to their common occupations . . .. Thus, the communication on all roads was closed. Thousands of enemies were on the spot though not a single one could be discovered; no courier could be dispatched without being taken; no supplies could set off without being attacked; in short, no movement could be effected without being observed by a hundred eyes. At the same time, there existed no means of striking at . . . a combination of this kind. The French . . . were obliged to be constantly on their guard against . . . the incessant molestations of an invisible enemy . . ..[23]

As well as in the Tyrol, it was essentially resistance of this kind that the French faced in Catalonia for much of the war, and in Galicia and northern Portugal in the spring of 1809. The example of Galicia is particularly interesting. Throughout 1808, the Galicians had, as we have seen, remained notoriously apathetic, whilst they had shown open hostility to the army of Sir John Moore when it retreated into the province en route for the sea in December 1808. With the British evacuation, the French soon obtained the sub-

23 H. von Brandt, *The Two Minas and the Spanish Guerrillas* (London, 1825), pp. 56–8.

mission of all the local civil and military authorities. Faced by the reality of occupation, however, the populace sprang to life. Soon every French patrol, column and supply convoy was liable to attack, every French post vulnerable to a surprise attack, and every French force cut off both from other forces and from the rest of Spain. Punitive expeditions were dispatched in all directions, garrisons were scattered throughout the province, villages were burned on all sides, and insurgents were executed by the hundred, but, if anything, matters grew worse rather than better: the French only controlled the ground they occupied, whilst each act of repression served to provoke further hostility. In short, the result was that substantial forces – some 17,000 men – were tied up in a long and demoralising struggle that had little prospect of resolution, the French eventually retreating in disgust in June 1809.

Yet this is not the end to the story. Dramatic though the Galician insurrection was, closer examination reveals that it only succeeded as a result of exceptional circumstances. Thus, in both Calabria and the Tyrol – where resistance was essentially very similar – the rebellions were eventually put down. In the former case, the British garrison in Sicily made little attempt to harass the French, who were therefore able to concentrate their entire resources on hunting down the brigands. Unable to prevent the advance of substantial enemy columns, the Calabrians witnessed the loss of one base after another. Constantly harassed, they were also subjected to starvation with anyone – even children – found carrying food being shot. Increasingly desperate, the bands either dwindled away, or were forced to launch suicidal attacks on targets that were too strong for them. By November 1811, the problem was all but at an end: brigandage continued, of course, but the last of the great partisan leaders had been caught and executed, and Calabria was proclaimed to be pacified. And as in Calabria, so in the Tyrol. With the Austrian withdrawal from the war following the battle of Wagram, the Tyroleans were left badly exposed. For a while they continued to win surprising victories, but they could not fight on for ever: food was short, disillusion spread rapidly and there were increasing difficulties in keeping the men in the field. With ever greater numbers of enemy troops moving in from all sides, by the end of the year resistance had collapsed.

In the Iberian peninsula, too, there is little doubt that mass insurgency of the Galician variety could have been quelled. Though the armed peasantry were a thorn in the flesh of the French, they could only very rarely stop the movement of their forces – marching on Oporto in March 1809, for example, Marshal Soult was able without difficulty to sweep aside the crowds of *ordenança* who harassed his movements. Forced to retreat into Galicia by the British two months later, moreover, Soult devised a plan based on a combination of garrisons, blockhouses and punitive columns that would have represented a deadly threat to the insurgents there. However, there simply were not sufficient forces available to carry this scheme into operation: even in Galicia the French also had to provide against the skeletal Spanish regular forces that had survived throughout the winter in the mountains straddling the Portuguese border, whilst by the summer of 1809 central Spain was threatened with invasion by the victorious British. Too few to cope with every threat at once, the French responded by evacuating Galicia altogether. What made irregular resistance so effective in the Peninsula, in short, was the constant presence of regular forces – not just Anglo-Portuguese but also Spanish – for, so long as they had to face these opponents, the French could never send all their troops against the guerrillas in the same way as they had done in Calabria and the Tyrol.

In any case, the picture in Spain is complicated by the fact that the mass insurgency of 1808–9 did not survive, or at least not in its original intensity. Instead, there was a strong tendency for the armed peasantry to coalesce in permanent bands. Some of these, their ranks often swelled by deserters from every army in the Peninsula, were never more than bandit gangs in the first place, whilst others increasingly acquired this character. However, a substantial number soon acquired an increasingly regular shape and it was in fact these forces that bore the brunt of *la guerrilla* for most of the struggle. The factors that produced this development were numerous. On the one hand, eager both to foment opposition and to gain control of the situation in the countryside, the central government sent a number of officers out into the occupied provinces to organise irregular resistance, these officers naturally seeking to form conventional units as quickly as possible. At the same time, too, individual regiments of regular troops, and sometimes even entire divisions, were told off for guerrilla operations. Meanwhile, the various chieftains who had emerged to head the struggle from amongst the populace on account of local influence, physical courage or sheer strength of character were also quick to appreciate the benefits of militarisation, for, as well as allowing them to secure a greater measure of success against the French, it also enabled them to win greater credit with the government and the British (and thus to obtain more in terms of arms and supplies), to obtain regular commissions for themselves, to boost their personal prestige, and to overawe rival leaders in their neighbourhood.

There thus emerged the guerrilla bands familiar to students of the Peninsular War, the most well-known being those of Espoz y Mina, El Empecinado, Julián Sánchez, Francisco Longa, Jerónimo Merino, Juan Diaz Porlier and José Durán. Able to wage protracted campaigns and to mount operations that were far more ambitious than those of the armed peasantry, these forces enjoyed considerable success – by early 1813, for example, Espoz y Mina had rendered the French hold on Navarre all but non-existent. Yet there were still limits to what they could do. Until supplied with mountain guns by the British towards the end of the war, the guerrillas were for the most part quite incapable of reducing the numerous French garrisons that studded the countryside, whilst they could only rarely take on the forces sent against them with any chance of success. Still less could they do anything to halt the inexorable advance of the French armies (between the end of 1809 and the beginning of 1812 huge swathes of Patriot territory, and with them a series of vital Spanish bases, were captured by the French). Unable to win this territory back due to their inability to mount large-scale operations, they at the same time impeded the recruitment of the regular armies that might have done so by providing a haven for deserters and draft evaders, and reducing large areas of the country to complete chaos. What saved Spain was the presence of Wellington's well-disciplined and highly trained regular army in Portugal. Indeed, had Wellington's troops not been there it is difficult to see how final defeat could have been avoided – though impregnable Cádiz might have held out, once the last Spanish field army had been defeated the guerrillas would inevitably have been hunted down and crushed. Critics of this theory will doubtless cite the supposed union of the Spanish people with the guerrillas, but in fact the latter no longer lived amongst but rather off the population. Not only were they often even more rapacious than the French, but they could not even afford the populace any protection. For how long, then, could they have been tolerated?

In the last resort the fact remains that, militarily speaking, the Spanish guerrillas were no more successful than insurgents anywhere else. If Spain escaped complete conquest, she was only liberated by British intervention (though it is but fair to note that the Spanish guerrillas did play a major part in Wellington's victories). At best the only hope the guerrillas offered was that the French would become so disillusioned that they would evacuate Spain of their own volition, a prospect that the major problems caused the French by 'people's war' seemed to make entirely possible. In Calabria victory took them five years and 20,000 casualties; in Spain the time would certainly have been far longer, whilst one estimate puts the cost at 180,000 men by 1813 alone. In Spain, too, war ceased to pay for war: far from contributing to the treasury, it lost Napoleon at least 3,000 million francs. The domestic repercussions of such expense were naturally serious and all the more so as demands for conscription also greatly increased, whilst the army, too, was undermined. Amongst the rank and file, exposed as they were to appalling conditions and the ever-present risk of a horrible death, resentment and demoralisation grew apace, Parquin noting the common graffito, 'This war in Spain means death for the men, ruin for the officers, a fortune for the generals!'[24] Furthermore, the conditions in which the war was fought also increased the army's already serious tendency towards indiscipline, the troops becoming ever more inclined to mistreat the civilian population. Nor was this all. Throughout Europe the war gave hope to opponents of Napoleon. Used to stir up revolt in the Tyrol by Austrian propagandists, it was also seized upon by German patriots in general and the Prussian reformers in particular. Last but not least, the war also provided the British with a desperately needed opportunity both to show their military prowess on the Continent (thereby making themselves more attractive as coalition partners) and to breach the Continental System. Thus, to paraphrase Napoleon himself, the Peninsular War was indeed extremely 'ulcerous'. For all that, however, the emperor would not willingly give it up, for to do so would have been too great a blow to his prestige, the fighting therefore continuing until defeat in Germany and Russia finally made a peace settlement imperative.

AN EXAGGERATED PHENOMENON?

The conclusions that we have reached, then, are bold indeed. Though Europe experienced great suffering on account of the Napoleonic empire, only in certain areas did passive resentment and low-level unrest explode into active revolt. Where it did, moreover, it was fuelled by factors that were by no means always directly connected to French rule. Thus, in Calabria, Spain, Portugal and the

24 Cit. B.T. Jones (ed.), *Napoleon's Army: the Military Memoirs of Charles Parquin* (London, 1987), p. 126.

Tyrol alike, resistance had its roots in social discontent and discontent with the reigning dynasty. Devotion to the *ancien régime* was evinced everywhere (though less so in Calabria), but in fact this was a mere symbol. Indeed, in many respects it was just as repugnant as French rule: after all, Catholicism was as much offended by Joseph II and Charles IV as it was by Maximilian I and Joseph Bonaparte. The Napoleonic empire was objectionable certainly, but this was not so much because it was Napoleonic or even because it was French, but because it introduced or accelerated policies that broke down the autonomy of rural society, capitalised agriculture and favoured the emergence of a new class of bourgeois landowners.

As for the efficacy of popular resistance, it is all too clear that in itself it presented little threat to French domination. In the first place, none of the three major revolts had any serious popular echoes elsewhere – thus, if northern Italy witnessed a short-lived peasant rising in 1809, Germany remained completely passive. By the beginning of 1812 the Calabrian and Tyrolean uprisings had alike been overcome, whilst even the Spaniards were threatened by defeat. Despite the absence of Napoleon himself and the immense difficulties with which the French were faced – an extremely difficult supply situation, deep divisions in the high command in the Peninsula, much ill-judged interference from Paris, and the constant juxtaposition of regular and irregular warfare – until the end of 1811 they were winning the war in the Peninsula. Wellington was penned up behind the Portuguese frontier, and the Spaniards were gradually being deprived of the capacity for regular resistance by the steady advance of the French armies and the outbreak of revolution in their American colonies in 1810 (until then, these had been an important source of financial support). The guerrilla war continued unabated, of course, but the moment would sooner or later have come when the last Spanish army was defeated and the last Spanish province occupied. With the French thus enabled to use a far greater proportion of their forces for repression, there seems little reason to believe that they could not ultimately have overcome the guerrillas and then have marched on Portugal with overwhelming numbers (to the obvious objection that any larger force than they employed in the great invasion of 1810–11 would simply have starved, the rejoinder should be made that, with Spain crushed, their supply difficulties would have been much eased).

Even in Spain, then, popular resistance was not an insuperable force. All that was needed was an endless supply of reinforcements and replacements, and, until 1811, very large numbers of troops were indeed made available for service in the Peninsula. In 1812, however, everything changed: with Napoleon's decision to go to war against Russia, not only did fresh troops cease to arrive, but significant forces were actually pulled out for service with the *grande armée*. As a result, the tide of French expansion suddenly outran the resources that were necessary to sustain it, the occupying forces became overstretched, and Wellington was at last able to break the stranglehold and embark on the victorious campaigns that led to the liberation of the entire Peninsula. Even then, however, had Napoleon been victorious in 1812 or 1813, it is hard to see how Wellington's gains could have been maintained. The fact is, then, that the contribution even of the Spanish insurgents, let alone of their Calabrian and Tyrolean counterparts, to Napoleon's downfall was limited. What mattered far more were the errors of diplomacy and strategy that led Napoleon into what became an impossible situation, and opened the way for the powers to take their revenge upon him. Although in the struggle that resulted 'people's war' was once more to become an issue, it was one which must again be hedged around with serious qualifications.

5 PERFIDIOUS ALBION

AN ISLAND SET APART

Baby, baby, naughty baby,
Hush, you squalling thing, I say;
Peace this moment, peace, or maybe
Bonaparte will pass this way.[1]

For Britons today the term 'the Great War' signifies one conflict
only – the First World War of 1914–18. In 1914, however, the term
was synonymous with the struggle against Revolutionary and
Napoleonic France of 1792–1815. Whether in the form of nursery
rhyme – as above – schoolroom history, or edifying works of
patriotic myth presented at countless prize days and Christmases,
this war was a central plank in the formation of successive
generations of children. At the same time, it had also permeated the
very geography of the country: Waterloo Roads and 'Lord Nelson'
pubs were all-pervasive, as were monuments to the war's various
heroes and victories. If this was so, it was hardly surprising: not
only had the struggle been a veritable war to the death that had
taxed Britain's resources almost beyond endurance, but, alone
amongst Napoleon's opponents, she had never been invaded, still
less conquered, her forces in fact securing an unbroken series of
victories on both land and sea. In consequence, the Old Order had
appeared to have triumphed, and all the more so as 'Boney' had
been brought down without any fundamental reformation in either
Britain's way of making war or her system of government. For all
that, however, the impact of the Napoleonic Wars was far from
negligible. Beneath the surface the modern state was emerging in
early nineteenth-century Britain as much as it was anywhere else,
whilst society was marked by bitter dissension, the struggle with

1 Traditional, *cit.* I. and P. Opie (eds.), *The Oxford Dictionary of Nursery
Rhymes* (Oxford, 1951), p. 59.

France exacerbating the tensions already produced by the onward march of the Industrial Revolution. Though the Britain of 1815 was on the surface little changed from that of 1803, in fact the dissolution of the Old Order was beginning to gather pace.

FACING UP TO BONEY

If one begins with the absolute number of men placed under arms by Britain in the period 1803–15, it is tempting to jump to the conclusion that she was a Nation-in-Arms. Thus, by 1809, counting the regular army, the navy, the militia and the volunteers, over 786,000 men – some one-sixth of the adult male population – were available for service at home or abroad (indeed, it has even been calculated that for much of the wars Britain maintained a higher proportion of her manpower under arms than France). Furthermore, in theory at least, two Acts of Parliament – the Levy-en-Masse Act of 1803 and the Training Act of 1806 – had introduced compulsory military service for all men. In practice, though, these statutes were moribund from their very promulgation, the reality being that Britain continued to fight her war with the institutions of the eighteenth century.

Let us begin with the regular army, which from a start of 132,000 men in 1803 had been raised to a strength of some 330,000 by 1813. Impressive though this feat might appear, however, it is apparent that popular enthusiasm to take part in foreign wars, even against an enemy so generally execrated as Napoleonic France, was relatively limited. Essentially, the army obtained its recruits on an entirely voluntary basis, either from the public at large or from the militia, who, following the success of earlier experiments in 1799, from 1805 onwards were encouraged to transfer into the regular army (two Acts of Parliament of June 1803 and June 1804 did sanction conscription to recruit the ranks of the second battalions which most line regiments maintained at their home depots in the hope that the troops thus obtained might eventually be persuaded to volunteer for service abroad, but such was the hostility aroused even by this timid measure that it had soon to be abandoned; in all some 43,000 men were obtained by such means, of whom about one-half may have eventually seen active service). Yet though volunteering remained the basis of the army's strength in so far as active campaigning was concerned, from no source were sufficient recruits forthcoming: between June and December 1803 – a time of great patriotic enthusiasm – 360 recruiting parties sent out into the country raised the grand total of 3,481 men; few regiments could keep more than one battalion up to strength at any time; regiments which only had one battalion were prone to dwindling to mere skeletons; and in 1811 the net gain of recruits over casualties was precisely 865. Taking the period 1803–14 as a whole, in fact, the army received an average of only 22,700 men a year, of whom 9,000 were from the militia. Even then many 'volunteers' had to be obtained by foul means: the recruiting parties sent out by each regiment regularly used a wide variety of dishonest practices; contractors known as 'crimps' would effectively use kidnap as a weapon of enlistment; militiamen were browbeaten into joining the regulars by means of extra guard duties and fatigues; and in Scotland the tenant-at-will system (which left the crofters utterly at the mercy of their lairds) was ruthlessly exploited to fill the ranks of the numerous Highland regiments.

Why should genuine volunteering have been so slack? As we shall see, the war was by no means universally unpopular, whilst economic change and wartime privation should have encouraged enlistment. However, the fact is that neither the lurid anti-French propaganda of the establishment and its supporters, nor the improvements in conditions of service introduced by such officers as the duke of York and Sir John Moore, nor the introduction of such innovations as pensions and fixed-term enlistments, could overcome the opprobrium which had traditionally attached to the red coat. Thus, savage discipline – above all, the widespread use of flogging – poor food, low pay, lack of prospects, the misery of life in the field, and the evil reputation enjoyed by the common soldiery all combined to discourage enlistment. At the same time, the army was in constant competition with the militia and the Volunteers for recruits, both these forces offering not only significantly better terms of service in most respects, but also higher bounties for enlistment: in 1805 a man received between sixteen and seventeen pounds for enlisting in the infantry, whereas he could obtain as much as sixty as a substitute in the militia, even the navy often paying more.

Mention of the bounty brings us to a discussion of positive reasons for enlistment. As far as these are concerned, patriotism did not figure very highly. Whilst it cannot be said that no men enlisted out of a genuine desire to fight for king and country, such cases were certainly fairly rare. At best, some recruits may have been attracted by tales of high adventure and military glory, but for the most part motives were anything but altruistic. As usual economic desperation played a major role, as witness the relatively large number of framework knitters and handloom weavers who enlisted, not to mention the swarms of Irish peasantry (in 1797 the duke of York even went so far as to claim that 'almost the whole of the recruits of the infantry of the line are Irish'[2]). Also important were crime or personal failure, with men joining up to escape punishment or personal humiliation. For men serving in the militia, meanwhile, service in the field may sometimes have seemed preferable to the endless monotony of garrison and security duty at home, and all the more so as transfer to the regulars did at least bring with it a pension. And for all and sundry there was the promise of the bounty, and, with it, access to copious supplies of alcohol – to quote the duke of Wellington, 'English soldiers are fellows who have enlisted for drink. That is the plain fact – they have all enlisted for drink.'[3] As even the few recruits of better quality generally themselves became corrupted by the habits of their fellows, Wellington's notorious description of his men as the 'scum of the earth' does not seem over harsh. Fight hard though they may have done, even here other factors – fear of the lash, regimental feeling, devotion to particular officers, or small-group loyalty – were as important as patriotism. And, as for the population as a whole, the fact remains that, for the vast majority, service in the field did not commend itself at all.

Much the same must be said of service in the Royal Navy, in which, if anything, conditions were even more unpleasant and dangerous. Minor improvements on the lower decks and generous bounties failing to produce an adequate supply of willing 'Jack Tars', increasing resort had to be had to compulsion. Not only was the hated press gang very active, but many criminals were handed over by the courts, the result being that by 1812 no more than fifteen per cent of most crews were composed of genuine volunteers (initially the proportion was between one-half and one-quarter). Yet, despite a steady increase in manpower, there were still not enough men, all vessels sailing under-handed, and many actually having to be laid up in port. So desperate was the navy for recruits, in fact, that considerable use had to be made up of foreigners, many of them seized from neutral vessels – at Trafalgar HMS *Victory*'s complement of 703 seamen included some eighty-one such unfortunates.

---

2 Cit. R. Glover, *Britain at Bay: Defence against Bonaparte, 1803–14* (London, 1973), p. 131.

3 Cit. Earl of Stanhope, *Notes of Conversations with the Duke of Wellington, 1831– 1851* (London, 1889), p. 14.

Here again, the reason was simple, for seafarers knew that they could receive higher pay on merchant ships, greater prize money on privateers, and more freedom in the Sea Fencibles (the maritime counterpart of the volunteers). Furthermore, whilst conditions for seamen were universally appalling, only the navy made official – and very heavy – use of the lash.

Mention of the foreigners who served in the navy brings us to the somewhat exotic medley to which much of the increase in the British army after 1803 can be attributed. Throughout the 1790s Britain had made much use of foreign troops, employing a wide variety of Swiss and *émigré* regiments that, whatever their nominal designation, were in fact composed of stragglers and deserters from virtually every state in Europe. Following the renewal of hostilities in 1803, this policy was renewed and even extended. Here pride of place should be given to the King's German Legion, a force that eventually numbered ten infantry battalions, five cavalry regiments, and five artillery batteries (or, in theory, perhaps 16,000 men). Originally formed from officers and men of the old Hanoverian army who had fled the French occupation of 1803, it received many more such recruits during the short-lived British expedition to northern Germany in 1805, but thereafter the ranks had increasingly to be filled with whatever material came to hand – Germans, Frenchmen, Italians, Poles and even Croats, the vast majority of them deserters or prisoners of war. Meanwhile, seven other foreign regiments also saw service, though rarely with the same distinction as the Legion, which did at least establish a reputation for military excellence. But even this was not an end to Britain's use of foreign manpower: setting aside her colonial forces, which included a number of negro regiments, she also sanctioned the enlistment of numerous foreigners into units of her own line, the Sixtieth Rifles containing many Germans and the Ninety-Fifth a number of Spaniards. Counting all the various categories of foreign contingent, the result was that by 1813 the grand total of such recruits was at least 53,000.

If we turn to the manner in which Britain's battles were actually fought, the conservative nature of her war effort becomes even more apparent. Virtually alone among the powers, British commanders never abandoned the linear order of the eighteenth century. Whether on the attack or in defence, the infantry that formed the backbone of her forces habitually fought in line, the result being that discipline and training were far more necessary than would otherwise have been the case, for only the steadiest of troops could hope to operate successfully in such formations. Of course, the line did not await the advance of the French columns in isolation: on the contrary, Wellington, in particular, made considerable use of skirmishers to screen his close-order troops and to disrupt the enemy advance. However, the various light infantrymen employed in this capacity were no more than the direct descendants of the privileged specialists of earlier wars – élite troops who could be relied upon not to desert and who were sufficiently trained to operate beyond the immediate control of their officers (under the influence of Sir John Moore and a number of other reformers, the separate light-infantry arm that had emerged since the early 1800s had become imbued with an intense *esprit de corps*: in contrast to practice in the rest of the army, flogging was all but abandoned and the men encouraged to take a pride in both themselves and their units).

In so far as actual fighting was concerned, then, the brunt of Britain's war was born either by foreigners or by a despised and more-or-less isolated minority. As for technique, in the army at least, this was very much that of an earlier age in which order was everything, and enthusiasm nothing. Still, there is no gainsaying the fact that the armies commanded by Moore, Chatham and Wellington were much larger than their counterparts of the eighteenth century (Marlborough, for example, took only 15,000 British troops to Blenheim). At the same time, had the French ever crossed the Channel, it is clear that they would have been faced by a very different kind of war effort. Throughout the struggle an extraordinarily high proportion of Britain's military manpower was tied up in home-defence units. Here the most important force, militarily if not numerically, was the militia. Dating from the days of the 'trained bands' of the sixteenth and seventeenth centuries, it should not be thought that this force was in any sense conceived as an answer to military developments in France. Nor was it comparable thereto. In theory, the obligation to serve was universal, but in practice liability was limited: thanks to the ability either to hire a substitute or to pay a fine rather than serve, not to mention a host of exemptions, service was restricted to the poorer classes of society. Each county was in any case expected to provide only a fairly restricted quota assessed in accordance with the size of its population and as these quotas had not been reassessed since 1757, the burden of service had become extremely uneven. Nor was the force a national one: Scotland was more or less exempt, whilst in Ireland recruitment was entirely voluntary. Called out permanently in time of war, in 1796 the militia proper was reinforced by a second force known as the Supplementary Militia which was to receive a modicum of basic training, but was only to be called out in the event of actual invasion. Re-embodied in May 1803, the two militias reached a peak of 89,000 men in 1805, and till the end of the war constituted some twenty per cent of the armed forces.

Though never sent abroad, at least the militia was a force to be reckoned with. On balance, the same could almost certainly not be said of the volunteer units which constituted the third major component of Britain's land forces, these being described by one secretary of state for war and the colonies as 'painted cherries which none but simple birds would take for real fruit'[4]. Originally springing more or less spontaneously from the wave of popular counter-revolutionary fervour that swept the country in the wake of the execution of Louis XVI, the formation of units of local volunteers had been authorised by an Act of Parliament of 1794, and by 1800 some 200,000 men had been thus enlisted. Mostly demobilised with the coming of peace, in 1803 they once more sprang to arms in enormous numbers, some 440,000 being under arms by the end of the year. With the passing of the invasion scare of 1803–5, numbers and enthusiasm dwindled, but, even so, as late as 1807, whereafter the government was increasingly at pains to force them into a newly formed and far more systematic force entitled the Local Militia, there remained some 294,000. Drilled only on a part-time basis, the idea that they could have taken their place in the line of battle – the only service for which most of them were trained – stretches credibility, whilst, despite the air of bellicose patriotism which they affected, there must also be doubts as to their motivation. For the men of property who actually organised most of the units, the Volunteers represented defence not just against the French but also domestic disorder. Meanwhile, for the professionals, shopkeepers, artisans and clerks who constituted a large part of the rank and file, participation meant association with their social superiors and opportunities for profit. Such men also benefited from the guarantee of exemption from the militia ballot brought by enlistment, the same advantage applying to such representatives as they included of the labouring classes (by the same token, they could avoid having to leave their homes and families, many of the Volunteers openly stating that they were unwilling to

---

4 *Cit.* C. Emsley, 'The volunteer movement', in A. Guy (ed.), *The Road to Waterloo: the British Army and the Struggle against Revolutionary and Napoleonic France, 1793–1815* (London, 1990), p. 47.

defend anything other than their own localities). For such men, too, the pay received for each day spent in training was a useful supplement for meagre or uncertain incomes, whilst some of them may also have been subject to a degree of compulsion from employers and landlords. Finally, at every level the Volunteers offered conviviality, comradeship, excitement, and, above all, the right to wear a uniform that was frequently as splendid as it was impractical.

If Britain was a Nation-in-Arms in the Napoleonic period, then, it was in form alone, a large part of her forces being at best part-time soldiers. Indeed, such was the nature of her mobilisation that she was actually starved of fighting men. Not only were large numbers of men who might otherwise have joined the regular army enticed into the enormous home-defence forces, but the latter were not even judged to be capable of taking the place of the regulars. Thus, as late as in November 1811 56,000 troops were deployed in the British Isles. With between 50,000 and 75,000 more men constantly deployed in the colonies, successive governments found that few troops were left to strike at Napoleon. With even Wellington never given more than 60,000 British troops, it is quite clear that Britain could not possibly have competed in the large-scale warfare seen in central Europe. From this it followed that Britain would have to pursue her objectives through other means – above all, naval power, coalition diplomacy and the exploitation of her economic muscle.

Let us begin with the Royal Navy. Concentrating on the clash of battle fleets as it does, the traditional naval historiography of the Napoleonic Wars has been very narrow in its focus, the experience of most British seamen in the Napoleonic period in fact being one of long years of patrolling. Nevertheless, the fleet actions at which the British so excelled – or, after 1805, the unwillingness of the French to risk them – remain important in that it was they that brought the control of the seas on which everything else depended. We must therefore first examine the factors that made Trafalgar such a foregone conclusion.

In naval terms, Britain began the Napoleonic Wars with a considerable strategic advantage. During the Revolutionary Wars a series of victories had greatly reduced the naval power of France and her allies, whether real or potential. Thus, by 1801 the number of French men-of-war alone had been reduced from sixty-five to forty-one. Meanwhile, thanks largely to the general social and political chaos, the rate of French naval construction was roughly halved. By contrast, by 1801 captures and new building had raised the number of British ships-of-the-line in service to 108, there being about another eighty in reserve, repair or construction. Desperate efforts were made by Napoleon to close the gap during the peace of Amiens, but want of adequate stores made progress slow, and when the war resumed, although some forty-five new vessels were under construction, even counting the small and obsolescent vessels of the Dutch navy, the number of men-of-war was still no more than about fifty, of which only twenty-three were available for immediate service. Even these forces were widely dispersed and low in morale, whilst there was also a desperate shortage of both officers and men. At the same time they were badly outnumbered: by March 1804 the British had over eighty ships-of-the-line in service, the average figure thereafter being around one hundred. Though on the surface matters were soon altered by the re-entry of Spain into the war in December 1804, in practice this made little difference: most of Spain's thirty-two battleships could not put to sea, whilst the chaos in her finances and administration was such that it would take many months to improve the situation.

Grim though this picture was, all was not lost for Napoleon: Britain's commitments were wide-ranging; it was extremely difficult to blockade every enemy port at once; timber was in short supply; and the strain of the constant patrolling inflicted a heavy toll on the Royal Navy's ships which also suffered heavily from dry rot, enforced reliance on unsatisfactory substitutes for Baltic timber reducing the average life of a seagoing warship to a mere eight years. Meanwhile, safe in port and assured of a virtually limitless supply of timber and other maritime stores from the resources of Continental Europe, the French navy could only grow in size, and, wartime losses notwithstanding, by 1814 its 104 ships of the line actually outnumbered the ninety-nine then available to the British; still worse, French ships were for the most part larger, better built and more heavily gunned.

With many French ports exceedingly difficult to blockade for geographical reasons, it was simply not possible physically to prevent Napoleon's squadrons from putting to sea in frightening strength (at Trafalgar, the combined Franco-Spanish fleet actually outnumbered that of Nelson). However, numbers were far from everything. Confined to port as they were for long periods of time, the French crews were deficient in seamanship, whilst their officers and admirals had little practice of manoeuvring in formation (in the Spanish fleet, things were still worse, many of the men who fought at Trafalgar not being sailors at all). For similar reasons their gunnery was also weak, British superiority in this respect being reinforced by a number of simple technical innovations such as the introduction of a flintlock firing mechanism for naval guns. Equally, their tactics were increasingly outdated: whereas the French relied on the formal line of battle, the British tended to sail in close and aim for an all-out mêlée. Last of all we come to the question of leadership, the British being favoured with a galaxy of talent that was at least as impressive as, if not more so than, anything which the French possessed on land.

As a result of such factors, fleet actions between the opposing sides were unlikely to be in much doubt, as shown by the overwhelming victory at Trafalgar. Faced by such might, Napoleon was in the short term forced to relinquish any attempt to contest control of the sea, thereafter, with the exception of sporadic colonial resupply missions, ordering his ships-of-the-line to stay in port until such time as the Royal Navy was finally outbuilt. Left to rule the waves, meanwhile, Britannia made use of her naval superiority to counteract the Continental System, consolidate her financial and industrial base, and amass the sinews of war. In the first place, of course, the seas could be rendered safe for British trade: though raiders sallied forth from virtually every coast in Europe, not to mention bases as far away as Java, the organisation of a proper convoy system, the capture and destruction of hostile frigates and privateers, and the gradual elimination of such havens as Mauritius kept losses down to a figure of about one-fortieth of the total amount of shipping involved (though this is not to say that the damage was not considerable – in 1810 alone some 619 merchant vessels were lost to enemy action). In the second, the ability to enforce the blockade and the Orders-in-Council gave Britain a virtual monopoly of seaborne commerce as the ships of her opponents were captured and forced to keep in port: thus, France had some 1,500 ocean-going merchant ships in 1801 and only 179 in 1812. At the same time, seapower could also bring an expansion of trade in its own right, as one by one the various French and Dutch colonies were recaptured and transformed into new markets and sources of raw material, a variation on this particular theme being the manner in which Britain was increasingly able to supplant Spain and Portugal with regard to trade with Latin America. Meanwhile, it was the Royal Navy, too, that allowed Britain to maintain offshore *entrepôts* such as Sicily and Heligoland through which a steady flow of colonial goods could be channelled to the hungry markets of Napoleonic Europe.

Vital to the British war effort as it was, seapower also opened up important strategic opportunities. As far as the naval war was concerned, Napoleon's creation of a battlefleet could be slowed down through such exploits as the pre-emptive capture of the Danish navy at Copenhagen in September 1807 (an alternative here was the capture and destruction of French naval bases such as Antwerp as attempted in the Walcheren expedition of 1809). Meanwhile, mention of Walcheren brings us to the dispatch and support of amphibious expeditions that was the second major contribution of British naval power to offensive operations. Time and again Britain was able to land field forces around the periphery of the Continent to exploit major strategic opportunities, encourage, reassure and generally support coalition partners, or protect flagging allies. Equally, it was British seapower that was the ultimate guarantee of the safety and upkeep of such armies (in the Peninsula, in particular, it was also put to good use in their campaigns, as in 1812 and 1813 when Wellington employed small amphibious forces to tie down large numbers of French troops in northern and eastern Spain). And, finally, it was British seapower that allowed the dispatch of copious supplies of arms, uniforms, supplies and money to such penurious allies as Spain and Prussia.

In the last resort, however, none of this was enough. Absolute though Britain's control of the sea undoubtedly was, on its own it could neither defeat Napoleon, nor prevent him from implementing a strategy of blockade that was at the very least extremely dangerous, if not fatal. For such goals to be achieved, Britain needed an army capable of operating in northern and central Europe in conditions very different from the unique circumstances that pertained in the Iberian Peninsula. Unable to amass an army large enough to operate with safety on its own, Britain's only hope lay in the construction of a stable anti-French coalition from amongst the great powers. Recognised from the very inception of the French Wars in 1793, such a conclusion had been reinforced by the collapse of the two coalitions of the 1790s, the demise of these alliances having given ample illustration of the impotence of British arms once left to themselves. From 1803 onwards, then, the central theme of British diplomacy was to persuade the other great powers that their chief interest lay in putting aside their many differences in order to resist Napoleon. Although any power would have been welcome as an ally, the linchpin of this strategy was an alliance with Russia, the great power seen as being least vulnerable to French military pressure, such a position being reinforced by the general perception that Prussia was untrustworthy and Austria weak. Thus, believing that Alexander I might be more persuasive in the counsels of Austria and Prussia than Britain (of whom there was much suspicion), Pitt's strategy in the formation of the Third Coalition in 1804–5 was to win Russia's support and then to leave the tsar to work on Vienna and Berlin. Under the 'Ministry of the All the Talents' of 1806–7 support for coalition diplomacy waned on the grounds of the somewhat specious words of the chancellor of the exchequer, Lord Petty, that it 'was ridiculous to talk of saving Europe, if Europe could not save herself'.[5] However, the result was the catastrophic treaty of Tilsit (Sovetsk), and, desperate measures to avert this having failed, under the Portland Ministry and its successors the principle was adopted that any power that took up arms against Napoleon should receive the fullest support. As for Russia, in particular, in the period immediately after Tilsit, great care was taken that no action should be taken that might permanently alienate her (such as a Copenhagen-style strike against her Baltic fleet), whilst in 1808 Canning showed himself to be perfectly willing to sacrifice the interests of Britain's last Baltic ally, Sweden, which was then embroiled in a desperate war with Denmark, France and Russia, if such an act would restore Russia to the fold (by contrast, little encouragement was given to the Austrians when they began to move in the direction of a new war in 1808, though, once hostilities had actually broken out, Vienna received over £1,000,000 in aid as well as the rather dubious assistance of the Walcheren expedition). Following the defeat of Austria, however, there was for some time little that could be done, the only hope being to continue the Peninsular War in the hope that something would eventually 'turn up'. Indeed, so pessimistic was the government with regard to the state of the Continent that even the successive war scares of 1811 did not persuade it to adopt a more active policy, though prompt support was offered to Prussia when it briefly seemed inevitable that Napoleon was again going to force her into war. Only after 1812 did the situation improve, but, though Britain now gained fresh allies, her problems were still not over, there being no guarantee that the powers would remain united or agree to the minimum British objective that Napoleon should be confined within France's pre-1792 frontiers. In consequence, the British government had to devote considerable energy to winning the confidence of her

---

5 Cit. C. Hall, *British Strategy in the Napoleonic War, 1803–1815* (Manchester, 1992), p. 139.

allies and persuading them of her point of view, the problem proving so difficult that the foreign secretary, Lord Castlereagh, was eventually left with no option but to travel to allied headquarters in January 1814, remaining there until the end of the war.

Throughout the war, then, the formation of a coalition of the great powers with Russia at its heart was central to the struggle against Napoleon. Unfortunately, however, numerous obstacles stood in the way of this objective. As we have seen, Britain was deeply unpopular in Europe, being suspected of using the war as a means to pursue her own interests. At the same time, the war aims that Britain tried to sell to her allies – the confinement of France to her old frontiers and the establishment of a zone of medium-sized buffer states backed up by the great powers as a barrier against future French aggression – took no account of the real interests that Austria, Russia and Prussia had elsewhere. Above all, whilst being eager for the support of foreign powers, Britain seemed to offer little in return: maintaining hundreds of thousands of men under arms for home defence seemed irrelevant from the perspective of Vienna, Moscow and Berlin; the blockade appeared as no more than a cover for the expansion of British trade; and the Peninsular War was quite clearly little more than a sideshow. Only by dispatching a large army to confront the French in northern or central Europe could the British possibly hope to prove that they were truly in earnest, and yet, even had the men for such a force been available, there was little hope of repeating, say, the campaigns of the duke of Marlborough until Britain was sure of a powerful continental alliance. Although it was not always appreciated – the actions of the Talents were particularly disastrous in this respect – it was therefore essential that attempts to attract coalition partners should be backed up with concrete incentives.

As we have seen, the very limited military force at Britain's disposal could sometimes be used to make some gesture to counteract foreign suspicions. A good example is the decision in 1805 to disembark an expeditionary force on the Italian mainland to protect Naples following the discovery that the Russians believed that the British wanted, in Czartorysky's words, 'to embroil Europe in a war only to escape from their own, which had become too burdensome'.[6] On the whole, however, there was generally very little that could be done in this respect, and we in consequence come

---

6 *Cit.* W. Flayhart, *Counterpoint to Trafalgar: the Anglo-Russian Invasion of Naples, 180–1806* (Columbia, South Carolina, 1992), p. 61.

to the exploitation of her economic potential that formed the third prong of Britain's war against Napoleon. More will be said about the economic background of the struggle at a later point, but, in brief, it is quite clear that by a variety of means Britain was able to sustain a level of expenditure that far outstripped that of every other country in Europe – it has been calculated that, although her population was only half that of France, Britain's war expenditure was more than twice as great, rising from £29,000,000 in 1804 to over £70,000,000 in 1813, the overall cost of the war in terms of loans and taxes amounting to over £1,500,000,000.

Achieved, as it was, in the face of a sustained effort on the part of Napoleon to procure Britain's bankruptcy, the question must be answered of how this feat was accomplished. Much emphasis has traditionally been placed on increased trade and the Industrial Revolution which are together held to have substantially increased the amount of capital available for government borrowing and taxation, but on its own mere economic growth was not enough; the government also needed the means to turn this to good effect. In consequence, reforms in the fiscal structure were crucial: between 1798 and 1815 no less than sixty-four per cent of the extra revenue required by the French Wars came from taxation; furthermore, less than one-tenth of the money thus raised came from an increase in the pre-war tax base. Pride of place here must be given to rises in taxes that had already been in existence in 1789, these producing fifty-five per cent of the increase in tax revenue. Thus duties were raised on a wide variety of staples such as sugar, tea and tobacco, such indirect taxation eventually producing a total of over £230,000,000, whilst the so-called 'assessed taxes', levied on such items as horses, servants and carriages and therefore tending only to affect the propertied, were trebled. Meanwhile, a further source of revenue was also found in improved procedures for administration and collection: as chancellor of the exchequer, for example, Spencer Perceval succeeded in saving some £350,000 by consolidating the forest of regulations concerning the levying of stamp duty into a single Act of Parliament in 1809. More famously, however, fresh sources of revenue were found in new taxes, though these in fact raised only thirty-six per cent of the total required. Of these measures, many continued to be concerned with customs and excise and therefore fell most heavily on the lower classes, but William Pitt, in particular, believed that it was essential in terms of both fiscal practicality and social justice for greater use to be made of direct taxation (only twenty-five per cent of the total in 1792). A start was made with the introduction of a tax on legacies in 1796, but the major change came three years later. With the old land tax hopelessly outdated (it had not been reassessed since 1692 and made no provision for anything other than direct ownership), some form of income tax was essential, and in 1799 a graduated levy was introduced on all incomes over £60, the top rate being two shillings in the pound. Remodelled in 1803, this covered four-fifths of all the income raised by new taxation and eventually contributed twenty-eight per cent of the cost of the war.

With further very large sums raised by government borrowing, it can be seen that successive British administrations strained every nerve to exploit the very real prosperity enjoyed at least by the propertied and the commercial classes in the course of the war. At the same time, too, one sees an acceleration of the drive for efficiency that had been under way since the 1780s, a good example here being the enquiry launched by Lord St. Vincent into the administration of the navy in 1802. Needless to say, the bulk of the income thus released had to be spent on Britain's own armed forces and other defences, such as the chain of 'martello towers' built along the coasts of Sussex, Kent and Essex, but the increase in revenue was nevertheless a valuable reinforcement to British foreign policy: if Britain could not send armies to the Continent, she could at least bolster her diplomacy with money and *matériel*. Already much used during the Revolutionary War, subsidies once again became of crucial, and, indeed, growing importance (whereas in the 1790s there had been some degree of selectivity as well as an attempt to use loans rather than subsidies, the principle was now established that every potential ally was to be offered money and that there should be no question of repayment). Thus, as early as July 1803, Addington was promising Russia and Prussia substantial sums if they would agree to go to war against France, whilst in June 1804 Pitt agreed to fund the Third Coalition to the tune of £5,000,000. Thereafter, as we have seen, opportunities for coalition building were limited until 1812, and the bulk of money paid over to foreign powers was made to countries that were already in alliance with the British. Nevertheless, the amounts involved were still substantial, and undoubtedly played a vital role in keeping Spain and Portugal, in particular, in the field, especially as they were in part paid in kind. As the leading industrial power, Britain was in a unique position to assist her allies with such commodities as weapons, uniforms and equipment: during the campaign of 1807 forty artillery pieces and 100,000 muskets were dispatched to the

Russo-Prussian forces in East Prussia, whilst in 1808 another 35,000 muskets were sent to Sweden; meanwhile, in the first year of the Peninsular War alone, Spanish ports saw the arrival of 155 artillery pieces, 200,000 muskets, 60,000 swords, 90,000 uniforms, 340,000 pairs of shoes, and innumerable other items including ammunition, shirts, sheets, canteens, cartridge belts, shakos, tents, hospital equipment and medical supplies.

Having essentially kept the war going until such time as fresh opportunities arose for coalition building, British subsidies also played a major role in the formation of the Sixth Coalition. Russia, of course, did not have to be bribed to enter the war, whilst Prussia was offered no incentive to do so, apparently because it was never realised that there was a chance that she might join the Allies. However, Sweden and Austria were both enticed to join the new coalition, each of them being offered £1,000,000 for the year 1813 alone. At the same time, British gold also had a major part in keeping the grand alliance in the field: after 1813 foreign subsidies never fell below £7,500,000 per annum, total payments in the period 1813–15 amounting to over £26,250,000 as compared with £39,500,000 for the period 1793–1812.

It is important to keep the question of British subsidies in proportion: not only was Britain rarely able to satisfy all the demands made upon her, but it should be noted that such payments represented a much smaller proportion of war expenditure than might be thought, the cost of maintaining Wellington's army alone amounting to more than twice the total subsidies paid out in the period that it was in the field. Nor can it be denied that the armies that Britain sent to the Continent were more impressive than ever before. Yet, such qualifications aside, the fact is that, in the absence of a French invasion, the war that Britain actually fought essentially resembled those which she had fought in the eighteenth century, the operations of relatively small regular forces being used to supplement overwhelming naval power and the workings of coalition diplomacy. Fundamental to the whole edifice, however, was economic strength, it being to this subject that we must now turn our attention.

BOOMING TO VICTORY

'In carrying the late war', wrote Thomas Malthus, 'we were powerfully assisted by our steam engines'.[7] According to

7   *Cit.* F. Crouzet, 'The impact of the French Wars on the British economy', in H. T. Dickinson (ed.), *Britain and the French Revolution, 1789–1815* (London, 1989), p. 209.

Wordsworth, meanwhile, the key was 'capital and the mechanic arts'.[8] At the same time, not only had 'capital and the mechanic arts' boosted the war, but the war had boosted 'capital and the mechanic arts': as Malthus remarked after the coming of peace, 'In no twenty-two years of our history . . . has there ever been so rapid an increase of production and consumption . . . as in the twenty-two years ending with 1814.'[9] Challenged though the latter view has been by a succession of economic historians, it is clear that Wordsworth, at least, was right, and, further, that, subjected to a most demanding test, the British economy emerged triumphant.

Let us first examine the caveats that must be raised with regard to any discussion of the role of the British economy in the defeat of Napoleon. In the first place, a number of statistics suggest that the Napoleonic Wars retarded the growth of the British economy or even led to its temporary stagnation. Not only was unemployment always high, but, whilst growing in overall terms, taxation can be shown to have derived a reduced proportion from trade, industry and the professions, falling from £34,850,000 in 1803 to £34,400,000 in 1812, the decline being even greater in such industrial areas as Lancashire. In some industries, moreover, output clearly fell, or at least failed to expand as rapidly as before. Foreign trade, too, did not experience the dramatic expansion that might have been expected, at their greatest extent exports managing an increase of only £9,000,000 on the level attained during the peace of Amiens. Furthermore, the average rate of growth for imports, exports and re-exports was two thirds lower between 1802 and 1814 than it had been between 1792 and 1802. Statistics aside, a number of other arguments can be advanced in favour of slower growth. With regard to agriculture, wartime conditions – and especially the steady rise of food prices as a result of rapid rise in the population, decrease in supplies from the Continent, and increase in the cost of shipping and insurance – led to a great increase in investment, the Napoleonic Wars witnessing the peak of the enclosure movement and a considerable increase in the area under cultivation. By such means production was raised by a factor of perhaps one-quarter, but at the same time the proportion of overall national output represented by agriculture rose from thirty-three to thirty-six per cent in the period 1803–11, the result

8. *Cit.* A. D. Harvey, *Collision of Empires: Britain in Three World Wars, 1793–1945* (London, 1992), p. 43.
9 *Cit. ibid.*, p. 28.

for the economy as a whole being problematic given that much capital was thereby diverted away from industry. Meanwhile, government orders for war material, though great, were not so significant as to provide a substantial boost to production – the iron industry, for example, seems to have devoted only seven per cent of the new capacity it acquired during the war to military production – whilst heavy taxation and borrowing together further 'crowded out' investment in industry, possibly by a factor of as much as one-half.

Persuasive though all this is, the argument that economic growth was retarded by the Napoleonic Wars is marred by numerous flaws. Unemployment is explained by population growth – the United Kingdom had 15,846,000 inhabitants in 1801 and 18,044,000 in 1811. Similarly, thanks to bureaucratic errors, tax evasion and the large number of small businesses exempted on account of their limited turnover, the profits of trade and industry were significantly underestimated – indeed, by 1811 it is estimated that losses due to tax evasion alone may have amounted to half the sum that was actually collected. Trade, too, may have fluctuated, but it was nevertheless sufficient to sustain a merchant fleet that, taking English vessels alone, grew from 13,446 ships in 1802 to 17,346 in 1815. And, in so far as arguments about the 'crowding out' of investment are concerned, if the twenty-five per cent rise in production achieved in agriculture secured a rise of only three per cent in the contribution of agriculture to the economy as a whole, then it is clear that industry must still have been growing very rapidly. Finally, it has rightly been pointed out that heavy taxation did not prevent the propertied classes from enjoying a most comfortable standard of living. Nor was this surprising, for income tax was moderate by modern standards, not to mention patchy in its application (as we have seen, business incomes escaped comparatively lightly, whilst salaries for the most part got off altogether). At the same time, opportunities for profit were very great, especially as Pitt's decision to abandon the gold standard in 1797 tended to increase the availability of credit. Commerce and industry may have been highly uncertain – the successive opening and closing of different markets in accordance with the vagaries of the war was particularly disruptive – but, for the fortunate, immense fortunes might still be made. Government borrowing, which had hitherto drawn largely on foreign financiers and now had perforce to turn to domestic sources of revenue, created not just a minority of millionaire speculators such as David Ricardo, but a growing number of relatively humble 'fund-holders'. And in agriculture the combination of rising food prices and the subsidising of the wages of farm labourers by the rapidly spreading 'Speenhamland system' led to great prosperity amongst the large owners and tenant farmers – hence Cobbett's complaints of yeoman living above their station, and Henry Hunt's reports of a positive land rush: 'If a farm was to be let, scores were riding . . . over each other, ready to break their necks . . . to rent it at any price.'[10]

Hunt's observations confirm arguments that investment was diverted away from industry, whilst it would also be pointless to deny that considerable damage was inflicted by the Continental System, in 1811, especially, there was a severe economic slump. In brief, the origins of this crisis were both commercial and financial. On the one hand, trade was slashed by one-third and many speculators ruined due to the combination of the enforced entry of Sweden into the Continental System, Napoleon's attempt to break into the colonial trade (see below, p.250), the tightening of the American trade embargo, and the disruption caused by the Latin-American revolutions. On the other, thanks largely to the impact on the money supply of greater imports of wheat following the bad harvests of 1809 and 1810, there was a sudden failure of confidence, the result being, as occurred at about the same time in France, a wave of bank failures which in turn provoked a crisis in industry. Bankruptcies more than doubled in terms of their average over the previous decade, and wool, hosiery, cotton and iron were all hard-hit – 9,000 workers were thrown onto the poor rates in Birmingham and 10–12,000 in Manchester, whilst in Lancashire those mill workers who kept their jobs were reduced to a three-day week. As for such groups as the handloom weavers, their plight was very severe, it being no coincidence that 1811 marked the emergence of Luddism, though this had been pre-figured a few years earlier in Wiltshire.

Yet Britain did not collapse – however severe, the 1811 slump proved temporary, the government's very refusal to surrender even in this crisis leading to a restoration of confidence which was soon rewarded by a favourable shift in the pattern of trade. And, taking the war as a whole, there simply can be no doubt that the British economy prospered enormously. If we examine industrial production, in most sectors output rose considerably. In iron, for example, production increased to such a point that by 1812 Britain

---

10 *Cit.* A. D. Harvey, *Britain in the Early Nineteenth Century* (London, 1978), p. 337.

had become for the first time a net exporter of this commodity. In cotton, consumption grew from an annual average of 13,900 tons in the period 1791–1800 to 31,800 in the period 1803–12. Even in coal, where a variety of technological problems rendered progress comparatively slow, production grew some twenty per cent faster between 1790 and 1811 than it had between 1780 and 1790. There is, too, much evidence of innovation and mechanisation: by 1813, 2,400 power-looms had been installed in Britain, much to the detriment of the handloom weavers; steam power appeared for the first time in the iron industry, by 1815 half the motive power in its Birmingham branch coming from this source; gas lighting was used for the first time in some factories; and, even in agriculture, the first threshing machines came on the scene. Evidence of Britain's prosperity may also be found in the field of urbanisation with existing cities like Manchester, Liverpool and Birmingham growing rapidly, and such pioneering settlements as Rochdale, Oldham and Bradford expanding even more dramatically. Urban development was accompanied by substantial public works: the construction of extensive new docks in London, the rapid expansion and improvement of the road and canal network, and the development of many new horse-drawn tramways.

However one might qualify the situation, therefore, Britain was booming. The consequences for the war effort were dramatic. On one level Britain was provided with the capacity to meet the substantial demands for war material of all sorts which the struggle made on her. On another, and far more importantly, the immense cost of the war was met without the country sliding into the sort of bankruptcy that characterised many of the Continental powers, the government's credit remaining intact and the paper currency that it used to finance the war retaining a high proportion of its face value. As a result, British diplomacy found itself able to draw upon resources that were almost inexhaustible, whilst Britain herself was able to outlast Napoleon's desperate attempts to break her back. In short, whether she was getting richer, getting poorer, or getting richer more slowly, the heart of Britain's war effort was a power and prosperity that Napoleon could not hope to emulate.

THE CHALLENGE TO THE OLD ORDER

From the moment that Britain first went to war with Revolutionary France in 1793, the Establishment was activated by a strong fear of political and social dissent, William Pitt describing the conflict in 1795 as 'a war for the protection of property'.[11] Inflamed to great heights during the Revolutionary War by such developments as the formation of a large number of popular radical clubs such as the London Corresponding Society, the wide-ranging diffusion of the writings of Thomas Paine, the food and militia riots of 1795–96, the mutinies at Spithead and the Nore in 1797, and persistent reports of the emergence of a revolutionary underground, by the time that war resumed in 1803 fears of a 'British Revolution' had come to seem rather ephemeral. Severe government repression, not to mention the success of populist conservatism in the battle for the popular mind, had broken the back of organised popular radicalism, most of the corresponding societies and their fellows simply disintegrating under its weight. As for the revolutionary underground, to the extent that this was a real threat at all (and there is no doubt that many of the reports reaching the government on the subject were highly alarmist) this was now dealt a heavy blow with the destruction of the so-called Despard conspiracy. An army officer on half-pay embittered by unjust dismissal from his post, Despard had in the late 1790s become involved with a shadowy group of Irish revolutionaries and survivors from the corresponding societies who styled themselves the United Englishmen. According to the government's numerous spies and informers, this organisation was planning a mass uprising in conjunction with a French invasion, to which end it was swearing in thousands of adherents in such areas as Cheshire, Yorkshire, Nottinghamshire, Lancashire and Derbyshire, these reports being lent verisimilitude by a extensive series of mysterious nocturnal mass meetings known as the 'Black Lamp' that were taking place at this time on the hilltops of the Pennines. Imprisoned for sedition in 1798, in 1800 Despard emerged from prison even more determined than before, and for the next two years he devoted himself to organising a conspiracy in London which established links with the United Irishman, Robert Emmet, who in July 1803 headed a dramatic revolt in Dublin, and some of the 'Black Lamp' agitators. Nevertheless, all this came to naught: Despard was arrested in November 1802 and was later executed with six others, whilst the 'Black Lamp' also collapsed following the transportation of a few ringleaders.

11 *Cit*. P. K. O'Brien, 'Public finance in the wars with France, 1793–1815', in Dickinson, *Britain and the French Revolution*, p. 183.

Since all now for some time remained quiet, with the exception, of course, of the Emmet rising (which admittedly was a most serious affair that caused intense alarm), all the evidence suggests that, at least in England, at the beginning of the Napoleonic Wars the government had nothing to fear from revolution. Whilst the much-feared revolutionary underground may have been in touch with wider social and economic unrest, its membership was confined to a small minority of activists. Moreover, if peace had been welcomed in 1802, the resumption of war was on the whole accepted without protest, in large part because, with an invasion fleet quite visibly in preparation just across the Channel, Napoleon was such an obvious threat to Britons of every class. Politically, moreover, admiration for the French Revolution and its ideals had been rendered increasingly difficult by the manner in which the prophecies of Edmund Burke had come to pass, for Napoleon was the very personification of the sort of military despot which he had always argued would be its logical result. And, with despotism rampant in France, the way was clear for reformers and radicals to be reconciled with patriotism, and the populace to be united behind the war effort. Thus, Napoleon having seemingly betrayed all that they believed in, many of the erstwhile champions of British liberty became involved in the volunteer movement, in which they saw a British Nation-in-Arms. Meanwhile, popular attention could be focused on the liberty enjoyed by even the humblest citizen under the traditional English constitution (in this respect, Addington's decision to avoid a witch-hunt after the Despard plot and to relax the more draconian restrictions on civil liberties that had been introduced in the 1790s was also clearly helpful). The case advanced by loyalists during the Revolutionary Wars was therefore greatly reinforced, and after 1803 this continued to be put forward more or less unchanged. In essence, the common man was to be persuaded that, in defending the established order, he was protecting his own interests, or, as one doggerel verse printed in 1803 put it, that 'The cause of George and freedom is your own!'[12] Based not on abstract theories but on centuries of practical experience, the British constitution had not brought absolute equality, but, in the context of their own particular stations in life, it had given liberty, happiness and the rule of law to all. In consequence, to attack it would be as ruinous to the honest labourer, artisan or small shopkeeper as it

---

12 *Cit.* F. Klingsberg and S. Hustvedt, *The Warning Drum – The British Homefront Faces Napoleon: Broadsides of 1803* (Berkeley, 1944), p. 58.

would to the propertied and wealthy, whilst to defend it would be to earn still better conditions. As one commentator urged, 'Remember that by thus coming forward to aid . . . your richer superiors, they will contract a debt of gratitude, which . . . they will not fail to repay.'[13] Added to this was a strong dose of xenophobia, as witness the ditty *Britons Unconquerable*:

Afraid of the French and afraid of invasion?
Afraid of the men whom on every occasion
We've beat since our Edward gained so much renown,
By bringing the king of these Frenchmen to town?

Yes, afraid of the French we will be when the moon
Shines as clear and as bright as the sun does at noon;
When the stars in their places no longer will stay,
But turn into marbles, and boys with them play.[14]

Such appeals clearly did not fall on deaf ears as indicated by the renewed success of the volunteer movement. To say, however, that that there was no danger of a popular rebellion in the crisis period of 1803–5 is not to say that popular feeling remained unchanged for the duration of the struggle. On the contrary, within a few years political radicalism had once again emerged as a significant force, whilst by 1812 certain areas of the country were in the grip of a severe outbreak of industrial unrest. However, before dealing with these questions, it is first worth examining the extent to which the war affected the landed interest's control of the levers of social and political power, it in fact being difficult to conclude that it made much difference. Although the war greatly increased opportunities for men of education through the enormous expansion that it brought in the activities of the government, in the absence of such mechanisms as competitive entrance procedures the civil service remained a preserve of clientage, the consequence being that the middle classes were able to advance very little except to the extent that they were able to secure the patronage of some member of the ruling oligarchy. Much the same was true of the magistracy, appointments to the bench depending upon the favour of the Lord Lieutenant of each county. In politics, too, the middle classes made

13 *Cit.* C. Emsley, *British Society and the French Wars, 1793–1815* (Manchester, 1979), p. 117.
14 *Cit.* Klingsberg and Hustvedt, *Warning Drum*, pp. 67–8.

little impression. Amongst prominent government politicians, Addington, Canning, George Rose and Lord Eldon, it is true, were not of landed origin, but none would have advanced very far without the support of powerful patrons, whilst, as prime minister, Addington had to contend with the open distaste of many even of his own supporters. And, if Addington was scornfully referred to as 'the doctor', the brewer, Samuel Whitbread fared even worse, a common joke being that, since he dealt in beer, he could not be a man of spirit. This, of course, is not to say that there was no middle-class penetration of the political world, but even so the number of Members of Parliament of commercial origin remained static, whilst the aristocracy actually extended its control, the number of seats in its gift rising from eighty-eight in 1793 to 115 in 1816.

Perhaps the most obvious area in which the war might have undermined privilege was the composition of the officer corps of both the army and the navy, particularly in view of the massive expansion consequent upon the war (between 1793 and 1814, the number of line-infantry officers alone increased by 225 per cent). In this respect there was certainly no formal obstacle to a 'democratisation' of the officer corps – to become an ensign or cornet a candidate had only to prove that he was at least sixteen years old and could read and write, and to obtain the recommendation of a senior officer – whilst the much-derided purchase-system, whereby officers could buy their way upwards through the ranks as far as that of lieutenant-colonel, in theory opened the officer corps to all men of property rather than just the landed gentry. And, expensive though the purchase of commissions could be – prices for an ensigncy or cornetcy ranged from £400 to £1,600 according to the regiment concerned – once a man had actually gained a place on the ladder, it was no longer essential. As only those commissions which had actually been bought could in turn be sold – a figure that in the period 1810–13 represented some twenty per cent of the whole – for much of the time purchase played no part at all even in those parts of the army where it existed (in the artillery and engineers promotion was entirely dependent upon seniority). Given that it was difficult to subsist on an officer's pay without a private income, and, further, that, purchase or no purchase, each step in rank carried with it a substantial administrative fee, money was still important, but the fact is that many men of relatively humble financial background did manage to make their way in the army. And, last but not least, promotion from the ranks was not impossible, perhaps five per cent of first commissions being awarded to men who had distinguished themselves by long service or acts of valour on the battlefield.

In theory, then, the landed interest should not have enjoyed a monopoly of the army's officer corps, but, for all that, the latter undoubtedly became progressively more blue-blooded. Thus, whereas only two per cent of army officers were of noble birth by 1812, for generals the proportion was ten times as great. Furthermore, since progression from the rank of lieutenant-colonel to that of full general was all but automatic, it is clear that this disproportion must have extended much further down the ranks. With at least forty-six per cent of generals still coming from either the nobility or the landed gentry as late as 1854, the inference is obvious: for all the expansion that the Napoleonic Wars brought to the army, to its social structure they mattered very little. In the first place, despite a series of reforms introduced by the duke of York as commander-in-chief to ensure that officers should gain at least a modicum of experience before attaining field rank, the purchase-system remained a tool of the landed gentry as much as it was an *entrée* for the bourgeoisie, two examples of 'sprigs of nobility' who enjoyed a meteoric rise to high rank as a result of its workings being the duke of Wellington and his cavalry commander at Waterloo, Lord Uxbridge. Secondly, although the duke of York is claimed to have tried to ensure that seniority should be the major criterion for promotions outside the purchase system, political influence continued to play a role (as it in fact did for both Wellington and Uxbridge), there being bitter complaints of 'the omnipotence of parliamentary interest'.[15] Thirdly, the conviction that officers should be gentlemen, and, further, that the definition of a gentleman rested upon the possesion of land, remained extremely strong, ex-rankers and other men of unsuitable background therefore being 'frozen out' or shuffled off in the direction of service in colonial or foreign units. Fourthly, in the Revolutionary Wars at least, commissions had frequently been offered to those who could bring in recruits, and here again the advantage lay with the landed classes, Sir Thomas Graham obtaining a colonelcy on account of having raised a new regiment from his estates in Perthshire. As a result, for all those dependent on promotion by seniority rather than by purchase or influence, progress was extremely slow. With the predominance of the gentry also extending to the militia and the volunteers, thanks to

15 *Cit.* C. Oman, *Wellington's Army, 1809–1814* (London, 1913), p. 200.

the influence in the former case of the Lords Lieutenant and, in the latter, of the magnates and other gentlemen who had organised their units, it can be seen that the land forces did not constitute much of an opportunity for social advancement. Nor were matters much better in the navy, in which, indeed, the proportion of noble officers was nearly twice as high as in the army. Whilst there was no purchase and less cost, promotion from the lower decks was almost non-existent, whilst Nelson's 'band of brothers' has been described as a compact clique of 'country squires, and preponderantly squires from the southern counties of England'.[16]

In short, then, the predominance of the landed interest was not much touched by the war, the result being a resurgence of political dissidence as soon as the invasion crisis was at an end. Reasons for dissatisfaction were certainly numerous. A series of major scandals did nothing to inspire public confidence, whilst ministerial policy with regard to the war frequently seemed incompetent and, on occasion, immoral as well. Thus, the failure of the expedition to Buenos Aires, the convention of Sintra, the enforced evacuation (and in a most shocking physical condition at that) of Sir John Moore's army from La Coruña, and the disappointing end to both the Talavera campaign and the Walcheren expedition gave rise to a considerable outcry, whilst the attack on Copenhagen provoked genuine horror, the Liverpool radical, William Roscoe, denouncing its authors as 'recreants to a Briton's name'.[17] Moreover, such operations as Copenhagen tended to reinforce doubts about the reasons why Britain had gone to war, just as the repeated military failures seemed to confirm arguments that, as Britain could not hope to defeat France, to continue the war was completely futile, especially as Britain was not in danger (the 'Friends of Peace', as the radical critics of the war became known, were here strongly influenced by the belief that a people united in the defence of its liberty could never be defeated). Whereas in 1803 the war had been a defensive one, it had increasingly assumed an offensive, and, indeed, selfish, aspect that was rendered all the more intolerable by the fact that the absence of political reform showed that it was being fought in favour of a narrow élite. As doing so could not bring victory, and especially not in alliance with Iberian obscurantism or Austrian absolutism, continuing the war would be

16 D. Howarth, *Trafalgar: the Nelson Touch* (London, 1969), p. 35.
17 *Cit.* G. Chandler, *William Roscoe of Liverpool, 1753–1831* (London, 1953), p. 115.

disastrous. In the first place, an expansion of the power of the executive consequent upon the wartime growth in patronage was seen as a threat to the liberty of the subject; and, in the second, the result was predicted to be general ruination and impoverishment (peace, by contrast, would supposedly allow Britain to rule the seas unhindered, it being assumed that Napoleon would content himself with Europe). Here, of course, the Friends of Peace were supported by the serious disruption caused by the Continental System. With the parliamentary opposition of Grey and Grenville showing little interest in radical reform, it was hardly surprising that the forces that had been thwarted in the 1790s should have gathered for a fresh assault.

Already visible as early as 1805, this resurgence of dissent was at first held in check by the collapse of the Pitt administration following the death of its leader in January 1806, and its succession by the far more pacific Ministry of the Talents. With the formation of the Portland ministry, however, the course of British politics was enlivened by a series of attempts by one means or another to challenge oligarchic rule. Thus, in the general elections of 1807, Westminster, then the largest and most representative constituency in the country, returned two popular demagogues, Sir Francis Burdett and Lord Cochrane, on a platform of electoral reform. The activities of these two disgruntled members of the élite were being supported by the so-called Westminster committee, this being a group of artisans, merchants and professionals who had for the most part been involved with the radical clubs of the 1790s. In the capital, at least, therefore, radicalism acquired a new degree of political organisation that made it doubly effective: when Burdett was arraigned for contempt of parliament after the government had tried to prevent public discussion of the Walcheren enquiry in April 1810, large crowds assembled around the Palace of Westminster and blocked the way with barricades. In the event, however, despite protestations of support for Burdett from around the country, this affair fizzled out, a far more serious threat to the government being posed by the growing resentment of the war amongst the business community. With the textile industries of the West Riding and Lancashire temporarily suffering a severe slump on account of the initial impact of the Continental System and the Orders-in-Council, the result was a series of public meetings and petitions calling for peace, this movement in turn drawing attention to the case for political reform which from 1811 onwards was strengthened by the emergence of the so-called Hampden Clubs. Renewed with redoubled force in the seemingly desperate circumstances of 1812, the petition movement now gained a dramatic success with the revocation of the Orders-in-Council. Implicit in this affair was the emergence for the first time of the manufacturing interest as a powerful and organised voice in direct opposition to the old oligarchy. The chief weapon against the Continental System, the Orders-in-Council effectively decreed that maritime trade could be carried on only on Britain's terms and, very largely, in British ships. This was all very well as far as the control of trade went, but it laid manufacturers, who were increasingly conscious that their products were becoming far more important to Britain's foreign trade than her colonial re-exports, open to severe losses as neutrals retaliated by refusing to admit British goods, a development that could not but lead to the markets of Europe and America eventually developing their own sources of supply. Still worse, by 1812 the Orders were leading Britain into a war with the United States which could only make the situation even more ominous. Here, too, lay yet another cause for conflict, for, whereas progressives admired the United States, conservatives despised her as both ungentlemanly and uncivilised. Also highly influential was the influence of Dissent, which was opposed to the war on religious and philosophical grounds that now chimed perfectly with the economic interests of the manufacturers (it was no coincidence that the peace petitioning of earlier years had been at its strongest in areas where Methodism and other forms of non-conformism had become particularly strong, and that the businessmen who were the leading lights of the agitation of 1812 were without exception Dissenters). Though its resonance in this respect should not be overstated, Cookson and Harvey having shown that the contest was as much between the manufacturers and colonial and shipping interests, between 'ins' and 'outs' in municipal government, and between the provinces and London, as it was between the manufacturers and the landed élite, the campaign against the Orders-in-Council that now broke out can very much be seen as a clash between the 'new' Britain and the old. Certainly, it was extremely impressive. Under the inspiration of anti-war liberals and political reformers such as William Roscoe, trade organisations of various sorts in Liverpool, the Potteries, Sheffield and Leeds held public meetings to petition for the Orders' abolition, the document thus produced in Leeds very soon collecting 17,000 signatures. Meanwhile, much support for these developments was manifested in the provincial press, as well as in a wide variety of other manufacturing areas, such as Birmingham and Nottingham.

And, most effectively of all, the campaign was extended into parliament itself through the efforts of such radicals as Henry Brougham, who secured the establishment of a Select Committee on the question and then proceeded to deluge it with evidence so convincing that it could not be gainsaid.

Increasingly beleaguered, the government caved in surprisingly quickly, the Orders eventually being revoked in June 1812. However, signal though this success may have appeared, it did not represent the rout of the landed interest. Led above all by Dissent, whose ministers and congregations now mobilised themselves to become the vanguard of what they hoped would be a general peace movement, anti-war petitioning continued to the end of the year and, indeed, in some respects gathered pace: in less than six months Leicestershire, Nottinghamshire and Derbyshire produced sixteen different petitions with a total of 30,000 signatures. Yet, if one discounts certain revisions of the Test and Corporation Acts, this campaign won no concessions from the government (it is also notable that it received relatively little support outside the dissenting heartland of the East Midlands). And, if another demand of the extra-parliamentary opposition was met through the revision of the monopolistic East-India Company Charter in 1813, this was hardly a blow against landed property, which, moreover, felt no qualms in establishing a Commons committee – in the face, be it said, of much public protest – to look into the question of protecting the price of corn against, first of all, bumper harvests such as that of 1813, and, secondly, the growing danger of renewed foreign imports. In fact, the victory of 1812 was entirely fortuitous. In the first place, on 11 May 1812 the prime minister, Spencer Perceval, was assassinated by a disgruntled bankrupt, the result being a ministerial crisis that undermined the chances of successful resistance. In the second, the government's stability was already being threatened by the intrigues that resulted from Lord Wellesley's efforts to seize the premiership following his resignation as foreign secretary over the question of Catholic emancipation. And in the third, there was growing alarm at the serious social and economic discontent that Britain was now experiencing, Perceval's murder, which was, indeed, greeted with widespread popular rejoicing, being widely seen as a harbinger of revolution. In short, the government gave way because it was weak, rather than because the forces opposed to it were strong, the seismic shift in the balance of power that the revocation of the Orders-in-Council seemed to portend being many years off.

Thus far the agitation that we have examined has above all been a middle-class phenomenon, its leaders being representatives of the *haute bourgeoisie* such as William Roscoe, Josiah Wedgewood and Thomas Attwood, dissenting clergymen such as Charles Berry and Thomas Mitchell of Leicester, provincial newspapers such as the *Leeds Mercury*, and the small owners who dominated the chapels of the East Midlands. Underpinning such forces, however, was an entirely different social stratum that, whilst it may have coincided with the new élites in certain of its objectives and was involved in their campaigns, had an agenda that was entirely its own. We come here, of course, to the working classes. Ever since the publication of Edward Thompson's *The Making of the English Working Class* in 1963, this subject has engendered a wide-ranging and sometimes ferocious debate whose complexity far outstrips the limited attention which can be paid to it in the context of a general survey of the Napoleonic Wars. Without entering into these discussions, however, it seems clear that certain sections of the working classes were indeed radicalised in the course of the war, and that the protest actions in which they engaged cannot be dismissed as purely economic.

That said, the outbreak of machine-smashing and other disorders known as Luddism that constitutes the most important example of autonomous working-class militancy during the Napoleonic period undoubtedly had its roots in economic grievances. In the first place, it emerged simultaneously with the onset of the most serious trade depression of the wars. In the second, the groups most affected by it – the handloom weavers of south Lancashire, the framework knitters of the East Midlands and the wool shearers of the West Riding – had all been relatively prosperous artisans who were particularly affected by one form or another of industrial dislocation, whether it was the introduction of new machinery, the abrogation of apprenticeship regulations and other laws that protected standards, the reduction of piece rates, or the development of new techniques that favoured mass production and undermined craftsmanship. As such pressures mounted, the first decade of the nineteenth century had been marked by attempts to secure redress by legal, or, at least peaceful, means. Such methods were never totally abandoned – in 1812 under the leadership of Gravener Henson the framework knitters spent much time and effort on having a bill for the regulation of their industry introduced in Parliament – but by then it had long since become apparent that they were unlikely to produce much in the way of a result. Hardly surprisingly, following the onset of general economic crisis of 1811 the result was a wave of severe violence. Thus, from March 1811 onwards bands of framework knitters calling themselves followers of one 'General Ludd' commenced a series of nocturnal raids in the villages of north-west Nottinghamshire in the course of which they smashed frames of employers deemed to be undercutting standards (by contrast, those employers who had maintained the old ways, or who now agreed to do so, were left alone). Early in 1812 these disturbances ceased, in large part because the framework knitters had made a number of immediate gains and were now persuaded of the feasibility of getting Henson's bill through parliament, but almost immediately a new wave of disturbances began in Lancashire and Yorkshire with a series of serious food riots in and around Manchester, an attack on a mill at Middleton which left seven of the raiders dead, a full-scale assault on the mill of William Cartwright at Rawfolds, and the murder of a particularly unpopular employer named William Horsfall. Taking at face value widespread reports of oath-taking, nocturnal drilling and arms raids, Thompson provides an account of the next few months that is replete with excitement. Thus:

> In the summer of 1812 there were no fewer than 12,000 troops in the disturbed counties, a greater force than Wellington had under his command in the Peninsula. For months at a time these considerable forces were singularly ineffective . . . due to the superb security and communications of the Luddites, who moved silently through well-known terrain, while the cavalry trotted noisily from village to village.[18]

Setting aside Thompson's carelessness with regard to military detail – at the battle of Salamanca on 22 July 1812 Wellington had with him some 30,000 British troops – it is fairly safe to say that this picture is an exaggeration, the local military commanders consistently denying that there was any danger of insurrection. The north of England was neither in a state of armed rebellion nor even under martial law, and in fact the disorder quickly receded. Quite simply, all the owners who were open to coercion had now been brought into line, whilst the almost total lack of success enjoyed by the Luddites when it came to storming barricaded and well-defended factories quickly dissuaded them of the value of the tactic, and all the more so once machine-breaking had been made a capital offence

18 E. P. Thompson, *The Making of the English Working Class* (London, 1968), p. 617.

and a number of ringleaders hanged or transported. Meanwhile, *pace* Thompson, the authorities' practice of swamping rebellious districts with mobile patrols proved highly effective in deterring the movement of large bodies of rebels. Though Luddism was not dead altogether – there were further outbreaks at the end of 1812 and in 1814 – labour revolt had done its worst and had been faced down, the government soon feeling secure enough to withdraw most of the extra troops it had sent to the affected areas and the owners to withdraw most of the concessions that they had temporarily been forced to make.

As a revolutionary force, then, Luddism has been much exaggerated. To say that it was ineffective, however, is not to say that it was not revolutionary at all. Although the army officers sent to suppress it were on the whole convinced that Luddism was the product of economic distress, there is ample evidence that it did have a strong political aspect, particularly in its rhetoric. For example, notices appeared demanding the head of the prince regent, a leaflet that circulated in Leeds called all croppers and weavers and the 'public at large' to 'follow the example of the noble citizens of Paris', and a Luddite letter from Nottinghamshire spoke of throwing off 'our immense load of taxation, an unprecedented national debt, a corrupt and despotic government, [and] a multiplied train of undeserved sinecures and unmerited pensions'.[19] Thompson is therefore undoubtedly justified in claiming that Luddism cannot be 'compartmentalized' as a specifically economic dispute. Yet, for all that, it appears difficult wholly to conflate Luddism with wider demands for peace, political reform and the abolition of the Orders-in-Council. For example, the peace petitioning of 1812 awoke few echoes in Luddite Nottinghamshire, whilst worker participation in the campaign against the Orders was at its strongest in districts that remained quiet (indeed, Thompson suggests that, wherever 'the employers themselves . . . initiated demonstrations and petitions against the Orders-in-Council . . . working-class discontent remained largely within 'constitutional' forms'[20]). Moreover, the leadership of Nottinghamshire framework-knitters, who have been seen as candidates for leadership of the Luddites of that county, specifically stated that they had no interest in matters relating to the war per se, remarking:

19 Cit. Thompson, *Making of the English Working Class,* p. 609; F. K. Donnelly, 'Ideology and early working-class history: Edward Thompson and his critics', *Social History,* I, No. 2 (May, 1976), 220.
20 Ibid., p. 617.

'Tis not the Orders in Council, 'tis not the . . . power of Bonaparte, that . . . can ruin the trade of these counties. No! The evil arises from a different source: 'tis in the manufactory itself; 'tis in speculating, unprincipled individuals that have made fraudulent goods to cheat and rob the public.[21]

From this it follows that Thompson is right to point to the period of the Revolutionary and Napoleonic Wars as one in which the working classes began to develop a specific political consciousness of its own in opposition to the onset of *laissez faire* and the factory system. In this respect, Luddism is, in fact, a side issue. Far more important was the growth of trade unionism among considerable sections of the labouring population, and especially the skilled workers, the notorious Combination Acts of 1799 and 1800 seeming to have had little effect in this respect. This is not to say that unions escaped persecution, but, far from being crushed, unionism survived in the many trades where it was already well-established, and made fresh advances elsewhere. Nor is this surprising given that industrial wages tended to lag behind the steadily rising cost of living. For Thompson, it was axiomatic that the secrecy that often had to be employed, with its heady cocktail of bloodcurdling oaths and nocturnal meetings, could not but lead to revolutionary politics, but he himself admits that much of the work remained 'humdrum', whilst it is clear that for most organised workers, complicated though the picture was by the fact that the riot had always been a recognised method of wage-bargaining, the real way forward was not the uprising but the strike (as was recognised by many of the Luddites, the Nottinghamshire disorders of 1811 being followed by a revival of trade-union activity). In 1808, for example, following the failure of parliamentary attempts to secure a minimum wage, there was a major strike by the Lancashire weavers; in 1812 there was a six-week strike among Scottish weavers; and in 1813 the shoemakers of London successfully struck to protect the price of their products. As yet, of course, the organisation of the working classes was in its infancy, but, whether through its encouragement of trade unionism or the generation of a heroic myth, the struggle with Napoleon had undoubtedly given it a considerable boost.

---

21 *Cit.* Emsley, *British Society and the French Wars*, p. 156.

THE RECKONING

In Britain perhaps more than in any other country it is tempting to see the defeat of Napoleon in terms of the triumph of the Old Order. Whereas such states as Spain and Prussia had been shaken to their very core, on the surface the United Kingdom appeared much the same sort of society as it had in 1802. For the propertied classes, certainly, the moment was one of great satisfaction. Setting aside the defeat of France, which was itself a matter for immense pride, on the surface they had many grounds to be content. Income tax was abolished in 1816, and, thanks in part to the Corn Laws introduced the previous year, landed wealth had rarely seemed a better investment. Meanwhile, their hold on power seemed as secure as ever: if the Hampden clubs presaged a revival of the political radicalism of the 1790s, attempts to achieve political reform had achieved nothing, every motion brought before Parliament in this respect having been defeated without difficulty; successive waves of peace agitation had been faced down; and the serious revolutionary threat seemingly represented by Luddism had been overwhelmingly defeated. Yet, setting aside changes in society that were being wrought by the separate process of industrialisation, the struggle with Napoleon had accelerated a number of developments that could not but undermine the landed interest, perhaps the most important of these being the professionalisation of state service.

In whatever sphere of the state's activity we look, in fact, by 1815 the writing was on the wall for the gentleman amateur, however much, as Emsley puts it, 'the kind of men who had administered Britain at national and local level before the war remained in control'.[22] This was not, of course, a development linked only to the struggle with France – the apparatus of the state had in fact been undergoing a process of renovation ever since the 1780s – but there can be no doubt that the experience of the French Wars underlined the need for even more radical change. Let us look first of all at the machinery of government, in whose work the Napoleonic Wars had, of course, brought a very great expansion. There was, however, no such expansion in the size of the bureaucracy, which remained very small, even the largest government department – the war office – having no more than 120 clerks, whilst positions in its ranks were the fruit not of competitive entrance examinations but of ministerial patronage. If individual ministers were conscientious – and some, it has to be said, were not,

22 Emsley *British Society and the French Wars,* p. 177.

Lord Wellesley, for example, being extraordinarily lackadaisical in his behaviour as foreign secretary in the period 1809–12 – the result was that the burdens of office could become very considerable, Lord Palmerston complaining of his appointment as secretary at war that it would be 'a very great confinement and fag'.[23] As for the business itself, it clearly suffered, there being repeated complaints about the war office, especially, that it was in a state of mounting confusion and arrears. In recognition of this situation, there were some attempts at reform – at the war office Palmerston increased the working day from five hours to six, and in the treasury the organisation of the department was thoroughly overhauled, financial experts were appointed to the chief posts, and all new appointments subjected to a probationary period. In practice, however, progress was both limited and piecemeal, Britain not acquiring a fully professional bureaucracy until the middle of the century. Nevertheless, the fact remained that times were changing – to quote Emsley again, 'The increased business of government meant that the men of Lord Liverpool's administration were civil servants and politicians who maintained a front as landed gentlemen rather than the opposite tradition of the eighteenth century.'[24]

If we examine the situation into which local government had been thrust between 1803 and 1815 the precarious nature of traditional arrangements becomes even more apparent. Represented chiefly by unpaid representatives of the nobility, gentry and, on occasion, clergy, in the form of the the Lords Lieutenant and their deputies and the justices of the peace, with a lowly substructure of parish vestries and constables, it had already found itself under heavy pressure in the Revolutionary War, and now visibly sagged under the unprecedented burdens placed upon it. The anti-invasion preparations of the early years of the war, for example, were especially burdensome, with parish officials being expected to carry out detailed surveys of the number of men available for military service and to administer the recruitment of the militia and such bodies as the 'permanent additional force' of 1804. Added to this were a host of financial duties such as the supervision of payments to the families of men serving in the militia and of the workings of the poor relief and Speenhamland systems, not to mention the provision of billets and supplies for the thousands of troops who

---

23 Palmerston to Fanny Temple, n.d. October 1809, University of Southampton, Broadland Papers, BR24/1.
24 Emsley, *British Society and the French Wars*, p. 179.

were permanently on the move around the country. Small wonder, then, that several Lords Lieutenant gave up under the strain, that much government legislation was implemented in the most patchy manner, and that complaints from local magistrates and other officials rose from all sides. In the districts affected by Luddism, moreover, chronic overwork and insufficiency caused local government to collapse completely. With burdens increased still further by new legislation, increased judicial and military business and the need to enrol large forces of special constables – 1,500 at Salford alone – and informers was simply too much, and for a time the system broke down altogether, local military commanders perforce having to assume much of the responsibility that had been thus surrendered. As with Whitehall, nothing much was done to remedy matters – though the state did increase its representation in the kingdom as a whole through the appointment of such officials as tax and ordnance inspectors – but, once again, it was clear that change must come.

Despite the victories of the British army in the Peninsula and at Waterloo, even this most formidable of bastions of the gentleman amateur was under threat. In the period after Waterloo the duke of Wellington became a ferocious opponent of any changes in the recruitment and composition of the officer corps. Purchase, he declared, had ensured that officers were men of rank and property with a stake in the interests and fortunes of the government and the country. He argued that military academies would turn out arrogant pedants, whereas, if officers received the same broad education available to any ordinary gentlemen, they would be more attuned to society and better fitted for the wide variety of roles – administrative, political and diplomatic as well as military – that they might encounter in the service. Last but not least, men promoted from the ranks would be unlikely to be able either to earn the respect of their subordinates – it was a common belief that the ordinary soldier preferred to be commanded by a gentleman – or fit in with their fellow officers, being all too likely to end up by turning to drink. Yet, if his every interest and prejudice propelled him in the direction of such sentiments, during the war Wellington had often been unremittingly scathing about the sort of men with whom reliance on untutored privilege had saddled him. For example:

> I have no hesitation in attributing the evil [of the chronic misbehaviour of the rank and file] to the utter incapacity of some officers at the heads of regiments to perform the duties of their situation, and . . . to

the promotion of officers . . . by regular rotation, thus holding forth
no reward to merit or exertion, and leaving all in a state of equal
indifference and apathy . . .[25]

At the same time, it should be pointed out that such vices were not
just limited to 'some officers'. On the contrary, for Wellington, at
least, the problem was general. Thus: 'Nobody in the British army
ever reads a regulation or an order as if it were a guide for his
conduct . . . every gentleman proceeds according to his fancy', or,
even better, 'How can you expect a court [martial] to find an officer
guilty of neglect of duty when it is composed of members who are
all more-or-less guilty of the same?'[26] Notoriously sweeping in his
opinions though the duke was, there is ample evidence that the
officers of the army were all too often inclined to place their status
as gentlemen before their duties as officers, a good example here
being the manner in which every winter Wellington was deluged
with requests from officers eager to return to England on what were
very often the slightest of pretexts. Such unmilitary habits were even
visible on the battlefield, a number of cavalry regiments being
massacred when their commanders threw control to the winds and
allowed their men to gallop helter-skelter at the enemy in the style
of a giant fox-hunt. As for Britain's generals, experience showed
that the system threw up far too many incompetents and
mediocrities, many of whom ended up thanks to influence or
seniority as field commanders. Perhaps the worst example was Sir
William Erskine, who, though both all but blind and mentally
unbalanced, served for a time as commander of the Light Division in
the Peninsula. Even if they were not clearly unfitted by their lack of
talents, many senior officers had seen very little active service: in
forty-five years in the army, Sir Hew Dalrymple had seen action
only in one campaign when he was sent to supersede Wellington in
Portugal in August 1808. Well might Wellington complain, 'Really
when I reflect upon the characters and attainments of some of the
general officers of this army . . . I tremble.'[27] As with other
branches of state service, there were some limited attempts to reform
the situation – as commander-in-chief in the period before 1809 the
duke of York strove to ensure that every officer should at least be

25 *Cit.* G. Davies, *Wellington and his Army* (Oxford, 1954), p. 51.
26 *Cit.* G. Rothenberg, *The Art of Warfare in the Age of Napoleon* (London,
1977), p. 177; L. James, *The Iron Duke: a Military Biography of Wellington*
(London, 1992), p. 168.
27 *Cit.* Davies, *Wellington*, p. 52.

instructed in arms drill and company and battalion manoeuvres, whilst between 1799 and 1802 he had founded the precursors of the Staff College and Royal Military Academy. Nor were all the army's officers so bad: the quality of the lower and middle ranks had improved dramatically in the course of the wars, and it is probable that by 1815 the British army was one of the best officered in Europe. For all that, however, the basic problem remained: though it was to take the disaster in the Crimea finally to prove the point, the demands of war were fast outstripping the capacity of the Old Order to meet them.

Given that we have already given much attention to the manner in which the Napoleonic Wars galvanised opinion among the middle classes and stimulated the emergence of an autonomous labour movement, it might be thought that this chapter would close upon the determinist claim that the impact of the period 1803–15 was essentially 'progressive' in its consequences. Whilst this may be so, the picture may also be more complex. In his study of war and society in Revolutionary Europe, Geoffrey Best entitled his chapter on Britain 'The Not-So-United Kingdom'.[28] Apposite in so far as the divisions in society that we have examined are concerned, this description overlooks a possibility that is more intangible. Although Britain did not fight her war in anything other than an eighteenth-century manner, for the purposes of home defence and internal security she yet mobilised a force of unprecedented size. Given that many militia regiments, in particular, were forever being shifted about the country from one posting to the next, this must for the first time have given the hundreds of thousands of men involved a vision of Britain that encompassed more than just their village, market-town or county. Added to this was the impact of constant propaganda, both official and unofficial, that sought to associate all classes in the struggle against France, to establish the victories of Wellington and Nelson as triumphs in which all might share, and to establish George III as a focus of national loyalty. Less directly linked to the conflict, though just as important, were the establishment of new newspapers in areas that had as yet been untouched by the press, the latter's general growth, and the steady rise in literacy. Of the result, there can be no doubt: for the first time war had become a truly national event. In consequence, if the mobilisation of the militia and the volunteers had suggested that the

28 G. Best, *War and Society in Revolutionary Europe, 1770–1870* (London, 1922), p. 122.

landed oligarchy were in the last resort dependent upon the people, it had also drawn the latter into closer integration with the state. What the Napoleonic Wars 'made' in Britain was in short not so much the working class, but, as Linda Colley has recently argued, the nation.

6 THE EMULATION OF THE FRENCH

LEGITIMISM LIBERALISED?

> As Napoleon extended the imperium of his will . . . his military
> enemies – though by no means all of them – recognized that he must be
> conquered by his own instruments of victory; their own strength, in
> part at least, must be made similar to that of France. The . . . armies
> with which they had been accustomed to playing fine games of strategy
> were no match . . . for this onward sweep of fire-spreading crusaders
> . . ..[1]

As Alfred Vagts implies, the reforms that affected Europe in the
Napoleonic period were not confined to the French empire.
Confronted by the reality of French military power, the continental
powers were sooner or later themselves forced to embark upon a
process of change. The extent of this process remains a matter for
debate, however. In the perception of contemporaries, reform was
dramatic, one French observer going so far as to remark that what
occurred was an 'exchange of standards, so to speak, which placed
the flag of authority and the monarchical principle on Napoleon's
side, and on that of the legitimist monarchs the liberal flag on which
was written "the liberation of all the nations"'.[2] Nor have historians
been unwilling to echo this judgement, Blanning, for example,
claiming, 'As Napoleonic France slipped into military dictatorship, it
was the old-régime states which introduced programmes of modernisation, mobilised citizen militias, declared total war and used the
rhetoric of liberation.'[3] Yet perhaps the key word here is 'rhetoric',
for change was limited. In Prussia – seat of by far the most radical

---

1 A. Vagts, *A History of Militarism: Civilian and Military* (London, 1959),
p. 129.

2 Marquis de Noailles (ed.), *The Life and Memoirs of Count Molé, 1781–1855*
(London, 1923), I, p. 151.

3 T. C. W. Blanning, 'The French Revolution and Europe', in C. Lucas (ed.),
Rewriting the French Revolution (Oxford, 1991), p. 206.

of the reform movements – reformers such as Stein soon became bitterly disillusioned, whilst elsewhere the basic structure of government and society was for the most part altered not a whit. Tempting though it is to explain the downfall of Napoleon in terms of the adoption of the Nation-in-Arms by his opponents, we should, perhaps, exercise more caution. As Hew Strachan observes, the *ancien régime* 'preferred to adopt the trappings of the Nation-in-Arms rather than its essence'.[4]

SPAIN: THE ERA OF GODOY

As a response to French power, reform predates Napoleon, and therefore cannot neatly be fitted into a timescale restricted to the Napoleonic Wars. Taking Spain first of all, it may here be dated from the end of the War of the First Coalition of 1793–95. As has already been noted in another context, the royal favourite and chief minister, Manuel de Godoy, responded to the defeat of Spain in this conflict with a sustained attempt at modernisation. To recapitulate, in order to stimulate Spain's staggering economy and keep the national debt within bearable limits, a start was made on the expropriation of the lands of the Church and new taxes imposed upon the propertied classes, including the nobility. At the same time, substantial efforts were made to erode provincial privilege and strengthen the authority of the state. Central to this project, however, was an attempt at military reform. With peace with France guaranteed by the Family Compact of 1761, Charles III (1759–88) had been able to concentrate on building up Spain's maritime strength in order to stave off the British. Denuded of strength, the army had therefore been overwhelmed by the *levée en masse*. Extremely mistrustful of the French, and convinced that Spain must restore her land forces if she was not to be eclipsed as a great power, almost from the very moment that peace was signed, Godoy was urging the importance of military reform, the alliance that he signed with France in 1796 being a device designed to allow him to gain time for this project. As for what needed to be done, Godoy's goals included a new system of recruitment and organisation, modern tactics, and better training for officers and men alike.

Impressed by the arguments of his favourite, in April 1796 Charles IV agreed to the formation of a special commission whose

---

4 H. Strachan, 'The Nation-in-Arms', in G. Best (ed.), *The Permanent Revolution: the French Revolution and its Legacy, 1789–1989* (London, 1989), p. 63.

task should be to elaborate a comprehensive programme of reform. Far-reaching though its purview was, however, even those of its members who were genuinely committed to the cause of change soon showed that they had little interest in a fundamental renovation. Whilst they displayed some hostility to such privileged formations as the overblown royal guard, and desired to end the exemptions that had saved many provinces and cities from conscription, in line with conventional eighteenth-century thinking they argued that citizen armies were militarily ineffective, and, further, that conscription should not be allowed to affect those who could contribute more effectively to the state by other means. Far from looking to the French model, they therefore suggested that Spain should retain the old selective ballot with all its exemptions, whilst adopting the Prussian system whereby conscripts spent the bulk of each year in their own homes, the hope being that this would render military service less obnoxious. However, modest though these proposals were, they were still sufficiently radical to demonstrate the obstacles faced by reform. Not only was Godoy regarded as an upstart by large parts of the court and military establishment, but his plans also offended numerous vested interests, and thus it was that they were for the most part blocked and Godoy himself forced to resign as secretary of state in 1798. As for results, these were at this stage minimal, all that had really been achieved being to extend recruitment of the provincial militia to the hitherto-exempt province of Valencia.

However, notwithstanding the fall of Godoy, it was not long before military affairs once more became the centre of attention. In 1801 French pressure led to Spain being forced to attack Portugal, Godoy being appointed to take command of the army assembled for this purpose. Although the Portuguese were soon beaten, the campaign still left much to be desired: mobilisation had taken a considerable time, and there had been serious supply problems. At last persuaded of the need for substantial improvement, the king now made Godoy generalissimo and ordered him to undertake fundamental reform, the result being the successive reorganisation of the infantry, cavalry, engineers, artillery, royal guard and provincial militia, and the introduction of French tactics (in this respect it should be noted that the war of 1793–95 had already seen a large increase in the number of light-infantry regiments). Yet in practice no more was achieved than before. Not only was there a constant air of improvisation, with several of the new ordinances having, at the cost of much confusion, almost immediately to be completely recast, but major issues such as recruitment were left entirely untouched, the only change in this respect being to extend the old *sorteo* to the whole of Spain. Yet so disliked was this system that it was never imposed in peacetime, the result being that, with service in its ranks as unpopular as ever, the army had in practice to rely on a mixture of press-ganged vagabonds and convicts and foreign flotsam-and-jetsam and remained badly understrength. Nor was very much achieved even in the way of military effectiveness: for all Godoy's efforts, the army remained short of cavalry and artillery, outmoded in its tactics and poorly officered, as well as being dogged by serious logistical difficulties. In part, all this was the fault of Godoy, the favourite lacking in intellectual grasp and absurdly complacent. At the same time, too, his numerous personal faults – he was notoriously venal and licentious – alienated potential allies and drove them into the camp of his opponents, whilst also ensuring that many of his collaborators were mere toadies. In mitigation, however, it has to be said that his position was very difficult. He was the object, as we have seen, of bitter hatred within the court, and his many enemies spared no effort to blacken his reputation and misrepresent his actions. Within the army, too, his very reforms angered as many as they pleased, the royal guard becoming a particular source of enmity after he reduced it by half in 1803. Meanwhile, the only basis for his continued prominence was the favour of the king and queen. Setting aside the damaging rumours of his relationship with the latter, this placed distinct limitations on his actions. Terrified of anything that might prejudice the loyalty of the armed forces, Charles IV and Marie Louise constantly acted as a brake on reform, repeatedly interfering with his plans. And, finally, as if all this was not enough, the state of Spain's finances was not such as to facilitate reform, thanks to the combination of the British blockade, soaring inflation, French rapacity and the need to engage in such operations as the war against Portugal.

In short, reform in Spain achieved very little. On the one hand, Godoy's attempts to raise more money were nullified by the implications of his foreign policy, whilst on the other his efforts to strengthen the army were frustrated by vested interests, political opposition, and the hesitations of his own sponsors. Whilst still managing to stir up a hornet's nest, the favourite had in reality succeeded in doing no more than tinkering with a few details. As a result, had the troops he attempted to mobilise in March 1808 really come to blows with the forces of Marshal Murat, it is hard to see how a Spanish Jena could have been averted.

AUSTRIA: THE FAILURE OF THE ARCHDUKE CHARLES

In Austria, too, though reform again began in the 1790s, little progress was achieved. Here consideration must first be given to the character of the emperor, Francis II, who came to the throne just prior to the outbreak of war with France in 1792. No tyrant, genuinely humane, by no means unintelligent, sympathetic to many of the aims of Joseph II – he was, for example, a sharp critic of the nobility's treatment of the peasantry – and very much concerned to give his subjects good government, the general upheavals of the period 1788–90 and the outbreak of the French Revolutionary Wars had left him in no doubt of the need for internal stability. Meanwhile, he was certainly more cautious than Joseph, being much inclined to put off difficult decisions and to listen to men who were themselves circumspect in their disposition, a prime example being his erstwhile tutor, Prince Colloredo, who was until 1805 secretary of his personal *kabinett*. Distrusting the consequences even of Josephinianism, he was therefore hardly the man to preside over a fundamental recasting of the institutions of the Habsburg state, his first reaction on being told of a certain Austrian patriot therefore being to demand whether he was 'a patriot for me'.[5]

Under Francis II, therefore, the political and social development of the empire was extremely inhibited, if not actually frozen, as witness the de facto abandonment of many of Joseph's political and social policies. In most areas of government the clock was not actually turned back, but no advance was made on the situation that had rtained when Francis came to the throne. Thus, the various provincial diets were allowed to remain in existence, whilst the compromise worked out with Hungary under Leopold II in 1791 was respected, further concessions, most of them fairly minor, being made to a specially convened meeting of the diet when Francis was crowned king of Hungary in 1792. Thus, whilst, except in Hungary, real power lay in the hands of the imperial bureaucracy, the nobility's position in the state was recognised, the threat to the survival of their privileges lifted, their economic interests conciliated (*malgré lui*, Francis was forced to tolerate an increase in the services demanded of the peasantry), and their manorial jurisdiction allowed to remain untouched. In order to discourage any movement of the rural population to the towns, meanwhile, controls were imposed on the growth of industry. Last but not least, no attempt was made to encourage popular identification with, or involvement in, the affairs

---

5   *Cit.* A. J. P. Taylor, *The Habsburg Empire, 1809–1918* (London, 1948), p. 25.

of state, the empire becoming marked by rigid censorship, police surveillance and clerical indoctrination. With many former *illuminati* themselves hastily backing away from support for reform, there thus perished the vibrant intellectual movement that had underpinned Viennese absolutism before 1792, and might now have been crucial in pushing through further reform.

Yet, for all that, it was not long before it had become clear that abandoning Josephinianism could not be reconciled with Austria's needs as a great power. In this respect, three problems presented themselves. First of all, Vienna had neither the finances nor the troops for a major conflict. With regard to the former, nowhere did the land tax that was the chief source of revenue draw adequately upon the resources of the nobility, especially in Hungary. In consequence, Vienna had no option but to rely on a mixture of foreign and domestic loans, of which the latter involved the issue of large quantities of paper money, or *bankozettel*. At the very end of his reign Joseph II had tried to introduce a unified land tax, but this had aroused such resistance that Leopold II had withdrawn the scheme, and it had not been resurrected by Francis. Insufficient to meet the requirements of the Habsburg state in time of peace – by 1790 the national debt amounted to 399,000,000 guilders – the old system was quite outstripped by the demands of the French Wars. Despite British loans and subsidies, the issue of fresh *bankozettel*, a slightly less intransigent attitude on the part of Hungary, and appeals for voluntary donations, between 1792 and 1801 the national debt rose by fifty-seven per cent, matters being made still worse by growing inflation (by 1803 prices in Vienna were 300–400 per cent higher than their 1790 level, whilst between 1801 and 1805 alone the cost of living trebled). As a result of these factors, as early as 1797 the Habsburg forces were reported to be 'in the most pitiable state'.[6] Furthermore, with the coming of peace in 1801 the military budget had to be cut by some sixty per cent, very large numbers of troops having to be sent home on unpaid leave.

Even as it was, the army was extremely short of men, recruitment resting on a mixture of selective conscription and voluntary enlistment. Volunteers were willingly accepted for all its branches, and some units – generally speaking, those recruited in areas such as Italy that were exempt from conscription – relied on them completely. However, in the hereditary Austrian lands and

---

6 *Cit.* K. Roider, *Baron Thugut and Austria's Response to the French Revolution* (Princeton, 1987), p. 232.

Galicia – the recruiting areas of the so-called 'German' regiments – all males were theoretically subject to conscription by ballot, though in fact there were the usual exemptions on the grounds of status, occupation or place of residence (many towns escaped very lightly whilst several provinces were exempted altogether). Meanwhile, in Hungary, men were raised by voluntary enlistment in accordance with a (generally very limited) figure agreed by the diet. And, last but not least, in time of war the Tyrol and the Military Frontier – the Slav region bordering the Ottoman Empire – supplied irregular militias that were theoretically composed of every able-bodied male. Yet in practice none of this was sufficient. Because service was for life the army could never gain sufficient volunteers, whilst conscription was hated by rich and poor alike. Joseph II had struggled to tighten up the system in the German lands, to end the exemption of such areas as the Tyrol, and to force the Hungarians to accept it or at least to increase the size of their contribution, but to no avail, having been forced to back down by massive popular resistance. Still worse, the number of men liable for conscription was reduced by the emancipation of the crown serfs in 1781 as this tended to increase the number of peasants enjoying personal exemption. Meanwhile the Military Frontier's system of enrolment was breaking down, only 13,000 men out of a theoretical total of 57,000 appearing for service in 1792. Much reliance therefore had to be placed on attracting recruits in the minor states of Holy Roman Empire, at least one half of the manpower of the 'German' units coming from this source. Even with this assistance, the army was badly understrength in 1792, mustering only 225,000 men out of a theoretical total of 300,000. As the wars went on, matters grew still more difficult. Peasant resistance to conscription increased sharply with at least 27,000 conscripts fleeing their homes to avoid being drafted, and recruitment fell away in Germany, eventually ceasing altogether when states such as Bavaria, Baden and Württemberg attained full independence under Napoleon. In the face of this situation, minor increases in the Hungarian quota and the formation of a few rather unreliable battalions of patriotic volunteers made little difference, the army never succeeding in attaining even its theoretical peacetime strength.

Added to the questions of finance and numbers, there was also that of the empire's extremely cumbersome system of governance. In the Austrian lands Maria Theresa and Joseph II had made considerable strides in the rationalisation of the administration, diminishing the influence of the estates and placing local government in the hands of six *gubernia* responsible to the 'Bohemian and Austrian Court Chancellory'. Yet devolution was minimal, even the most inconsequential matters having to be referred either to the relevant ministries of state – foreign affairs, defence and finance – or to the emperor himself, in which case they were first discussed by his personal council, the *Staatsrat* (to make matters even more complicated, the members of this latter body reported to the monarch individually via his personal secretariat, the *kabinett*). Even when matters were dealt with at ministerial level, action was often very slow due to the fact that there were no responsible ministers as such, but rather 'colleges' of senior officials who took decisions in council (or, with depressing frequency, chose rather to request a decision by the emperor). As can be imagined, immense quantities of paper were generated by the system. Thus, in 1802 some 2,000 reports are supposed to have been awaiting Francis's decision, whilst when the Archduke Charles became war minister he found no fewer than 187,000 documents awaiting attention; meanwhile, in 1808 the president of the *gubernium* of Lower Austria protested that the government was issuing so many rules and regulations that 'the most retentive memory cannot hold even the titles, let alone the contents'.[7] Clumsy though this system was, it did not even extend to the whole monarchy, the Italian, Flemish and Walloon provinces and the Military Frontier having remained aloof from its introduction, and Hungary having thrown it off.

As for the empire's military administration, this was just as complicated. In theory, the *Hofkriegsrat*, or palace war council, was responsible for all matters pertaining to the army's internal administration, finance and supply, and yet in practice a whole series of specialised agencies had grown up that dealt with parts of its remit whilst yet remaining independent of its control. Meanwhile in 1792 Francis had ordered that a special section of the *Staatsrat* should be created to look at military affairs, thereby undermining its supremacy. At the same time, the *Hofkriegsrat* frequently discussed strategic planning, even though this role was theoretically allocated to the quartermaster general staff. The whole system was weighed down by paperwork – Leopold II complained bitterly of its 'many useless, superfluous and burdensome reports, returns and accounts', and Thugut that it was overburdened with 'details and military pedantries'.[8]

7 *Cit.* C. Macartney, *The Habsburg Empire, 1790–1918* (London, 1969), p. 159.
8 *Cit.* G. Rothenberg, *Napoleon's Great Adversaries: the Archduke Charles and the Austrian Army, 1792–1814* (London, 1982), p. 19; Roider, *Thugut*, p. 27.

Not only was the system intolerably cumbersome, but the armies of bureaucrats which it supported were notoriously inefficient. Frequently owing their appointments to clientage and nepotism and guaranteed a secure future by the fact that promotion rested entirely on seniority, they had no formal training and, at the lower levels at least, often had an unenviable reputation for sloth, venality and incompetence. The chances of the system ridding itself of corruption were considerably lessened by the fact that the inflation brought by the war had reduced the value of its salaries almost to nothing. At the same time, of course, it discouraged independence, too many officials taking the easy way out by referring as many decisions as they could to their superiors. Finally, with a few exceptions, the bureaucracy had been notoriously hostile to the more populist aspects of Josephinianism, and it was futile to expect that it should change its attitude in the midst of a war with Revolutionary France.

Compared with these problems, the various deficiencies of the army itself – lack of skirmishers, inadequate military education, noble predominance within the officer corps, ageing commanders, and outdated field guns – were relatively insignificant: after all, the Austrians all but defeated Napoleon himself at Marengo in 1800. Yet although they were hardly the heart of the matter, it was at first only in such terms that reform was discussed. In the mid-1790s, for example, we therefore find officers such as Baron Mack and Francis II's younger brother, the Archduke Charles, advocating more use of the tactical offensive (though even then both skirmishers and the column were rejected in favour of the line), and the introduction of a corps system. However, no thought was given to the wider aspects of reform, Austria's defeats generally being attributed to the failings of the high command. The idea that the army should be composed of anything but a force of long-service professionals attracted particular hostility. In the words of the Archduke Charles, for example, 'Popular risings, arming the people, rapidly gathering untrained volunteers and such, can never provide reliable troops.'[9] When Francis established a special reform commission in 1798, the only result was therefore the formation of a few new regiments.

Yet, as witness the crushing defeats of 1800, this was not enough, Francis in consequence appointing the Archduke Charles

---

9 G. Rothenberg, 'The Archduke Charles and the question of popular participation in war', *Consortium on Revolutionary Europe Proceedings*, 1982, p. 219.

president of the *Hofkriegsrat* and ordering him to formulate a detailed and comprehensive plan of military reform. Though anything but a radical, Charles at least saw that military and domestic issues could not be separated, and was deeply concerned at the failings of the empire's governance, believing that these were so bad that they might even precipitate a revolution. Nor was the archduke alone in his opinions: not only were several of his brothers, including the Archdukes Rainer and Joseph, pressing for a revival of Josephinianism, but the new foreign minister, Cobenzl, was agreed on the need for major rationalisation, whilst even Colloredo had come to the conclusion that matters could not go on in the same fashion. As he wrote to Cobenzl:

> I tremble when I think . . . about what I see . . . .. All is in flux . . . general confusion, no co-operation, a total lack of direction, no energy for grappling with business . . . .. Oh God, where will it all end?[10]

Under Charles' influence, there therefore followed a real attempt to tackle the problem of government. Starting at the summit of the régime, the *Staatsrat* was abolished, and replaced with a new *Staats und Konferenz Ministerium* that, through regular meetings of the various ministers, was supposed to co-ordinate the whole work of government. Subordinate to this body were three ministries – interior, war and navy, and foreign affairs – each of which was headed by a responsible minister, whilst for the first time their responsiblities were extended to the entire empire (the ministries were later increased to four with the creation of a ministry of finance). Even the *Hofkriegsrat* was reduced to the role of an executive arm of the war and navy ministry (of which Charles himself became the head). At the same time great efforts were made to increase administrative efficiency, Charles pressing for a purge of the bureaucracy and remodelling the *Hofkriegsrat* on a simpler basis whilst a series of officials in the foreign ministry put forward plans for financial reform.

Better than nothing though all this was, Charles' outlook remained exceedingly cautious. Opposed to a revival of Josephinianism per se, he was quite prepared to tolerate continued Hungarian autonomy provided that the Hungarians stayed loyal to the dynasty. Indeed, allowing the peoples of the empire to retain

10 *Cit.* K. Roider, 'The Habsburg foreign ministry and political reform, 1801–1805', *Central European History* (hereafter, *CEH*), XXII, No. 2 (June, 1989), 165.

their traditional institutions was all to the good, for, as Charles wrote, 'The German soldiers could then be utilized successfully to smash any uprising in the Hungarian kingdom, and the Hungarian soldiers . . . to crush the Germans or the Bohemians.'[11] With regard to Hungary, then, all that Charles was prepared to do was to demand that she should contribute more men and money to the empire. When the Hungarian diet met in May 1802 it was therefore requested to increase permanently its quota of recruits from 56,000 to 64,000 men, to introduce conscription, and to vote a cash contribution of two million guilders. Only when the diet proved recalcitrant did Charles suggest more drastic measures based on the suppression of Hungarian autonomy, and in the event he did nothing to push matters to extremes.

As for the army, Charles enacted a number of minor technical reforms and held a series of large-scale manoeuvres, but as before he refused to do anything that would affect its nature, in March 1804 telling Francis that making 'the whole nation . . . an army . . . would ruin industry and national prosperity, and disrupt the established order'.[12] Though he turned his attention to the system of recruitment, the most that he would do was to reduce the term of service from life to between ten and fourteen years, depending on the arm of service, in the hope that this would reduce hostility to conscription, large numbers of the old exemptions being retained. Care was certainly paid to questions of morale, with Charles supporting some relaxation of discipline, an improvement in the treatment of the rank and file by the officer corps, and the stimulation of greater initiative on the part of the common soldier, but it is clear that all this was directed to strengthening the professional *esprit de corps* that he held to be the key to success against the French.

Setting aside his own shortcomings, the archduke was also hampered by the insecurity of his position within the régime. In particular, Francis greatly disliked his brother, and distrusted the military, remembering, perhaps, the *condottieri* of the Thirty Years' War. At the same time, he believed the *Staats und Konferenz Ministerium* to threaten his control of the administration, the consequence being that it was soon allowed to fall into desuetude. Many of Charles's appointments, moreover, were highly unpopular

11 *Cit.* J. Vann, 'Habsburg policy and the Austrian war of 1809', *CEH*, VII, No. 4 (December 1974), p. 298.
12 *Cit.* Rothenberg, 'Archduke Charles', p. 220.

– indeed, possibly unwise, especially in the case of his chief civilian collaborator, Matthias von Fassbender – whilst his prominence attracted the jealousy of numerous generals and other court figures. Yet more trouble was provoked by the emergence of a war party following the resumption of hostilities between France and Britain in 1803, Charles being convinced that Austria should avoid war at all costs. With Francis predisposed to turn against him, Charles was soon outmanoeuvred: in January 1805 the *Hofkriegsrat* was removed from the control of the war ministry and within a few months his chief collaborators had been forced to resign. Charles himself stayed on as war minister, but he found that he was now deprived of any real power. Reform did not come to an end – on the very brink of war in 1805 the new quartermaster-general, Baron Mack, introduced a number of changes in tactics and organisation – but the only result was disorder and confusion, whilst Mack's efforts did nothing to address the real issues, the army therefore going down to catastrophic defeat.

In terms of the empire's domestic politics, Ulm and Austerlitz gave reform a new impetus, the Archdukes Rainer and Joseph once again bitterly criticising the inefficiency of the administration and demanding the introduction of a more equitable system of taxation. Though little attention was paid to their arguments by Francis, the emperor did at least somewhat reluctantly appoint Charles general-issimo of the Austrian armed forces on 10 February 1806. Unlike in the period 1801–5, however, Charles did not concern himself with administrative matters and instead devoted himself to the question of the army's quality. Thus, efforts were made to improve the training of the officer corps through the issue of a series of pamphlets on tactical problems and the publication of a new technical journal; a new code of discipline was introduced that abjured physical brutality and stressed the need for motivation and *esprit de corps*; a number of new light-infantry battalions were formed, and the third rank of line battalions authorised to deploy as skirmishers; columns of attack were introduced, as well as a new formation known as the 'battalion-mass' that was designed to allow infantry to manoeuvre in the face of enemy cavalry; the artillery was reorganised so as to phase out the old regimental guns and concentrate all field pieces into proper batteries; and a system of permanent divisions and corps was introduced. Yet the political impact of these measures was non-existent. Nothing was done to renovate the composition of the officer corps; the system of recruitment remained unaltered except for the addition of two reserve battalions composed of supernumerary conscripts to each of the forty-six 'German' foot regiments; and, as for the concept of the Nation-in-Arms, Charles continued to decry all militias and other such bodies on the grounds that they 'make it appear as if we have a large mass of combatants and so induce a false sense of security'.[13] Outside the army, moreover, a number of measures were taken that were positively regressive, the towns being stripped of their right to elect their own councils and the central government of much of the co-ordinating machinery that Charles had sought to give it in 1801. Last but not least, a very cautious attitude continued to be adopted towards Hungary, even though its diet offered only the most grudging and limited response to the régime's demands for men and money.

In practice, then, reform in Austria after 1805 was distinctly unimpressive, but, for all that, it has often been treated with much *éclat* by historians. In large part the reason is the flirtation that now took place with German nationalism. Nationalism had in fact been growing amongst the German intelligentsia of the empire since the 1790s. Initially stimulated by the growing reaction against the intellectual hegemony of the *philosophes*, it was now reinforced by nostalgia for the vanished Holy Roman Empire. Until 1805 expression of such sentiments had been kept firmly under control, but under the impact of Austerlitz Francis authorised a dramatic change in policy, appointing Count Johann Stadion as foreign minister. As an erstwhile imperial knight, Stadion identified Austria's chief interest as the restoration of the Holy Roman Empire, which Francis had been forced formally to dissolve (in fact, since 11 August 1804 he had already been styled Francis I of Austria). To achieve this aim he was only too happy to avail himself of the services of nationalism, the period 1806–9 therefore seeing a general relaxation of censorship. Meanwhile, albeit from a slightly different perspective, Francis' youngest brother, the Archduke John, who was deeply influenced by Romanticism and inclined to idolise the German people as the personification of virtue, had also been attracted to the nationalist cause.

Aided and abetted by Francis' third wife, Maria Ludovica (a member of the branch of the Habsburg family recently ejected from Tuscany by Napoleon), Stadion and John now encouraged a great outpouring of German national sentiment, exiles such as Schlegel, Gentz and Hormayr calling for German unity, a war of revenge

13 *Cit.* Rothenberg, *Napoleon's Great Adversaries*, p. 68.

against Napoleon, and revolt in the Tyrol. At the same time, such men were aided by a growing press that filled its pages with exaggerated accounts of Spain's resistance to Napoleon and the glorification of the German national character. By 1808, moreover, it appeared that their efforts were bearing fruit, for on 9 June 1808 Francis sanctioned the formation of a citizens' militia, or *landwehr*, that was in theory expected to produce over 200,000 men. And, once war with France finally broke out in 1809, it was accompanied by a series of grandiloquent and widely distributed proclamations whose language was ostensibly strongly nationalist. As that of 8 April put it, 'Our cause is the cause of Germany.'[14]

Such language, and, indeed, the formation of the *landwehr*, has encouraged incautious commentators from Clausewitz onwards to imagine that the war of 1809 was the first example of the 'people's wars' by which Napoleon was supposedly ultimately overthrown. However, nothing could be further from the truth. Amongst the German bourgeoisie and intelligentsia there was certainly some enthusiasm for the struggle. A number of volunteer battalions were formed in Vienna and the capital was briefly the scene of immense patriotic excitement. Yet in reality the régime remained as hostile as ever to the idea of arming the people. Even the bellicose Maria Ludovica, for example, doubted the propriety of raising the Tyrol against the king of Bavaria, who was, after all, now its legitimate sovereign. Equally, well before the battle of Wagram, the Archduke Charles – at best a reluctant convert to the new war – was warning that no reliance should be placed upon the *landwehr* and that the army might be needed to restore order. At the same time, the new militia was not raised by universal conscription – Hungary and Galicia were exempted and the ballot restricted to those who were liable to service in the regular army anyway – whilst relatively few even of those men who were eligible were actually put into uniform, there also being some attempt to restrict the formation of volunteer battalions. As for political and social reform, meanwhile, this too languished in abeyance with the power of the police remaining as unchecked as ever, the towns being offered no form of self-government, and the peasantry left subject to the *corvée*.

If the dynasty was reluctant to arm the people, the people were reluctant to be armed. Despite the fact that the soaring inflation brought by the wars had greatly benefited the peasantry, except in

14 *Cit.* W. Langsam, *The Napoleonic Wars and German Nationalism in Austria* (New York, 1930), p. 68.

the Tyrol, where the *schützen* had turned out willingly enough in the campaigns of 1796–97, there had been little enthusiasm for fighting the French prior to 1809. Conscripts remained sullen and unwilling and volunteers for the regular army almost non-existent (a few volunteer *freikorps* did appear, but their tendency to disintegrate as soon as the prospect arose of going into action suggests that their motive for enlistment was the desire to play at soldiering so characteristic of the European bourgeoisie in this period). Vienna was inclined to panic at the merest rumour that the French were approaching and there were frequent bread riots and demonstrations of anti-war feeling, with such figures as the bellicose Thugut, who was chancellor from 1793 to 1801, being stoned and jeered whenever they appeared in the streets (in contrast to the countryside, in the cities the runaway inflation did cause severe hardship). Nor did anything much change in 1809: there was some ephemeral excitement and much patriotic posturing, but the bulk of those *landwehr* who were raised – as many as seventy-five per cent in some cases – deserted, the Poles and the Magyars were frankly hostile, whilst it was not long before the people of Vienna had put aside their initial defiance to fraternise with their conquerors.

Not surprisingly, then, with the exception of the Tyrol, Austria made war with her old army alone, this in turn ensuring that in 1813–14, especially, her generals followed cautious eighteenth-century style strategies designed to avoid a decisive battle. And, with Clemens von Metternich in the saddle as chancellor thereafter, never again did the régime go even so far as it had been prepared to do in 1809: though by no means the arch-conservative of legend, Metternich was genuinely obsessed with the fear of revolution, whilst being extremely unwilling to risk alienating his master, Francis. In point of fact, reform did not come to a complete halt. The flood of patriotic propaganda was ended, strict censorship reimposed and the Archdukes Charles and Rainer excluded from exerting any more influence, but there were nonetheless a number of changes, some of them of great importance. A new civil code that incorporated many Josephinian concepts was promulgated in 1811. Francis' hostility to economic development was abandoned in favour of an economic liberalism that produced such measures as a reduction in the privileges of the guilds and the abolition of laws forbidding the import of machinery and the establishment of new factories. Drastic efforts were taken to check the onrush of inflation through the issue of a new currency and in 1812 the Hungarian diet was dissolved when it made difficulties over financial reform,

Hungary to all intents and purposes being ruled on the same basis as the rest of the monarchy from then until 1825. In the final analysis, however, all this meant little enough: with all attempts to bind the population more closely to the régime effectively at an end, Austria had already embarked on the road that led to 1848.

RUSSIA: ALEXANDER I, THE UNOFFICIAL COMMITTEE AND SPERANSKY

Unlike in Spain and Austria, the beginnings of reform in Russia coincide far more neatly with the advent of Napoleon. Paul I (1796–1801) favoured greater centralisation, an increase in the efficiency of the army and a reduction of the privileges of the nobility, but such practical results as he achieved were ended by his assassination by a clique of disaffected aristocrats in 1801. The new tsar, Alexander I, quickly rescinded many of the measures that his father had introduced and amnestied the many noblemen who had incurred his wrath. For all that, however, Alexander still favoured reform, though in this he was not inspired by fear of France: he at first desired to retreat into neutrality, and greatly admired Napoleon. What motivated him was rather his own character and experience. A somewhat insecure young man who craved affection and popularity, he had been much influenced by the education in the ideas of the Enlightenment that he had received at the instigation of his grandmother, Catherine the Great. Appalled by the behaviour of his notoriously brutal father, and much influenced by an idealistic young official named Basil Karazin, Alexander became possessed of vague dreams of doing good.

In practice, all this meant very little. If Alexander had enjoyed a progressive education and acquired a number of friends who were strongly influenced by ideas of reform, he had been horrified by Paul's assassination, was so strongly influenced by military models that he was described as suffering from 'paradomania', and also much admired the ferocious Alexei Arakcheev, a narrow-minded, rigid and sadistic soldier who inspired universal dread. It has even been argued that the new tsar's supposed liberalism was in fact a piece of self-deception designed to make him feel better about safeguarding his own prerogatives as autocrat. That said, however, Alexander's accession was followed by some relaxation in the political atmosphere: the secret police was abolished, censorship relaxed, and discussion of political and economic ideas positively encouraged (much attention was paid to education, the period witnessing the establishment of several new universities and the beginnings of a system of secondary education). At the same time the new tsar summoned his old tutor, Laharpe, back to Russia, encouraged Karazin to ply him with ideas for educational and social reform, and gathered four trusted friends – Adam Czartorysky, Pavel Stroganov, Nicolai Novosiltsov and Victor Kochubey – around him in a so-called 'unofficial committee' to discuss what needed to be done. Yet, for all Alexander's misty dreams, this group soon agreed that Russia could not be other than an autocracy: none of the reformers conceived it otherwise, whilst Laharpe, who had served in the Helvetic Republic's directory, had now become violently anti-Jacobin. In theory it was agreed that the powers of the autocrat should be bound by the law, but, if work began on a new legal code and the minister of justice was asked to elaborate a constitution, nothing came of this. Similarly, extensive discussions were held with regard to serfdom, but here, too, nothing could be agreed other than a few minor palliatives. In so far as progress was achieved at all, it was in the field of government. A scheme to impart order and regularity to the administration, and in particular to ensure that the will of the tsar was properly implemented by his officials, by strengthening the power of the senate – the supreme council of administration and justice set up by Peter the Great in 1711 – was rejected, but this was not in itself a sign of regression: on the contrary, it represented a move away from the old collegial system which had long since been shown to be extremely cumbersome. Instead, as of September 1802, Russia was to be administered by eight clearly defined ministries, each of which was to be responsible to a single head. To discuss common business and co-ordinate their work, the ministers would furthermore come together in a central committee presided over by the tsar. But there was no prime minister, nor sense of collective responsibility, whilst the old colleges were allowed to survive inside the new ministries, thereby ensuring that their work would be greatly slowed down. Meanwhile, such full-time officials as held posts on a lower level were ill-trained and remarkably few in numbers, local government remaining entirely in the hands of the nobility. And, if the senate was given the right to challenge any government decree that it objected to, this was almost immediately withdrawn, it being realised that to do otherwise would be to hand substantial powers of obstruction to the very noble élite whom Alexander was determined to subordinate. In short, change was extremely limited, and in any case the 'unofficial committee' very soon ceased to meet, the régime also increasingly showing signs of returning to the police methods that had characterised the rule of Paul I.

Defeated by Napoleon in 1805 and then again in 1807, Alexander's attention was soon once more focused on 'constitutionalism', meaning the establishment not of *representative* government, but of *efficient* government – the introduction into Russia, in short, of order, system and method. Coming in 1807 almost by chance across the talents of a brilliant reformist official in the ministry of the interior named Mikhail Speransky, Alexander was so impressed that he made him his de facto chief minister (in this respect it is also probably no coincidence that, unlike the 'unofficial committee', Speransky was a man of obscure and humble origin who could not in any way be associated with the traditional élites). Under Speransky's influence, reform once again came to the fore. Essentially Speransky was a strong advocate of free enterprise who believed that it was the task of the régime to educate Russia in preparation for her economic modernisation. Politically a believer in a balanced monarchy in which autocracy would be tempered by the rule of law and kept in touch with its subjects, he was also deeply aware of the need for further institutional reform, these concerns being reflected by the draft 'Statute of State Laws' that he produced in 1809. In brief, this recommended a pyramid of triennial municipal, district, provincial and national assemblies of notables that would elect administrative councils at each level and advise the executive on such measures as it might choose to put before them, the State Duma that occupied the apex of the system also having the right to reject unconstitutional laws and impeach ministers who were guilty of misconduct. As for the executive, the tsar would remain at its head, but he would be assisted by a council of state headed by a 'state secretary' – to which post Speransky was himself eventually appointed – and a council of ministers. In addition to all this, the functions of each ministry were to be refined on a rational basis, the workings of local government reordered, and the justiciary freed from the control of the bureaucracy.

Impressive as Speransky's plans may have seemed, they contained many flaws. Although they rested on the idea that the tsar should be bound by the law, they neither delineated the parameters of government, nor established real obstacles to the exercise of arbitrary power, nor defined the liberties of the citizen, nor did anything to address the problem of serfdom, the 'Statute of State Laws' therefore amounting to no more than a scheme for the better ordering of despotism. Even then, it was not fully implemented, the only features to appear being the council of state and the revised organisation of government ministries. To be fair, these measures were not without importance, whilst Speransky also made great efforts to improve the training of the bureaucracy and to end the privileges enjoyed by the nobility within its ranks, to stabilise and reorganise the finances of the state, and to introduce a new code of law (modelled, incidentally, on the *Code Napoléon*). Nevertheless, in the absence of even the limited degree of popular participation hoped for by Speransky, any hope that autocracy might somehow be liberalised simply faded away.

Turning more specifically to the situation of the army, here, if anything, change was even more restrained. In the first place, matters were not helped by the fact that Alexander, who was perennially dogged by guilt at the murder of his father, for a long time remained under the sway of Arakcheev, one of the few generals who had remained absolutely loyal to Paul. First as inspector general of the artillery and then as war minister, Arakcheev introduced a number of substantial improvements, totally re-equipping the artillery after the battle of Austerlitz, and placing relations between war ministry, general staff and tsar on an orderly basis. However, his views on how armies should be run were entirely those of the Prussia of Frederick the Great, Arakcheev being renowned for his emphasis on uncomfortable Prussian-style uniforms, parade-ground drill, the use of the linear order, and savage discipline: screaming and swearing at officers and men alike, he is supposed even to have torn off moustaches. Terror, brutalisation and the complete suppression of the individual were everything, and in this system Alexander at first readily complied.

Yet, if Alexander never questioned Arakcheev's military judgement, he was concerned by his obscurantist politics, and, in particular, his hostility to Speransky. In January 1810 Russia therefore acquired a new war minister in the person of the far more humane Barclay de Tolly. Deeply opposed to the manner in which discipline in the Russian army seemed to rest entirely on the lash, he by contrast looked to encouragement rather than terror, arguing that officers should seek to understand and care for their men. In consequence, some attempt was made to secure some amelioration in the treatment and condition of the soldiery, but in practice very little changed. Conscription continued to be for twenty-five years and to fall exclusively – and extremely capriciously – upon the serfs, amongst whom it was universally feared and hated, other sources of recruits being convicts, foundlings and soldiers' children; Russian tactics remained clumsy and uninspired (so poor was the general level of initiative that skirmishers were almost non-existent); regimental officers were notorious for their ignorance; promotion was difficult without favour at court; and the general atmosphere remained one of fear and brutality. Nor was Arakcheev wholly eclipsed, retaining the tsar's ear, and in 1811 persuading him to try out his famous scheme to 'plant' the army in the self-sufficient agricultural 'colonies' that were to acquire so evil a reputation after 1815.

Any idea, then, that under Alexander the empire was transformed is wildly removed from reality. At most a greater efficiency was brought to the workings of the state. Far from emulating the Nation-in-Arms, in fact, with the origination of the idea of military colonies the empire was actually moving in the direction of its antithesis. Nor did the greatest proponent of reform survive for very long. The son of a penniless village priest, Speransky had never really been personally accepted at court, whilst matters had not been improved by his cold, arrogant and supercilious character. Many of his reforms had infuriated the nobility and it was not long before he had attracted a considerable number of enemies. Speransky being heavily influenced by French models, he was quickly tainted by the growing unpopularity of the alliance that Alexander had signed with Napoleon at Tilsit, and attacked for being 'un-Russian', the fact that he was a mason being particularly damaging. Last but not least, Speransky was hated not only by Arakcheev, but by the tsar's favourite sister, the Grand Duchess Catherine. As Alexander's rift with Napoleon deepened so this coterie of opponents worked continually to poison the tsar's mind against the state secretary, but their vague allegations of treason would probably have borne little fruit but for the gulf that existed in Alexander's mind between intention and reality. Speransky's plans containing the possibility of a diminution in his own power, in the last resort they could not be allowed to go ahead, with the result that on 29 March 1812 the state secretary was suddenly arrested and sent into internal exile. In Russia as in Spain and Austria, then, there were limits on the extent to which the *ancien régime* was prepared to revitalise itself through the pursuit of enlightened absolutism, let alone through the adoption of new models of social and political organisation. For any movement to take place in this direction a major shock was needed in the form of military defeats so catastrophic as to create a situation in which necessity temporarily overcame inhibition, and even then, as we shall see, change was to prove both reluctant and partial.

PRUSSIA: THE GREAT REFORM MOVEMENT

For the rulers of the *ancien régime* military power and dynastic prestige were paramount, there being, at bottom, no other basis for their rule. When overwhelming military disaster struck, therefore, sheer desperation propelled them in directions that they would not otherwise have contemplated, and thus it was that reform movements appeared that seemed to base themselves not on the patterns of the eighteenth century but on the liberalism and nationalism of the future. Setting aside the ephemeral Austrian experiment of 1809, the only real example that we have of such a development comes from Prussia, which in 1806 was struck by one of the greatest disasters ever to befall one of France's opponents. Here as nowhere else the army was identified with the state. And, not only was the Prussian army the foundation of the Prussian state and social system – for the position of nobility, burghers and peasants alike were essentially defined by military considerations – but it was still regarded as the finest in the world, victory over Napoleon being widely regarded as a foregone conclusion. When war came, however, it was a very different story. Whilst many individual formations fought well enough, at Jena and Auerstädt the main Prussian forces were routed in circumstances of the most discreditable confusion. Still worse, as the French pursuit fanned out across Germany, fortress after fortress surrendered without a fight, as did most of what was left of the army, often to mere handfuls of the enemy. Meanwhile, not only was there no popular resistance of any sort, but the local authorities everywhere collaborated with the French without demur (not that they were encouraged to do anything else, the governor of Berlin proclaiming, 'The first duty of the citizen is now to be quiet'[15]). Furthermore, when peace came in 1807 Prussia was stripped of all of her provinces west of the Elbe and all of her possessions in Poland, the result being that her population was reduced from 9,700,000 to 4,900,000. The cost in revenue was even greater, much of the territory left to Prussia being notoriously barren and infertile. In addition, she was placed under military occupation, prohibited from having an army larger than 42,000 men, and mulcted of the usual indemnity (which in this case was never even assigned set limits). And, last but not least, the rump state left to Frederick William III was strategically indefensible. Well might Clausewitz lament, 'God, what a spectacle for us!'[16]

15 *Cit.* R. Parkinson, *Clausewitz: a Biography* (London, 1970), p. 77.
16 *Cit. ibid.*, p. 85.

Under such blows even the most rigid of absolutists could not remain inert, there following a significant change of policy. Until 1806 Prussia's experience of reform had been very much that of Spain, Austria and Russia, except that, if anything, still less had been achieved. If this was the case, it was not for want of discussion. Unusually, there existed in Germany a flourishing military press which produced a plethora of journals, pamphlets and tactical manuals, many of which showed considerable awareness of the changes in warfare brought about by the Revolution. By far the most important influence in this development was a Hanoverian officer, Gerhard von Scharnhorst, who had become convinced of the importance of the Nation-in-Arms. Transferring to Prussian service in 1801, Scharnhorst immediately submitted a sheaf of proposals for reform to Frederick William, and helped form the so-called 'Military Society', a group of like-minded officers who met on a weekly basis to discuss new currents in military affairs. Aside from Scharnhorst, to name but a few of the most prominent, those involved included Carl von Clausewitz, Ludwig von Boyen, August von Gneisenau and Carl von Grolman. Needless to say, the Prussian army was subjected to scathing criticism, much emphasis being placed on the need for more flexible tactics and a greater proportion of light infantry, the logical corollary of such demands being better treatment of the common soldier, and, indeed, the creation of a soldiery imbued with patriotic enthusiasm. From here, of course, it was but a short step to the Nation-in-Arms, the reformers also putting forward plans for universal conscription and the formation of a citizen's militia, Scharnhorst, in particular, arguing that only thus could Prussia ensure her security. However, if the population as a whole was to fight, it must clearly be given something to fight for. Implicit in such ideas was therefore a wholesale programme of political and social reform encompassing better education, religious emancipation, political representation, the abolition of serfdom, the opening of the officer corps – hitherto almost entirely restricted to the *junker* – to all classes of society, and an end to all restrictions on occupation and the ownership of property.

Yet, although the number of officers involved in the Military Society grew rapidly (to a maximum of about two hundred), very little came of their deliberations. In the first place, many of its own members did not accept the reformist critique, Clausewitz, for example, complaining that his fellow, General Rüchel, 'was convinced that . . . determined Prussian troops, employing Frederician tactics, could overrun everything that had emerged from the unsoldierly French Revolution'.[17] Outside, meanwhile, the picture was one of complete gloom. Many officers reacted to the reformers with alarm and hostility, whilst, though aware of the need for change, the king was suspicious of anything that might subvert the social order or undermine the state. As a result little was done. The army already possessed twenty-seven specialist light-infantry battalions, and in October 1805 it was agreed that the third rank of each line battalion could be trained to fight as skirmishers; some improvement was made in the training of staff officers and the foundations laid for a permanent general staff; a local militia – the Provincial Reserve – was formed from a mixture of time-expired soldiers and men exempt from conscription; the regular army was given a first reserve by training more conscripts than were actually required; attempts were made to cut down on baggage; and on the very eve of war in 1806 the army was organised into permanent divisions. Yet none of this changed the nature of the army, and still less that of Prussia, whilst many of the changes were either never fully implemented, or were actively harmful, the new divisional system in particular being very poorly thought out.

Setting all this aside, the success of military reform in Prussia was as dependent as it was anywhere else on an improvement in the governance of the state. In this respect Prussia was particularly backward. Executive power was in the hands of the eight ministers who made up the General Directory of War and Domain, but the tasks of these men were apportioned in a most confusing fashion, with some dealing with all matters of state as they affected individual provinces and others dealing with one particular matter as it affected the whole kingdom. For historical reasons, meanwhile, the important province of Silesia had its own administration, whilst the army was effectively entirely independent (although the latter was theoretically covered by a department of the General Directory, in practice this had almost no power, responsibility for the military administration being shared by a supreme council of war and – unofficially – the king's own military advisers). At the head of the whole edifice was the king and his personal suite, the *kabinett*, the ministers of the General Directory having no authority of their own. As the state council that was supposed to draw all the threads of the system together rarely met, all this made for immense confusion, and all the more so as Frederick William combined a refusal to

17 Cit. C. E. White, *The Enlightened Soldier: Scharnhorst and the Militärische Gesellschaft in Berlin, 1801–1805* (New York, 1989), p. 75.

delegate authority with inordinate procrastination. Still worse, in the eyes of radical reformers, it also constituted yet another obstacle to the emergence of a patriotic spirit. As Baron vom Stein – later to become the most important civilian representative of the Prussian reform movement – put it, 'A necessary consequence of the incompleteness of the arrangement and the choice of persons is the dissatisfaction of the inhabitants of this country with the government, the decline of the sovereign's reputation in public opinion, and the necessity of an alteration.'[18] Stein's solution – the creation of an executive council of ministers and the rationalisation of the ministries themselves – was rejected, however, as were a variety of other similar proposals, Prussia therefore going to war unreformed.

As the French armies marched across Prussia, so the arguments of the reformers became unanswerable: aside from anything else, the claim that nobility was the guarantor of military prowess had been laid low by the capitulation without a fight of one impeccable aristocratic pedigree after another. Struggling to rebuild his battered forces in the remote fastness of East Prussia, Frederick William therefore issued a series of decrees that enjoined his generals to fight with a new vigour, advised the adoption of French tactics, announced condign punishment for all officers found to have behaved dishonourably, threatened draconian measures against any repetition of such conduct, and temporarily opened the officer corps to promotion from the ranks. So desperate was the king, indeed, that he even considered the formation of a mass army in East Prussia, though in the event a lack of arms and supplies led to the plan being abandoned, its only vestiges being a few small-scale partisan operations in Silesia.

With the coming of peace, improvisation was replaced by a sustained campaign of reform, the first step being the establishment of the so-called 'Military Reorganisation Commission' in July 1807. Although at first only two of its five members – Scharnhorst and Gneisenau – held reformist views, by the end of the year the commission had been entirely won over to the reformist cause. As to the direction that this should take, Scharnhorst and Gneisenau were in no doubts. As the former wrote to Clausewitz, in November 1807, 'We must inspire the nation with the feeling of self-dependence, give it the opportunity of acquiring self-knowledge and self-control; only so will it learn to respect itself and force respect

18 *Cit.* J. R. Seeley, *Life and Times of Stein* (Cambridge, 1878), I, p. 271.

from others.'[19] Gneisenau, too, is also worth quoting in this respect, especially as he makes plain the influence of Revolutionary France. Thus:

> These new times . . . require fresh action . . . . The Revolution has set into motion . . . the entire French people . . . on an equal social and fiscal basis, thereby . . . abolishing the former . . . balance of power. If the other states wish to re-establish this balance, they must . . . use these same resources.[20]

If the reformers needed any further encouragement in such views, it was provided by the insurrection that broke out in Spain in 1808. Accepting the bombastic outpourings of Spanish propaganda with regard to its success at complete face value, they believed that it could be emulated in Germany. Thus Gneisenau dreamed of repeating the feats of the defender of Zaragoza, José Palafox, who had fought off the French for two months at the head of the armed citizenry; 'insurrectionary committees' were organised to prepare the way for revolt, and Stein and Scharnhorst pressed Frederick William to sanction a general uprising in the event of a war between Austria and France and even discussed his overthrow should he stand in their way. In the event all this came to nothing – Stein himself was dismissed after the French intercepted a most incautious letter relating to plans for revolt, whilst the series of insurrections attempted in Westphalia in 1809 proved a fiasco – but, be that as it may, the Spanish war remained a constant source of inspiration, Gneisenau and Clausewitz dreaming up further plans of insurrection in August 1811.

To discuss the impact of the Spanish revolution is to anticipate events, however, for in fact reform was already well under way before it broke out. As might be expected, attention was first concentrated on the performance of the Prussian officer corps in 1806, a lengthy enquiry being conducted into this subject. Superficially, the results were dramatic: 208 officers were cashiered, and many others compulsorily retired or placed on the inactive list – of 142 generals, 885 field officers, and some 6,500 junior officers, the numbers retained were respectively twenty-two, 185 and 1,584. Although a useful pretext was provided by the French-enforced reduction in the size of the army, all this suited the reformers' views

19 *Cit.* Seeley, *Stein*, II, p. 117.
20 *Cit.* White, *Scharnhorst*, p. 132.

on the officer corps: the *junker* were notoriously ill-educated, whilst twenty-five per cent of regimental and battalion commanders and fifty-four per cent of generals were aged over sixty, the consequence being entrenched conservatism and a general want of dynamism. However, what was needed was not just a thorough purge. For the reformers it was axiomatic that the officer corps' status as a preserve of the nobility should be ended, for only thus could war be made an affair of the nation (prior to 1806 it had been argued that only *junker* could make good officers, the proportion of commoners having been reduced to less than ten per cent). Angered by the events of 1806, Frederick William made no objection and on 6 August 1808 an order was duly issued to the effect that henceforward access to the officer corps, and promotion within it, were to depend entirely on merit without regard to social status. To buttress this system – which required that all appointments and promotions should in normal times be decided by examinations – two schools for officer cadets, three more for commissioned officers, and a general staff academy were established under the supervision of a single director of military education. Needless to say, erstwhile members of the Military Society played a prominent role in teaching, one of the lecturers at the staff academy being Carl von Clausewitz. With officers better trained, moreover, a more modern system of tactics was possible: instead of the rigid Frederician battle line, in July 1809 the army adopted a flexible mix of skirmishers, lines and columns.

The interest of the reformers was not just confined to the officer corps, but also extended to the rank and file. No longer were soldiers to be mere automata driven to fight by fear of the lash, nor conditions in the army so severe that the population would not willingly join its ranks. In August 1808, then, new disciplinary regulations greatly reduced the incidence of corporal and capital punishment, and enjoined greater personal respect for the common soldier. Drill was simplified, training improved, and marksmanship, initiative and self-reliance encouraged. Meanwhile, the introduction of French-style tactics in itself lessened the need for the incessant drilling and brutalisation of the Frederician army. At the same time, the new treatment afforded to the common soldier in theory laid the basis for a much increased use of skirmishing: whereas before 1806 this had on the whole been left to trusted specialists, all line-infantrymen now began to be trained to fight in open order.

All these changes in training and discipline, however, were but a preliminary step to a far more radical change. For men such as Stein the ultimate goal was the creation of a Nation-in-Arms, this in theory implying that all Prussian citizens, regardless of their rank and social station, should be liable to military service on an equal basis. As yet, however, this was not achieved: once the desperate crisis of 1807 was past, Frederick William's instinctive opposition to arming the people, and, indeed, to anything that might undermine the regular army, resurfaced, whilst the definitive peace treaty with France – the treaty of Paris of September 1808 – specifically prohibited the organisation of a militia. Though the reformers continued to repeat their demands for such a force thereafter, Frederick William remained adamant, the result being that the old cantonal system was left untouched. All that was done, in fact, was to release small numbers of trained soldiers on furlough so as to create a trained reserve and allow fresh conscripts to be trained without breaking the terms of the treaty of Paris (which limited the army to 42,000 men). In no way did this process – the so-called *krümper* system – create the basis of a Nation-in-Arms, however, no more 13,500 extra troops having been created in this fashion by 1810.

A further factor in the failure of the reformers to obtain universal conscription was Stein's sudden removal from office on the orders of Napoleon in November 1808. An imperial knight from western Germany, Stein had entered Prussian service in 1780. Becoming a minister in 1804, he introduced a number of major innovations, forming a bureau of statistics, revising the salt monopoly, reducing the number of internal customs barriers, tightening control of the national bank, and eroding the fiscal privileges of the nobility, whilst in 1806 he had, as we have seen, proposed a complete reworking of the state machine. Following the disasters of Jena and Auerstädt Frederick William offered him the foreign ministry, but Stein would only accept on condition that the king abjured his personal *kabinett* in favour of a responsible council of ministers and in consequence fell from favour. In the catastrophic aftermath of Tilsit matters were very different: deciding that he was indispensable, in October 1807 Frederick William made him de facto chief minister, the chief idea, as Stein put it, being 'to arouse a moral, religious and patriotic spirit in the nation . . . and to seize the first favourable opportunity to begin the . . . struggle'.[21]

---

21 *Cit.* G. S. Ford, *Stein and the Era of Reform in Prussia, 1807–1815* (Princeton, 1922), pp. 122–3.

Such words certainly suited the mood of Stein himself. A convinced German patriot, he was determined to overturn France's hegemony. In order for this to be achieved, Prussia had not only to be made more efficient, but the people drawn into the workings of the state. As he wrote in the political programme that he penned whilst out of office in June 1807 (the so-called Nassau Memorandum):

> My own official experience . . . has given me a deep and lively conviction of the great advantage of properly constituted estates, and I regard them as a powerful instrument for strengthening the government through . . . giving the forces of the nation a free activity and directing them to the public good . . .[22]

From the moment that he came to power, then, Stein busied himself with the reordering of the state. Beginning at the top, government was much simplified by the creation of five new ministries (including for the first time a ministry of war) and a ministerial council. At a lower level, meanwhile, Stein concentrated on involving the propertied classes in the administration through the creation or revivification of representative institutions, seeing this as a means of instilling not only greater patriotism but also greater efficiency. By the propertied classes, moreover, he did not just mean the nobility, for Stein was determined to bring forward the whole nation and was in any case inclined to regard the *junker* as selfish and ignorant. As he wrote in the Nassau Memorandum, the voice should be heard of 'significant property owners of all types'.[23] Ultimately, such representation should operate on a national level, but for the time being a host of factors – the opposition of the king and the nobility and the need to avoid provoking French suspicions of a national revival – led to this aspect of affairs being neglected. Yet it was in any case clear to Stein that a national assembly could not come straight away – as he wrote to his fellow statesman, Hardenberg, 'The transition from the old state of affairs to a new order must not be too sudden . . . Men must be gradually accustomed to act on their own initiative before they are . . . entrusted with great issues.'[24] Initially, then, Stein's focus was more parochial. At a

22 *Cit.* Seeley, *Stein*, I, p. 315.

23 *Cit.* R. Berdahl, *The Politics of the Prussian Nobility: the Development of a Conservative Ideology, 1770–1848* (Princeton, 1988), p. 111.

24 *Cit.* W. Simon, *The Failure of the Prussian Reform Movement, 1807–1819* (New York, 1971), p. 30.

provincial level he intended that the existing diets – which rarely met – should be convened on a regular basis and bolstered by representatives of the peasants and burghers, but for the time being this could be only done in East Prussia, the rest of the country being occupied by the French. Thus in February 1808 the traditional noble diet, augmented by some representatives of the free peasants, who for historical reasons formed a substantial body in the region, was summoned to approve plans to meet the French indemnity by the alienation of significant areas of domain land and the imposition of a general income tax. A year later the Kurmark's diet also met, but, with Stein now out of office, no concessions were made to wider representation, the *junker* remaining firmly in control. As a result, the only area in which his ideas made real progress was that of local government. In the course of the eighteenth century the towns and cities had lost all their rights to self-government, being administered by councils appointed by the General Directory. To Stein, of course, all this was anathema, and, although he does not at first seem to have taken any action on the matter, when plans were evolved in Königsberg (Kaliningrad) for a reform of city government, he fell upon them with enthusiasm, the result being the so-called 'City Ordinance' of 19 November 1808, which provided for the creation of elected local councils and the restoration of civic autonomy.

For all that Stein remains the most well-known figure in the civil aspects of the Prussian reform movement, he was not directly responsible for its most famous achievement – the emancipation of the serfs. On the contrary, the initial pressure here came from the unlikely figure of Frederick William, who was convinced that serfdom was economically indefensible, and had already secured its abolition in the crown lands and the territories annexed from Poland in the 1790s. Much alarmed by the fact that serfdom was on the point of abolition in the neighbouring Grand Duchy of Warsaw, he was now in a position to go much further, and by the time that Stein came to power the 'Edict of Emancipation' was ready for promulgation. Introduced with Stein's full approval on 9 October 1807, this laid down that, from Martinmas (i.e. 11 November) 1810, all peasants would become personally free, that all land could now be freely bought and sold (so that, say, nobles could acquire peasant land, and the bourgeoisie noble land), and that all social limitations on occupation should be lifted. At the same time, to all intents and purposes all distinctions between the bourgeoisie and the peasantry were abolished, so that Prussian society now consisted simply of nobles and commoners. Much praise has traditionally been heaped upon this document, but in fact its limitations were numerous, especially as serfdom had not just been a system of exploitation. If the peasants owed a variety of fees and services to the *junker* and were tied to the land – a fundamental requirement of the army's system of recruitment – they also enjoyed considerable security of tenure and were further protected by customary stipulations that their lords should repair their dwellings, provide them with assistance in times of hardship, and supply them with seed and implements. Some of the proponents of emancipation had wanted to sweep all this away, but Stein, who genuinely wanted to protect the peasants as property-owners, secured a compromise that maintained existing peasant rights unless permission was granted for their abrogation by the provincial authorities. Yet the law did not lay down the conditions under which this might be done, and in addition failed to establish which services the peasants owed in consequence of their personal serfdom and which they owed by virtue of their tenancies. Nor was anything said about manorial jurisdiction or the abolition of other noble privileges. Much clarification being needed, in February 1808 Stein issued a supplementary decree providing guidance on some of these issues, only to be forced to make further concessions: though he again strove to protect the peasants, the best that he could do was to limit the circumstances under which land might be taken from them and try to establish some compensation for its loss.

In so far as the peasantry were concerned, then, the fall of Stein represented a considerable blow. Whether it made much difference to the direction taken by the reform movement is a moot point, however, for few of his fellow reformers had ever shared his social radicalism. For most of the military reformers, in particular, it was axiomatic that officers should be gentlemen, and soldiers peasants, artisans or labourers. Prepared though they were to agree that the bourgeoisie might have as much right to be regarded as gentlemen as the *junker*, there was never any suggestion that the nobility should serve in the rank and file. Nobles in any case continued to be treated on a favourable basis, official instructions to the new examining boards implying that such qualities as 'propriety in his deportment' were as important in a prospective officer as 'knowledge and scholarship'.[25] Meanwhile, the bourgeoisie were also to be favoured: in a memorandum of 31 August 1807

---

25 *Cit.* G. Craig, *The Politics of the Prussian Army, 1640–1945* (Oxford, 1955), p. 44.

Scharnhorst suggested that all able-bodied men who could meet the cost of arming and clothing themselves should be enrolled in a citizens' militia, and that those who could not should form the professional army, the inference being that the propertied would enjoy better conditions of service than the commonalty. As to the idea that the whole of the people should be armed, Scharnhorst specifically argued against the creation of a militia that involved the lower classes, whilst Clausewitz after the war frankly admitted that arming the people had been highly dangerous.

With the fall of Stein, then, if the Prussian reform movement did not collapse, it certainly acquired a new direction, developments now revolving around the figure of Baron Karl von Hardenberg. Appointed chancellor in June 1810 after a brief period of 'caretaker' government, Hardenberg was a devotee of absolutism who had little time for Stein's dreams of involving the people, or at least the whole of the propertied classes, in government. Taking first of all the question of popular representation, the new chancellor regarded this with great suspicion, warning Frederick William that 'such matters must be handled with the greatest caution to ensure that popular participation remains compatible with a monarchical constitution and to prevent it from degenerating into something revolutionary'.[26] Although he formed an 'assembly of notables' in December 1810 composed of sixty-four representatives of the bureaucracy, the nobility and the peasantry, and later a 'provisional national assembly', which sat from 1812 to 1815, he was determined that neither was to be allowed any authority, their sole purpose being to assist in the execution of his plans (indeed, even that role was frequently denied to them: so unimportant was the latter in Hardenberg's eyes that it was rarely consulted about even the most important measures). For Hardenberg, in short, the goals of reform were very different, their real purpose being to weld Prussia into a centralised state rather than a collection of provinces, and to break the power of the *junker* (by 1810, as we shall see, noble resistance to the reform movement had become extremely powerful). Meanwhile, though Hardenberg certainly wished to subordinate the *junker* to the state, as a doctrinaire economic liberal, and, indeed, a large landowner, he was inclined still further to erode protection of the peasantry.

So important is the question of emancipation to the Prussian reform movement that Hardenberg's actions in this respect must be

26 Cit. Simon, *Failure of the Prussian Reform Movement*, p. 33.

examined in some detail. In essence the edicts of 1807 and 1808 had plunged the country into turmoil. Much anger had already been caused by the threat to the nobility posed by the reform of the army, which *junker* such as Yorck put down to 'feeble yielding to the view of . . . cosmopolites'.[27] Watered down though they were, the emancipation edicts provoked general fury, this being all the better articulated by the fact that the political vacuum brought about by the French occupation had of necessity revitalised the nobility's county and provincial assemblies. Thus, petition after petition reached the government to the effect that the state had no right to interfere in the rights of property, that the *junker* would be ruined, and that the fall of the nobility would produce the downfall of the state. Protest though they did, however, many of the *junker* also made use of the opportunities provided by the legislation to dispossess their peasants, whilst in some cases simultaneously trying to suppress news of emancipation altogether, the result being that large numbers of peasants rose in revolt, especially in Silesia. Intermittent outbreaks of resistance continued till at least 1811, on several occasions the disturbances being so severe that both French and Prussian troops had to be called in to restore order. Yet the nobility were by no means cowed. Determined to secure his aim of subordinating the nobility to common institutions and at the same time to rationalise the state's finances and maximise its revenue, in October 1810 Hardenberg introduced the far-reaching 'Finance Edict'. In brief, this imposed heavy duties on luxury goods, eliminated all exemptions from the land tax, subjected all property owners to taxation on an equal basis, and abolished the guilds and all other monopolies, including those that the nobility enjoyed with regard to milling, brewing and distilling. The response being a fresh wave of protest, Hardenberg gave way in the area that mattered least to him, a new edict of 14 September 1811 in essence establishing that non-hereditary peasant leaseholders – the majority of the erstwhile serfs – could become freeholders, and thus relieve themselves of all further labour obligations, by ceding half their land to their lords and agreeing to pay over a further sum in either cash or kind in accordance with a further process of 'regulation'. Needless to say, all of this was extremely unfavourable to the peasants, who found themselves stripped of large quantities of land and were often left with plots that were too small to support a family. Even this was not enough for the *junker* – who objected to

27 *Cit.* Simon, *Failure of the Prussian Reform Movement*, p. 154.

the very principle of peasant proprietors, claimed that the lower classes had become disrespectful, and protested that it was really the nobility that had been deprived of property rather than the peasantry – but it is clear that the ideals that had originally underpinned emancipation were now dead.

To Hardenberg, however, this was of little account, whilst it certainly did not imply that he had abandoned the cause of reform. On the contrary the Finance Edict had given notice that he was determined to press on with a programme of classic enlightened absolutism that would sweep away corporate privilege, and in the process unlock financial and economic resources that were desperately needed by the bankrupt Prussian state. With the guilds and the provinces already overthrown, on 11 March 1812 the Jews were admitted to full civil rights, in the process being stripped of all status as a separate community (it should be noted in this context that the aim of Hardenburg, and his minister of religions, Wilhelm von Humboldt, was effectively to turn the Jews into Germans of Jewish faith). More importantly, perhaps, Hardenberg now at last moved against the nobility's administrative powers and patrimonial jurisdiction, which so far had been left untouched. Thus, the 'Gendarmerie Edict' of 30 July 1812 abolished the county assemblies of nobility which had until then constituted the heart of local government, deprived the *junker* of their right to appoint the local clergy, scrapped the old manorial courts, and established an entirely new judicial and administrative system that effectively stripped the *junker* of all their traditional functions. In the event, however, none of this saw the light of day: so great was the opposition that the new edict had still not been implemented when war broke out again in 1813, whereupon such was the need to conciliate the *junker* that it was promptly abandoned.

So far as the Prussian reform movement is concerned, one must conclude that, though arguably far more effective, once Stein had been dismissed from office, it was not in fact so very different from the movements we have examined elsewhere, under Hardenberg in particular becoming essentially congruent with the same enlightened absolutism that lay at the heart of reform in Spain, Austria and Russia. This is not to say, of course, that there were no changes from the patterns of the past. Unlike their conservative opponents, most of the leading figures of the reform movement saw Prussia as a figurehead that would inspire reform in the other German states and one day lead them to unification, whilst, willingly or unwillingly, they were prepared to mobilise the entire nation to achieve their goals. The exception, however, was Hardenberg whose thinking was always directed far more towards Prussia than towards Germany as a whole. Seeing reform in traditional eighteenth-century terms, he presided over an administration whose goals were very different from that of Stein, whilst proving no more able than the latter ultimately to overcome the resistance of the privileged classes.

THE SURVIVAL OF THE OLD ORDER

To conclude, then, the Revolutionary and Napoleonic Wars stimulated a considerable wave of reformist activity amongst the various monarchies that at one time or another opposed the French: whether it was in Spain under Manuel de Godoy, Austria under the Archduke Charles, Russia under Alexander I, or Prussia under Stein and Hardenberg, the massive increase in French power consequent upon the Revolution and Napoleon provoked a more or less desperate attempt to keep pace with developments west of the Rhine. In the ensuing turbulence, much prominence was secured by the repeated calls that were made for the French to be overthrown by means of a 'people's war' and by the efforts of such men as Stein and Speransky to involve a wider spectrum of the population in the affairs of state, the result being that it has been widely argued that the French were being resisted with their own weapons, or, in short, that the *ancien régime* had itself been revolutionised.

In fact, the truth was rather different. In Spain such ideas were specifically rejected at a very early date by the reformers themselves, whilst in Russia Speransky's desire to reach out to the whole of the propertied classes was never allowed to come to fruition. Briefly given their head in both Austria and Prussia, meanwhile, the minority of genuine radicals soon found that they were excluded from power or simply disregarded, the reform movements in fact following an agenda that was entirely traditional. As witness the steady erosion of peasant rights in Prussia, the failure of Scharnhorst and Gneisenau to secure universal military service, and the lukewarm use made by the Austrian authorities of the *landwehr*, everywhere the idea of an appeal to the people came to be eclipsed. In general, the goal of reform was to strengthen the power of the state, to rationalise the workings of government, to secure greater revenue, to humble the privileged corporations, and to develop more efficient armies, there being nothing here that would have been startling to any of the monarchs of the eighteenth century. In so far as 'the people' were to play a role at all, it was to be through the extension of traditional systems of conscription that bore no relation to the Nation-in-Arms, the prospect that they might be armed en masse, or, still worse, that they might take up arms on their own account stirring fear in the breasts even of the more radical reformers.

What we witness in the Napoleonic era is, in short, the last, and frequently not very impressive, gasp of enlightened absolutism (in Austria and, to a lesser extent, Spain and Russia, monarchs in fact refused to emulate the radicalism of their predecessors). Herein lies an interesting paradox, however. The reforms of Alexander I, the Prussian reform movement, and the Archduke Charles have traditionally been seen as an attempt to defeat France with her own weapons – in other words, to fight 'people's war' with 'people's war'. Faulty though this parallel is, another such mirror image may be inserted in its place. If Napoleon was not a man of the Revolution, but rather a terrible reincarnation of Louis XIV, fire was, in fact, still fought with fire. Confronted with enlightened absolutism writ large, the emperor's opponents sought a similar improvement in their own states, and in the case of Austria, Russia and Prussia did just enough to open the way to ultimate victory. Whilst certain individual reformers may have been disappointed with the end result, to speak of the 'failure' of reform is therefore to misinterpret its objectives.

7 REVOLUTION AND THE FRENCH

TRANSFORMATION AT THE PERIPHERY

> Spaniards! The word 'Fatherland' must no longer be an . . . empty word for you. In . . . your hearts it must signify the place where law and custom are inviolate, a place where talent is allowed to flourish and virtue is rewarded. Indeed, Spaniards, the day will soon dawn when the monarchy is given a solid and lasting foundation . . .. You will then possess basic rights which will hinder . . . the growth of arbitrary power and foster law and order . . .[1]

If we wish to discover radical social and political change amongst Napoleon's opponents, we should not look to the great powers. Whilst adopting various measures designed to strengthen the state, Austria, Prussia and Russia in practice made few concessions to liberalism or nationalism, the Old Order emerging from the wars fundamentally unchanged. For evidence of genuine political upheaval we must look elsewhere, above all to Spain, Sweden and Sicily, in all of which the Napoleonic Wars opened the way for revolution, the establishment of constitutional monarchies, and the implementation of more or less wide-ranging programmes of liberal reform. At the heart of this process was constant reference to the wishes of the people and, in Spain especially, to the concept of 'people's war'. Spain, of course, was the seat of the famous *guerrilla*, Sweden witnessed a considerable amount of irregular resistance in Finland, whilst Sicily witnessed real fears that the people would sooner fight for the French than for the Bourbons. Whereas the Prussian reformers had been concerned to draw the population into the struggle by means of political and social reform, in these peripheral states the position was therefore reversed, the involvement of the populace in the struggle acting as a justification

---

1 Proclamation of the Junta Supreme Central, 26 October 1808, *cit.* W. Hargreaves-Mawdesley (ed.), *Spain under the Bourbons, 1700–1833: a Collection of Documents* (London, 1973), I, p. 223.

for change. Yet in each case 'the people' were but poorly rewarded for their efforts, the real beneficiaries of liberal reform being élites – whether noble or bourgeois – who seized the initiative and pursued their own interests. Liberal though they may have been, the Napoleonic revolutions were therefore anything but popular.

SPAIN: MEDIAEVALISTS AND LIBERALS

The first state to be affected by a crisis that acted as a catalyst for fundamental reorganisation was Spain. Here the insurrection of May 1808 was of its very nature an act of revolution, amounting, as it did, to a denial of the rights of the Bourbons to dispose of the throne without reference to the Spanish people. Such an action being argued to have no legitimacy, it followed that sovereignty had reverted to the people and that the latter had the inalienable right to determine its own destiny. Though traditionalists might argue that sovereignty had been resumed solely to restore it into the hands of Ferdinand VII, on this point there was general agreement. As even Gaspar Melchor de Jovellanos, who throughout remained a bitter opponent of liberal arguments, frankly admitted:

> The people . . . created [the juntas] in open insurrection, and I know that in tranquil times this right cannot be conceded . . . without destroying the foundations of the constitution . . .. But to deny this right . . . to a people . . . basely delivered into the hands of a tyrant whom they hated . . . would . . . be a monstrous political error . . ..[2]

Needless to say, the voices of the various foci of genuine liberalism scattered across Spain were fully in agreement. On 22 September 1808, for example, the *Semanario Patriótico* – the organ of the liberal poet, Manuel Quintana – declared, 'Only the nation can . . . reconstruct the executive power left in a disorganized state by the absence of the king.'[3] This being the case, it followed that some form of popular representation was essential. Initially this want was supplied by the thirteen provincial juntas

2   G. M. de Jovellanos, *Memoria en que se rebaten las calumnias divulgadas contra los individuos de la Junta Central del Reino, y se da razón de la conducta y opiniones del autor desde que recobró su libertad* in *Obras publicadas e inéditas de D. Gaspar Melchor de Jovellanos,* ed. Biblioteca de Autores Españoles (Madrid, 1963), I, p. 509.
3   *Cit.* G. Lovett, *Napoleon and the Birth of Modern Spain* (New York, 1965), II, p. 422.

which had sprung up to head the insurrection in those areas of Spain that were free of the French, these being composed of a *mélange* of representatives of the administrative, military and ecclesiastical institutions of the Old Order – now acting as representatives not of the monarch, of course, but of the people – as well as representatives of the local landed and commercial oligarchy. Significantly, where attempts were made to challenge this new orthodoxy, they collapsed in failure, the explicitly legitimist dictatorship established by the Captain-General of Old Castile, Gregorio García de la Cuesta, being quickly overthrown. Moreover, not only was it agreed that the people were sovereign, but it was also clear that reform was essential. Whatever their other views, all Spaniards could agree that no Godoy, who was now seen not only as an incompetent wastrel, but also as a traitor, could ever be allowed to trouble Spain again, and, further, that all traces of his rule – generally referred to as 'ministerial despotism' – should be swept away, this in turn implying that some curb should be placed on the free will of the monarch. Then, too, there were the demands of the war, although this problem was not at first particularly prominent, being obscured by the wild euphoria generated by such early Spanish successes as the capture of an entire French army at Bailén, which were wildly exaggerated and mistakenly ascribed to popular heroism.

When the Junta Supreme Central – essentially a committee of all the provincial juntas – assembled at Aranjuez as the new government of Spain in September 1808, it could not but reflect these perceptions, the first proclamation that it issued promising that its objectives would include economic, fiscal, legal, educational and constitutional reform. Such was the vagueness of this document that virtually all educated Spaniards could unite behind it, but in fact, as was shortly to be revealed, the pressure for reform embraced very different perspectives and objectives. After much discussion, and an impassioned public debate facilitated by the decision of the Junta Central to allow a very wide degree of press freedom, it was agreed that the obvious way forward was to summon a national assembly, or *cortes*, but there was no agreement as to the form that this should take, the alternatives being to resurrect the traditional estates or to adopt some new model of representation. In June 1809 the Junta therefore invited the submission of ideas on the form that the new assembly might take, and, indeed, on the wider question of reform in general. In the event, some 150 answers were received from a wide variety of institutions and individuals, these revealing a substantial degree of disunity. Almost all were agreed on the need for some kind of reform, most called for the establishment of a *cortes*, and, interestingly in view of the general antipathy with which the army had been regarded prior to 1808, many expressed particular interest in changes in the military estate, there being widespread agreement on the need for the subordination of the military to the civil power, the exclusion of the army from the administration, the gainful employment of the troops in peacetime, the opening of the officer corps to all classes of society, the introduction of universal military service, and the suppression of the army's numerous privileges. Yet beyond these points of consensus, it is clear that opinion was deeply divided, at least three different positions revealing themselves, albeit in a manner that gave rise to much confusion.

Of these three positions, the most coherently expressed and argued was that of the liberals. Underpinning this was a classic combination of political perception and economic interest. Under the influence of Rousseau and Adam Smith, a growing minority of the Spanish educated classes had come to argue the need for a thorough renovation of society, the starting point of their theory being that in the Middle Ages Spain had enjoyed an age of liberty – and hence felicity – which had then been eclipsed by centuries of despotism. To restore this 'golden age' it was necessary to take account of the basic rules that the Enlightenment had shown to govern human conduct – first that all men were employed in the pursuit of happiness, second that the only possible measure of happiness was material wealth, and third that all men were created equal. From this it followed that the role of government was to create a society in which prosperity could be pursued by all men on an equal basis, this in turn requiring that all men should enjoy equality before the law and have the absolute right freely to acquire, own and dispose of property as they saw fit. Given the War of Independence, however, all this was doubly important, for the liberals argued that the people had risen against the French not to sustain the rights of despotism, but to recover their own liberty. As Quintana put it, 'To suppose that the Spaniards . . . had no intention of gaining any internal advantages by such prodigious efforts . . . is an absurd dream.'[4]

According to liberal rhetoric, Spain owed such success as she had won in the war to the people, from which it followed, firstly,

4 *Cit.* J. Aymes, *La guerra de la independencia en España, 1808–1814* (Madrid, 1975), p. 26.

that the privileged estates had lost their right to pre-eminence, and, secondly, that reform was the key to victory, every defeat being blamed on failure to maintain its momentum, and thus to keep popular devotion at white heat. But reform was not just necessary for the present, but also for the future. Thus:

> The Spaniards are fighting to be independent, to be free. And, for these . . . objectives to be achieved, is it enough for them to . . . face death with serenity and exterminate the French? Assuming that the latter are expelled . . . if we did not establish a system of . . . just, wise and beneficent laws, if we did not banish from amongst ourselves the multitude of errors . . . that have reduced us to the level of animals, if we did not augment the nation's wealth by diminishing the unproductive classes . . . would we be able to . . . feel ourselves safe from . . . the usurper, or any other power that sought to impose a tyranny upon us?[5]

In *ancien-régime* Spain, however, liberty was an impossibility, for extensive quantities of territory were held in perpetuity by the Church and the nobility, which also enjoyed a monopoly of direct entry to the officer corps, whilst freedom of economic opportunity was restricted by the guilds. Meanwhile, too, there was no semblance of equality before the law, with the Church, the nobility, the army, the military orders, the guilds and the Basque provinces all enjoying their own *fueros* and large areas still being governed by seigneurial jurisdiction. What was required was therefore the destruction of all forms of privilege, the creation of a free market in land with all its attendant property rights, the sale of the lands of the Church, the abolition of all restrictions on economic activity, and the establishment of a unitary state. Also vital was a written constitution that would guarantee basic freedoms, impose limits on the power of the monarchy, and provide for the representation of the people on the basis of proportionality rather than of privilege (the old estates would therefore be swept away in favour of a unicameral assembly). Finally, the Church would have to be reformed so as to reduce the power of the papacy and purge it of the Inquisition and the religious orders, thereby making it both more 'national' and less oppressive and burdensome.

Thus far Spanish liberalism appears a model of patriotic altruism, but in fact it dovetailed neatly with the interests of sub-

---

5 *Diario Redactor de Sevilla*, 9 December 1812, n.p., Servicio Histórico Militar, Colección Documental del Fraile, CXXXII.

stantial elements of the propertied classes. For all their exaltation of the people, few even of the most radical could conceive of their direct participation in politics. Products of a cultured élite, the liberals were terrified of the unruly mobs who had overthrown the Old Order in 1808 and were determined to defend private property, their arguments being a reflection of powerful economic interests. Thus, by 1808 Spain was witnessing the emergence of a prosperous oligarchy of non-noble notables. Reinforced by the influx of wealth brought by the commercial boom of the late eighteenth century, these *nouveaux riches* had sought to capitalise upon their prosperity through the acquisition of status, land and office, and had benefited greatly from Godoy's disamortisation of large quantities of Church land in the period leading up to 1808, whilst also acquiring substantial interests as government creditors (it was in large part their money that had financed the large issues of paper currency on which the favourite had increasingly relied). Clearly, then, the creation of a free market in land acquired a new significance, for in the Spain of 1808 it implied the entrance into the market of enormous territories that had never been available before. Spain, in short, was to be reordered for the benefit of a new élite, the much-lauded Spanish people actually having little stake in the future for which they were supposedly fighting.

Between this programme and that of the second position revealed in the debates of 1808 and 1809 there was a surprising amount of common ground despite the fact that the latter may essentially be described as legitimist. Prior to the uprising Spain had not been the backward state of legend but a vibrant and reformist monarchy in which successive Bourbon rulers had sought to foment economic development, stimulate the growth of public knowledge, rationalise the administration, centralise the state at the expense of the privileged orders, provinces and corporations, and subordinate the Church to the throne. In the course of the uprising of 1808 many of the ministers and officials who had been active in this tradition had given their allegiance to Joseph Bonaparte, but some yet chose the Patriot cause, the most notable being Jovellanos and the aged Conde de Floridablanca. With the death of the latter in December 1808, the chief proponent of this position became Jovellanos, and it was largely due to his influence as one of the representatives for Asturias that the Junta Central acquired the reputation for conservatism with which it has ever since been burdened. Yet in fact Jovellanos shared many of the liberals' perceptions. In terms of economics, for example, Jovellanos was heavily influenced by the work of Adam Smith, and he had therefore condemned such phenomena as entail, the prohibition of enclosure in favour of the rights of pastoralists, and the survival of communal property. With regard to religion, meanwhile, he was very much a Jansenist, demanding the hispanisation of the Church and the abolition of the Inquisition (or at least the transfer of its powers to the episcopate). Like the liberals, too, he opposed provincial privilege, and, above all, he was deeply committed to progress in the realms of science and education, calling for freedom of the press, a reduction of illiteracy, and the wider study of agronomy and economics. Where Jovellanos differed from the liberals, however, was in his political analysis. Terrified by the French and Spanish revolutions alike and unable to conceive of a society that could function without the guidance of the nobility and the Church, he never argued for the abolition of entail per se but merely suggested its limitation. At the same time, still less did he desire a new concentration of the land in the hands of wealthy oligarchs, looking rather to the creation of a settled and prosperous peasantry. Faced by the events of 1808 he had perforce concurred in the resumption of sovereignty by the nation, but he had only done so with the greatest reluctance, and now demanded that the *cortes* should meet by estates, or at least preserve some form of separate representation for the old élites, whilst opposing the radical programme of political and institutional reform proposed by the liberals: for him, in fact, Spain already had a constitution in the form of the fundamental laws that she had inherited from the mediaeval era, all that it was necessary to do to abolish despotism being to restate them.

Cautious though this programme was, it remained a marked contrast with that of the traditionalist party who now emerged as the third main element in Patriot politics, though in fact they had already made their mark before the uprising in the coup that had brought down Charles IV and Godoy at Aranjuez. Thus, the aristocrats amongst the court cabal that had assembled around the future Ferdinand VII had seen support for him as a means of hamstringing the monarchy, the weak and vapid crown prince essentially being envisaged as a puppet who would dance to the tune of the grandees. With all their gains swept away by Napoleon's overthrow of the Bourbons, they had sought to revive them by fighting the French – in Zaragoza, José Palafox, a young guards officer who had been involved in the Aranjuez mutiny, staged a revolt and set himself up as dictator of Aragón in the apparent hope that the entire country would rally behind his leadership. Outflanked by the simultaneous revolt of the rest of the country, Palafox's gamble proved a failure, but he was by no means an isolated figure, substantial elements of the clergy and nobility being bitterly hostile to regalism, disamortisation and the decline of aristocratic influence. Throughout Spain, this group from the start strove to interpret the rising in terms of a crusade for Church and king, thereby short-circuiting arguments in favour of radical change. Nor did they limit themselves to mere propaganda, indulging in a series of intrigues against the liberals that culminated in the overthrow of the Junta Central in January 1810.

In the event the establishment by the collapsing Junta Central of a regency of its own choice in Cádiz outmanoeuvred the conspirators, but the political programme that they espoused had by no means been dispelled. As exemplar of its many advocates, we have the figure of Juan Pérez Villamil, a senior official of the admiralty. Though as much enamoured of popular heroism as any liberal – following the Dos de Mayo, for example, he had issued from the village of Móstoles a stirring call for a national uprising – for Pérez Villamil the past was still valid, liberty (and, indeed, a constitution) lying in the existence of the fundamental laws inherited from the past. Far from being overthrown by the introduction of dangerous foreign innovations – it was a constant theme of traditionalists that the ideas of the liberals were drawn from the French Revolution – these should rather be reinforced. We thus return to the position adopted by Jovellanos, but, for all that, it would be a mistake to believe that Pérez Villamil was in agreement with him. On the contrary, for Pérez Villamil and his fellows, given the threat that it represented to corporate privilege, the royal reformism that the erstwhile minister represented was just as much a cancer as the ideas of the liberals, the solution being to turn back the clock: in 1810, for example, we find the future traditionalist deputy, Francisco Borrull, not only defending the rights of the nobility but also demanding the restitution of the Valencian *fueros* overthrown by Phillip V in 1707.

With Spain in a state of the most utter confusion, it was not until the convocation of the *cortes* in September 1810 that a measure of order was restored to the country's political affairs through the triumph of the liberals. Often attributed to the fact that circumstances had forced the new assembly to meet in the port city of Cádiz – in January 1810 the French had occupied the whole of Andalucía – this development rested above all on simple muddle.

Few of the priests, lawyers, functionaries, writers, academics and army officers who constituted the majority of the deputies were strongly committed to any one of the three basic political positions outlined above, but all were agreed on the need for reform. At the same time, meanwhile, one cannot but be struck by the extraordinary amount of common ground that existed even between the liberals and the mediaevalists. Thus, all shades of opinion coincided in defending the sovereignty of the people, denouncing 'ministerial despotism', and calling for a return to a mythical mediaeval 'golden age', the consequence being that the revolutionary nature of the liberal position was simply not apparent. With the liberals further assisted by the fact that they alone had a measure of political organisation, their leaders having often known one another for many years, not to mention the favourable circumstances afforded by Cádiz, which possessed a flourishing press and had always been a centre of the Spanish Enlightenment, their triumph was assured.

Thus it was that the *cortes* embarked upon the course of reform encapsulated by the constitution of 1812. Taking the constitution first of all, great stress was placed on the idea that it was a reflection of tradition, but in reality this was a mere fiction: for all the liberals' claims, the constitution's roots lay firmly in the Enlightenment, establishing, as it did, all the basic civil liberties except that of religion, and in general dealing a heavy blow to corporate privilege. Thus, the *cortes* itself, being unicameral, made no recognition of the estates, whilst there was to be equality before the law, freedom of economic opportunity and employment, and equal liability to taxation and military service. Meanwhile, the principle of the separation of powers was declared, the nation proclaimed to be sovereign and the most severe restrictions placed upon the power of the king. Real power therefore belonged to the *cortes* which was to meet each year and to enjoy complete control of taxation as well as a dominant role in legislation. Last but not least no changes in the constitution would be permitted for at least eight years, Ferdinand being expected to swear an oath of loyalty to the entire document as soon as he returned from exile.

Hostile to the throne though it was, in many respects the constitution followed the goals of enlightened absolutism. Thus, provincial privilege was removed and Spain declared a unitary state, her governance being completely remodelled. The king was to be aided by a council of state, and the network of councils that had stood at the apex of administration and justice was replaced by seven new ministries. As taxation was to be assessed in an equal and proportionate fashion, it followed that the nobility and the Church, and indeed, such favoured provinces as the Basque territories, would now lose their fiscal exemptions and have to contribute their full share of revenue. And, last but not least, in contrast to the confusion that had characterised the *ancien régime*, Spain would henceforth be administered according to a uniform pattern of civil governors and town councils.

Dramatic though all this was, however, it meant very little with regard to the social and economic position of the population as a whole, one form of privilege simply being replaced by another. Already visible in the constitution, which effectively limited political power to the propertied by denying the vote to such groups as domestic servants, the indigent and the illiterate and setting up a complicated system of indirect elections, this is even more visible in the various pieces of social legislation by which it was accompanied. If we look, for example, at the abolition of the feudal system on 6 August 1811, we find that the peasantry gained few benefits, their erstwhile *señores* being enabled to convert most of the old fees into rent by the fact that they were confirmed in their property rights. Nor did the rural masses do any better from disamortisation. Seizing the property of the municipalities, of those religious communities – and there were many – whose monasteries or convents had been destroyed by the war, and, when they abolished it in February 1813, of the Inquisition, the liberals placed immense amounts of land on the market without taking any practical measures to ensure that even a proportion of it was acquired by the peasantry. As a result, wherever the Patriot cause held sway, existing proprietors consolidated their position and were joined by new men from the towns and cities, the peasantry in the meantime being subjected to rent rises, eviction and exclusion from the vital commons (hence the bitter social disorder in southern and eastern Spain noted in our discussion of the guerrillas).

Inequitable though liberal social and economic policy was, it did have a powerful rationale in that Spain, as we have seen, was bankrupt. Alongside disamortisation, the other central component of liberal financial policy was therefore fiscal rationalisation. Here, too, we see the influence of Bourbon reformism in that the model selected for reform had been proposed as early as the 1750s. In brief, the aim was to simplify the collection of revenue and impose a uniform system of taxation. On 13 September 1813 a new financial structure was therefore duly introduced, which formally abolished all fiscal privileges and exemptions, and suppressed the complex array of direct and indirect taxes that had hitherto been levied in favour of a single 'direct contribution' assigned to each province on the basis of a quota based upon its population, the payment of the individual citizen being decided according to his income.

Although the liberals continued to enjoy a surprising amount of support on many issues, as time wore on opposition to their rule began to grow. As might have been expected, the catalyst for this development was the question of religion and, in particular, the Inquisition. Identifying the Holy Office as a key obstacle to Spain's liberation, the liberals were determined to secure its disappearance. To the vast majority of political and ecclesiastical opinion outside the *cortes*, not to mention a large number of its own deputies, such a move was quite out of the question, however, and all the more so in view of the increasingly anticlerical flavour of much of the Cádiz press. Having already fought hard to restrict the freedom of the press, its supporters therefore made a determined attempt to have the Inquisition reinstated. In the event the liberals were triumphant, the Holy Office formally being abolished on 22 February 1813, but the debate had served to clarify issues that had hitherto been elided. Though the constitution might proclaim Catholicism to be Spain's faith, freedom of the press and the abolition of the Inquisition together stripped the Church of its defences, the liberals therefore no longer being able to hide behind the fig-leaf of traditionalism. With public opinion greatly inflamed, for the first time there coalesced a definite traditionalist party, known scornfully by the liberals as *los serviles* – the servile ones.

As a result of these developments, the period 1812–14 was marked by a deepening political crisis. Ostensibly, the root of this crisis was ideological in that criticism of the liberals was for the most part couched in terms of a defence of throne and altar (though Spain's continued prostration did produce numerous claims that the *cortes* had also neglected its duties with regard to the conduct of the war). Thus, no opportunity was lost to compare the work of the liberals with that of the French Revolution, the constitution was denounced, the liberals themselves were vilified as heretics, disaffected generals were courted and extolled, repeated efforts were made to persuade the duke of Wellington (since January 1813 commander-in-chief of the Spanish army) to overthrow the liberals, and there was widespread clerical resistance to the *cortes'* religious policy. Faced by these developments the liberals responded with official pressure: in March 1813 the Regency was purged; in June the generals in command of the Spanish forces based in Galicia (a hotbed of traditionalist feeling) were dismissed from their posts; in July the papal *nuncio* was expelled from Spain; and attempts were made throughout to build up a force of loyal troops in Cádiz, to pack the local administration, and to delay the holding of new elections and the transfer of the *cortes* to Madrid (now finally evacuated by the French).

At the heart of the liberals' resistance, of course, was their claim to speak on behalf of the Spanish people. Yet on the whole the people remained profoundly hostile: although the liberals did receive some popular support in such cities as Cádiz and Madrid, the resistance of traditionalist bishops, clerics and nobles was heartily seconded from below. Large-scale disorders, as we have seen, took place among the peasantry; in Vizcaya the local commander's fear of popular resistance was such that he for some time refrained from proclaiming the constitution; and in Palma de Mallorca in April 1813 crowds assembled chanting, 'Long live the Faith! Death to the heretic traitors!' By the following year, moreover, the liberals were even more isolated, in the first few months of 1814 serious disturbances taking place in Vitoria, Zaragoza, Valencia, Toledo and Seville. Yet this does not imply that popular resistance was necessarily motivated by ideology. Thus, in the early stages of the war, even when specifically called out to fight for Church and king rather than the 'liberty' of liberal propaganda, the population had often remained quiescent until the French actually arrived amongst them. Nor is this surprising, fighting for the Old Order implying fighting for the hated *señorios*. For the roots of popular opposition to the constitution we must therefore look to other factors, and above all to the threat that liberal policy posed to popular economic interests: having offered the people nothing – indeed, less than nothing – the constitution of 1812 could expect nothing in return.

On their own, however, neither the people nor even the *serviles* were likely to be able to overthrow the constitution. What really mattered was military force, this being something the liberals simply did not have. As we have already noted, most shades of opinion in Patriot Spain were strongly antimilitaristic, the political and social pre-eminence enjoyed by the army in Bourbon Spain having been the subject of much resentment. For the liberals, however, such antipathy was particularly virulent, their language having been characterised by the utmost venom: for example, *El Patriota* blamed the succession of military disasters that had afflicted Spain on the 'shameful madness' of giving the command to an 'infinite succession of generals, each of them more idiotic and culpable than the last' when what should have been done was to employ nobody but 'leaders formed . . . in the revolution'.[6] Coupled with scorn for the regular army was respect for the people, this being much reinforced by the defeat of Napoleon in Russia, which was attributed to the fact that 'Russia's war has become as national as that of Spain'.[7] As Flórez Estrada wrote, 'The people . . . destroyed the barbarous legions of our enemies . . . and upset the plans . . . of the Tyrant. It is the people, the people, and only the people who are the principle authors of these prodigies.'[8]

With the liberals content to rely upon popular heroism, their policy towards the army concentrated upon such issues as the formation of a national guard and of a 'military constitution' that would conciliate the army's ordinances with the social and political norms of the new Spain. In adopting this line, however, it can only be said that they were flying in the face of reality, for the period between the beginning of 1810 and the beginning of 1812 was in fact marked by a series of disasters that involved the loss of most of what little of the country remained unoccupied. Though the guerrillas, aided by 'flying columns' of regular troops, fought on, by the time that the constitution was passed all that was left was Galicia, the area around Alicante, the besieged city of Cádiz and certain enclaves in the interior of Catalonia. Barely capable of defending such territory as remained in their hands, the armies, meanwhile, were desperately short of men, munitions, clothing, transport and supplies, and unable to make good their wants – though Spain was still in receipt of copious aid from Britain, there could be no substitute for the reconquest of the land lost to the French. Guerrillas or no guerrillas, then, Spain was losing the war, the situation only being reversed when the impending war against Russia ended the endless stream of reinforcements that the French needed as the price of victory. Suddenly over-extended, they were no longer able to keep the Anglo-Portuguese army of the duke of Wellington penned up in Portugal, the result being that in the course of 1812 they lost the crucial border fortresses of Ciudad Rodrigo and Badajoz and were forced to evacuate all of southern Spain. Yet even this did not solve the problem. On the contrary, swarming with

6 *El Patriota*, No. 1, 4–5, Hemeroteca Municipal de Madrid (hereafter HMM.) AH1–5, No. 158.

7 *La Abeja Española*, 23 November 1812, 188, HMM. AH6–5, No. 1250.

8 *El Tribuno del Pueblo Español*, 22 December 1812, 206–07, HMM. AH1–4, No. 120.

deserters, guerrillas, bandits and bands of mutinous peasants, the Patriot zone was in a state of utter confusion. With the civil authorities completely helpless, conscription and taxation languished. For the army, this meant continued relegation to the sidelines, Spanish troops playing only a limited role in the decisive campaigns that finally drove the French from most of Spain in 1813.

Essentially, then, for the last three years of the war the army had to take second place to the Anglo-Portuguese, its sense of humiliation being increased when the liberals, impelled by the need to gain British support against a particularly dangerous intrigue on the part of the *serviles*, appointed the duke of Wellington commander-in-chief. Meanwhile, it had also to endure the most extreme privations, whilst also seeing most of the privileges that it had hitherto enjoyed being ruthlessly swept away. In this climate liberal rhetoric was at best irrelevant and at worst downright insulting, matters not being helped by the arrogant behaviour of certain of the constitutional authorities. Though a constituency that might easily have been won over to the liberal cause, large numbers of officers having no interest in seeing the return of the conditions that had marked the Bourbon army, the officer corps was therefore propelled in the direction of *servilismo*. Yet this did not make the army absolutist per se. During the period 1810–14 examples may certainly be found of senior officers opposing the liberals on grounds that were clearly ideological, but over and over again what came to the fore were concerns that were explicitly professional, whether it was Wellington's appointment to the command-in-chief (which prompted an attempted military coup in Granada in October 1812), the abolition of military privileges, the subordination of the captains-general to the civil authorities, or the neglect of the army's physical needs. Ideology, then, was unimportant, but, for all that, the army was in fact becoming intensely politicised. As a succession of military pamphleteers began to argue, the military estate was vital to the nation's independence and general well-being, it therefore following that its needs should be satisfied and its members treated with respect, or, to put it another way, that the interests of the army were synonymous with those of the nation. As the guardians of the national interest, it further followed that the army had the right, and, indeed, the duty, to intervene against any government that failed to meet these criteria, Spain therefore being launched on the slippery slope that led via a succession of military coups to the civil war of 1936.

More immediately, of course, the Spanish revolution was

doomed. With the army disaffected, the liberals could neither impose their will on Spain nor stave off a vengeful monarch. And that Ferdinand was vengeful there was no doubt, his having been horrified by such news as he had heard from Spain. Released by Napoleon in a desperate effort to cut his losses in March 1814, he returned to Spain to find that the liberals were completely isolated and that for the most part military opinion was decidedly opposed to them. Disobeying the orders of the *cortes* that he proceed directly to Madrid, he therefore turned aside to Valencia and began to lay plans for the restoration of absolutism. In the last resort, however, this was the work not of the king himself, but of the willingness of the garrison of Valencia to 'pronounce' in favour of absolutism and march on Madrid. With mobs now rioting on all sides and the *serviles* calling for the overthrow of the constitution, everything turned on the response of the rest of the army. As to this there was no doubt: although a few commanders were loyal to the liberals, they knew that they could not trust their subordinates and therefore attempted little in the way of resistance. In short, the revolution was dead.

Though absolutism had been reinstated, nothing had been resolved. In essence, Ferdinand had been restored through the forces of traditionalism and corporate privilege. Thus, on the one hand the chief statement of *servil* intentions – the so-called *Manifesto of the Persians* – was a clarion call in defence of the Church and the nobility that demanded respect for traditional institutions, an end to 'ministerial despotism', and the convocation of the *cortes* by estates, whilst on the other the army had made it quite clear that in future its support for any régime would be conditional upon its treatment. Whatever the ideas of the Bourbons, in short, the days of absolutism were numbered.

SWEDEN: THE DOWNFALL OF THE VASAS

As in Spain, in Sweden war brought political upheaval. Until 1805, Sweden had played little part in the French wars. Gustav III (1771–92) had been a bitter opponent of the Revolution from the very beginning – on hearing of the convocation of the Estates General in 1789, he had exclaimed, 'The King of France has lost his throne, if not his life!'[9] – and over the following three years he made

9 *Cit.* R. N. Bain, *Gustavus III and his Contemporaries, 1746–1792* (London, 1894), p. 104.

repeated efforts to forge a powerful anti-French coalition. In the event, however, his dreams of a march on Paris came to nothing, for on 16 March 1792 he was assassinated at a masked ball by a group of aristocratic conspirators. Under the subsequent regency – being only thirteen, his son, Gustav IV, did not assume the throne until 1796 – all interest in fighting France lapsed, the economic advantages of neutrality soon becoming obvious, and in fact Sweden became the first European power to recognise the Republic. After 1801 a variety of circumstances conspired to draw her into the conflict, however. Eager to stay on good terms with Britain (which was, after all, the destination of between forty and fifty per cent of the iron ore that was Sweden's most important product), Gustav was also determined to restore Sweden to her erstwhile position as a great European power and was increasingly obsessed with a pathological hatred of Napoleon, whom he came to identify as the beast of the Apocalypse. In October 1805 Sweden therefore entered the war, though she played little part in the fighting other than to defend her possessions in Pomerania when these came under attack in 1807. Stubbornly refusing to make peace despite the fact that Tilsit had left Sweden in a very vulnerable state, in February 1808 Gustav was attacked by Russia, war also being declared by Denmark, which had in October 1807 signed an alliance with France following the British sequestration of her fleet at Copenhagen.

Hardly surprisingly, the war did not go well for Sweden, whose forces were badly unprepared. Most of Finland was overrun by the Russians, invasion forces were soon massing in both Denmark and Norway, and the powerful fortress of Sveaborg (Suomenlinna) outside Helsinki was surrendered without a fight. Meanwhile, though his refusal to make peace had been understandable given that Sweden must thereby have lost her highly lucrative status as Britain's chief *entrepôt* in the Baltic, as a war leader Gustav proved to be a disaster. As Sir John Moore, the commander of the British expeditionary force sent to aid him, noted:

> The king . . . proposes measures which prove either derangement or the greatest weakness of mind. He has no minister but governs himself, and, as he has neither the habits nor the talents requisite, Sweden . . . is only governed by fits and starts. The king is perfectly despotic . . .. He does not see the perilous position that he is in, and nobody dares represent it to him.[10]

---

10 J. Maurice (ed.), *The Diary of Sir John Moore* (London, 1904), II, pp. 209–10.

Thus, although Sweden's military position could hardly be more serious, the king demonstrated a complete lack of realism. Calling up a *levée en masse* of 30,000 men for whom there were neither arms nor supplies, he produced a series of ever-wilder plans for offensive operations, and responded to the refusal of Moore to have anything to do with these schemes by placing him under arrest. Not content with alienating his allies, he also disgusted his own forces by dismissing a series of generals and publicly disgracing the entire royal guard (probably justifiably, as they were notoriously lacking in training and discipline). As for the war, although the Finnish peasantry rose against the Russians (and possibly, too, in an attack on the local magistrates and landowners, most of whom collaborated with the invaders), by early 1809 Russian troops had entered northern Sweden and the country was bankrupt and exhausted.

With matters in this state, in March 1809 Gustav was overthrown in a palace revolution. Traditionally attributed to the king's personal failings, the origins of this coup in fact lie in his domestic policy, the disasters of the war being a mere pretext. Mentally unstable and no great military commander as he was, in the thirteen years since his accession he had introduced a series of important administrative and financial reforms that had facilitated the work of government, increased revenue, and cut expenditure. Very much an enlightened absolutist, Gustav IV continued in the traditions of his father who had consistently sought to break the power of the nobility (hence his assassination in 1792). Meanwhile, under the influence of agricultural reformers such as Rutger Maclean, he also introduced legislation that opened the way for the complete reorganisation of Swedish agriculture through the consolidation of the peasantry's scattered strips into proper farms, an increase in their share of the land, and the commutation of their labour services. Further irritated by reductions in court expenditure, Gustav's tendency to appoint non-nobles to high office and the rupture with France – on the whole the diplomatic and military establishment had always been in favour of a revival of the traditional alliance with Paris – by 1808 a powerful faction of the nobility was openly at odds with the crown, the war providing them with the perfect opportunity to gain their revenge. Motivated by a mixture of dismay and disaffection, a group of conspirators came together in Stockholm to plan the removal of the king, a complete reversal of Sweden's foreign policy, and the utter destruction of Gustavian absolutism, the plot soon gaining a number of adherents amongst the commanders of the various Swedish armies. Matters

233

came to a head on 9 March 1809 when the commander of the Swedish forces on the Norwegian front, having first arranged a local armistice with his opponents, set off for Stockholm at the head of his troops. Immediately Gustav turned to the royal guard for assistance, only to discover that it was no longer reliable: exactly as had occurred in Spain just a year earlier, the guard showed its propensity to be the instrument not of the crown but of the nobles who monopolised its officer corps. Thus, on 13 March six guards officers arrested Gustav without there being the slightest attempt at resistance, this event being followed by the proclamation of a regency under his uncle, Duke Charles, and the summoning of the traditional estates, or *riksdag*. In June, moreover, Charles – who had long since shown himself to be an opponent of traditional Gustavian policy – was elected king as Charles XIII, Gustav being forced into exile.

For proof that the coup was at least as much the fruit of domestic political considerations as it was of Sweden's military situation, we need only to turn to its aftermath. When the *riksdag* assembled on 1 May 1809, it was completely dominated by Hans Järta, a nobleman who had been one of Gustav's bitterest opponents, the constitution that it evolved therefore reflecting the interests of the nobility and consciously basing itself upon the Glorious Revolution of 1688. Thus, the aim was on the one hand to check royal despotism and on the other to oppose the threat from below, which was felt to be considerable, not only on account of the emancipation of the peasantry but also because of the emergence of a whole range of non-noble 'persons of standing' such as merchants, iron masters and bureaucrats whose very existence was a threat to the traditional order. In the words of Michael Roberts, in fact, the nobility might speak 'the language of freedom', but 'its concept of liberty had become narrow and sterile: political liberty for the upper classes, and a whiggish distrust of the monarchy'.[11] As a result the constitution had more than one echo of the programme of the *serviles* in Spain, Järta even specifically declaring that it 'was not patterned after any of the social costumes in fashion . . . in the rest of Europe, but after the ancient Swedish dress'.[12] Though the king was declared to rule the kingdom alone, he had now to consult a nine-member council of state, to abjure the advice of private

---

11 M. Roberts, 'The Swedish aristocracy in the eighteenth century', *Essays in Swedish History* (London, 1967), p. 284.

12 *Cit.* F. Scott, *Sweden: the Nation's History* (Minneapolis, 1977), p. 297.

favourites who had no responsible position, and to summon the *riksdag* at least once every five years. As to the *riksdag*, this was to determine taxation, legislate jointly with the king, and hold the members of the council of state individually responsible for their actions. Certain liberal features, such as freedom of the press and of employment, were introduced into the constitution, but in composition the *riksdag* remained exactly the same as before, meeting in its four separate estates of clergy, nobility, burghers and peasants. Moreover, the whip-hand was very much held by the nobility, as witness the various measures that were immediately implemented to protect noble property. And, last but not least, the leaders of the revolution were also able to secure the election of their nominee, Prince Christian August of Augustenburg, as successor to the throne.

This victory on the part of the so-called 'men of 1809' did not put an end to the turbulence gripping Sweden. In the first place, their hopes that they might be able to secure a *rapprochement* with France and Russia were soon dissipated: far from agreeing to a cease-fire, Alexander pressed home his advantage without any hindrance from Napoleon, the Swedes eventually being forced to sue for peace and to sign the treaty of Frederikshamn (Hamma), whereby they were stripped of the Åland islands, Finland and a strip of territory in the far north-east. Also forced to enter the Continental System, the conspirators suddenly discovered that perhaps Gustav's foreign policy had not been so unwise after all. Meanwhile, discontent at the peace settlement was reinforced by a variety of domestic grievances with many representatives of the old 'court' aristocracy continuing to identify with the cause of Gustav, and the peasantry and the bourgeoisie much disgruntled by their failure to gain any increase in their representation in the *riksdag* (the constitution had, in fact, only been passed in the teeth of heavy resistance). Nor were matters helped when Christian August suddenly dropped dead in May 1810, this event provoking violent disturbances in Stockholm in which the leader of the Gustavians and erstwhile royal favourite, Count Axel von Fersen, was murdered.

For a variety of reasons, Swedish attention at this point turned in the direction of France. Within the régime, awareness of Napoleon's growing differences with Russia produced an inclination to exploit them with a view to regaining Finland; the leaders of the 'democratic' faction seem to have decided that the choice of a Frenchman would facilitate a liberalisation of the constitution; and many army officers were infatuated with the glories of French arms. There followed a series of approaches both unofficial and offical, and the eventual result was the election of Marshal Bernadotte as the new heir apparent (for a variety of reasons that need not concern us here, Bernadotte, who had commanded the imperial forces stationed in Denmark during the war of 1808–9, had made himself extremely popular in Sweden).

Arriving in Sweden in October 1810, Bernadotte adopted the Lutheran faith and the name, Charles John, and busily applied himself to the task of winning the approval of all and sundry. As Charles XIII was increasingly old and senile, moreover, it was not long before he was effectively acting as regent and preparing Sweden for a new war to secure compensation for the losses of 1809 (in 1811, for example, French-style conscription regulations were introduced). Politically speaking, however, he quickly showed that the hopes that liberals had placed upon his election were unmerited. Though well known for his Jacobinism in earlier years, he was now determined to uphold the power of the monarchy against the *riksdag*. Yet, given that he was not prepared to tolerate the pretensions of the nobility, or to reverse the social and economic reforms that had brought down Gustav IV, or even to pursue a French alliance, it can be seen that the revolution of 1809 had ultimately been a failure, one enlightened absolutist simply having been exchanged for another. In Sweden as much as in Spain, in short, the palace revolution had become an irrelevance.

SICILY: THE BARONS AND THE BRITISH

For our third example of reform from below, we must turn to Sicily. Here, again, war acted as a catalyst for change, but in this case pressure for change did not only come from within Sicilian society. Thus, although domestic Sicilian factors played a major role in the developments that eventually led to the promulgation of a constitution and abolition of feudalism in 1812, pressure from outside in the shape of British intervention was just as important. Before going on to examine the political situation that produced reform in Sicily, then, we must first examine Britain's relationship with her smaller allies.

Frequently isolated as Britain was in her struggle with Napoleon, she found that even the weakest European states could represent useful allies. Portugal, for example, became the key to the continuation of the struggle in Spain; after 1807 Sweden was a vital channel for the evasion of the Continental System; and Sicily was an important naval base, *entrepôt* and bastion against French expansion in the Mediterranean and the Levant. Great efforts were therefore made to support them, but this in turn persuaded the British that they had the right to demand stable, efficient and loyal government from the régimes which they were upholding. When this appeared to be lacking, the British responded by pressing for reform. For instance, the duke of Wellington bombarded the council of regency that governed Portugal during the Peninsular War with demands for such measures as a forced loan, an increase in the property tax, the introduction of a graduated income tax, the reinforcement of local government, and tighter management of the universally excoriated commissariat. Combined with this pragmatism, however, there was a streak of cultural superiority, and even, in unofficial circles at least, of imperialism. Thus, not only was there a tendency to assume that the application of British models was a panacea for the ills of a wide range of benighted foreigners, but it was hoped that this might lead to an extension of Britain's political and commercial influence. Meanwhile, as patronising of the lower classes as they were contemptuous of the upper, many British observers contended that Portuguese, Spaniards, Sicilians or Greeks might be made into excellent soldiers if only they were given British officers (as, of course, was actually done in the case of Portugal). Not all such influences operated at every level – the Perceval and Liverpool administrations, for example, were strongly opposed to wild talk that Sicily might be annexed as a colony whilst the Sicilian opposition's eventual adoption of British constitutional models was opposed by the British embassy and generally ridiculed at home – but the fact remains that in this fashion Britain became almost as strong an influence for reform as France.

Needless to say, British suggestions were not always heeded. In Portugal, for example, Wellington's demands were pointedly ignored, whilst in Spain the British came to be thoroughly detested by liberals and *serviles* alike, the Latin American revolutions (for which Britain was held responsible) raising such hostility to fever pitch. In Sicily, however, matters were very different, long-standing friction between the monarchy and the aristocracy, growing resentment of the Neapolitan domination of Sicily, and a somewhat affected anglophilia among the educated classes all combining to give Britain a unique degree of leverage. Thus, ever since the 1780s successive Bourbon administrations had been attempting to restrict the feudal jurisdiction and fiscal privileges enjoyed by the Sicilian barons. As the traditional Sicilian estates had continued to function in the face of Bourbon absolutism, meeting once every four years for the vote of supply and the presentation of petitions, the barons' opposition soon acquired a strongly constitutionalist focus. However, resentment of the Bourbons was not just based on concern for corporate privilege. From the late eighteenth century onwards educated Sicilian opinion had increasingly objected to Neapolitan rule on the grounds that Sicily was being both neglected and exploited, the events of the Revolutionary and Napoleonic Wars greatly strengthening this feeling. Asked to pay huge sums to uphold the Bourbon cause against Napoleon, the Sicilians were afforded proof positive that their rulers had little interest in them, the attitude of the court being disdainful in the extreme when it was forced to flee to Sicily in 1798 and again in 1806. Nor was the presence of the court of much benefit, for, though it certainly stimulated the economy of Palermo, the cost was very heavy – Maria Carolina, in particular, was wildly extravagant, showering gifts upon a circle of more or less dubious favourites and lavishing money on an unceasing campaign to regain control of Naples – whilst the court and administration was heavily dominated by Neapolitan and French *émigrés* at the expense of the local nobility.

Aristocratic constitutionalism and outraged patriotism led in turn to the emergence of a strongly pro-British tendency. The roots of this development were strongly antiquarian, resting on the coincidence that both England and Sicily had experienced a Norman conquest, but it was reinforced by the influence of writers such as Young, Smith and Blackstone and by the obvious contrast that could be drawn between British prosperity and Sicilian backwardness. Meanwhile, ever since the British had sent a garrison to Sicily in 1806 the relationship between their military commanders and the court had been extremely turbulent, the Sicilian régime being regarded as decadent and untrustworthy (so much did Maria Carolina hate the British that she was not above negotiating in secret with Napoleon). In the opinion of Sir John Moore, for example, the queen was 'violent, led by her passions, and seldom influenced by reason', King Ferdinand 'an indolent man, hating business', and the chief minister, Circello, 'quite an old goose'.[13] In consequence, Britain's representatives in Sicily were frequently loud in their demands that it should intervene to secure a change of régime, realising which the opposition became even more inclined to praise British models (indeed, in some circles the belief that

13 Maurice, *Diary of Sir John Moore*, II, p. 126 *passim*; cf, especially pp. 141–6, 188–92.

imitation is the sincerest form of flattery was taken to the extent of speaking Sicilian with a British accent).

With the stage set in this fashion, a coincidence of political and military crises in 1810 precipitated dramatic change. Short of money as ever, in January 1810 Ferdinand demanded a much larger subsidy from the estates than was customary, only for the barons to respond by persuading their fellow chambers to join with them in halving the sum required and proposing a radical reform of the tax system. As the abolition of noble privilege was inherent in this decision – henceforward there was to be a single levy of five per cent payable on the value of all landed property, irrespective of ownership – some comment is required on the barons' motives. In part the result of genuine patriotic fervour, the move was also the fruit of shrewd economic calculation. Thus, Sicilian feudalism, of which the right of the nobility to determine the level at which it should be taxed was part and parcel, was in fact fast becoming an embarrassment in the eyes of many of its beneficiaries. Thanks in large part to the British presence, Sicily was experiencing a great economic boom. Perennially in debt, the barons were eager to benefit from this situation, and yet they were precluded from doing so by a variety of factors connected with the feudal system. Being entailed, for example, estates could not be sold or rationalised; mining rights were often restricted or shared with the crown; there was no free market in corn; and the peasantry enjoyed a variety of irritating rights with regard to pasturage and water courses. Finally, economics aside, feudalism also brought serious disadvantages with regard to the barons' relationship with the crown, for, as fiefs, all estates reverted to the crown in the event of a noble house failing to produce an heir.

In making their counterproposal, then, the baronial opposition were both asserting their economic interests and identifying themselves with the cause of the nation. Faced by this rebellion, the king appeared at first to back down, making some judicious changes in the personnel of the government and promising to forego the increased levies he had demanded, activities which paid off when the opposition was defeated in a second session of parliament in August 1810. Yet this was not an end to the matter: still desperate for money, in February 1811 Ferdinand quite unconstitutionally established a national lottery, imposed a one per cent tax on all commercial transactions, and expropriated and put up for sale considerable quantities of Church and municipal land. The result was uproar, the new measures encountering extensive resistance, but this time the régime stood firm, pressurising the deputation charged with the defence of the constitution when the assembly was not in session into declaring Ferdinand to be within his rights, and imprisoning five of the opposition's most important leaders. The royal triumph was to prove short-lived, however, for, at the very time it was outraging the barons, the court had also alienated the British. Thus, in September 1810 Murat had attempted an assault on Sicily across the Straits of Messina. In the event, this had proved a fiasco, but the Sicilian response at every level had been one of apathy, whilst it at the same time became clear that Maria Carolina was in contact with both Napoleon and Murat. Much enraged, and fearing that the court was now so unpopular that it might provoke a pro-French revolt, the British determined on intervention.

In resolving on intervention in Sicily, the British government's aims were three-fold. First of all, Maria Carolina was to be eliminated as a threat to the alliance; secondly, peace was to be restored to relations between crown and country through a programme of domestic reform; and, thirdly, mainland Italy was to be encouraged to revolt against the French through the example of a new and beneficent administration in Sicily. As the instrument for this policy, whose obvious corollary was a change of government in Palermo, London selected a vigorous soldier and administrator of liberal views, Lord William Bentinck. Arriving in Sicily as both ambassador and commander-in-chief in July 1811, Bentinck at first tried persuasion, only to be faced by a flat refusal to co-operate. After returning to London for fresh instructions – it had not been made at all clear just what steps could be taken to enforce the wishes of his masters – Bentinck now applied considerable pressure, threatening to withdraw the British subsidy unless the administration was remodelled to include a respectable proportion of prominent Sicilians, the exiled barons freed, the court and government purged of treacherous elements, and the British ambassador appointed commander-in-chief of the Sicilian army. Faced by this challenge, the court essayed resistance, only to cave in when Bentinck ordered the military occupation of Palermo, Ferdinand agreeing to withdraw from the government in favour of his son, Francis, who was henceforth to act as prince regent.

As Francis quickly released the exiled barons and rescinded the unconstitutional measures taken by his father the way now seemed clear for reform. In fact, however, the road was still to prove distinctly rocky, for Ferdinand and Maria Carolina had no intention of letting their son have a free hand, and strove by every means available to block the advent of reform. Their relations with Bentinck were therefore in a state of permanent crisis, the latter eventually having to go so far as virtually to deport the queen. Yet, step by step, progress was made. In March 1812 a new ministry was formed which included the reformist leaders, Belmonte and Castelnuovo; in May new elections were called; and on 20 July the basis of a new constitution was agreed by the assembly. True to form, this document, drawn up by the antiquarian cleric, Paolo Balsamo, purported to be an exact copy of the British constitution. Thus, there was to be a House of Lords and a House of Commons; parliament was to meet on an annual basis and to have the power of legislation; ministers were to be appointed by the king but responsible to parliament; all taxation had to originate in the Commons; the monarchy lost its estates in return for a civil list; and Sicily was to enjoy the principle of the rule of law and trial by jury. Moreover, feudalism was now specifically abolished: baronial jurisdiction vanished, the old fees were in theory swept away, and the estates of the nobility were converted into freeholdings. And, last but not least, Sicily's status with regard to Naples was carefully defined, the two being declared to be completely independent of one another (thus, were Ferdinand to return to Naples as its monarch, he would have to leave Francis behind as king of Sicily).

What, however, did all this signify? Hailed by Bentinck as a great victory for Sicilian patriotism, it rather appears as a coup on the part of a faction of the nobility eager to break the power of the monarchy and advance their own economic interests. Thus, the abolition of feudalism, as elsewhere, meant almost nothing in social terms. In effect, the peasants were left free to be dispossessed of numerous vital customary rights, deprived of access to the commons, and encumbered with greater burdens than ever (though all feudal dues were supposedly abolished, the decision as to what was and what was not a feudal due was left to litigation). By contrast, meanwhile, the nobility, as well as gaining immensely from the unrestricted control they now possessed of their estates, had also to be paid compensation for what they were deemed by the courts to have lost. Furthermore, although a free market in land was created, entails per se were never abolished, the estates of the nobility therefore being guaranteed.

Yet the predominance of the barons proved disastrous for the cause of constitutionalism, the political crisis of 1810–12 having exposed deep divisions in Sicilian society. Economically speaking, the nobility had since the late eighteenth century been being challenged by a non-noble oligarchy that had been able to derive considerable income from usury, leasing land from the barons, or estate management, this threat having been sharpened by new fortunes made during the war. Alongside this basic economic rivalry there also existed tension between greater and lesser nobles, between different regions of the country, and even between individual cities. In protest at the obvious sectionalism of the constitutionalists, there therefore emerged a radical movement which took as its inspiration the French Revolution and the *cortes* of Cádiz. Thanks in large part to the rapid process of disintegration that now affected the baronial party on account of personal differences between Belmonte and Castelnuovo and of second thoughts about the wisdom of abolishing feudalism, the radicals were able to seize control of the assembly. Demanding universal suffrage, a single chamber and the abolition of entails, they proceeded to block all supply, the result being that parliamentary government had soon completely broken down. Social disorder was meanwhile on the increase, with bread riots in Palermo and serious anti-seigneurial disturbances in the countryside. By October 1813 Bentinck was therefore left with no alternative but to dissolve parliament and impose martial law in the hope that he might somehow 'hold the ring' until such time as the Sicilians could be brought to a greater pitch of political maturity, whilst in the meantime implementing the various administrative reforms that had been blocked by the parliamentary impasse (in particular, it was intended to replace the old system of seigneurial jurisdiction with new courts and legal codes). In May 1814 new elections were duly held which eased matters slightly in that, thanks to heavy official pressure, a constitutionalist majority was elected to the Commons, but the hostility between Belmonte and Castelnuovo prevented the formation of a stable ministry and the nobility were by now so thoroughly frightened that the House of Peers had become a bulwark of absolutism. With matters once again in a state of deadlock, Belmonte eventually decided that the only way out was to invite the king to resume his power as monarch, the hope being that this would in turn win back the support of the barons. Eager to secure the approbation of the great powers so as to ensure the return to Naples – Murat's decision to change sides in January 1814 had thrown this into doubt – Ferdinand was for the time being quite happy to play the part of a constitutional monarch, and on 5 July 1814 he duly returned to power.

Despite the king's protestations of good will, in reality he was as much of an absolutist as ever, the survival of the constitution in effect depending upon continued British protection. Yet Bentinck, who persisted in his enthusiasm for a popular rising in Italy long after London had dropped all thought of such a course for fear of upsetting Austria, was rapidly falling out of favour, whilst there was in any case a general recognition that Sicily could not be kept constitutional by force. Though he was allowed to retain command of the army, Bentinck was stripped of the embassy, whilst it was made clear that his successor, A'Court, was to do no more than to endeavour to support the constitution in general terms. With the initiative now entirely in the hands of Ferdinand, he could afford to bide his time until he could be sure of regaining Naples. In March 1815, however, the charade finally came to an end: fearing that the allies intended to depose him, Murat seized the opportunity provided by the Hundred Days to secure his throne by means of a nationalist revolt, only to be defeated at Tolentino on 3 May and forced into exile. With the road to Naples free – for the allies promptly agreed to his restoration – Ferdinand lost no time in securing his revenge, dissolving parliament on 17 May and returning to his old capital. Six months later, moreover, Naples and Sicily were proclaimed a unitary state – the kingdom of the Two Sicilies – the separate Sicilian constitution thereby being implicitly abolished.

ABSOLUTISM TRIUMPHANT

In Spain, Sweden and Sicily alike, then, war led to revolution. In each case, moreover, the origins of the political turmoil into which they were plunged can be seen to lie in the clash between enlightened absolutism and corporate – above all, noble – privilege that had characterised the eighteenth century. Thus, in Spain the economic pressures engendered by the French wars caused an already reformist régime to accentuate its efforts at modernisation, this in turn provoking opposition amongst a faction of the nobility who seized upon the limp figure of the heir to the throne, Prince Ferdinand, as a figurehead in whose shelter they could pursue aims that were wholly sectional. Driven to desperation by Napoleon's decision to turn against the Bourbons, they frantically sought security in the military coup at Aranjuez that led to the overthrow of Charles IV and Godoy on 19 March 1808. With the French unwilling to be bought off by a grovelling Ferdinand VII, the plot did not succeed, and when Spain subsequently exploded in revolt its coadjutors found themselves submerged in a welter of grievances that completely transcended their original interests. Nevertheless, in the aftermath of the rising, *frondeurs* such as the Palafox brothers, the Conde de Montijo and the Marqués de la Romana continued to work for a dictatorship that would confirm the supremacy of the nobility, whilst the defence of noble privilege was also implicit in the traditionalist wing of the wider revolutionary movement that now developed. In Sweden, too, the overthrow of Gustav IV, whilst justified in terms of the disastrous leadership displayed by that ruler during the war against Russia, was directly related to the long struggle between the Vasas and the Swedish nobility, this having been accentuated by the efforts of the monarchy to reform agriculture. There was a further parallel with Spain in that the royal guard – the very same instrument was used to bring down Charles IV – was the chief tool of the rebel leadership. Finally, in Sicily resistance to Ferdinand IV and Maria Carolina, though aided and abetted by the British, was from the start centred on the nobility, which wanted to advance its economic interests and felt threatened by the reforms introduced in the late eighteenth century, not to mention the prolonged presence of the Bourbon court in Sicily.

In each case, then, the nobility were at the heart of the initial conflict, their longstanding concern at the advance of absolutism being reinforced by the developments generated by the war. And in each case, too, it was the war that provided the catalyst for an attempt to rein in royal power. Yet in no case did matters transpire exactly as the conspirators planned. Nor is this surprising: whether in Spain, in Sweden or in Sicily, in the first place the nobility cannot be regarded as a single entity possessed of a single political consciousness, or, indeed, of a clear view of its economic interests. On the contrary, the nobility was everywhere a highly fissiparous body. Often divided by degrees of wealth or status, it was also frequently riven by personal rivalries and lacking in any forum for the expression of its views (in this respect Sicily was an exception). Further problems were caused by the attraction of the court, which, however hostile to corporate privilege, yet functioned as a source of dignity, employment and reward. Whilst small groups of individual noblemen were therefore able to come together to oppose, and even to overthrow, reformist absolutisms, having once seized power they were invariably confronted by political divisions within their own estate. Thus, in Spain many nobles opted for King Joseph, whilst others became liberals; in Sweden Järta and his colleagues were opposed by the 'old Gustavians'; and in Sicily the barons were not only fragmented between absolutists and constitutionalists, but also between Belmontists and Castelnuovists. In consequence, the aristocratic reaction was never able to impose its solutions. In Sweden, certainly, the constitution of 1809 reflected the interests of the dissident nobles, but this victory did nothing to reverse the long-term emancipation of the middle classes and the peasantry and was to a degree nullified by the arrival of the dynamic Bernadotte. In Sicily, meanwhile, administrative reform and reliance on the English model produced a House of Commons strong enough vociferously to challenge baronial predominance. And, finally, in Spain the pressures of the war combined with circumstance to create a situation in which the conspirators of 1808 were eventually reduced to complete irrelevance and the country remodelled in the image of the revolutionary bourgeoisie.

As to the survival of the new constitutions thrown up by the war in Spain, Sweden and Sicily, this was from the start jeopardised by the political weakness or unreliability of their progenitors. Thus, in Sweden and Sicily the majority of the nobility abandoned revolution in favour of an alliance with the throne that would guarantee their social pre-eminence. Yet the example of Spain shows that liberalism was equally lacking as a revolutionary force. With its tenets – or at least their practical manifestation – anathematical to its supposed beneficiaries, the people, the political minority who came to dominate patriot politics were as powerless as the *frondeurs* whom they supplanted, and all the more so once they had lost the support of the army. But here we come to a question that is central not just to the histories of three particular states during the Napoleonic era, but also to that of the entire Restoration period. In Spain, absolutism was overthrown and then restored by a military coup; in Sweden Gustav IV was brought down by an army revolt; and in Sicily, where the domestic military force was negligible, political change ultimately came to rest upon British bayonets. In short, whether we are speaking of the eighteenth-century struggle between corporatism and absolutism, or the nineteenth-century struggle between absolutism and liberalism, the Napoleonic period clearly demonstrated that, at least until such time as an era of mass politics might develop, the final arbiter of political change in Europe would be the proverbial man on horseback.

8 THE DOWNFALL OF THE FRENCH

A PEOPLE'S WAR?

> The downfall of Napoleon is a trilogy of which Moscow, Leipzig and Fontainebleau are the successive pieces and Waterloo the epilogue . . .. It is a truism to point out that the moral of this titanic trilogy is the victory of the national spirit over the alien tyranny which educates and fosters its destroyer.[1]

With these words Herbert Fisher encapsulated an explanation for the defeat of the Napoleonic empire that has persisted to the present day – that, first in Russia and then in Germany, Napoleon was confronted by a foe that even he could not vanquish in the form of mass armies fired by outraged nationalism. If many historians have written thus over the past 150 years, they are only advancing an opinion that was common amongst those who participated in the French Wars. Thus, a French observer could remark of Leipzig, 'It was plain that the will of the masses was making itself felt to the sovereigns who up to that time had been all-powerful.'[2] From the opposing camp, meanwhile, Clausewitz wrote, 'In Spain the war became of itself an affair of the people . . .. In Russia, in 1812, the example of Spain . . . was taken as a pattern . . .. The result was brilliant.'[3]

Dismissing the traditional picture of the so-called 'Wars of Liberation' would therefore be an act of folly, and yet problems remain. If Prussia put six per cent of her total population into the field in 1813 – rather more than twice the percentage that she had managed in 1806, and far more so if the large number of foreigners in the army at that point is discounted – her forces continued to experience resistance to conscription on a massive scale. If her army,

---

1 H.A.L. Fisher, *Napoleon* (London, 1912), pp. 189–90.
2 Duc d'Audiffret-Pasquier (ed.), *A History of my Time: Memoirs of Chancellor Pasquier* (London, 1894), II, p. 103.
3 C. von Clausewitz, *On War*, ed. A. Rapoport (London, 1968), p. 385.

certainly, was greatly altered from the days of Jena, the same did not apply, or at least not as much, to that of either Austria or Russia. And, finally, if nationalist feelings were emerging amongst the educated classes in Germany and Italy, the practical results of this development were minimal. What, then, did bring down Napoleon? In the first place, the answer must be the overwhelming numbers generated not so much by 'people's war' as by the emergence of such a coalition as the emperor had never had to face before. In the second, however, we must also look at developments in France herself: to focus on the actions of Russians, Germans and Italians misses the point that the empire as much collapsed from within as it was overthrown from without. Last but not least, we must also consider the emperor himself, who, as we shall see, repeatedly rejected a compromise peace in favour of a total victory that was ever more unattainable.

DISINTEGRATION ON THE HOME FRONT

In 1799 Napoleon had come to power as the man who would bring peace, stability and order to France, whilst satisfying the interests generated by the Revolution. Implicit in his rule was therefore the concept of a social contract: having made the *notables* the found- ation of his rule, it was imperative that he should retain their support by respecting their interests. Whether in terms of their riches or their sons, they had to be treated gently, whilst they had also to be allowed to prosper and to be protected from disorder; further- more, nothing could be attempted in terms of foreign policy that would jeopardise their security. As for the people, meanwhile, the utter disorder of the 1790s suggested that at all costs taxation and conscription had to be kept within tolerable limits, living standards maintained, and the Catholic Church treated with due respect.

Such were the ground rules for stability in Napoleonic France, but by 1814 Napoleon had long since broken all of them. Let us start with conscription. For a number of reasons this was always certain to be a delicate issue. In the first place, it was an area in which the regime could not relax its demands, for an adequate supply of manpower was central to Napoleon's survival. In the second, it was a development that was both recent and innovative, conscription to the regular army having been unheard of before 1793. In the third, it was, as we have seen, hated by the peasantry (amongst the urban lower classes, by contrast, it seems to have been rather less unpopular, perhaps because they were more vulnerable to unemployment and less sedentary in their habits; numerically, however, there were far fewer of them than there were peasants). And, finally, for the *notables* conscription was no less alarming. Unlikely though they were actually to have to face the prospect of service in the ranks, they disliked the unpopularity incurred by the task of administering the draft, had a strong interest in protecting agricultural labour, and felt directly threatened by the desertion that figured among its consequences (penniless, cut off from their homes, and desperate for food and shelter, the growing numbers of deserters – over 50,000 a year by 1811 – frequently turned to crime as a necessary means of survival). Needless to say, the result was widespread resistance: between December 1804 and July 1806 there were no fewer than 119 disturbances arising from the draft, whilst the number of those attempting to evade service between 1799 and 1805 has been estimated at 250,000. Many of these men received the assistance not just of their families but also of the local authorities (being sheltered and supported in or near their home communities, draft evaders were far less threatening than deserters, whilst also representing a valuable source of labour).

Despite the obvious need for caution, however, the régime's demands became heavier and heavier. Between 1800 and 1807 the average number of men called up in any one year was 78,700, and in only two cases was any attempt made to call up under-age men from future 'classes'. From 1808 onwards, matters were very different. In the period February 1808–January 1809 alone, 240,000 men were drafted, whilst the number taken between then and 1812 amounted to another 396,000. In short, the annual average had increased to 127,200, whilst men were now being taken not just from the current year-group, but also from those which had already been balloted or were still under age. Nor was this increase sweetened by dramatic victories (there is some evidence that resistance to conscription was temporarily lessened by the news of Ulm and Austerlitz). On the contrary, the chief theatre of the war was now the Iberian Peninsula with all its reputation for horror and cruelty. Still worse, service was becoming ever harder to escape. Increasingly, the administration of the ballot was taken out of the hands of local officials, the right to employ substitutes was restricted, efforts were made to put an end to the exemption from military service enjoyed by married men, and the minimum height requirement was relaxed. Meanwhile, the families of *réfractaires* were fined or had troops billeted upon them; those who assisted fugitives or otherwise connived at draft evasion were heavily punished; and, from February 1811 onwards, columns of troops were dispatched into the countryside to hunt down the 139,000 men estimated to be missing from the ranks at that point.

On the whole such measures were successful. By early 1812 the number of *réfractaires* had been reduced to less than 40,000, whilst the vast majority of new conscripts were coming forward without undue protest. In consequence, as late as 1813 Napoleon was remarkably complacent about the situation on the home front, evidently believing that he had nothing to fear from resistance. In reality, however, conscription was no more popular than before. Whilst local communities might now be convinced that hiding *insoumis* was more trouble than it was worth, with a few exceptions the attitude to the draft was at best one of sullen resignation. Moreover, resistance was still evident: not only did many men continue to inflict the most appalling injuries on themselves rather than serve, but the exemption for married men continued to be abused on a massive scale (in Flanders a boy of eighteen even married a woman of ninety-nine).

Napoleon's rapacity in terms of manpower would possibly have been less objectionable had his rule continued to offer obvious benefits to France, but from 1810 onwards this was less and less clear. Until this time, the emperor's wars had more or less funded themselves, industry had been expanding, and there had been a modest improvement in living standards. For a variety of reasons, however, the picture now changed dramatically. In the first place, certain problems began to become apparent with regard to Napoleon's grand design to turn the rest of Europe into a captive market for French industry. Prior to the imposition of the Continental System large areas of central and eastern Europe had been heavily dependent on the export of raw materials and agricultural products to Britain. This trade, however, was now cut off, whilst France was both unable easily to import bulk goods and self-sufficient in many of the products involved, the result being that agricultural prices, and with them purchasing power, could not but fall. Yet, at the same time, French imports were disproportionately expensive, given on the one hand the technical deficiencies of French industry, and on the other France's enforced reliance on land transport. As French production rose – as it did quite dramatically – so a crisis of over-production came ever closer, this being finally sparked off by new developments in the imposition of the Continental System. By 1810 it was clear to Napoleon that he could not close the coasts of Europe to British goods, and, further, that the expansion of French industry was constantly dogged by the high price of colonial raw materials. In response, the emperor decided that the only solution was to open up direct links with Britain, issuing a series of decrees that on the one hand authorised the importation of colonial goods, and on the other restricted this trade to France alone. In order to enforce this French monopoly, moreover, from November 1810 onwards the huge stocks of colonial contraband that existed in many German, Dutch and Italian cities were seized and sometimes publicly destroyed.

In promulgating the decrees of 1810, Napoleon's aims had been threefold – in the first place, to profit from a trade that he could not stop; in the second, to boost French industry; and, in the third, to secure France a monopoly not just of industrial production, but also of the distribution of colonial goods. Rather than advancing the cause of French prosperity, however, the decrees had precisely the opposite effect. Speculation in colonial imports having become rife, the events of 1810 brought general ruin, with French merchants undercut by the new imports, and foreign ones stripped of their stocks. Inside and outside France alike, the consequence was a wave of bankruptcies and a squeeze on credit, the latter ensuring that the crisis would spread to industry (many manufacturers had had no option but to borrow very heavily to survive the general fall in prices).

There followed a period of general depression. In cotton and silk, production fell by four-fifths, whilst in wool the fall was about one-half. Nor was the disaster limited to textiles, one-fifth of the workers and artisans employed in the Parisian luxury trades also being laid off. As if all this were not enough, the period 1809–11 was marked by abnormally severe winters, together with cyclones, droughts and flooding, the crops on which large parts of French industry depended being slashed by between a half and two-thirds and the price of food soaring by as much as 100 per cent. All this, meanwhile, was inflicted on a country already burdened by steadily increasing taxation. No longer able to make his wars pay for themselves, Napoleon had had no option but to raise taxes, the yield from indirect taxation rising four-fold between 1806 and 1812.

Faced by this crisis, the imperial régime did not remain inert. On the contrary, a stream of orders and decrees attempted to rectify the situation. Major programmes of public works were undertaken, and artisans and craftsmen assisted through government contracts, the establishment of national workshops, and even the issue of new regulations concerning the dress to be worn at court (each new suit being a boon to some small tailor). Meanwhile, welfare efforts were also increased: in May 1811 Napoleon ordered 300,000 francs to be given to charitable committees in Paris, whilst large quantities of soup were distributed to the poor. Finally, desperate efforts were made to secure the supply of grain. Yet, except in Paris, all this was to no avail, many parts of France being afflicted with the greatest misery and distress. The death rate rose dramatically, hospitals and charities were overwhelmed, and large parts of the population were rendered destitute – in the Gard nearly one-third of the population were being fed from soup kitchens early in 1812, whilst even in Toulon, where the worst effects of the depression were staved off by the presence of the great naval yards, 2000 people were in receipt of such relief. Not surprisingly, France in consequence once more began to experience serious problems of public order. Bread riots took place in many parts of the country, Luddism made an appearance in the north, mendicity became endemic, large bands of beggars terrorised the countryside, and widespread brigandage reappeared for the first time since the early days of the consulate.

As before, meanwhile, the general turmoil was being fuelled by the question of religion. By means of the concordat of 1801 Napoleon had bought peace with the Church, but this was soon in jeopardy. By 1809 disputes with Pius VII over the extent of papal authority had led to the annexation of Rome and the Papal States. There followed a spiral of reprisal and counter-reprisal that ended with Napoleon excommunicated, Pius incarcerated, and the French Church in crisis. How far these events were linked to the growing disorder is a moot point – on the whole the clergy did not preach armed resistance, whilst popular dissidence tended to be expressed through participation in the pietistic traditionalist sect known as the *petite église* – but it is at least probable that the growing turmoil helped spread disquiet and uncertainty even amongst the *notables*.

And that the *notables* were turning away from the empire there can be little doubt. As yet, overt political opposition remained muted. If the imprisonment of the pope had acted as a stimulus to royalism, the results were not very impressive. Certainly the crisis led to the foundation of a new royalist secret society, the Chevaliers de la Foi, in 1809, but, except in the field of propaganda, in practice its activities remained restricted to a cloak-and-dagger conspiratorialism of the most juvenile kind. More practically, other royalists made common cause with disgruntled republicans, and this development led to the formation of an elaborate conspiracy in the south-east which aimed to raise a revolt at Toulon and Marseilles, only for these plans eventually to be uncovered in the winter of 1812–13. And, most dramatically, there was the affair of General Malet in October 1812 in which a handful of conspirators came within an ace of establishing a provisional government in Paris. The work of a tiny minority though all this was, the fact that the vast majority of the *notables* played no part in active opposition to the empire does not necessarily imply that they were ardent in its support. Many, indeed, had throughout done their best to eschew direct involvement in its workings, whilst by the end of 1812 it was being generally reported that even the régime's officials were in general inclined to act more out of self-interest than of devotion to the emperor. In short, the 'masses of granite' on which Napoleon had once depended had increasingly been reduced to shifting sand.

DISASTER IN RUSSIA

If Napoleon's hold on power in France, and, indeed, the rest of Europe, was fragile, it was not yet under serious assault. What changed the situation, of course, was the disastrous Russian campaign of 1812, it also being the events of this campaign that really gave birth to the myth that the First Empire was overthrown by 'people's war'. In fact, however, it is difficult to make such an argument stick. To achieve victory in Russia, Napoleon had but one hope – to destroy the bulk of the Russian regular army whilst yet retaining sufficient strength to terrify Alexander into making peace (for arming the serfs in a genuine *levée en masse* would have been politically and socially quite unthinkable). From this it in practice followed that such a victory must be achieved, as Napoleon planned, relatively close to the frontier, for a march into the interior would inevitably bring with it such losses as ultimately to denude the invasion of all threat. If the Russian victory really was due to popular participation in the struggle, it must therefore be shown that this played a major role in the absence of a new Friedland somewhere in the western borderlands.

Superficially, at least, the evidence for a Russian 'people's war' seems quite compelling. In the first place Alexander responded to the French invasion with a series of dramatic appeals to the populace, such as that of 18 July, which proclaimed, 'We call on all our civil and religious communities to co-operate with us by a general rising against the universal tyrant'.[4] Such appeals were

---

4 Cit. R. Wilson, *Narrative of Events during the Invasion of Russia by Napoleon Bonaparte and the Retreat of the French Army* (London, 1860), pp. 46–8.

buttressed by stage-managed events exemplified by the assemblies of the merchants and nobility which were convened when Alexander visited Moscow in July 1812, not to mention a general change of atmosphere in the régime. Ever since 1801 there had been a recrudescence of the perennial debate in Russia between 'westerners' who sought solution to Russia's problems in foreign models of government and society, and 'easterners' who believed that Russia must rather seek salvation in her own traditions and institutions, it being the former tendency that had hitherto had most influence over Alexander. Once the tsar had broken with Napoleon, however, the easterners came back into favour: Speransky was dismissed in March 1812 and replaced with Admiral Alexei Shishkov, whilst Count Fyodor Rostopchin was appointed Governor of Moscow. Bitter opponents of Speransky, both men were obsessed with the defence of the nobility and the protection of Russian language and culture from what they saw as corrupting foreign influences, and were associated with a growing Romantic tradition with strong roots in the Orthodox faith. Under their influence traditionalism was restored to fashion and attempts made to hound out enlightened thinking and whip up patriotism to fever pitch, whilst Alexander himself, who was in the throes of religious conversion, made great show of his devotion to the Orthodox Church, the war in general being portrayed as a holy crusade. Furthermore, on 20 August the 'German' Barclay de Tolly was replaced by Prince Mikhail Kutuzov as commander of all the forces facing Napoleon, Kutuzov being ideally placed to exemplify the spirit of a genuinely 'Russian' war (in earlier years he had been a collaborator of the leading general, Alexei Suvorov, who had advocated a specifically Russian mode of waging war based on the so-called 'cult of the bayonet').

From the start, then, the régime presented the war as a patriotic struggle and by one means or another sought to conciliate public opinion, which was, moreover, no longer to be ignored (not only was much concern expressed at the constant retreats of the first two months of the campaign, but the appointment of Kutuzov was forced upon Alexander by popular demand). To what extent, however, was there a genuine echo amongst the population? Amongst the élite, certainly, the war produced much excitement. Thus, French plays were jeered in the theatres of St. Petersburg, French itself was shunned (its use among the nobility had hitherto been habitual), and the events of the campaign were avidly discussed in school and salon. Much material support was also forthcoming.

A certain number of young men enlisted as patriotic volunteers, the merchants of Moscow pledged over two million roubles in money, and the Church and nobility offered huge sums in plate and jewels and 'gave' many thousands of serfs for service in the army or the militia. All this, perhaps, was to be expected – the nobility were terrified that Napoleon might free the serfs, whilst the Orthodox Church was unremitting in its hostility to French 'atheism' – but what of the people? Here, too, we have some evidence to suggest real engagement in the struggle. In the army the Russian, Kutuzov, was certainly far more popular than 'Germans' like Barclay, whilst the extraordinary ferocity displayed by the troops throughout might perhaps be interpreted as evidence of new-found patriotic enthusiasm. As for the common people, Madame de Staël claimed that the peasants 'volunteered with enthusiasm', their masters 'only acting as their spokesman' in giving them away.[5] Meanwhile, vast crowds saluted the tsar when he visited Moscow in July, whilst the evacuation of the city by the vast majority of its population in the face of French occupation two months later can rightly be pointed to as an event for which there was no previous parallel in European warfare. Last but not least, there is no doubt that, particularly in the latter half of the campaign, at least some peasants did indeed take up arms and exact a horrific vengeance on those invaders unfortunate enough to fall into their hands.

Yet, despite all this, the evidence remains dubious. If the Russian army fought well, this was nothing new, Russian armies having been noted for their courage and resilience even in the eighteenth century. The Russian forces may have grown enormously in 1812, but this was on the whole achieved by compulsion: the traditional system of conscription – decrees levying so many 'souls' on every hundred serfs – was used extensively, no fewer than three such levies being decreed in 1812, conscription also being used to raise the 223,000 militiamen eventually called up for service with the newly-formed *opolchenie* (in giving up large numbers of serfs to the army and militia, moreover, the nobility had by no means lost sight of self-interest, continuing, as before, to use military service as a way of ridding themselves of the lazy, the incompetent, and the troublesome). Nor are the eight volunteer *jäger* regiments, the forty-seven new regiments of cossacks (so-called: many of these units were actually bourgeois town guards or troops of volunteer cavalry)

---

5 *Cit.* A. Brett James (ed.), *1812: Eyewitness Accounts of Napoleon's Defeat in Russia* (London, 1966), p. 69.

and the nine regiments of Tartars, Kalmucks, Bashkirs and other assorted nomads that also appeared in the course of 1812 much more interesting. The *jäger* clearly came from the well-to-do, and the cossacks either from the same source or from the same free peasants as their original namesakes. As for the Tartars and the like, they were effectively tribal mercenaries with no sense of identification with Russia. All that can be said with regard to the serfs, meanwhile, is that, *pace* Madame de Staël, conscription – which still carried with it the full term of twenty-five years – was, at best, accepted with passive acquiescence, and, at the worst, outright hostility: not only did it continue to produce general lamentations, but in December 1812 serious disorders broke out amongst the militia regiments that had been raised in the province of Penza. Nor did hostility to serfdom disappear: not only did a number of serfs wait upon Napoleon to petition for emancipation, but there were serious risings against the local landlords in Lithuania, as well as around the towns of Vitebsk and Perm. Even when they did take up arms, moreover, whether they were fighting out of a sense of patriotism is another matter: as in Calabria, or, indeed, Spain, loot, self-defence, the desire for vengeance, and sheer necessity must be all regarded as highly plausible alternatives. In so far as they had a choice, in fact, the peasantry appear rather to have remained aloof from the struggle, and to have refrained from participating in the sort of scorched-earth policy which has generally been cited as the third main pole of the supposed 'people's war'. Thus, whilst villages were certainly destroyed, crops burned and wells poisoned, this was again in large part the work of the cossacks and the regular army (when the French penetrated into areas through which the retreating Russians had not passed, these were often found to have remained untouched). In consequence, claims of massive popular backing for the struggle are clearly open to question.

Nor would the régime itself have welcomed a spontaneous *levée en masse*. As one of Alexander's proclamations specifically stated, 'I have delegated the organization of the levies to the nobles of every province'.[6] With the nobility terrified of a servile insurrection, in short, the populace was to be kept in its place; indeed, Rostopchin even welcomed the fact that the bulk of the militia had to be armed with pikes on the grounds that these weapons were 'useless and harmless'.[7] Near Moscow, moreover, peasants who took up arms

6   Cit. Wilson, *Invasion of Russia*, p. 48.
7   Cit. E. Tarle, *Napoleon's Invasion of Russia, 1812* (London, 1942), p. 118.

against French foragers were accused by the local nobles of being mutineers. In fact, not even the notables were to be permitted any opportunity to voice their opinion: when Rostopchin discovered that certain Moscow nobles wished to question Alexander about the war effort, he condemned their initiative as 'impertinent, improper and dangerous'.[8] When the guerrilla warfare in which the Russians engaged in the latter half of the campaign is examined, we therefore find that, though some individual officers undoubtedly did encourage the peasants to rise, its main agents were not the people at all, but cossacks and regular cavalry.

Even if all such doubts are set aside, it will still be found that 'people's war' played little role in the defeat of Napoleon. As will become clear, Napoleon had probably already lost the war by the time that he reached Smolensk, and certainly by the time that he reached Moscow. If this be the case, then the whole question becomes an irrelevance. Not only does there seem to have been little peasant resistance before the *grande armée* reached Smolensk, the appeals of an Orthodox régime cutting little ice amongst the Catholics and Jews of the western border lands, but, however many men Alexander called up, few such recruits reached the Russian armies until quite late in the year: by the time of Borodino, in fact, the troops facing Napoleon had been joined by no more than 25,000 fresh conscripts and perhaps 15,000 embodied militia.

Why, then, did Napoleon fail? On paper the chances of a rapid victory seemed very great when war broke out on 24 June. Setting aside the mostly Prussian and Austrian forces he had deployed to cover his flanks, Napoleon had at least 375,000 men concentrated on the river Niemen (Neman) on the seventy-five mile front between Kovno (Kaunas) and Grodno, and another 80,000 in reserve in the rear, the grand total of all the troops he had available for service coming to over 600,000. Facing these forces were no more than 175,000 Russians, backed up by only a motley collection of depot formations (though the substantial forces of regular troops that had been released by the recent diplomatic agreements with Sweden and Turkey were also slowly making their way towards White Russia). Deployed in two separate armies over far too wide a front, their command arrangements were in complete disarray, such strategic plan as had been adopted was inherently weak, and there was nothing to suggest that the quality of the army was any better than it had been at Austerlitz and Friedland. Yet, for all that, the rapid

8 *Cit.* Tarle, *Napoleon's Invasion*, p. 117.

victory that Napoleon was expecting was not obtained. Hampered by poor roads, inadequate reconnaissance – the French cavalry was soon falling by the wayside in droves, some formations losing a quarter of their mounts by the beginning of July – commanders who were out of their depth, and its sheer size, the *grande armée* moved with none of its customary celerity. Meanwhile, Napoleon himself was no longer the dynamic leader of earlier years, being increasingly corpulent and rather unwell. The results were predictable. Evading French envelopments on no fewer than three occasions, the Russians eventually succeeded in concentrating their forces at Smolensk, leaving the *grande armée* to lumber slowly along in their wake. And as Napoleon advanced so his forces began to disintegrate. In the first place matters were not helped by the weather, periods of blazing heat being interspersed by torrential downpours. In the second the logistical situation soon collapsed into chaos, the troops outstripping their supply trains and discovering that the poor and thinly populated borderlands, devastated as they had been by the retreating Russians, were unable to meet their requirements. As a result, the 375,000 men amassed by Napoleon had by the time they reached the vicinity of Smolensk lost around 100,000 to disease or desertion, whilst another 90,000 had been detached to guard the emperor's line of communications with the border. There remained but 182,000 front-line troops, losses of cavalry horses and draft animals having proportionately been even worse. Nevertheless, all was not lost. Though the two Russian armies had at last succeeded in coming together at Smolensk, they still numbered no more than 120,000 men, whilst they had been under almost as much strain as the French. In short, a heavy blow might still have been decisive, for, with the defenders of Smolensk – the bulk of the Russian field army – gone, the chances were that Alexander might yet have made peace, the genuine popular mobilisation that would have been necessary to replace the regulars being as impossible as ever.

In fact, however, Smolensk witnessed no such victory, still more fumbling on the part of Napoleon and his senior commanders allowing the Russians to disengage their outnumbered forces and retire to the east. With them there probably went Napoleon's last chance of victory. As Alexander still refused to make peace, the emperor had no option but to march in pursuit in the hope that, by threatening Moscow, he might yet force a decisive battle. Of this, however, there was now little hope, the emperor being even less likely to secure a decisive victory after the wastage consequent upon a march 280 miles further east had been added to the 20,000 men he had lost at Smolensk and the 16,000 more that he was forced to detach to protect his line of communications. And so it transpired, especially as the *grande armée* now began for the first time to encounter significant irregular resistance. By the time that Kutuzov reluctantly decided to give battle at Borodino, some seventy miles west of Moscow, the odds against him had been reduced still further, Napoleon's army now amounting to no more 130,000 men.

Even now a cheap and crushing victory might still have brought success, and for a moment this again seemed to be in the emperor's grasp, Kutuzov having not only deployed his army in such a position that it was in grave danger of being outflanked from the south, cut off from Moscow and trapped against the river Moskva, but having also disposed of its command in a manner that can only be described as bizarre. Fortunately for him, however, on this occasion Napoleon's generalship was even worse. In the first place, for no very good reason the emperor rejected the idea of a strategic envelopment of the Russian left flank, and instead settled upon a series of massive frontal assaults that demanded the very most of his exhausted and demoralised troops and could not but lead to heavy casualties, especially as there had been a significant change in French tactics since the halcyon days of 1805–7. Thus, as the ranks filled up with new conscripts, there was a tendency for finesse to be eclipsed in favour of brute force, the French now tending to attack in huge divisional columns that were difficult to manoeuvre and presented enemy artillery – and Russian artillery was notoriously well-served, heavy in calibre, and lavish in quantity – with the choicest of targets.

With such a battle plan, the only hope of victory was that the Russian army would break in panic, but this was something that was most unlikely: setting aside Kutuzov's efforts to imbue his men with religious and patriotic fervour and the fact that the Russian position was so congested that the soldiers literally could not move, Russian troops were so brutalised that they did not have the initiative to run away – as one British observer put it, 'Taken from a state of slavery, they have no idea of acting for themselves when any of their superiors are by.'[9] As a result the French were confronted with the most obstinate resistance. Furious attacks were met by even more furious counterattacks, key positions were taken and retaken several times, and even the most experienced observers were shaken by the savagery of the fighting. Gradually, however, even the

9 *Cit.* A. Palmer, *Russia in War and Peace* (London, 1972), p. 106.

Russians were overborne and by mid-afternoon their line was beginning to crack, Napoleon in consequence being repeatedly begged to commit the 18,000 men of the Imperial Guard who constituted his last reserve. With his one hope a decisive and crushing victory, the emperor had no option but to throw in every man he possessed, but, determined to keep at least one formation intact for future use, this he would not do even though a mere 18,000 men would have made no difference if the Russians were not now firmly beaten. Tired and ill, the fact was that he had either hopelessly misjudged the real situation, or had simply lost his nerve.

When fighting gradually drew to a close in the early evening, the French had succeeded in driving the Russians from all their front-line positions and had inflicted terrible damage on most of their formations. Twenty-three generals were down, perhaps 44,000 men had been killed or wounded, many others had been separated from their units, the artillery was out of ammunition and had lost much *matériel*, and the survivors were dazed and exhausted. Yet the French were in no better shape. Their own losses had been at least 28,000 men, and they, too, were utterly prostrated. Though one more effort might have broken Kutuzov, the latter was in fact able to slip away and make a more or less orderly retreat.

In short, for all Napoleon's efforts, the main Russian field army remained intact, the war now being definitively lost. Though the French now entered Moscow without a fight, Napoleon could do no more – as Clausewitz tartly put it, 'He reached Moscow with 90,000 men, he should have reached it with 200,000.'[10] With Moscow immediately set alight by agents of Count Rostopchin, partisan activity springing up all around him, supplies desperately short, Kutuzov's army being rebuilt a mere seventy-five miles to the south, substantial regular forces closing in on his thinly protected lines of communication from north and south, the discipline and morale of the *grande armée* at breaking point, and no more than 95,000 men available for action, Napoleon's position was clearly desperate.

When once it became clear that Alexander would not make peace, retreat therefore became inevitable, the troops actually beginning to move out on 19 October. Initially the plan was to move southwards so as to gain access to a route to Smolensk other

---

10 C. von Clausewitz, *The Campaign of 1812 in Russia* (London, 1843), p. 255; in fact, Napoleon had 95,000 men, having lost 28,000 at Borodino and dropped 7,000 more off to protect the last few miles of road.

than that traversed by the army during the summer, but on 23 October the French advance guard ran into Kutuzov's forces at Maloyaroslavets. In a fierce action the next day the French secured a tactical success that ought to have secured Napoleon's objective of a retreat on Smolensk via the towns of Medyn, Yukhnov and Yelnya. Yet, apparently because he feared that marching westwards from Maloyaroslavets would invite Kutuzov to attack his flank, Napoleon instead ordered the army to head north for the same road that had been taken before.

There followed the 'retreat from Moscow', which, thanks to the futile Maloyaroslavets affair, now got off to a very bad start, the lengthy diversion that this had incurred having wasted not only precious supplies but also a week of reasonably fine weather. Harried by cossacks and bands of peasants every foot of the way, the *grande armée* was also from the beginning of November assailed by heavy snow and bitter cold. Meanwhile, Kutuzov's army repeatedly cut the column in two, the result being that one corps or another would suddenly have to retrace its steps to rescue the beleaguered forces at the cost of yet more desperate fighting. With the army encumbered by immense caravans of baggage and non-combatants, food, warm clothing and proper footwear in short supply, and the troops on the march day after day, formation after formation lost all cohesion as their men died by the hundred or fell away to join the ever-growing crowd of stragglers. Barely escaping complete destruction when they were attacked from all sides at the river Berezina in the last week of November, the survivors staggered on under the command of Marshal Ney (Napoleon himself left for Paris on a fast sleigh on 5 December), but they were forced to leave behind almost all the remaining guns and baggage and, by the time that the frontier was reached early in December, numbered barely 20,000 men.

To conclude, the Russian campaign had produced, in Clausewitz's words, 'the most complete result conceivable'.[11] In the retreat, the 140,000 men whom it had involved (counting not just the troops who had started from Moscow, but also the many thousands who had been picked up along the way), had suffered at least 120,000 casualties, French losses in the campaign as a whole amounting to perhaps half a million men. How had this disaster come about? Whilst popular involvement in the struggle may to a certain extent have increased the scale of the catastrophe, far more

11 Clausewitz, *Campaign of 1812*, p. 212.

instrumental were questions of climate and geography and the physical and organisational limitations of the *grande armée*. With the only chance of victory an early triumph that would have forced Alexander to the peace table, in essence, the campaign was a gamble that should never have been made, and, indeed, an object lesson in the need for Napoleon to curb his demands on the rest of Europe. Realism being something that had by now effectively deserted Napoleon, however, he did not heed the warning, and thus it was that he was now to lead France to fresh disasters from which even he could not emerge intact.

THE WAR OF LIBERATION

With the remnants of the *grande armée* driven across the frontier and the Russian armies poised to invade Poland, it might be thought that Europe would now have risen in wholesale revolt. Yet such a revolt did not occur: just as the defeat in Russia had been the work not of the people but of the régime, what defeated Napoleon in 1813 was not the people of Europe, but the great powers.

At first sight such a judgement might seem surprising, for in both Germany and Italy the Napoleonic period had witnessed the emergence of a nationalism that was above all defined by its opposition to French domination. Taking the case of Germany first of all, even before the French Revolution arguments had begun to be heard that the Germans had a 'national character' that was different – and infinitely more attractive – than its French counterpart, whilst French neo-classicism was being challenged by the *sturm und drang* movement. Inspired at first by little more than simple irritation at the predominance of the *philosophes*, this cultural nationalism had received a strong theoretical justification in the writings of Johann Herder. Thus, according to Herder it was ridiculous to lavish attention upon French models as if they possessed some universal truth, the reason being that every nation was a unique organic community differentiated by history, culture and language. We come here to the influence of Romanticism. For such men as Friedrich Schleiermacher, Heinrich von Kleist, Adam Müller, Friedrich Jahn, Joseph Görres, Ernst Arndt and Johann Fichte, Germany's salvation lay in a revival of the ancient Teutonic practices and culture now threatened by French-inspired reform. Bolstered by the growing vogue for folklore, they demanded that the German people be educated in their 'Germanness'. French influence must be rooted out from the language, the racial purity of the

261

nation maintained, and a cult of national greatness inculcated through constant references to the glories of the past. Particularly influential in this respect was the figure of the Teutonic chief, Arminius, who had destroyed several Roman legions at the battle of the Teutoburgerwald in AD9. Idolised as 'Hermann' and compared with such Spanish heroes as Palafox, this warrior was now seized upon as a pattern for resistance to Napoleon, von Kleist going so far as to produce an epic poem entitled *Die Hermannschlacht* which almost openly called for a national uprising. 'Hermann's battle' was also recalled by Fichte's famous *Addresses to the German Nation*, a series of lectures delivered at the University of Berlin in the period 1807–8. Thus:

> When you hear my voice, you are at the same time hearing the voices of our forefathers. They offered their lives to stop Roman aggression . . . . They are calling you and begging you not to lose your birthright . . . .[12]

Moved by such rhetoric, some of the Romantics began actively to prepare for war, pride of place here belonging to the Berlin schoolteacher, Friedrich Jahn. Initially an enthusiast for the Prussia of Frederick the Great, he was disillusioned by the events of 1806, in consequence switching his attention to the *volk*. Convinced of its strength, he believed that it should be called forth in a great national militia, to which end he launched a patriotic gymnastic league whose aim was to inculcate military values and turn out healthy young soldiers. In addition, Jahn also founded a new secret society, the Deutscherbund, with the aim of preparing a revolt, a similar society known as the Tugenbund having already been founded in Königsberg (Kaliningrad) in 1807.

From well before the time of the Russian campaign, then, Germany witnessed the emergence of a violent anti-French nationalism that to a large extent stood outside the traditional order, and which looked to the German people themselves for liberation. Meanwhile, much hardship had been caused by the general economic depression and, in Prussia especially, by the *grande armée*'s march to the Russian frontier, all this occasioning great resentment – as Jerome wrote in December 1811:

12 *Cit.*, S. Heit, 'German romanticism: an ideological response to Napoleon', *Consortium on Revolutionary Europe Proceedings*, 1980, I, p. 188.

There is profound unrest . . .. The example of Spain is being recommended, and, if war breaks out, every country between the Rhine and the Oder will be the scene of an active insurrection.[13]

At first it seemed as if these fears might prove justified. Even before news came of Napoleon's defeat, the war against Russia had occasioned numerous manifestations of discontent. When Frederick William of Prussia agreed to conclude a treaty of alliance with Napoleon preparatory to joining in the invasion, a number of the erstwhile Prussian reformers, including Boyen and Clausewitz, went so far as to travel to Russia to take up arms against the French. Here they were joined by Stein, who had been summoned from his Bohemian exile by Alexander, and throughout the campaign this group exerted what influence it could to stir up anti- French feeling in Germany, whilst organising a special unit known as the Russo-German Legion as a spearhead for a national uprising.

Whilst not without an echo in Germany – there were, for example, a series of anti-French disturbances in East Prussia in the winter of 1812 – the efforts of Stein and his fellows to prepare the way for revolt had little concrete effect. In the first place the clique of Romantic intellectuals who clamoured for a war of national liberation were a minority within a minority. Almost by definition, the cultural élite to which they belonged was cut off from the constraints of traditional society by its university education, whilst even the minority represented by the German intelligentsia was not united behind the call for a *völkisch* anti-French crusade. Of the Romantics, Goethe remained fascinated by the figure of Napoleon as hero, whilst others, such as Novalis and Holderlin, conceived of a national revival as something spiritual rather than material. And not all intellectuals were Romantics, just as not all nationalists were anti-French. Hegel, for example, believed that Germany's revival could only be achieved through the intervention of a dictator on the Napoleonic model, whilst to the very end numerous intellectuals remained firmly attached to the liberal ideals embodied in the Confederation of the Rhine, a good example of such loyalty being the stance adopted by the literary reviews of Halle and Jena, these being generally regarded as the leading artistic periodicals of the day. As Napoleon's power and ambition visibly became ever more unbridled, so disillusionment with his imperium spread, but, even so, as late as 1813, men of the stamp of Jahn and Arndt remained but one strand of opinion among many.

13 Cit. G. Rudé, *Revolutionary Europe, 1783–1815* (London, 1964), p. 275.

If the intelligentsia were split on responses to French domination, how much more was this true of the wider community? With particularist loyalties still very strong – in 1815, for example, the Saxon army mutinied in protest at the despoliation of its country by Prussia – nationalism was a concept of the most limited force, it being well said that there were as many Germanies as there were princes. This, of course, did not preclude loyalty to Prussia, in particular, from acting as a powerful stimulus to outraged patriotism, but even this had its limitations. Humiliating though the Prussian treaty of alliance with Napoleon was (by its terms, the rump of the Prussian state was subjected to French occupation and effectively demilitarised), von Treitschke tells us that only twenty-one Prussian officers resigned their commissions, and Clausewitz that 'there was hardly a man who did not set down this temper of mind for a semi-madness'.[14] Nor is this passivity surprising. Terrified of agrarian disorder, the *junker* had always distrusted the reformers' talk of popular insurrection and were currently engaged in repressing the peasant reprisals occasioned by the depredations of the *grande armée*. As for the bourgeoisie, far from eagerly welcoming the plans of Scharnhorst and others to conscript them into the army, they had been utterly horrified: as the historian, Niebuhr, wrote, soldiering should be left to the common people, for 'the rough peasant will not mind the service much'.[15] Last but not least, in view of what was to occur in 1813, serious doubts must also be entertained with regard to the attitude of the lower classes, the peasantry showing as much hostility towards the *junker* as they did towards the French and seeking only to protect their homes and their crops.

On the whole, then, Germany remained quiet, and would doubtless have remained so had not the events of the Russian campaign caused Frederick William briefly to lose control of his own state. In this respect, the first step was taken by the commander of the Prussian troops in Russia, Johann von Yorck, who, having been placed in a most difficult position by the retreat of the French army, on 30 December signed a treaty of neutrality with the Russian forces at Taurroggen (Taurage), thereafter withdrawing to Königsberg

---

14 Clausewitz, *Campaign of 1812*, p. 1; Craig claims that the number of officers involved was 300, but neither von Treitschke nor Clausewitz are likely to have let such a figure pass without comment. Cf. H. von Treitschke, *History of Germany in the Nineteenth Century* (London, 1915), I, p. 461; G. Craig, *The Politics of the Prussian Army* (Oxford, 1955), p. 58.

15 *Cit.* W. Simon, *The Failure of the Prussian Reform Movement, 1807–1819* (New York, 1971), p. 156.

(Kaliningrad) where he was followed first by Wittgenstein's Russians and then by Stein. Appointed by Alexander to mobilise the resources of the liberated territories, Stein lost no time in organising the 'people's war' of which he had so long dreamed. Convoking an informal meeting of the estates, he persuaded them to decree the establishment of a *landwehr* recruited by universal conscription. Needless to say, all this placed Frederick William in an impossible position. Terrified of Napoleon, who still seemed very strong despite the Russian *débâcle*, highly suspicious of Russia, and as hostile as ever to the radical military reform now under way in East Prussia, he at first sought to remain on good terms with the French whilst yet decreeing general mobilisation in case this proved impossible. However, the defeat of Napoleon having caused great excitement amongst the educated classes, the reformers were able to deluge the king with warnings of civil war and revolution, whilst many even of the more conservative generals, such as Blücher and Yorck, were now eager to seize the chance to avenge the disasters of 1806. Thus assailed, and with many of his doubts assuaged by Russian guarantees that, in exchange for significant territorial concessions in Poland, Prussia would be restored to a size equivalent to that of 1807, Frederick William therefore finally agreed to an alliance.

With the French forces, other than a few garrisons, now out of the way across the Elbe, on 16 March Prussia declared war, thereby initiating the so-called *befreiungskrieg*. With the first-line forces that he had had at the beginning of 1813 consisting of a mere 65,000 men, Frederick William now had no option but to adopt the full programme of the reformers. Thus, on 3 February it was decreed that young men who could meet the cost of providing their arms and equipment could enlist in volunteer *jäger* battalions; on 9 February that all exemptions from conscription to the regular army were henceforth abolished; on 18 March that a *landwehr* should be formed by ballot from all those men aged between seventeen and forty who were not required by the army; and on 21 April that the remainder of Prussia's manpower should serve in the *landsturm*, an emergency home-guard that was supposed to launch guerrilla resistance in territories occupied by the French. Meanwhile, on 18 March the king issued the grandiloquent *Appeal to my People* in which he proclaimed that 'our independence and the honour of the *volk* . . . will only be secured if every son of the fatherland participates in this battle for . . . freedom'.[16]

16 *Cit.* J. Sheehan, *German History, 1770–1866* (Oxford, 1989), p. 315.

In purely numerical terms the results were dramatic. By June 1813 the regular army, including the *jäger*, had been increased to 150,000 men, whilst the *landwehr* numbered another 120,000. How far, however, was this the result of genuine popular enthusiasm? Von Treitschke, as one might expect, is replete with edifying stories of devotion to the war effort, this picture being to some extent borne out by contemporary observers – the British diplomat, Sir George Jackson, for example, describes the people as 'an army without leaders, all impatient to rush *pêle mêle* upon their foes . . . in the excess of their joy at the prospect of being freed from the clutches of the French', whilst, as one *landwehr* officer wrote, 'In the conviction that . . . whole nations could achieve their destiny by great effort and noble deeds alone, everybody was resolved to do every manly action . . . to help liberate the Fatherland.'[17] Most dramatic of all was the reaction of the intellectual community which indulged in a great display of patriotic enthusiasm, and in some cases rushed to join up, being especially associated with the *freikorps* – independent mobile columns which fanned out across Germany in an attempt to stir up resistance, gaining their greatest success in Hamburg where a popular revolt declared for the Allies on 18 March (i.e. six days after the French had evacuated the city). Finally, much encouraged by the reforms of Hardenberg, many middle-class Jews also took up arms.

There is, then, no smoke without fire. Yet there is, too, considerable evidence that this picture of a popular crusade is a myth. In so far as the middle classes are concerned, the reaction to conscription was as often hostility and horror as it was enthusiasm. Both Breslau (Wroclaw) and Königsberg (Kaliningrad) protested against the extension of conscription to the bourgeoisie, such disaffection also being widely mirrored in the press. Nor do the bourgeoisie seem to have been especially willing to take up arms, even on the most preferential terms. Thus, there were never more than 12,000 *jäger*, whilst most of the *freikorps* were composed of cossacks and Prussian regulars, the few volunteer units that they did include being recruited in large part from labourers and artisans who had been driven to enlist by poverty and despair. By contrast, the *landsturm* did awaken much enthusiasm, but in this connexion it

---

17 *Cit.* Lady Jackson (ed.), *The Bath Archives: a Further Selection from the Diaries and Letters of Sir George Jackson, K. C. H., from 1809 to 1816* (London, 1873), II, p. 55; cit. A. Brett-James (ed.), *Europe against Napoleon: the Leipzig Campaign, 1813, from Eyewitness Accounts* (London, 1970), p. 42.

must be pointed out that, with the French in full retreat to the west and south, it was unlikely to see much service. Meanwhile, ambivalence amongst the bourgeoisie turned to outright hostility amongst the common people, except, perhaps, in devastated East Prussia. Elsewhere, flight and resistance were common, the situation in this respect being particularly bad in Silesia: hitherto absolutely free of conscription, by June 1813 it had raised fewer than one-half of its quota of recruits. Throughout the Prussian forces, meanwhile, desertion became a serious problem, no fewer than 29,000 *landwehr* disappearing in the period March–June 1813 alone. As for Stein's Russo–German Legion, it obtained few willing recruits, having eventually to be converted into an ordinary line-infantry regiment.

The fact is, then, that, as the Prussian general staff was later forced to admit, the population had to be compelled to go to war in 1813, notions of a national crusade being further undermined when one considers the manner in which the Prussian government visualised the struggle and the degree to which the structure of society remained untouched. Thus, if the proclamation of 18 March summoned all the king's subjects to fight, they were addressed not as 'Prussians', but as 'Brandenburgers, Prussians, Silesians, Pomeranians [and] Lithuanians' and reminded of 'times gone by, of the Great Elector and Frederick the Great'.[18] Equally, officers and men alike might wear the new 'iron cross' instituted by Frederick William on 10 March, the dead might be honoured and have their families cared for, and a few deserving soldiers might be promoted from the ranks, but in practice little had changed, the social and economic position of the *junker* being in so far as possible respected. Thus, setting aside the manner in which they had been favoured by the emancipation of the serfs, not only did the *junker* continue to dominate the officer corps, but the common people were kept firmly under control, as shown by the fate of the *landsturm*, which was first placed under a series of regulations that were so tight as virtually to defeat its central purpose, and then to all intents and purposes abolished. Meanwhile, similar qualifications have to be made with regard to the role of nationalism in the campaign, in that if Alexander and Frederick William backed up their campaign with appeals for a national insurrection, it is quite clear that their aim was first and foremost to pressurise the other German rulers into

18 H. Kohn, *Prelude to Nation States: the French and German Experience, 1789–1815* (Princeton, 1967), pp. 279–80.

abandoning Napoleon, neither of them having any interest in a united Germany.

If the popular conception of the *befreiungskrieg* is so seriously to be called into question, what did defeat Napoleon in 1813? The answer is simply that his whole system of making war now collapsed. Thus, until 1813 all his campaigns had been predicated upon the elimination of one opponent at a time. In 1813, however, matters changed. In a remarkable feat of improvisation, Napoleon assembled a new army of over 200,000 men in Germany, and with these troops was easily able to hold his own against the roughly similar number of Prussians and Russians available for service against him at this time, inflicting serious checks upon them at Lützen and Bautzen. Nevertheless, although Alexander and Frederick William had been pushed to the point of collapse, the *grande armée* proved incapable of following up its success – thanks to Napoleon's inability to replace the tens of thousands of horses lost in the Russian campaign, there were too few cavalry; the raw conscripts who had been called up to fill the ranks were too young to withstand the rigours of the campaign; and the French generals were manifestly past their best. As a result, the Russians and Prussians survived, the emperor letting them off the hook by the offer of a temporary suspension of hostilities, there following the two-month armistice of Pläswitz of 4 June–13 August 1813.[19]

We now come to the turning point of the campaign, for the armistice ended with the entry of Austria into the war, this action not only adding the Austrian army to the forces facing Napoleon, but also the Swedes, whom a canny Bernadotte had hitherto deliberately kept well clear of the conflict despite the military alliance that he had signed with Alexander in April 1812. Having rather unwillingly been forced to take part in the invasion of Russia, Metternich was desperate to maintain a balance between France and Russia, conceiving that an outright victory for either could not but spell disaster for the Habsburgs, and greatly fearing the nationalistic effervescence that Stein and his adherents were attempting to provoke across the whole of central Europe. In these circumstances the only hope seemed to be to reach some compromise peace, and all the more so as such a course promised to restore Austria's

19 This armistice is known under a bewildering variety of names, including those of Parchwitz, Pläswitz, Plaeswitz, Pleiswitz, Plasswitz, and Pleschwitz. Of these, Pläswitz seems the most likely; it has unfortunately proved impossible to trace its current British name.

prestige and independence, the chancellor therefore withdrawing from his alliance with France and proffering Austria's services as a mediator. When Prussia entered the war, moreover, there was even more reason to secure a settlement, for the terms on which she had done so made it quite clear that she would be offered fresh territory in Germany, the inference being that Austria was in real strategic danger (not only was the only practical source of such territory Saxony, but Frederick William would now be bound firmly to Alexander through sheer cupidity). Though Metternich was offered generous terms by Alexander to enter the struggle, he therefore kept Austria neutral, and made a concerted attempt to persuade the opposing sides to enter negotiations, in the meantime mobilising the Austrian army and struggling to afford such protection as he could to those smaller states which, like Bavaria and Saxony, now found themselves subjected to Prussian bullying.

To achieve his aims, Metternich would have liked to arrange a general peace conference, but in the event he was forced to settle for face-to-face discussions with first Alexander and then Napoleon. Ratified in the convention of Reichenbach (Dzierzoniow) of 27 June, the result of his discussions with the Allies was that, unless Napoleon agreed to surrender the Illyrian provinces to Austria, recognise the independence of the states of the Confederation of the Rhine, evacuate his possessions in Germany, return the territories taken from Prussia in 1806, and dissolve the Grand Duchy of Warsaw, Austria would enter the war on 20 July. Confronted with these terms at Dresden, Napoleon brushed aside Metternich's attempts to present them in a favourable light and swore that he would fight on. Nevertheless, eager to win more time so as to bring up the largest possible number of reinforcements and improve the training of his inexperienced forces, the emperor did agree to take part in a conference at Prague, whereupon Metternich, who was still eager for peace, unilaterally extended the armistice to 10 August. However, even when the chancellor offered to waive Austria's claim to the Illyrian provinces, it soon became clear that Napoleon had no intention of giving way, and in consequence on 12 August Metternich was left with no option but to declare war.

Confronted by the odds that he now faced, even Napoleon would have been hard put to survive. Counting the troops of his remaining allies, he could muster some 335,000 men in the main theatre of operations in Saxony. However, facing him were a minimum of 515,000 Allies. Yet these forces were not the product of some military revolution. In Prussia, as we have seen, universal conscription had been introduced, but even now the regular army remained the mainstay of operations, over half the *landwehr* never seeing anything other than garrison service, and most of the *landsturm* never being mobilised at all. In Russia, certainly, there had been heavy conscription, but this had been carried out in the traditional manner and in no way represented a true mobilisation of the nation, whilst brutality and corporal punishment remained as common as ever. As for the Swedes and the Austrians, military reform had affected them hardly at all. Notwithstanding Bernadotte's adoption of the French model of conscription, the army that he landed at Stralsund in March 1813 had to be brought up to strength by pressing large numbers of Germans from Sweden's erstwhile Pomeranian outpost. Meanwhile, Austria's mobilisation was achieved entirely through reliance upon existing legislation, Hungary being once again left comparatively untouched and the *landwehr* of 1809 broken up and pressed into the regular army at a rate of two battalions to each line regiment. Nor was anything else to be expected from Metternich, who had, after all, in large part joined the coalition to ensure that ideas of national revolution did not get out of hand: so far, indeed, was he from supporting such a position, that in March he had crushed a conspiracy to raise a new insurrection in the Tyrol, whilst it was directed that official propaganda should contain nothing 'that savours of German liberty in the sense that members of the Tugenbund use that phrase'.[20]

Not only has the change in nature of Europe's armies been exaggerated, but even their individual size was not much greater than before. Counting every man that they possessed, Prussia had some 272,000 men available for the campaign, Russia 296,000, Austria 250,000, and Sweden no more than 50,000, these figures in fact having risen comparatively little from the figures of 1805–7. If there was a difference it was that the armies that faced Napoleon in 1813 were largely made up of men who had but lately been pressed into service, or who had, as was often the case in Austria, received a bare modicum of military training before being dismissed on permanent leave. Nor were the troops any longer tightly buttoned and neatly coiffured mannikins, the Prussian army, in particular, going to war in a bizarre medley of British and Prussian uniforms and semi-civilian clothing. The old professional armies of the eighteenth century were therefore clearly no longer a necessity, and

20 *Cit.* W. Langsam, *The Napoleonic Wars and German Nationalism in Austria* (New York, 1930), p. 160.

all the more so as all the opponents of the French now used variants of the column formations that had served their enemies so well as a means of employing raw troops on the battlefield.

If talk of Nations-in-Arms is clearly premature, numbers were nonetheless crucial to the defeat of Napoleon. Dividing his forces so that he could strike out in several directions at once, he succeeded for a short period in staving off disaster, but, so used were France's generals to the emperor's guiding hand that few of them were capable of independent command, several of them now being heavily defeated. Where Napoleon himself was in charge, things were better, as at Dresden where the emperor secured a considerable victory on 27 August, but the Allied generals eventually agreed to refuse battle whenever he was present, the result being that all his offensives achieved was to exhaust his own troops. Meanwhile, the Allied armies were closing in upon him, and eventually the emperor was compelled to adopt a defensive position around the city of Leipzig. There followed the largest, bloodiest and most dramatic battle of the Napoleonic Wars, with the 177,000–strong *grande armée* facing an initial total of over 250,000 Allies. On 16 October Schwarzenberg and Blücher launched simultaneous attacks from north and south, but were successfully repulsed. At this point Napoleon might yet have got away to the west, but he was expecting 14,000 fresh troops to arrive the following day, and decided to stay put, apparently in the expectation that he could secure a genuine victory. However, though the Allies were dared to attack, 17 October proved quiet as they were waiting for the 140,000 reinforcements who were coming up under Bennigsen and Bernadotte. The fighting was therefore not resumed until the next day when 300,000 men were launched against the French from virtually every point of the compass. Thanks in part to bungling and irresolution on the part of the Allies, the *grande armée* held its ground, but its position was clearly not going to be tenable for very much longer, and in consequence Napoleon ordered a withdrawal during the night. With the only way out of the trap a long and narrow causeway across a marshy river valley, this was an extremely dangerous manoeuvre, but at first all went well: disorganised and exhausted, the Allies did not react until the retreat had been under way for many hours, and even then they were held at bay on the outskirts of the city by the French rearguard. Many of Napoleon's troops therefore escaped, and even more would doubtless have done so but for the fact that the causeway was mistakenly blown up early in the afternoon. As a result what could have been a skilful end to an unfortunate campaign was converted into catastrophe, at least 30,000 French troops who might easily have got away intact now being either killed or captured, and the Allies also taking immense quantities of stores, artillery and baggage. Added to the 38,000 casualties the French had suffered over the previous three days, not to mention the many thousands who had been lost earlier in the campaign, this was a blow from which recovery was simply impossible.

Allied casualties had also been very high – at least 50,000 men – but the victory was to prove cheap at the cost, Napoleonic control of central and northern Europe now evaporating overnight. With the *grande armée* fleeing for the Rhine, those of Napoleon's German satellites that had not already come over to the Allies – Mecklenburg had changed sides in March and Bavaria early in October – either collapsed or deserted the French cause, whilst many of the German units still serving with imperial armies crossed the lines en masse or had to be disarmed. Also lost at this time was Holland, which the French evacuated in the first week of November, leaving a group of influential merchants and politicians hastily to establish a provisional government so as to maintain order. Finally, Denmark was now invaded by Bernadotte and forced to make peace in January 1814.

With the French driven across the Rhine, the *befreiungskrieg* now finally acquired the the unequivocal appearance of a war of nations, especially given the fact that most of France's erstwhile allies hastily authorised the formation of substantial forces of volunteers and militia. But, again, all was not what it seemed. The western *landwehr* and *landsturm* were only formed at all because the Allies demanded them as the price of continuing independence and even then only under much protest, whilst nationalist agitators such as Görres very soon discovered that they were no longer *personae gratae*. As for the population at large, the evidence is at best mixed. On the one hand, it seems clear that public opinion did become greatly excited, the French ambassador to Munich, for example, writing of the Bavarian decision to join the Allies that Maximilian I 'could not fight single-handedly against that public sentiment which had arisen throughout Germany, dominating the situation to such an extent that [he] would have been dethroned had he acted otherwise'.[21] Yet, on the other, there does not seem to have

21 G. Hellman (ed.), *Memoirs of the Comte de Mercy Argenteau, Napoleon's Chamberlain and His Minister Plenipotentiary to the King of Bavaria* (New York, 1917), p. 148.

been much enthusiasm actually to take up arms. In Hamburg, for example, a large part of the new troops raised in the revolt of March 1813 were actually drafts from the King's German Legion sent out from Britain, despite the fact that that one British observer described its inhabitants as being 'certainly as . . . willing to exert themeselves in aid of the good cause as any people I ever saw in my life'.[22] Nor were things any better when, later in the year, those Prussian territories that had been liberated from the French, together with the *rheinbund* states, began to raise new armies for the Allies: having already discovered that the behaviour of their liberators was frequently just as bad as that of the French, they now found that they were to called up at a rate that far exceeded anything demanded by Napoleon (for example, to meet the quotas set by the Allies – generally set at four per cent of their population – France's erstwhile allies had to abolish the the right of substitution). Not surprisingly they therefore proved most unenthusiastic soldiers: during the Waterloo campaign of 1815, at least 10,000 Rhinelanders fled the Prussian army. As for Napoleon's defeat in Germany, it is quite clear that nationalism had played very little role in his downfall. Popular support for the war had been limited, and only Prussia had made any real changes in her military institutions until after the French had been overcome at Leipzig. Even then, moreover, the introduction of universal conscription and the formation of the *landwehr* had not prevented near disaster at Lützen and Bautzen, the day having been saved only by the entrance of Austria and Sweden into the war and the arrival of substantial British aid (from 1812 onwards British aid to Napoleon's opponents assumed a magnitude that was quite unprecedented: between 1812 and 1814 Prussia received £2,088,682, Austria £1,639,523, Russia £3,366,334, and Sweden £2,334,992). Throughout the campaign of 1813, meanwhile, the emperor displayed a confidence that was all but unlimited. From the evacuation of East Prussia and the Grand Duchy of Warsaw onwards, French garrisons that eventually amounted to over 100,000 men were left scattered in the *grande armée*'s receding wake in the assumption of an eventual counter-offensive. Offered peace terms that would have stripped France of her German annexations, Westphalia, Berg, the Illyrian provinces, and the Grand Duchy of Warsaw, but given her her natural frontiers, Holland and the Kingdom of Italy, Napoleon chose rather to bring Austria down upon his head. Having thus gratuitously

22 *Cit.* Jackson, *Bath Archives*, II, p. 70.

doubled the forces facing him, Napoleon then insisted on retaining Saxony as his base of operations even though it was so badly exposed as to be all but indefensible. At Leipzig, too, he held on to the last minute when retreat on 17 October would have brought safety. And, last but not least, when Metternich offered him terms – the so-called Frankfurt proposals – that would have offered him the natural frontiers, Napoleon rejected these as well. Underlying the entire campaign, in fact, we see a failure to perceive any limits to what the emperor could ask either of France or of his much tried troops, a constant tendency to underrate the quality of the enemy armies and to forget the deficiencies of his own, and, above all, a belief that somehow the entire continent could be imposed on simultaneously. In short, for total victory, everything was risked, and, in the end, thrown away.

Of course, it was not just in Germany that the frontiers of Napoleonic power were receding in 1813, but also in Spain and in Italy. Here, too, there is plenty of material to suggest that over-blown language is not in order. Whilst in Spain it is true that guerrilla resistance made a significant contribution to the successful liberation of most of the Peninsula by the duke of Wellington in 1813, popular insurrection played no part in the defeat of the French in Italy at all, even though she, too, was witnessing the emergence of the first shoots of nationalism. Thus in perhaps no other area in Europe had the Revolution elicited such enthusiasm. However, with the experience of French occupation, the Italian revolutionary movement had split. Whilst many of its members continued to see the future in terms of collaboration with the French, others began to look to the creation of a single Italian state. By the time that Napoleon came to power, then, a school of thought had emerged that believed that genuine liberty could only be achieved through the ejection of the French – and, indeed, all other foreigners – and the establishment of a united Italian Republic. Yet the liberalism which this tendency represented was not the only source of Italian nationalism, the policies pursued by the French and their collaborators also stimulating the emergence of a strong Romantic tendency, which aimed to return to the corporate society of the Middle Ages, and was therefore as opposed as the liberals to the rule of Napoleon. Having once emerged, this burgeoning opposition to the empire found expression in longstanding Italian traditions of political and social association. Ever since the mediaeval period the Italian peninsula had been characterised by numerous secret associations whose aims ran the gamut of virtually every form of social – and antisocial – activity. Imbued as it was with a tradition of secrecy and conspiracy, few models could have been better suited to a revolutionary underground drawn from a narrow social and intellectual élite, whilst it was now given a major boost by the French encouragement of freemasonry.

In consequence, all over Italy there now emerged a bewildering variety of anti-French secret societies. Chief among these groups were the Sanfedisti, the Trinitari, the Calderari, the Filadelfi, the Adelfi, the Guelfi, and, above all, the Carbonari. To some extent, these groups can be given a political typology – the Sanfedisti and the Calderari were militantly Catholic and traditionalist, and the Filadelfi and Carbonari republican and liberal – but in practice at this stage they all embraced a wide range of views, being brought together by their common opposition to the French. With the emergence of such an underground, it might be thought that Italy would have been on the brink of revolt by 1813, but in fact no such revolt occurred. Typically formed from men of property and education, the secret societies could not but look askance at such examples as that afforded by Calabria, and were in practice loath to unleash such a spectre, knowing, as they did, that they would inevitably become a target for the insurgents. In consequence, they did little to foment peasant unrest, whilst the populace remained utterly indifferent to all but their own social and economic concerns, the events of 1813 therefore awaking but the feeblest of echoes. Although the secret societies received an influx of support from erstwhile collaborators with an eye to the future, the people rallied neither to the Austrians when they invaded Venetia in October 1813, nor to the substantial Anglo-Sicilian army that landed at Livorno in March 1814 (it is true that anti-Bonapartist rioting did break out in Milan on 20 April, but by that point Napoleon's viceroy, Prince Eugene, had already signed an armistice). In so far as there was any response at all, it came from the rather unlikely figure of Joachim Murat who had changed sides in January 1814 in the belief that only by championing Italian nationalism could he now hope to survive, but his movements were in any case so dilatory that his army played no effective role in the campaign. In consequence, Eugène was able to hold out in Lombardy without difficulty, fending off the rather ineffectual efforts of his Austrian opponent, General Hiller, until the very end of the war.

To conclude, then, the campaign of 1813 was by no means marked by a great 'people's war' against Napoleon. Whilst it is true that in Spain the guerrilla war reached a peak of effectiveness in the winter of 1812–13, Italy remained completely inert, whilst in Germany mass armies were only raised, even in Prussia, by means of compulsion, and then only at the cost of serious popular opposition. As for Austria and Russia, such expansion as took place in the size of their armed forces was not marked by any change in their nature. 'People's war', in short, was simply not an issue.

NAPOLEON AT BAY

By the end of 1813, then, Eugene's beleaguered domains aside, the frontiers of the French imperium stood roughly at the Pyrenees and the Rhine, all that was left to Napoleon being the resources of the 'natural frontiers'. Opposed on every front by means that were potentially incalculable, his own forces had once again been reduced to a mere skeleton. In order to survive, he would therefore have to call forth sacrifices on a scale not seen in France even in the days of the Terror. Already, however, he had asked too much, and in consequence he was now to be deserted.

Let us begin with a consideration of the impact of the Russian campaign upon French opinion. Since Napoleon's failure was blamed on the climate, it does not seem in itself to have had too serious an impact on confidence in the empire. The Bourse, for example, held firm, whilst to quote Marbot:

> The majority of the French nation . . . accustomed to regard the emperor as infallible, and having, moreover no idea of what had really happened, saw only the renown which the capture of Moscow had shed on our arms . . ..[23]

Nevertheless, many of the educated classes were now beginning to have serious doubts as to the future. As Count Molé reflected after watching Napoleon review some new conscripts, 'The more I saw of him, the greater was my conviction . . . that death alone could set a limit to his plans and put a curb on his ambition'.[24] Moreover, such private misgivings were soon translated into public discontent by the measures which Napoleon now took to recruit his forces. Between January and October 1813 no fewer than 840,000 fresh troops were summoned to the colours, large numbers of these

---

23 J. de Marbot, *The Memoirs of Baron de Marbot* (London, 1892), II, p. 350.
24 Marquis de Noaillles (ed.), *The Life and Memoirs of Count Molé, 1781–1855*, (London, 1923), I, pp. 148–9.

unfortunates being men who had previously escaped service or who had succeeded in securing 'cushy billets' of one sort or another. For the first time, too, large numbers of married men were taken due to the mobilisation of the National Guard for service in the field. Nor did the wealthy escape: in April Napoleon gave the prefects the power arbitrarily to designate young men of good family to serve in a new 10,000-strong cavalry force, which was, moreover, to clothe, mount and equip itself at its own cost. And all this, meanwhile, was imposed at a time of continued economic hardship – as Pasquier wrote, 'Not a day passed, but that money became tighter, and, as fears for the future led the most well-to-do families to curtail their expenses, there was, as a result, a considerable decrease in the employment of labour.'[25]

Such was the habit of obedience that the Napoleonic régime had succeeded in instilling into the nation with regard to conscription that on the whole all these levies were met (thereby incidentally encouraging Napoleon to fight on to the bitter end in Germany). Yet, for all that, they nevertheless engendered immense resentment, particularly amongst the propertied, who now for the first time felt the real impact of conscription and in addition found that the money they had invested in substitutes in previous years was now wasted. Even now, especially in areas where imperial policies had been particularly paternalistic, the régime was not wholly without popular support, but sacrifices of the sort Napoleon was now demanding far outstripped the pool of willing manpower, whilst Leipzig had stripped military service of the last vestiges of glory and dealt a fatal blow to his credit. Yet, convinced that fresh troops would continue to be forthcoming willy-nilly, when he got back to Paris Napoleon ordered two further levies of 150,000 men apiece, as well as imposing an increase in several taxes and a twenty-five per cent cut in official salaries. All this was just too much. To quote Pasquier again, 'A general anxiety prevailed . . .. There was no faith in anything anymore, and every illusion had vanished.'[26] Needless to say, this attitude could not but undermine the loyalty even of the régime's own personnel, who as *notables* inevitably had much to lose as well as no desire to return to the days of Jacobinism and the *levée en masse* which a desperate emperor now seemed to be trying to revive (not only was the rhetoric of the régime increasingly echoing that of 1793, but Napoleon had sent out a

25 Pasquier, *Memoirs*, II, p. 67.
26 *Ibid.*, p. 108.

number of extraordinary commissioners in the style of the old *deputés en mission*, introduced a number of measures intended to redistribute a certain amount of land to the peasantry, and decreed the formation of a volunteer militia drawn from unemployed workers in Paris and other towns of northern France). Such doubts were reinforced by the popular reaction to the new levies. Draft evasion once again became a serious problem, fewer than half the new levies appearing at the depots, whilst for the first time since the 1790s serious anti-conscription riots broke out, these in some cases attaining an additional political dimension (in Belgium, for example, there were demonstrations in support of a return to Austrian rule, whilst at Hazebrouck rioters proclaimed that they were fighting for 'Louis XVII'). At the same time, too, with thousands of draft evaders and deserters once again taking to the forests and turning to banditry, the *notables* seemed threatened with a renewal of the disorder that had marked the last years of the Directory. With a royalist restoration no longer a serious threat in social and economic terms – on 1 February 1813 Louis XVIII had issued a well-publicised declaration in which he promised generally to respect the status quo – the political establishment had no reason to support a fight to the finish and every reason to make peace. Already in December 1813 the *corps législatif* had effectively demanded that Napoleon make peace immediately. Meanwhile, further signs of disaffection appeared in the administration, the prefects and their deputies now beginning to refuse to carry out their orders, to connive at draft evasion and the non-payment of taxes, and even to abscond altogether.

With the political machine in a state of disintegration, the war effort could not long have been maintained. Yet even now Napoleon would not give up, seeking fresh salvation in an escape from the Spanish imbroglio. Thus, the captive Ferdinand VII was offered his throne in exchange for promises that the British would be expelled from the Peninsula, and the 60,000 veteran troops that still held northern Catalonia and a number of beleaguered fortresses in other parts of eastern Spain allowed to return to France. Implicit in this arrangement was the possibility of a war between Britain and Spain, Napoleon having got wind of the serious difficulties that had been besetting their alliance ever since the outbreak of the Latin-American revolutions in 1810. Had the scheme worked, it might indeed have led to great things – the 100,000 troops who were facing Wellington and the Spaniards were the last substantial force of veterans to whom the emperor had access – but yet again

Napoleon was demonstrably completely lacking in judgement: whatever the state of relations between Britain and Spain, the latter was certain to reject Napoleon's terms out of hand, as she in fact immediately did.

In the end Napoleon was reduced to releasing Ferdinand without any conditions, but the gesture was as futile as it was desperate. At best, Napoleon had no more than 85,000 men to defend the eastern frontier against an initial total of at least 350,000 Allies. In the south-west, meanwhile, 40,000 Frenchmen faced 90,000 British, Portuguese and Spaniards, the only fronts that were remotely secure being Catalonia and Italy. As for the quality of the French forces, not only were the bulk of the troops composed of raw recruits or such miscellaneous sweepings as invalids, customs guards, sailors and *gendarmes*, but experienced officers and NCOs were desperately few in number, the emperor even having had to plunder the Invalides to provide cadres for some of the new guard regiments whose formation he now decreed (in the last years of the empire, the Imperial Guard grew enormously, Napoleon seeking to boost morale amongst his raw conscripts by drafting them straight into its ranks). Also lacking were arms, uniforms and equipment of all sorts, whilst, amongst the senior ranks in particular, demoralisation was rampant, many of the marshals now begging Napoleon to make peace on whatever terms he could get.

Instead of listening to such advice, Napoleon chose to fight on in the hope of improving his bargaining position, striking hard and fast at a succession of Allied commanders as they invaded eastern France. At first it seemed he might succeed: suffering no fewer than five major defeats in three weeks, the shaken Allies offered peace on the basis of the frontiers of 1792. But once again Napoleon had been too successful for his own good, electing to fight on in the hope of forcing the resurrection of the Frankfurt proposals. It was his last mistake: though his improvised armies had performed prodigies of valour, starving and exhausted as they were, little more could be expected from them. As for the rest of France, even the few enthusiasts for Jacobinism who still remained had not been taken in by the attempt to recall 1793, whilst the bulk of the population was desperate for peace. As a result, guerrilla resistance only took place when the more unruly elements of the Allied forces got out of control: if anything, in fact, the depredations of the half-starved French army, which was now living almost entirely by pillage, made the populace downright hostile. Nor, of course, were the *notables* any more enthusiastic than before, the result being that on all sides expressions of support for the restoration of the Bourbons began to multiply dramatically. Last but not least, Napoleon's intransigence had driven the Allies closer together, an agreement reached at Chaumont on 1 March committing all four of the great powers to fighting on until the emperor had been defeated.

With matters in such a state, the end came quickly. Once fighting resumed early in March, though Napoleon continued to fight and manoeuvre relentlessly, he could in the end achieve little, and by the end of the month the Allies were bearing down on Paris. Meanwhile, on 12 March Bourdeaux had proclaimed Louis XVIII, its authorities having first made sure that they would be immediately relieved by the Anglo-Portuguese army. At this point, the army finally broke as well: mutiny and desertion were now rife; at Lyons Marshal Augereau simply abandoned his headquarters and fled; and in Paris Marshal Marmont first surrendered the city to the Allies without much of a fight on 31 March, and then led his troops over to the enemy. With Alexander I and Frederick William III both in the capital, the initative was now seized by the erstwhile foreign minister, Talleyrand, who had been living there in semi-retirement and was convinced that France's only hope was the restoration of the Bourbons. Defying Napoleon's orders that all high-ranking dignitaries should evacuate the capital, as soon as the Allied monarchs arrived he set about persuading them that Napoleon had to go. Though the hand of a rather doubtful Alexander (who hated the Bourbons) had to be forced by some hastily organised demonstrations of support for Louis XVIII, on 1 April the Allied monarchs issued a declaration that they would no longer treat with Napoleon or any of his family, and that, in so far as the future government of France was concerned, they would respect the wishes of the French people as expressed by an immediate meeting of the Senate. Stage-managed by Talleyrand, this event could have but one end: on 2 April the sixty-four members of the Senate who were both present in Paris and willing to attend proclaimed Napoleon to be deposed and formally invited Louis XVIII to return to France.

Meanwhile, Napoleon was at Fontainebleau with some 60,000 men. Though the emperor was still ready to fight on, his remaining commanders would take no more, on 4 April Napoleon therefore being waited upon by Macdonald, Ney, Lefebvre, Berthier and Oudinot, and bluntly informed that he must abdicate. After a brief attempt at bluster, he agreed to step down in favour of his son, and, two days later, to surrender the throne altogether. The war was not yet quite over – if only because news of the armistice did not reach him in time, Wellington had to fight one last battle against Soult at Toulouse on 10 April, whilst various isolated garrisons also held on for some time – but on 28 April the emperor sailed for his Elban exile.

THE LIMITS OF THE POSSIBLE

The surrender of the last few diehard garrisons did not, of course, quite mark the end of the Napoleonic Wars. In February 1815 for a variety of reasons Napoleon embarked on a desperate atttempt to reconquer France at the head of the miniscule army that had been allotted him by the Allies (bored and frustrated, he was being starved of money by Louis XVIII, and he may also have come to believe that there was a plot against his life). Landing at Cannes on 1 March, within a few weeks he had forced the Bourbons into exile and mobilised an army of 280,000 men. After a nominal effort to keep the peace, on 15 June Napoleon struck into Belgium in a desperate effort to secure the defeat of his nearest opponents before the full weight of Allied power could once more fall upon him, only to be heavily defeated by the duke of Wellington at Waterloo. This was the end: sporadic fighting followed as the Allies invaded France, but as early as 22 June Napoleon was persuaded once again to abdicate, eventually giving himself up to the British at Rochefort. Less than one month later he set sail for his final exile on Saint Helena.

The reasons why Napoleon was defeated at Waterloo – his physical infirmities, the incompetence of his subordinates, the tactical brilliance of the duke of Wellington, the staunch support offered to the 'iron duke' by Marshal Blücher, and the shortcomings of the French army – need not concern us here. What matters rather more is to point out that even had Waterloo been a victory, it is difficult to see how it could have brought security: at the Congress of Vienna news of the escape from Elba led to the powers patching up their considerable differences, resolving to overthrow Napoleon once and for all, and abjuring a separate peace. Faced by a coalition which included virtually every state in Europe, Napoleon's only ally was Murat, who, in a desperate bid to save his throne, attacked the Austrian army in northern Italy, only, as we have seen, to be defeated at Tolentino. In short, Napoleon had once more committed France to a seemingly endless struggle against impossible odds.

Whether France would accept this was a moot point. Certainly, Napoleon initially secured a considerable measure of support, but it is unclear for how long this approval would have been sustained.

From the very beginning it is evident that the hard core of the popular Bonapartism of the Hundred Days came from the ranks of Napoleonic veterans. In the first place, large parts of the army had not shared the miseries of 1814, the many thousands of men tied up in the isolated garrisons that had held out to the end coming home convinced that they were undefeated. Sharing their sense of betrayal, meanwhile, were the masses of prisoners of war who now returned from an exile that had frequently been quite appalling. For the most part demobilised, such men now frequently found themselves homeless and unemployed, whilst they were joined in misery by at least 20,000 officers who were stripped of their posts and placed on half pay. Meanwhile, even those officers and men fortunate enough to secure a place in the new army had to suffer the humiliation of watching hundreds of Bourbon favourites being promoted to high rank and awarded the Legion of Honour. With the despair and exhaustion of Napoleon's last campaigns increasingly shrouded in a haze of glory, it was hardly surprising that Bourbon army and demobilised veterans alike should have rushed to join Napoleon in 1815.

In so far as the rest of the population is concerned, the picture is less certain. In Napoleon's favour was the fact that, whereas in 1814 the Bourbons had not appeared so bad an option, perceptions of the Restoration had now changed. In complete contrast to the moderate views that Louis XVIII had been espousing in 1813, the *notables* found themselves threatened with loss of employment and land alike: not only were many officials sacked, but alarming noises began to be heard with regard to the *biens nationaux*. With the régime clearly favouring the nobility in its appointments, moreover, the principle of the career open to talent also seemed at risk, whilst still further discontent was aroused by signs of renewed clerical influence. Nor did such policies do anything to reassure committed liberals, this group having already been alienated by the deletion of the principle of the sovereignty of the people from the constitution drawn up by the Senate in April 1814. Lower down the social scale, the peasantry, too, were concerned for such land as they had acquired during the Revolution, as well as being rife with rumours that the tithes and feudal dues were to be restored. Finally, assailed by post-war depression, the urban workers were suffering severe unemployment, and in consequence regretted the paternalism that had, however imperfectly, shielded them under the empire. And, last but not least, for all classes of society, the experience of foreign occupation had frequently been an extremely unpleasant one, particularly in those regions traversed by the Prussians and Russians.

In consequence, excitement at Napoleon's return was very great. But whether this support could ever have been translated into enthusiasm for war is doubtful – the number of civilian volunteers who offered themselves for service was no more than 8,000, and, when the emperor again made a superficial attempt to revive the spirit of 1793 through such measures as the appointment of Lazare Carnot as minister of the interior, this alarmed many of those who a few days before had been rejoicing at his return. Whilst they did not want a return to the social and economic norms of the *ancien régime*, they had no desire to see a return to the requisitioning and compulsion of 1793 either. In consequence, it was not long before peasant resistance had once again emerged: though royalist attempts to raise rebellions in the Midi proved abortive, the Vendée rose in revolt and *chouannerie* once again swept the west, whilst in many areas the peasantry slipped back into the sullen disaffection of 1814. Certainly popular support continued in the shape of the *fédéré* militia whose formation Napoleon now permitted, but this was restricted to the towns and cities, and even then was not entirely solid, there being report of riots or other serious disturbances in Paris, Lyons, Dunkirk, Nantes, Marseilles and at least thirteen other towns. Nor was much effort made to turn it to good use: on the one hand the emperor continued to distrust popular levies and Jacobin insurrection alike, whilst on the other he was unwilling to alienate the *notable* and bourgeois support he was seeking to attract through his adoption of a liberal constitution (the so-called Additional Act of 22 April). Yet this gesture achieved almost nothing, the emperor's new-found regard for parliamentarianism being generally derided, particularly in the press (which was now left virtually uncensored), and large numbers of local officials indulging in passive non-cooperation or even actively stirring up opposition to the new régime. Though Carnot attempted to remedy the situation by a series of wholesale purges, getting rid of sixty-one prefects alone, such new men as he brought in for the most part proved no more enthusiastic and rather less competent. Still worse, whipping up fresh resentment as they did, the purges only added to the problem, which was in any case also being inflamed by schoolteachers, the Church and even the judiciary. With the entire country seemingly sliding into anarchy and even some of Napoleon's own ministers, such as Fouché, playing a double game, whether the sort of war that France would now have again to fight was ever a feasible possibility must remain an open question.

In the 'Hundred Days' of 1815, in short, we see in microcosm the faults that brought Napoleon to his downfall. At the heart of the problem was, in Napoleon's own words, his belief that the impossible was 'the spectre of the timid and the refuge of the coward'.[27] Invading Russia in 1812, he had set himself a task that was in practice beyond the capabilities of the *grande armée*, and had then made disaster certain by persisting even when it was clear that victory was beyond his grasp. Similarly, in Germany in 1813 he had rejected every possibility of a compromise peace, and, in search of total victory, taken risks with his forces that had culminated in the catastrophe at Leipzig. And, finally, having already made demands of France for which she was psychologically quite unprepared, in the winter of 1813–14 he once again gambled on military success. Meanwhile, France was being thrown back more and more on her own resources, so that in 1814 she was finally confronted with the necessity of once again becoming a Nation-in-Arms. That she would acquiesce in this prospect Napoleon had no doubt – hence in part his continued belligerence – but in fact the emperor's real power-base was his de facto promise to safeguard the revolutionary settlement without recourse to the extremities of 1793. The latter being no more acceptable in 1814 than they had been twenty-one years earlier, particularly in the context of what appeared to be studied Bourbon moderation, both people and *notables* fell away. Did France, then, betray Napoleon? Though such a claim is an important component of the Napoleonic legend, in fact it would seem that the reverse is true. If the emperor fought on, he did not do so because France, the principles of the Revolution, or even his own dynasty, were in danger. On the contrary, he fought on because he could not accept the limitations that the powers were now determined to place on his influence. Far from France betraying Napoleon, then, it was rather Napoleon who betrayed France.

Before we conclude, there is one last question that must be dealt with. Tempting though it is to argue that France was somehow beaten down through the adoption of the very weapons that she had used to subjugate Europe, the armies that confronted Napoleon in the period 1812–14 were essentially conventional. With popular resistance of only limited importance, what really changed the situation was the fact that the emperor was forced for the first time to fight all the great powers simultaneously. As this was entirely his own fault, we are once more thrown back on the emperor's refusal to restrict himself to the limits of the possible. From here we return

27 *Cit.* Molé, *Memoirs*, I, p. 149.

to Clausewitz. Whilst *On War* seemingly made much of the idea that war is by definition an absolute struggle waged with the full weight of the national power, in reality Clauscwitz believed war was rarely, if ever, total, being effectively limited by the need to wage it in accordance with a political object. If he had ever recognised this necessity, however, Napoleon had lost sight of it by 1812, and, in losing such a sense of what was possible, he finally lost his throne as well.

9 THE IMPACT OF THE NAPOLEONIC WARS

THE NAPOLEONIC WARS AND THE IDEA OF PROGRESS

> There are some battles . . . which claim our attention . . . on account of their enduring importance, and by reason of the practical influence on our own social and political condition, which we can trace to the results of those engagements. They have for us an actual and abiding interest . . ..[1]

As John Keegan points out in his masterly study, *The Face of Battle*, with these words, which are taken from the preface to his *Decisive Battles of the World*, the Victorian historian, Sir Edward Creasy, gave intellectual justification to an abiding fascination with the details of military conflict that both then and later seemed entirely to contradict the prevailing ethos of the western world in general and the historical world in particular. To quote Keegan:

> Creasy's formula provided every historian who wished to write about battles with the excuse he needed. Battles are important. They decide things. They improve things.[2]

For us, of course, the question that now arises is to establish exactly what the Napoleonic Wars decided. In simple political terms, we might argue that the occupation of Paris in 1814 finally put an end to the ambitions entertained by successive French rulers since the days of Louis XIV of exercising a preponderant influence in the international affairs of western Europe, whilst in addition confirming Britain's victory in the long struggle in which Britain and France had been engaged for commercial and maritime supremacy. The historical community having long since moved on from the narrow confines of diplomatic history, however, the issue must

---

1 E. Creasy, *The Fifteen Decisive Battles of the World from Marathon to Waterloo* (London, 1851), p. viii.
2 J. Keegan, *The Face of Battle: a Study of Agincourt, Waterloo and the Somme* (London, 1978), p. 60.

needs be addressed in another fashion. Thus, it might also be argued that the chief result of the Napoleonic Wars was to usher in a new age of revolution, or, to put it another way, that they had in fact decided nothing, in that, although the Old Order once again seemed in firm control of Europe's destiny, the changes that had been wrought by Napoleon and his armies were such that the peace settlement of 1814–15 was inherently unstable. In other words, if the Napoleonic Wars matter, it is because they brought fundamental change to European society. As the East German historian, Walter Markov, puts it:

> [Napoleon] could not simply shake off the legacy of the Revolution, which clung to him like some lascerating hairshirt. Wherever his campaigns took him, he was obliged to expunge feudalism, to topple monarchs and to flout tradition. He thus continued to find himself the executor and bailiff – as well as the beneficiary – of a great upheaval.[3]

Though the Marxian tradition from which Markov stems has been increasingly challenged, to pretend that the Europe of 1814 was the same as that of 1803 would be to tilt at windmills. Napoleon did bring change to Europe, it being in large part through the onward march of his armies that the French Revolution was exported to the rest of the Continent. Yet to accept this is not the same as to accept, say, that the period from 1803 to 1815 brought about a full-scale bourgeois revolution, Karl Marx himself making it quite clear that in Germany at least no such development had occurred – thus: 'While in England and France feudalism was entirely destroyed [by 1848] . . . the feudal nobility in Germany had retained a great portion of their ancient privileges.'[4] In this concluding chapter, then, we must make some attempt to establish the limits of change, and to decide, in short, whether Napoleon really was, as he has been called, 'one of the fathers of modern Europe'.[5]

THE PRAGMATIC LEGITIMISTS

Once upon a time it was all very simple. On Napoleon's defeat in 1814, the powers met at Vienna and devised a peace settlement that

---

3 W. Markov, *Grand Empire: Virtue and Vice in the Napoleonic Era* (New York, 1990), p. 57.

4 K. Marx, *Revolution and Counter-Revolution*, ed. E. Marx Aveling (London, 1971), p. 3.

5 J. Godechot, 'The sense and importance of the transformation of the institutions of the Napoleonic epoch' in F.A. Kafker and J.M. Laux (eds.), *Napoleon and his Times: Selected Interpretations* (Malabar, Florida, 1989), p. 295.

not only swept aside the principles of nationalism, but ensured that a French Revolution could never again endanger the peace of Europe. Internally, meanwhile, they overturned French-style reforms, brought back absolute monarchy, restored the privileges of the Church, the nobility and the guilds, and presided over a period of black reaction whose ultimate product was the revolutions of 1848. In short, the clock had been turned back to 1789, it taking a further series of seismic upheavals of the sort witnessed in that year to allow a return to the process of social and political progress that characterised the Napoleonic era.

As with all such myths, this has a certain basis of truth. Culturally speaking, the Restoration era was certainly one of counter-revolution. In the aftermath of the Napoleonic Wars the French Revolution inspired far more fear than it had ever done at the time of its occurrence, the consequence being a powerful religious revival that sought both to buttress the monarchies of Europe against the threat of revolt and to restore the influence of the Church. Hence, the calls by such figures as Friedrich Schlegel, Joseph de Maistre, Louis de Bonald and Hugues de Lamennais for a return to an idealised theocracy in which secular rulers would owe their allegiance to the pope, and the Catholic Church enjoy complete independence, as well as unrestricted powers of censorship. Hand-in-hand with this development there went a widespread attack on freemasonry and, above all, Jewry, with such writers as Friedrich Rühs demanding such measures as forcible conversion, enslavement and even extermination. With at least some of Europe's monarchs only too happy to co-operate with any force that promised to secure them against the Jacobin spectre, the result was that the Catholic Church, especially, found that the veritable war that had been waged against it in many states during the eighteenth century was now suspended, many of its powers now being restored by a series of concordats. At the same time, there was a more or less severe political reaction with the overthrow of liberal constitutions in Spain and Sicily, the disappearance of the institutions of representative government that had been possessed by such defunct satellites as Westphalia and the Kingdom of Italy, the restoration of absolutism in Piedmont and the Papal States following their reappearance as independent countries, and, above all, the formation of the Holy Alliance under the guidance of Alexander I in September 1815. Finally, socially, too, there was a considerable reaction, there being a widespread tendency to restore the power of the guilds, to rescind the concessions that had been made to the Jews, and, whether formally or informally, to buttress the position of the aristocracy (in Spain, for example, Ferdinand VII was notorious for favouring titled grandees who had done little or nothing in the war against France at the expense of commoners who had fought for years to uphold his rights; equally, in Prussia the Gendarmerie Edict was quietly abandoned and the bourgeoisie once again increasingly excluded from the officer corps).

At the same time, 1814–15 was also a period of 'White Terror'. Expressed at the highest level in a number of arrests and executions – the imprisonment and subsequent trial of numerous liberal sympathisers in Spain, the execution of Marshal Ney and a number of other army officers in France – at a lower level the mob took the law into their own hands. Throughout Spain, for example, the days that followed the coup of May 1814 were marked by a series of riots and other disturbances as constitutionalist officials were chased from town halls and terrorised into falling in line with the dictates of Ferdinand VII. In France the Hundred Days had a bloody sequel in parts of the south as royalist *miquelets* murdered Protestants, Jacobins and public figures associated with the empire, such as the governor of Toulon, Marshal Brune, whilst in Strasbourg there were disturbances against the Jews. In Italy anti-Bonapartist riots broke out in Milan after the surrender of Eugene de Beauharnais and in Germany there were further demonstrations of anti-Semitism, with Lübeck and Bremen both expelling all their Jews.

When all this is said, however, the observer cannot but be struck by the patchy and pragmatic nature of the Restoration. Let us look first of all at the question of territorial organisation. Whilst the Congress of Vienna clearly took no account of national susceptibilities – Poland remained partitioned, Belgium was awarded to Holland, Norway to Sweden, Finland to Russia, and Lombardy and Venetia to Austria – it yet made no attempt to return to the territorial chaos that had marked central Europe. If Italy regained much the same appearance that she had possessed in 1789 except for the incorporation of Genoa into Piedmont and the annexation of the erstwhile Venetian Republic by Austria, the same was not the case with Germany. Here, though Austria regained the Tyrol and Salzburg and certain other districts from Bavaria, whilst Prussia took back the lands that she had lost in 1807 and annexed much of Saxony and the Rhineland as well as Swedish Pomerania, the middling states were allowed to retain the territories which they had acquired in the course of Napoleon's reorganisation of the Holy Roman Empire, whilst the ecclesiastical states, the free cities and the imperial fiefs were not restored to their former status. Indeed, few even of the princely states that had disappeared were restored (the exceptions include Hanover, Brunswick and Saxe-Weimar). Nor, of course, did the old Empire make a reappearance, the confederation of German states that replaced it being organised on an entirely different basis. With Austria giving up Belgium in exchange for her gains in Italy, in short, considerable progress had been made in the direction of the modern concept of the state as a homogeneous block of territories encompassed by a single frontier. In all this, we see the influence of war: the miserable performance put up by the Dutch, the Piedmontese, and, above all, the *reishsarmee* in the Revolutionary Wars had not been forgotten, there now being a strong emphasis on ensuring that France's immediate neighbours would never again cave in in the manner that they had done in the 1790s (thus, far from being a gesture in the direction of German nationalism, the German Confederation was above all envisaged as a military device that would in wartime bind the forces of the small German states in a single army, and their rulers in a permanent alliance).

In terms of internal government, too, the post-Napoleonic era did not witness a single-minded attempt to turn back the clock. Participation in the Napoleonic Wars having convincingly demonstrated the value of professional bureaucracies and uniform systems of government controlled from the centre, few examples can be found of rulers who had introduced such measures abandoning them in 1815, Prussia being the one exception. In the same way, rulers who returned home to discover the new system in place made little attempt to change it, just as others who did not enjoy its benefits often introduced it for themselves. Thus, in France, Louis XVIII retained the departmental system untouched; in Piedmont Victor Emmanuel I attempted to abolish it, but quickly saw the error of his ways; in Holland the constitution of 1814 emasculated the Estates General, abandoned the principle of federalism, and retained the fifteen departments into which Holland and Belgium had been divided under the empire; and in Naples Ferdinand IV retained the reforms introduced by Joseph Bonaparte and Joachim Murat and in 1816 extended the departmental system to Sicily. Finally, in Saxony, Frederick Augustus' fear that Prussia intended to swallow what little territory was left to him after the Vienna settlement convinced him of the need to abandon the pronounced hostility to reform that he had hitherto shown. From 1815 onwards, then, the Saxon ruler incorporated all those parts of his realm that still enjoyed juris-dictions of their own into the centrally ruled hereditary lands, eventually dividing the country into fourteen French-style prefectures. At the same time, too, the chief minister, Detlev von Einsiedel, embarked upon a far-reaching reform of the apparatus of central government that is directly comparable with that undertaken in so many other states during the war years. Last of all, even in ultra-reactionary Austria and Spain, respect for the Old Order was not sufficiently great completely to overcome monarchical self-interest. Thus, we find Francis I failing to restore the privileges of which the Catholic Church had been deprived by Joseph II and governing Hungary without any recourse to its Diet from 1811 to 1825. Ferdinand VII in theory annulled all the legislation passed by the *cortes*, but in practice allowed much of it to survive (on 30 July 1814, for example, it was announced that the monarchy would retain the right to appoint administrative and judicial officials to all villages that had hitherto been *señorios*).

Turning away from strictly administrative matters, we find that constitutionalism was far from dead. Here, too, pragmatism dictated that concessions must be made, there being a common feeling that, in the wake of the wars of the period 1812–15, public opinion could not simply be ignored: whether it was in Russia in 1812, Germany and Austria in 1813, or France in 1814, educated opinion had become more engaged in the course of events than ever before. Thus, France, Sweden, Holland, Finland, and 'Congress Poland' – that part of the Polish lands which was handed over to Russia at Vienna – either retained or were given constitutions, whilst very soon after 1814 these also started to appear in many of the South German states. With regard to France, of course, the 'charter' of 1814 was essentially a device designed to ensure political stability and prevent another revolution, but elsewhere constitutionalism was quite clearly intended as a means of involving at least the educated classes in the fortunes of the state (to return to Saxony, if there was no advance on the archaic constitutional arrangements in force in 1814, it is nonetheless notable that Einsiedel made extensive efforts to justify the government's record and actions to the population).

As for the reordering of society, reaction to the Napoleonic era was once again patchy, in part because there was often little need to turn the clock back. Taking emancipation as a case in point, the abolition of feudalism had in practice generally been relatively painless, if not downright advantageous, to the European nobility. In consequence, with the exception of – in theory – Spain and one or two minor German states such as Hanover and Hesse Darmstädt, there was no question of a formal refeudalisation of rural society where emancipation had taken place, the period after 1815 even witnessing an extension of reform in such states as Baden and Württemberg. What is the case, however, is that the position of the nobility was sometimes further reinforced. Thus, in Prussia in 1816 a fresh ordinance undermined peasant chances of gaining full emancipation by establishing a minimum size of holding as a *sine qua non*, this being set at a level that was unreasonably large. Meanwhile, in a further move to buttress the *junker*, who had, of course, already been reconfirmed in their administrative and judicial capacities, in 1823 the Prussian government introduced a revised model of the old estates that confirmed their political predominance.

With regard to the guilds, and, indeed, to the growth of industry in general, we see rather more ambivalence. Unlike emancipation, there was a considerable reaction against the introduction of laws concerning industrial freedom, the abolition of the guilds being identified as a genuine threat to the social order, the result being that in such states as Hesse-Cassel, Hanover and Oldenburg, their privileges were restored in full. Elsewhere, however, as, for example, in Bavaria, Hesse-Darmstädt, and the Prussia of 1807–13, restrictions on the power of the guilds were allowed to stand, the same being the case for areas that had been under French rule like the Palatinate and Prussia's new Rhenish provinces, where they had been swept away altogether (in Holland, too, we find that their 1808 abolition was never rescinded). Nor, indeed, did the Restoration preclude fresh blows against corporatist practices, further measures being brought in against the guilds in certain states as early as 1819.

In only one field, in fact, can there be said to have been a wholesale reaction against the experience and perception of the Napoleonic era. Given that the Vienna settlement, and, indeed, many of the domestic policies of the Restoration era, rested upon a desire for strength and security, it is, perhaps, somewhat ironic that this area should have been that of armies and land warfare. However, if there was one concept that really was anathema to the monarchical governments of the Old Order, it was that of the Nation-in-Arms. True though it was that some of them had flirted with it in the latter days of the struggle with Napoleon, in practice they remained hostile. In the first place, it was linked inseparably with the threat of revolution, not only because, as one Prussian nobleman put it, 'To arm a nation means merely to organize and facilitate opposition and disaffection'[6], but because the very existence of large armies was held to make international conflict more likely, there being general agreement that the concomitant of a new war must be revolution (hence the genuine attempt to keep the peace of Europe by means of the so-called Congress System). In the second, large armies were an expensive burden that an exhausted Europe could sustain only with the greatest difficulties, demobilisation therefore being an economic necessity. In the third, wherever it had been employed, large-scale conscription had aroused such widespread resentment that it could not be regarded as anything other than a threat to the security of the state. And, in the fourth, the vast majority of senior officers had genuine concerns about the military value of large masses of improvised citizen-soldiers, whether it was in Spain in 1808, Austria in 1809 or Germany in 1813, new levies having given at best only a moderate account of themselves. At the same time, of course, the very idea of soldiers who thought for themselves rather than obeying orders remained a very threatening one, 'the deliberating soldier' being, as one Prussian officer put it, 'no longer a soldier, but a mutineer'.[7] Finally, there was also the question of political reliability, a resentful and angry French army having rallied en masse to Napoleon in 1815. There was, in fact, no evidence that the argument was valid – after all, in France in 1789, in Russia in 1801, in Spain in 1808, and in Sweden in 1792 and 1809, old-style professional armies, or at least their officers, had been agents or allies of political revolution, whilst in 1814 a mass conscript army had overthrown Spanish constitutionalism – but in the atmosphere of 1815 it seemed axiomatic that small forces of long-service veterans made by far the best political sense, and all the more so as the post-war period was one of severe hardship, a variety of bread riots and peasant uprisings being reported from around Europe.

So far so good. However, the reaction inherent in such thinking faced a major problem in that, like it or not, the Napoleonic Wars *had* involved armies of a very considerable size that were often composed of men who possessed minimal training and experience. As John Gooch puts it, 'The conundrum which now faced most of the rulers of Europe was how to reconcile military efficiency, which

---

6 Cit. H. Strachan, *European Armies and the Conduct of War* (London, 1983), p. 69.

7 Cit. G. Craig, *The Politics of the Prussian Army, 1640–1945* (Oxford, 1955), p. 80.

meant a large conscript army, with reliability, which required a small, élite, professional force.'[8] Not much time was wasted on the problem, however, the answer that was found being to argue that military efficiency did not require a large conscript army at all. Thus, in France, in part perhaps because they could not but remain politically suspect, the many Napoleonic generals who had now found renewed employment under the Bourbons argued that the chief lesson to be learned from the wars of their erstwhile master was that mass armies did not pay off. The contrast, say, between the Austerlitz campaign and that of 1812 showed that as the French army had grown bigger so its quality and capabilities had declined dramatically. Wastage had increased due to the inability of raw conscripts to endure the rigours of life in the field; supply problems had multiplied; manoeuvrability had fallen off; and battle tactics had become ever more bludgeon-like. As a result, from the precision instrument of 1805–7, the grande armée had degenerated into a lumbering monster that had ultimately collapsed under its own weight. Equally, in Prussia even at the height of the reform period there had always been numerous officers who maintained that Jena and Auerstädt had been lost through bad luck and incompetence rather than the sort of fundamental military weakness condemned by Scharnhorst and his fellows. In the period after 1814, encouraged by Frederick William's increasing irritation with the reformers, who were not only generally arrogant and insubordinate, but had spent the befreiungskrieg and its aftermath pressing a highly nationalistic foreign policy upon him, such men took every opportunity to portray the mass army that had been raised in 1813 as being undisciplined and unreliable, pointing especially to the mounting evidence that the landwehr had become extremely inefficient (although this was true enough, it should be noted that it was being starved both of adequate training and experienced officers). Finally, in Austria, for commanders such as Schwarzenburg and the Archduke Charles, the very survival of the empire was proof enough that the traditional military system was entirely adequate, the moral being that, as the latter put it, what counted was 'not the number of soldiers . . . but their efficiency and mobility'.[9]

It is such thinking that explains the fact that the leading military thinker of the period after 1815 was not the 'mahdi of the mass',

8   J. Gooch, Armies in Europe (London, 1980), p. 50.
9   Cit. G. Rothenberg, 'The Austrian army in the age of Metternich', Journal of Modern History, XL, No. 2 (June, 1968), 163.

Carl von Clausewitz, but Antoine Henri Jomini. In essence, if Jomini was influential, it was because he was saying what his audience wanted to hear. A Swiss of humble origins, Jomini had become a staff-officer in the Napoleonic army, serving at Jena and Eylau, in the Peninsula, and finally in Germany in 1813, at which point a combination of personal animosity and self-interest led him to change sides and join the Russians. Devoting himself thereafter to writing commentaries on the art of war, he produced a theory of warfare whose keynote was revulsion at the age of Napoleon. In this respect, the Spanish and Russian campaigns had both been particularly shocking. On the one hand, Spain had afforded him a vision of 'people's war' taken to its worst extremes – of a land ravaged not only by hostile armies, but also by gangs of guerrillas-cum-bandits in which normal life had completely broken down and famine and atrocity were the norm. On the other it had done little to persuade him of the value of 'people's armies' in that the crowds of raw recruits fielded by the Spaniards were defeated on almost every occasion that they took the field, whilst the small, professional, eighteeth-century-style army of the duke of Wellington had been well-nigh invincible. From the Russian campaign, meanwhile, Jomini drew a further lesson in the horrors that could result from involving the people in armed conflict – the peasantry may not have been central to the defeat of Napoleon in 1812, but they had nevertheless on occasion carried out atrocities that were as terrifying as they were bestial not to mention in the problems that could result from armies becoming over large. Finally, from the Napoleonic Wars as a whole, Jomini drew a further lesson in that he saw very clearly that Napoleon had committed France to a war to which there was no end except total victory, remarking, 'One might say that he was sent into this world to teach generals and statesmen what they ought to avoid.'[10] The emperor's failure to limit his objectives being a major reason for the brutalisation of conflict to which Jomini so objected, the latter believed that it would be necessary to return to an age in which the object of war would not be the total destruction of the enemy, but simply the pursuit of dynastic interests. As he frankly admitted:

As a soldier . . . I acknowledge that my prejudices are in favour of the good old times when the French and English guards courteously invited each other to fire first . . . preferring them to the frightful

10 *Cit.* B. Liddell Hart, *The Ghost of Napoleon* (London, 1933), p. 109.

epoch when priests, women and children throughout Spain plotted the murder of isolated soldiers.[11]

As a result of these prejudices, Jomini produced an argument that was decidedly partial. Flying in the face of the considerable evidence to the contrary, he argued that the key to Napoleon's art of war was not battle but manoeuvre, pointing out that his greatest successes – Lodi, Ulm, Marengo and Jena – had all been won through the use of the famous *manœuvre sur les derrières*, whereas his failures – Eylau, Aspern, Borodino and Waterloo – had all been the fruit of blind frontal assaults. Furthermore, to be successful, the art of manoeuvre rested on a number of basic principles which in their essentials boiled down to speed and concentration. However, if this were so, then individual field armies had by implication to be relatively small, for large forces could neither move quickly nor supply themselves with any ease. At the same time, they would also have to be well-trained, for only thus could they make up for their lack of size. Needless to say, this was the conclusion at which Jomini had been aiming all along, the idea of the army that was 'small but good' therefore gaining a real measure of theoretical justification.

Thus reinforced, the war ministries of Europe set out both to create the armies of which Jomini dreamed and to ensure that they were kept well apart from the civilian population, thereby shattering such tenuous links as had indeed developed between armies and their respective nations. Thus, in France the first reaction to the Hundred Days was to purge the officer corps and disband the army altogether, the latter being replaced by a new force composed of a powerful and highly privileged royal guard, a few Swiss regiments, and a number of volunteer 'departmental legions' intended, as Paddy Griffith puts it, 'to give some expression to the legitimist faith in a decentralised rural society based on *noblesse oblige*'.[12] In the event, however, it was discovered that only about 3,500 volunteers were forthcoming per year, the result being the reintroduction of conscription by means of the Loi Saint-Cyr of 1818, this amounting to a copy of the old Napoleonic system. However, as the annual quota for recruits was kept extremely low, the term of service set at eight years, and many veterans induced to re-enlist, France thereafter had what amounted to a professional army, as in effect did

11 *Cit.* Strachan, *Conduct of War*, p. 61.
12 P. Griffith, *Military Thought in the French Army, 1815–51* (Manchester, 1989), p. 7.

Russia, Austria and Spain which all retained or reverted to the old selective systems of recruitment that had been in use under the *ancien régime* (in Spain, too, the large numbers of new regiments formed during the Peninsular War mostly disappeared, their men being disbanded and their officers placed on half-pay). Only in Prussia were matters any different, the *wehrgesetz* of September 1814 laying down that all young men would serve in the regular army for three years from the age of twenty before passing into first the army's active reserve and then the *landwehr* for a further fourteen. Yet even here the ethos, at least of the officer corps, was one of intense professionalism, whilst the *junker* remained predominant, and undoubtedly spared no effort to indoctrinate the rank and file and sequester them from contact with the outside world. With the *landwehr*, which the reformers had hoped to see become a separate 'army of the nation' that would bridge the gulf between the military estate and civilian society, from 1819 increasingly brought under the control of the regulars, the fact was that in reality Prussia was therefore little different from other states – certainly the verve with which her troops quelled popular disorders was quite notorious.

If one looks at the military experience, too, one is again left with the impression that the situation was not so very different from that of the eighteenth century. If soldiers were everywhere kept more apart from the citizenry as a whole, now being universally housed in purpose-built barracks – or, in Russia, the military colonies – and for the most part serving on a permanent basis rather than spending much of the time on leave, their treatment was not much improved. In Russia, Austria and Britain, corporal punishment, including sentences of hundreds of lashes, was still common, the troops therefore remaining motivated in large part by fear, whilst, even in armies such as the French and Prussian in which the soldiers were supposed to be led by encouragement and kindness, the reality of barracks life often seems to have been one of harshness and petty brutality. As for training, except perhaps in France and Prussia, this continued to emphasise proficiency on the barracks square – the very antithesis of the 'thinking soldier' – at the expense of tactical flexibility. And everywhere pay was low, food unpalatable and conditions generally grim, whilst soldiers remained as universally despised as they had been fifty years previously. For all the changes of the Revolutionary and Napoleonic period, in short, the common soldier's lot remained as unhappy as ever.

To conclude this overview of the Restoration, then, it is clear that there was indeed an absolutist reaction in the period after 1815. However, this was far more selective than has often been portrayed. Where the reforms of the Napoleonic era presented no threat or were positively beneficial to the power of the state, and, by extension, the dynasty, they were generally retained and even extended, and it was, in fact, only rarely that they were cancelled altogether, the chief area of wholesale regression being that of military organisation. Nor is this surprising. With Napoleon's goals in many respects being identical with those of the absolute monarchies of the eighteenth century, it was only natural that the reforms which he inspired should frequently have been seized upon by rulers who were only to eager to emulate his achievements. Far from undermining the Old Order, in short, the Napoleonic era may actually have reinforced its capacity to sustain itself.

A SOCIETY TRANSFORMED?

In examining the reaction of the monarchs, statesmen and generals of Europe to the legacy of the Napoleonic era, we have been dealing with developments that have a very clear context and causation – if, for example, there was a clear move away from the Nation-in-Arms in terms of military organisation, it can clearly be shown that this was a result of the fears which that spectre evoked. In charting the impact of the Napoleonic Wars on social and economic development, however, the historian is confronted with an immediate problem. Taking industry and commerce as an example, we can say that the period 1800–15 witnessed a rapid development in the cotton industry and the emergence of new foci of industrial development in the hinterland of Europe, but we cannot say with any certainty that these were not developments that would have happened anyway even without the influence of the Napoleonic Wars. Nevertheless, to believe that a series of conflicts that at one time or another mobilised millions of men for periods of up to fifteen years at a stretch, that were fought across the face of almost the entire continent, that involved a sustained attempt to wage wholesale economic warfare, and that provoked a range of major social reforms, had no impact on the fabric of European society would be to defy common sense.

Let us begin with the field of demography. Beyond any doubt whatsoever, the Napoleonic Wars were a human tragedy of the first order, albeit of incalculable dimensions. Actual battle deaths were not especially high – the British army, for example, lost only 16,000 men killed in action, or, in other words, some 4,000 fewer than those who died in the first day of the battle of the Somme in 1916 – but, despite the desperate efforts of such men as Baron Larrey in France and James McGrigor in Wellington's Peninsular army, standards of medical care, and, indeed, knowledge, were extremely poor by modern standards, whilst medical services were in general thinly stretched and poorly equipped. With insufficient numbers of ambulances and stretcher bearers, many casualties were left lying on the battlefield for days on end, whilst those that were rescued were treated in the most filthy and insanitary conditions by surgeons who were all too frequently poorly trained and overworked. If they survived the horrors of treatment – for many wounds the only possible treatment was amputation, and that without any anaesthetic – they were then consigned to hospitals improvised from such buildings as churches or monasteries. Left to lie on dirty straw, deprived of adequate treatment, comfort or stimulation, and liable to depression, gangrene, septicaemia, and the variety of infectious diseases that stalked such places, they then died in their thousands. Joining them in the hospitals were the casualties of the illnesses that were the constant accompaniment of military life in peace and war alike – cholera, typhus, malaria, syphilis, pneumonia and even plague all claimed numerous victims, as did drunkenness, hunger, thirst, cold and simple exhaustion. At any one time the total number of men listed as being 'sick' could amount to whole divisions – in July 1809, for example, Wellington's army of 26,539 men had 4,395 in hospital; equally, in January 1810 the figures for his French opponents were 44,254 out of 324,996 – or, indeed, armies, as during the miserable British occupation of Walcheren in 1809. For most of these men, the prospects were bleak – to take just one example, of 9,000 French soldiers hospitalised in southern Italy in 1806, 4,000 died – the overall figures for deaths from disease being far in excess of those suffered in action: in the Peninsula and southern France, for example, between Christmas 1810 and May 1814, 8,889 British soldiers died in action or from their wounds, and 24,930 from sickness. Still more deaths occurred amongst the many prisoners of war, who at this stage did not enjoy the benefits of the Geneva Convention. Harshly treated even in Britain, where thousands were confined in terrible conditions on the dreaded 'hulks', elsewhere their sufferings could be truly apocalyptic, perhaps the worst case occurring on the rocky island of Cabrera where the survivors of the army that had surrendered at Bailén were abandoned and effectively left to die of starvation. Even this was not an end to the 'butcher's bill'. So far we have looked only at military casualties, but some account must also be taken of the many non-combatants who also lost their lives. Mercifully, except in the Balkans and the Turkish frontier, the Napoleonic era was not one in which war was waged directly against the civilian population (though a number of massacres did occur, particularly in Spain, Portugal and Calabria). Nevertheless, caught up in sieges such as those of Zaragoza and Danzig (Gdansk), tramping along in the wake of the armies as camp followers, smitten by hunger and want, not to mention the epidemic diseases carried by the military, condemned to die of exposure and starvation by the destruction of their villages, or simply done to death by bandits or marauders, civilians died in their thousands. To take just two examples, 70,000 Portuguese peasants are believed to have died of hunger and disease after taking refuge behind the Lines of Torres Vedras during the winter of 1810–11, whilst at least 34,000 of Zaragoza's inhabitants died during the great siege of 1809.

What did such suffering really mean, however? In global terms, the number of war dead remains obscure, being further complicated by the fact that the few figures that exist – as, for example, the 1,400,000 generally agreed to have been lost by the French army between 1792 and 1814 – take the Revolutionary and Napoleonic Wars as a single whole. As a very rough guide to military losses, a list of eighty battles, sieges and other combats taken from every campaign except that of 1812 for which rough totals of killed, wounded, missing and prisoners of war are known gives a total of 1,550,000 casualties. If we assume that the total number of dead in the campaigns in which these actions took place amounted to about this figure (in other words, that the number of casualties who escaped with their lives roughly cancels out those who died from other causes such as illness or starvation), and add first the generally recognised figure of 800,000 men for all those lost in Russia, and then perhaps 500,000 to account for other losses not yet taken into consideration, it becomes clear that dead amongst the military alone could easily have amounted to nearly 3,000,000. Adding, say, another 1,000,000 for civilian losses, we come to a figure little short of 4,000,000 dead. This, of course, it must be stressed, is little more than an intelligent guess, but it nevertheless does not appear to be wholly implausible, the fact being that the Napoleonic Wars inflicted very grievous losses, and, further, that they are still remembered with horror even now (during a recent visit to Germany the author was told by the pastor of the small Thuringian village of

Hassinghausen that his community lost more dead in the period 1803–15 than it had in any other war in which Germans have been engaged since the seventeenth century).

That said, however, the Napoleonic 'blood tax' does not seem to have had any long-term demographic effects. Only in France was there any marked stabilisation in the population's rate of growth thereafter, and it is clear that this was not so much due to a shortage of young men as to the impact of the end of primogeniture in the countryside, this making it imperative to limit the size of families. Meanwhile, even as the wars still raged, deaths from battle and disease were being countered by the desperate effort of many young men to avoid conscription by getting married, not to mention the trail of illegitimate children which all armies left in their wake (in this respect it is possible that the wars' temporary erosion of social conventions may have contributed to the 'sexual awakening' believed by some commentators to have taken place in the first half of the nineteenth century). At all events, the Napoleonic Wars appear as a mere blip, if, indeed, they appear at all, in the statistics of the period, the population of Europe continuing to increase dramatically in the period after 1815. As growth was especially marked in Germany, whose losses from the war had probably been proportionately greater than those in any other area, one may assume that the death toll had little lasting impact.

Population growth, of course, was central to the coming of industrialisation, but the fact that the wars did not affect the former very much does not mean to say that they had no impact on the latter. On the contrary, the period 1800–15 witnessed the confirmation of a major change in the European economy that had been in train ever since war broke out between Britain and France in 1793. Thus, prior to 1789 the most dynamic sector of the European economy had been centred on the burgeoning colonial trade. Ports such as Barcelona, Cádiz, Lisbon, Bordeaux, Nantes, Antwerp, Amsterdam and Hamburg had been a hive of activity with a growing population engaged not only in the colonial trade itself, but also in a wide range of industries – cotton, linen, tobacco, distilling, provisioning, ship-building, rope-making, sugar-refining – that were in one way or another connected with it, such industrial activity often being extended deep into the peasant hinterland. At the same time, too, they had engendered a wealthy commercial and professional class whose good fortune was reflected in the construction of the fine residences and public buildings that can still be seen in them today. However, within the space of a few years, the Revolutionary Wars had ended this coastal boom: under the impact of the British blockade, port after port was closed and European shipping swept from the seas, the communities that depended on them sliding ever more rapidly into bankruptcy and despair. Perpetuated as this situation was in the Napoleonic period by the Continental System, by the time that the wars ended Britain was so far ahead that the maritime regions were never able to recover their former glory – as Crouzet comments, 'There was, of course, a revival of traffic in the [harbours], but, even where a fairly high level was attained, most of them had lost their position as international *entrepôts* and had become mere regional ports. As for their industries, they were relatively far less active.'[13]

As Crouzet remarks, much of this was probably inevitable in the long term, given the superior organisation and lower costs of the British economy, the war therefore merely speeding up and greatly accentuating the process. Nor did the tendency of the Napoleonic Wars to 'pastoralise' the Continent stop here. Thanks to the immense quantities of land that came onto the market throughout Europe, the large profits that could be made from supplying foodstuffs to the armed forces, the prevailing economic uncertainty, and, in *la grande France* and her satellites at least, Napoleon's insistence on making landed property the foundation of *notabilité*, investment in agriculture was extremely attractive. Exactly as had occurred in Britain, much capital that might otherwise have been invested in industry was diverted onto the land, whilst social prejudices against 'trade' were subtly reinforced.

Thanks once again to the wars, moreover, even when capital was invested in industry, it could not necessarily be turned to good account. In the first place areas that were under de facto French rule, but were excluded from *la grande France* herself, such as Holland, Westphalia, Berg, and the Kingdom of Italy, found that the considerable nascent industry which they possessed was constantly dogged by the impact of the highly protectionist tariff policy imposed by Napoleon. Nor was this necessarily much of an advantage to the areas covered by it. Always lagging behind Britain in technique and technology, foreign industrialists had been heavily reliant on the innovations that they observed in her industry to keep up to the mark. Frequently visiting British businesses and inspecting British products, they had attempted to copy every new development

13 F. Crouzet, 'Wars, blockade and economic change in Europe, 1792–1815', *JEH*, XXXIV, No. 4 (December, 1964), 572.

themselves. Needless to say, the Napoleonic Wars (and, of course, the Revolutionary Wars before them) to a very large extent brought such contacts to a close. Some borrowing persisted – the cotton magnate, Liévin Bauwens, managed to introduce machine-spinning to his works by smuggling a mule and five skilled workers out of Britain – whilst, particularly in the field of cotton printing, some domestic innovation did take place. Nevertheless, only in cotton, and then only to a limited extent, was there any real success in keeping up with the British, the technological advantage which the latter enjoyed increasing considerably. Heavily protected as their products were, the industries that made such progress in France, Belgium, the Rhineland, and elsewhere were therefore developing in a dangerously unstable environment, the result being that when British goods once again penetrated the European market on a large scale after 1814, there could not but be a major period of recession, certain major enterprises, such as those of Richard-Lenoir and Bauwens actually being wiped out. Last but not least, it should also be remembered that the cotton industry in particular laboured for the entire war under a variety of heavy burdens: raw cotton was always extremely highly priced and sometimes in short supply (in 1808, for example, imports threatened to dry up altogether), whilst there was a serious shortage of machinery, such jennies as were produced costing up to four times as much as they would have done across the Channel.

From all this it might be thought that industrial advance on the Continent would have been much faster had the Napoleonic Wars, and, above all, the Continental System, not supervened. Matters, however, are far from being so simple. Even before the French Revolution it had become apparent that almost no European manufacturers could hope to compete with the British Industrial Revolution in an open market, the textile industries of France, Saxony and Switzerland alike all having come under pressure that threatened to be fatal. Distorting though the Continental System may have been, it is therefore necessary to examine it in another light. As Crouzet has pointed out, 'By 1800 Continental Europe was threatened by pastoralisation and the fate of India in the nineteenth century',[14] the important Catalan cotton industry being a case in point. Booming right up till 1808, it was stripped of the protection offered by the Continental System, devastated by the Peninsular War, deprived of its traditional markets by the British penetration of

14 Crouzet, Wars, blockade and economic change, 579.

Latin America, and prevented from re-equipping its mills by the ban imposed by Britain on the export of textile machinery, the result being, as Harrison puts it, 'a period of lengthy stagnation.'[15] For all its disadvantages, the Continental System at least saved much of Europe from such a fate; indeed, in Crouzet's eyes, it was 'the only way to introduce the Industrial Revolution'.[16]

Bearing this in mind, let us examine the actual development of Continental Europe during the Napoleonic era. Needless to say, given the intensely francophile nature of the Continental System, progress was at its most dramatic in *la grande France*. As in Britain, the sector of the economy that made the most rapid strides was the cotton industry. Based in six major regions – Paris, Normandy, Flanders-Picardy, Alsace, Belgium and the Rhineland – the consumption of raw cotton and the production of finished cloth soared. Thus, in 1802 the figure for the former was 5,000 tons, but by 1804 it had risen to 10,800; equally, exports of cotton cloth rose by a factor of one thousand per cent in the period 1807–10, overall production roughly quadrupling in the same period. In terms of the number of spindles, meanwhile, by the end of 1810 Ghent, Lille, Roubaix and Tourcoing between them had 293,000, whilst in 1814, after some years of depression, Paris had 150,000 and Seine Inférieure 350,000. Coupled with this activity was a dramatic increase both in the number of enterprises engaged in the industry, and of the population of such towns and cities as Ghent, Mulhouse, Lille and Saint Quentin.

Nor was cotton the only industry which benefited from the economic boom. In Lyons and Saint Etienne, the silk industry was boosted by the development of the Jacquard loom, whilst in the Rhineland Kreveld may have doubled its production. Much stimulated by military demands, wool experienced some technological innovation, and began to be organised on a larger scale with important centres of production developing at Verviers in Belgium, Elbeuf and Louviers in Normandy, Rheims and Sedan in eastern France, and Aachen and Jülich in the Rhineland, older areas of domestic production by contrast suffering a marked decline. Moving away from textiles, there was considerable technological innovation in the chemical industry; the production of coal increased greatly in the North, where it rose by seventy-three per cent in the period 1807–9, and even more rapidly in Belgium, where output had by

15 J. Harrison, *An Economic History of Modern Spain* (Manchester, 1978), p. 58.
16 Crouzet, 'Wars, blockade and economic change', p. 579.

1810 reached 1,500,000 tons a year; the construction of machinery began in Paris, Mulhouse, Liège and Verviers; metal-working became important at Düren in the Rhineland; and by 1811 the production of pig-iron had more than doubled in Belgium since 1789, though in France it stagnated, remaining for the most part archaic in technique and small-scale in organisation. Finally, the squeeze on colonial imports even led to the emergence of a few new industries such as the extraction of sugar from beet and the development of a substitute for indigo.

Outside the frontiers of the French empire, the picture is complicated by the damage that was wrought by French protectionism, this undoubtedly leading to a decline in industry in such areas as northern Italy, Westphalia and Berg. Yet even here the picture is not completely black – the higher quality of their iron permitted the survival of metallurgical industries at Remscheid and Essen, whilst coal production rose steadily until 1812. Elsewhere, moreover, régimes had greater freedom to protect their industries, which were in any case often favoured by geographical and commercial factors. Thus, taking the example of Saxony as a case in point, we see that the Napoleonic period witnessed considerable development with regard to cotton. Already relatively well-endowed with a ready fund of expertise and experience, Saxony was situated at an important commercial cross-roads in the heart of Europe – the Leipzig trade fair was one of the most important on the Continent – and enjoyed the benefit of excellent communications as well as easier access to the cotton supplies coming from the Levant. Moreover, her king was an independent character who was not inclined simply to kowtow to the dictates of Napoleon and was therefore prepared to follow a tariff policy that severely undercut that of France. The result of these factors being that the raw material was significantly cheaper in Saxony than in France, a large-scale cotton industry developed with a total of spindles that had risen from 13,200 in 1806 to 255,900 in 1813, this being accompanied in Chemnitz (Karl-Marx-Stadt) by the emergence of light engineering based on the production of jennies. Though much more harassed and impeded by Napoleon, who seems to have been inclined rather to turn a blind eye to Saxony on account of its proven military efficiency, Switzerland, too, made much progress in the field of machine-spinning under the influence of the industrialist, Hans Esscher, who also developed the manufacture of the necessary machines. Finally, in Naples Joachim Murat made a serious, albeit ultimately unsuccessful, attempt to establish a modern textile industry, encouraging the immigration of foreign manufacturers and supporting them with free premises and much government patronage.

What, then, do we see? To argue that France, let alone the rest of Europe, experienced an Industrial Revolution under Napoleon would be palpably absurd. Large-scale factory production was concentrated in a very few areas and even then remained relatively weak, with artisanal methods and domestic industry remaining very common, if not the norm; technology often remained backward, with steam power appearing in only a tiny handful of not very successful examples; much of the wartime development proved vulnerable to post-war competition; Britain was allowed to increase the lead that she enjoyed in technique; large areas of the Continent were stripped even of such industry as they had; the bourgeoisie was encouraged to invest in land rather than industry; and the vast majority of the population continued to live in the countryside.

If Napoleon did not preside over a general process of industrialisation, he may yet be said to have played a major role in paving the way for such a development, as indicated by the changing relationship between the nobility and the bourgeoisie. On one level, the former may be argued to have weathered the storm of the Revolutionary and Napoleonic era remarkably well. Whilst they had often – but not always – been stripped of their legal privileges, their economic predominance had on the whole been preserved. Particularly in eastern Europe, their income had often been hit very hard by the disruption to the export of such products as grain and timber brought about by the Continental System, and in some cases this had forced them to sell a certain amount of land to the bourgeoisie. However, such developments were very much the exception rather than the rule: in France, Spain and Italy the nobility shared in the purchase of the *biens nationaux*, whilst in Prussia and the Grand Duchy of Warsaw the emancipation of the serfs was followed by the acquisition of much of their land; thus, thirty-nine per cent of the land sold in the Tuscan department of the Arno went to the nobility, whilst in Prussia the *junker* seized peasant holdings to the extent of a minimum of 400,000 hectares. Nor was this an end to the misery brought about by emancipation. Only in rare cases did emancipation mean that the peasantry were freed from their financial obligations to the nobility, as the dues owed as a result of land tenure rather than personal servitude were simply converted into rents, whilst the decision as to exactly what the peasant had been emancipated from was often left to the courts.

In some cases, indeed, the burden may even have increased thanks to the commutation of labour services and the revision of tariffs to the disadvantage of the peasantry. In Sicily and Naples, meanwhile, emancipation was followed by the wholesale exclusion of the rural populace from the grazing land and watercourses that had hitherto been essential to their well-being, whilst across wide swathes of the Continent the sale of the commons denied the peasantry access to important windfall crops as well as vital sources of pasture and firewood. With their income slashed and their security eroded, it is therefore hardly surprising to find that in Prussia, Poland, Sicily and Naples the rural populace was frequently reduced to the status of an agricultural proletariat. For all that, however, the impact of the age of Napoleon cannot be disregarded. Throughout *le grand empire* and in many other areas of the Continent as well, in the long term the position of the nobility had in fact been gravely undermined. Thanks to changes in the laws of property, largely, though not entirely, related to the imposition of the *Code Napoléon* and its derivatives, in large areas of Europe entail was a thing of the past, the result being that the nobility could no longer rest assured that it would enjoy its estates in perpetuity. In many areas where this was not already the case, moreover, there was no obstacle to the bourgeoisie acquiring, or at least speculating in, landed property, whilst there were now many fewer restrictions on its activities in the fields of commerce, industry and state service. This is not to say that progress was uniform, nor still less that there was no regression after 1814 – the *Code Napoléon* had, after all, never been introduced in much of Germany even in modified form, whilst in the wake of France's defeat it was abolished in such areas as the Papal States – but the fact remains that for the bourgeoisie, whether we look at France, Spain or Germany, the period after 1814 was one of growing power and prosperity.

To conclude, then, the social and economic effects of the Napoleonic Wars were broadly speaking fourfold. In the first place, Europe was given an important breathing space that may ultimately have secured her future as an industrial society, it being probable that the dislocation that she would have experienced without the Continental System would have been far worse than that which it brought in its train. In the second, a generation of entrepreneurs had received a vital lesson in the methods of industrialism which, especially in Germany, they were later to exploit to much better effect, being further enabled to do so by the attack which had been unleashed on the guilds and the changes that had been introduced in the laws concerning property. In the third, the economic map of Europe had been transformed, the chief focus of industry having migrated from the coast to new areas centred above all on the swathe of territory stretching from Belgium and the North southwards through the Rhineland, the Ruhr and Alsace-Lorraine, these containing major resources of coal, lignite and iron ore that were to form the basis for later industrialisation. And, last but not least, the predominance of the nobility had been dealt a blow from which it was ultimately never to recover. Post-war crisis or no post-war crisis, well might Eric Hobsbawm write, 'The foundations of a good deal of later industry, especially heavy industry, were laid in Napoleonic Europe.'[17]

A NEW AGE OF REVOLUTION?

The period from 1815 to 1848 was characterised by wholesale political turmoil, witnessing no fewer than three successive waves of revolution – in 1820, 1830, and, of course, 1848 – setting aside numerous more or less minor rebellions and other disturbances. Needless to say, these have in large part been ascribed to the reactionary policies of the Vienna settlement and the Restoration with their denial of the new gods of liberalism and nationalism, the inference being that the Napoleonic era unleashed a series of social, political and economic developments whose very existence made a headlong collision with the Old Order inevitable – in short that it had produced what Geoffrey Best has called an 'insurgent underground'.[18]

That such an underground should have existed stands to reason. Whilst the Restoration settlement took no account of national feeling, the Napoleonic era had greatly stimulated the rise of nationalism. Faced by the realities of foreign military occupation and stimulated by such stirring examples as the Spanish uprising of 1808, at least some Germans discovered for the first time that they *were* Germans, this being reflected in the emergence of the vociferous national movement that we have already examined. In this development, the fact that they had but rarely taken up arms to free themselves made little difference, events such as the battle of Leipzig creating a powerful myth that was to be exploited through-

17 E. Hobsbawm, *The Age of Revolution: Europe, 1789–1848* (London, 1962), p. 211.
18 G. Best, *War and Society in Revolutionary Europe, 1770–1870* (London, 1982), p. 257.

out the nineteenth century. In the same way, the Poles and Italians could take courage from the establishment of the Grand Duchy of Warsaw and the Kingdom of Italy, being further heartened by the performance of the troops of these states in the service of Napoleon. Nor should it be forgotten that the Napoleonic Wars actually generated a number of revolts that were seemingly overwhelmingly nationalist in character: thus, in 1804 the Serbs rose in revolt against the Turks under Karadjordje and established an independent state that survived until 1813, whilst in Latin America a series of revolts broke out against Spanish rule that were within a few years to have freed the entire Continent. If she had not yet risen against the Turks, moreover, Greece had also acquired a national movement, thanks in part to the influence of the Serbian revolt and the ideas of the French Revolution, and in part to the emergence of Napoleon as a prototypical hero of Greek independence – he had, after all fought the Turks in Egypt and 'freed' the Ionian Islands, poets such as Martelaos and Koraes hailing him as the 'God of the world' who would 'sever the shackles of the enslaved country'.[19] And amongst Rumanians, too, whether it was in Austrian Transylvania or Turkish Moldavia and Wallachia, certain elements of the intelligentsia and the nobility were led by a variety of factors to see Napoleon as a liberator, the result being the emergence of the so-called 'National Party'.

Closely connected with the rise of nationalism – for it was axiomatic that freed institutions could not be established except in the context of free nations – was the rise of liberalism. Thanks to the French Revolution and Napoleon, the new society that had been dreamed of in the eighteenth century had temporarily been given concrete form, albeit in a manner that was considerably less than perfect. However, despite Napoleon's betrayal of the cause of liberty, in liberal eyes the empire over which he had presided, not to mention the doomed constitutions of Spain and Sicily, had represented an alternative that was infinitely preferable to the black reaction which seemed now to have settled upon Europe. In the speeches and writings of such figures as Benjamin Constant, François Guizot, Charles de Rémusat, Friedrich Dahlmann and Karl Rotteck, voice was given to a powerful critique of the Restoration whose main theme was that individuals could only indulge in the pursuit of self-interest that was the key to general happiness in a

19 *Cit.* E. Kefallineou, 'The myth of Napoleon in modern Greek literature and historiography, 1797–1850', *Consortium on Revolutionary Europe Proceedings*, 1991, 109.

free society, this in turn requiring the establishment of representative institutions, responsible government, an independent judiciary, equality before the law, and complete freedom of person, speech, property, religion, and occupation.

To nationalists and liberals alike, meanwhile, the Napoleonic Wars were not only the cause of much nostalgia, but also the source of considerable inspiration for the future. In the first place, they had certainly done much to glorify war in the eyes of certain sections of the intellectual community, in which respect Napoleonic propaganda was undoubtedly of paramount importance. Under the empire, painters such as David and Lejeune had produced a succession of graphic canvases extolling the glories of Napoleon and his army, and, in a manner that could not but stir the enthusiasm of the Romanticism that dominated European culture at this time, generally portraying war as a triumph of the human spirit. With the emperor banished to Saint Helena, this development could only acquire further momentum as the growth of the Napoleonic legend inculcated nostalgia for his rule, and spread the belief that the empire had been an agent of the progress that had now been cruelly short-circuited. Nor, of course, was such a feeling confined to the French and their admirers: for German nationalists just as much, the battle of Leipzig had marked the birth of a new age. In short, in a manner that would have horrified most of the writers of the eighteenth century, the concept of armed struggle came to be regarded as both inherently glorious and politically valuable, such beliefs undoubtedly playing upon the emotions of a generation of young men frustrated by the fact that they were too young to have fought in the wars. As a result, dreams of freedom became hopelessly intertwined with dreams of war, this militarisation of progressive politics being further reinforced by the large numbers of ex-soldiers – both officers and men – who had been turned adrift with the coming of peace and now found themselves left with little hope of stable employment. Whether it was Italian veterans becoming involved with the Carbonari, Spanish veterans turning to political conspiracy, or British veterans sailing off to Latin America to aid San Martín and Bolivar, such men frequently found an outlet in revolutionary politics.

With insurrection and war thus enshrined in many minds as the way forward, it was again but natural that the Napoleonic Wars should provide the model for the action that must be taken. Thus, just as Scharnhorst and Gneisenau had dreamed of the German people emulating the Spanish uprising in 1808, so similar hopes were now entertained with regard to the political situation after 1814. It was expected that the peoples of Europe would simply rise up and overthrow their oppressors either directly or by means of guerrilla warfare, the success ostensibly achieved by such methods in the Greek War of Independence of 1821–29 naturally causing much excitement. Indeed, for some nationalists so strong was the impact made upon them by the Napoleonic example that it became axiomatic that a people could not achieve its liberty except through armed conflict, war becoming a vital process in the formation of the nation. In consequence, from 1815 onwards the hopes of revolutionaries everywhere were directed above all towards the mobilisation of the people, this period witnessing the publication of a whole series of works on popular insurrection. Also important in this respect was the work of the press, the Napoleonic era having given an immense boost to the publication of newspapers and the journalistic profession in general. Having sporadically been encouraged, whether in Austria in 1809 or Prussia in 1813, to propagate the ideas of liberalism and nationalism, the numerous writers who had thereby found employment and, in some cases, renown, now found themselves muzzled, denied opportunity, and, on occasion, forced to flee into exile, many of them now throwing themselves into revolutionary politics.

If it is therefore entirely fair to talk of the emergence after 1815 of a revolutionary movement dedicated to the overthrow of the Old Order, it is equally fair to note that, until 1830 at least, it remained singularly ineffectual. In the first place, it is abundantly clear that revolutionary politics remained confined to a narrow élite. Thus, whilst students, professors and journalists were often ardent revolutionaries – albeit sometimes of a distinctly 'armchair' nature – the bulk of the population remained aloof or positively hostile. In theory, of course, the bourgeoisie should universally have rallied to the banner of revolutionary liberalism, for, having in large parts of Europe been offered a period of considerable social and economic opportunity, whilst also being deliberately politicised by an Old Order desperate to secure victory in the titanic struggles of 1812–14, the advances that it had made were now being seriously threatened. Yet nothing of the sort occurred. Amongst many of the bourgeoisie, for example, the reforms of the Napoleonic period brought a sense not of opportunity but of danger. Attractive to rich industrialists and merchants, liberalism was far less so to small shopkeepers and petty entrepreneurs. Equally, for the thousands upon thousands of Germans who in one way or another derived their income from the courts of such cities as Munich or Stuttgart, the idea of German unification was anathema, whilst it should also be noted that the concept of a Bavarian or Württemberger state was in any case far more appealing than that of a German one (in this respect the Napoleonic Wars may actually have delayed the cause of German unification: not only had rulers such as Maximilian I of Bavaria and Frederick I of Württemberg sought by every means available to stimulate particularist loyalty, but in 1813–14 many Germans had gained first-hand experience of Prussian arrogance and bullying). Moreover, whether it was in Calabria, Spain or the Tyrol the bourgeoisie was well aware of the ferocity with which the people-in-arms – for which read the peasantry – were liable to behave towards them, whilst in France the *notables* had alarming memories of the horrors of the *grande peur* and the Vendée. As for the spectre of the red-bonneted, Jacobin *sans culotte*, it stalked the whole of Europe. In consequence, exactly as had been the case in 1813, even those elements of the middle classes who were drawn to revolutionary ideas were in practice terrified by their implications. Constant, for example, was as bitterly opposed to democracy (which he termed 'the vulgarization of despotism'[20]) as he was to absolutism, whilst a nationalistic Italian historian could later describe the Italian counter-revolutionary insurrections as 'terrible events in which the people showed what it was capable of, and with what insolence and audacity it knew how to impose itself on other classes.'[21]

And what of 'the people'? The peasantry of the Revolutionary and Napoleonic era having frequently risen against the assault which the French and their sympathisers had launched on traditional society, it was hardly likely that the peasantry of the Restoration would fight for the ideals which their fathers had striven so desperately to resist. Meanwhile, in so far as the urban lower classes are concerned, the belligerence of the *fédérés* of 1815 could be contrasted with the traditionalism of such groups as the Neapolitan *lazzaroni*, whilst even the artisanate, which now found itself under increasingly severe pressure thanks to the abolition of the guilds and the spread of machinery, was as likely to resist the cause of revolution as to rise in its favour (in the Vendée, for example, hand-loom weavers had figured heavily amongst successive waves of

20 *Cit.* J. Droz, *Europe Between Revolutions, 1815–1848* (London, 1967), p. 48.
21 *Cit.* M. Broers, 'Revolution and *risorgimento*: the heritage of the French Revolution in nineteenth-century Italy', in H.T. Mason and W. Doyle (eds.), *The Impact of the French Revolution on European Consciousness* (Gloucester, 1989), p. 88.

insurgents). Thus, if peasant uprisings, machine-breaking and whole-sale banditry abounded, the people were hardly the revolutionary force of which the underground dreamed.

Of course, by 1848 – indeed, even by 1830 – things had changed enormously, but in 1815 only one factor saved the pan-European revolutionary movement from complete eclipse. Whereas in the eighteenth century the guns – in the form of the 'cabinet armies' of that era – had all been on the side of the régime, this was no longer the case. Whether it was in Sweden in 1809, Prussia in 1812, and France and Spain in 1814, we can find example after example of armies intervening in politics to safeguard their own professional interests: irritated at Gustav IV's caprices and alarmed by his conduct of the war, the Swedish army had marched on Stockholm to overthrow him; desperate to save his forces, and possibly to provoke a war against France, Yorck had on his own initiative ended hostilities against Russia; in April 1814 Napoleon had been forced to abdicate by his own generals; and the following month the Spanish army, eager to avenge itself for years of military defeat and liberal antimilitarism, restored the absolute monarchy. In France no more than in Spain, however, did the events of 1814 presage the restoration of the indissoluble bonds that had once linked the throne and the army. On the contrary, when the restored Bourbon monarchies stepped out of line with military interests, their armies issued a sharp reminder of the limits of the possible: in Spain the first of a whole series of military risings against Ferdinand VII occurred as early as September 1814, whilst in France the Hundred Days was again the work of an outraged army.

Be it noted, then, that armies were not politicised in any given direction, the French wars simply imbuing them – or at least certain elements of their officer corps – with a sense of their own corporate interest, this frequently having been challenged in an unprecedented manner. At the same time, too, having been forcibly brought to the centre of public affairs, they had everywhere acquired a new self-importance. As Ford remarks, 'For better or for worse, Napoleon, his commanders and the commanders who fought against him had given the military . . . that combination of prestige and self-awareness needed to make it a genuine force in civil affairs.'[22] Even more insidious in its effects was the cult of the hero: whether it was such swaggering Spanish generals as José Palafox and Francisco Ballesteros, the dashing Russian partisan commander, Denis

22 F.L. Ford, *Europe, 1780–1830* (London, 1989), p. 302.

Davidov, or even Joachim Murat dying bravely before a Bourbon firing squad after a desperate attempt at a Hundred Days of his own in October 1815, the officer corps of Europe had gained a series of role models that encouraged many of their members in a fatal search for glory. This new self-consciousness did not necessarily operate on the side of revolutionary politics – in Prussia, for example, the traditionalist faction that had always enjoyed a latent dominance in the officer corps was after 1815 increasingly able to marginalise its reformist rivals and incline Frederick William in the direction of a policy of wholesale reaction, whilst in Austria the army remained completely loyal throughout the period 1815–48. However, in Naples, Piedmont and Spain, the experience of absolutist rule, with its cuts in the army, aristocratic favouritism and financial bankruptcy, inclined numerous officers to liberalism. Becoming closely involved in the network of conspiratorial and masonic groups that flourished in Restoration Italy and Spain, they provided the revolutionary movement with a vital spearhead without which it would have been doomed to failure, the Spanish, Neapolitan and Piedmontese revolutions of 1820–21 all beginning as military revolts in which the professional interests of the army were well to the fore. Equally, in Russia young officers returning from the wars in Germany and France were horrified by the contrast between the progress, prosperity and general sense of freedom that they had encountered in the west and the brutality, obscurantism and backwardness that characterised their homeland. Less influenced by purely military concerns than their counterparts elsewhere (although they strongly disapproved of the floggings and general mistreatment endured by the common soldiery and desired an army inspired not by fear, but by patriotism), they formed a number of secret societies in the hope that they might incline Alexander I in the direction of internal reform, and in 1825 eventually inspired a military revolt in Saint Petersburg in a desperate bid to prevent the accession to the throne of the much-feared Grand Duke Nicholas.

In the person of young officers excited by the experience of the French wars and frustrated by that of the Restoration, the revolutionary movement had therefore gained a powerful ally – indeed, well might Karl Marx write that 'the culminating point of the *idées napoléoniennes* is the preponderance of the army'.[23] In

23 K. Marx, 'The Eighteenth Brumaire of Louis Bonaparte', in S.L. Feur, (ed.), *Karl Marx and Friedrich Engels: Basic Writings on Politics and Philosophy* (London, 1969), p. 383.

one respect, however, this was deeply ironic for at the same time a different strand of political protest was emerging that could not regard such vainglorious figures as Rafael Riego, Guglielmo Pepe or Pavel Pestel as anything other than enemies. In a development that has proved rather more lasting than the alliance between political protest and military dissidence, the Napoleonic Wars gave birth to the modern peace movement. In theory, war had always been condemned by the Christian Churches and, in large part, the intellectual community alike, whilst small numbers of sectarian Protestants had from the seventeenth century onwards refused to take up arms. By the late eighteenth century, moreover, this latent antiwar sentiment had been given political form by the writings of the *philosophes*. For thinkers such as Jean Jacques Rousseau, Immanuel Kant, and Thomas Paine, it was axiomatic that man was naturally peace-loving, and war, by implication, unnatural, being the work of kings and their ambition. Meanwhile, for economic theorists such as Adam Smith, war was also an absurdity in terms of commerce and industry, being not only damaging in itself, but also a denial of the manner in which all humanity was linked in a great chain of mutual interest. Logically, then, it followed that war could be abolished, all that was necessary being to break the power of the Old Order, introduce representative political systems (for the people would supposedly never voluntarily agree to go to war), and put an end to all restrictions on international trade, it being argued that economic rivalry had no existence in itself but was solely the fruit of protectionism. As to such disputes as might still emerge, once taken out of the hands of selfish 'despots', these could easily be settled by rational discussion and international arbitration.

With these beliefs given widespread publicity by the publication of Tom Paine's *Rights of Man* in 1791, the horrors of the Revolutionary and Napoleonic Wars could not but provoke a reaction. Genuinely horrified by what they saw around them, and, in the case of the British merchants and businessmen who were prominent amongst them, mindful, first, of the damage that war was inflicting upon their profits, and, second, of the social conflict that was endemic between themselves and the landed aristocracy, in Britain and the United States in particular a number of individuals came together to work for a permanent end to war (as opposed to just an end to the Napoleonic Wars per se). As might have been expected, a leading role in events was played by the Quakers, who combined pacifist religious principles with an extraordinary degree of success in trade and industry, though Utilitarians and liberal economists were also of some importance. The result was the first peace movement: in the course of 1815, no fewer than three separate peace groups were formed in the United States, these later being united as the American Peace Society, whilst in 1816 the British Quaker, William Allen, founded the Society for the Promotion of Universal and Permanent Peace. In the course of the next few years further peace societies also appeared in Holland, France and Switzerland.

Brave though the efforts of these groups were, however, they remained a miniscule force confined to the Quakers and certain other non-conformist groups, which, on those rare occasions when they attracted any notice at all, were subjected to general ridicule. To the extent that their views had any influence, it was when they were adopted on purely utilitarian grounds by such figures as the leaders of the British free-trade movement, Cobden and Bright. Constantly agitating against expensive armed forces, aristocratic privilege and protectionism, they preached the gospel of Tom Paine with verve and fervour and attracted much public attention, but even they were to find that in reality their arguments bore little weight when it came to shaping the government's policy, all the fulminations which they could muster failing to prevent Britain from going back to war in 1854.

To conclude, then, the Napoleonic Wars presented the Restoration with a legacy of protest that was superficially dramatic, but in practice not as yet very threatening. Much inclined to wishful thinking and ideological confusion, the revolutionary underground remained confined to a small coterie of students, intellectuals, professionals and adventurers that had little popular support and could only have an impact to the extent that it could acquire allies within the officer corps of Europe's armies. Where this happened, they could become a real threat, but many officers had different interests to their civilan fellows, whilst they were by no means able to deliver the support of all their comrades, let alone to prevent their troops from being used for counter-revolutionary purposes. In almost every case where revolution actually broke out in the immediate post-war period, whether it was in Spain, Naples, Piedmont or Russia, the armed force needed to put it down could therefore easily be found. This is not to say, of course, that the Restoration settlement could be sustained indefinitely – seriously challenged in 1830, it was, of course, to collapse altogether in 1848 – but these events were related far more to social and economic developments after 1815 than to those of the Napoleonic Wars. In short, if the latter created a revolutionary movement, it did not create the conditions in which it could succeed.

INTO THE NINETEENTH CENTURY

What impact, then, did the Napoleonic Wars really have upon the course of nineteenth-century history? In a seminal article published in 1963, Franklin Ford argued that, whilst there are strong elements of continuity linking the pre-Revolutionary and post-Napoleonic eras, as, for example, with regard to the history of ideas, there were yet major changes that, in the aggregate, 'reveal a revolution in the fullest sense, a fundamental departure from some of the most important conditions of life before 1789'.[24] According to Ford, these changes were fivefold: a revolution in the structures of government; a dramatic change in the nature of warfare brought about by the introduction of the *levée en masse*; the increased involvement of public opinion in politics; the replacement of the measured neo-classicism of eighteenth-century art by the passion of Romanticism; and, above all, the definitive replacement of the traditional hierarchy of orders and estates by a new society based on wealth and merit. With the possible exception of his remarks on the Nation-in-Arms, there is very little with which one can disagree here, but even so to talk of a revolution seems to be a little excessive. The abolition of feudalism, the changes in the laws of property introduced by the Napoleonic codes, the acquisition of large amounts of landed property by the bourgeoisie, the introduction of the career open to talent, and the industrial development promoted by the conflict may all have contributed to a long-term erosion in the exclusive status of the nobility, but they did not create a truly revolutionary situation. Far from wanting to overthrow the Old Order, the new élites that had been thrown up by the war, and continued to be thrown up thereafter, wanted rather to be a part of it and to be accepted by it, whilst often fearing both economic change and the violence of the lower classes. As for the Old Order, it had in many ways been strengthened, the administrative reforms associated with the French in the Napoleonic period not only securing many of the objectives of the enlightened absolutists of the eighteenth century, but also greatly reinforcing the power of the state – indeed, in Continental Europe the modern state

24 F.L. Ford, 'The Revolutionary-Napoleonic era: how much of a watershed?', *American Historical Review*, LXIX, No. 1 (October, 1963), 28.

may even be said to be an invention of the Napoleonic era. Meanwhile, if the temporal power of the Catholic Church had in large part been broken, it remained a powerful force, as, indeed, did the nobility, it finally taking the far more demanding and traumatic conflict that broke out one hundred years after the downfall of Napoleon to overcome their last remaining bastions.

Yet it should not be inferred from this that the Napoleonic era was unimportant. In the first place, as Stuart Woolf has argued, whilst the Napoleonic era may have stifled conflict amongst the 'haves', it accentuated the gulf between the 'haves' and the 'have-nots', thus opening the way for a new era of social disorder that was to become ever more serious. In the second, far from integrating the Continent, Napoleon actually succeeded in injecting it with far greater divisions than those which had existed under the *ancien régime*. Thus, until the Revolution overflowed its bonds and spilled into Spain, the Low Countries, Italy and Germany, it had been generally accepted amongst the thinkers of Europe that it was possible to aspire to a system of universal law and a pattern of common government that would hold good for all men in all societies at every time. Firmly believing in such a vision, Napoleon had sought to impose it upon an empire that at its greatest extent stretched from the Portuguese frontier to Lithuania and from the northern coast of Germany to the southernmost tip of Italy. Needless to say, however, such a project could not succeed: throughout the French imperium, and, indeed, even in metropolitan France herself, parochialism remained a powerful force that was never overcome, whilst the experience of French rule stimulated the rise of a series of nationalist movements that, whilst ostensibly highly cosmopolitan, eventually could not but collide with one another. For the time being, it was in the interests of governments everywhere to avoid such collisions and to stifle the forces that led to them, but, once war had been stripped of the fear of revolution with which it was so closely associated in 1815, it was not long before it once more was to become an instrument of state policy that was to be rendered far more terrible by the fact that it was wielded in a era of industrialisation. Far from being the precursor to an age of general peace, in the long run the Napoleonic Wars were therefore the precursor of an age of conflict in which, much to the detriment of suffering humanity, the ideas of Clausewitz would finally be vindicated.

CHRONOLOGY

1803

18 May	Britain declares war on France.
23 May	Napoleon orders arrest of all British subjects on French territory.
26 May	French troops enter Hanover.
14 June	French forces enter Naples to occupy Puglia.
15 June	French army begins to mass at Boulogne for the invasion of England.
21 June	British forces capture Santa Lucia.
25 June	Batavian Republic signs treaty of alliance with France.
30 June	British capture Tobago.
27 July	Robert Emmet launches abortive rising in Dublin.
3 August	War breaks out in India between Britain and French-backed Mahratha Confederacy.
11 September	Lake defeats Mahrathas at Delhi.
20 September	British capture Demerara and Essequibo.
23 September	Wellington defeats Mahrathas at Assaye.
1 November	Lake defeats Mahrathas at Laswari.
28 November	Wellington defeats Mahrathas at Argaon; French garrison of Sainte Domingue capitulates to British at Cap François.
29 November	Insurgent leaders proclaim independence of Sainte Domingue as Haiti.

1804

15 March	Arrest of the Duc d'Enghien.
16 March	After two years of growing unrest, Serbs rise against their Janissary governors in defence of the rights of Selim III, and besiege Belgrade.
29 April	British land in Surinam.

5 May	Garrison of Surinam capitulates.
19 May	Napoleon creates the first eighteen marshals.
5 August	Serbs take Belgrade; although they permit the Ottomans to instal a garrison, they demand greater autonomy.
5 October	British ships attack Spanish treasure fleet.
6 November	Austro-Russian defence agreement signed.
2 December	Napoleon crowned Emperor of France.
12 December	Spain declares war on Britain.

1805

7 May	Selim III orders the Serbs to lay down their arms; when they refuse, Ottomans prepare for their subjugation by force.
25 May	France annexes Ligurian Republic.
26 May	Napoleon crowned King of Italy.
12 July	Serbs defeat Ottomans at Niš.
28 July	Britain and Russia agree formation of Third Coalition.
9 August	Austria joins Third Coalition.
18 August	Serbs defeat Ottomans at Ivankovać.
10 September	Naples signs convention with Russia.
23 September	Bavaria signs alliance with France.
1 October	Prussia mobilises after French troops occupy Ansbach; Baden signs alliance with France.
3 October	Sweden joins Third Coalition.
8 October	Württemberg signs alliance with France.
14 October	French commence evacuation of Puglia.
20 October	Capitulation of Ulm; Mack surrenders with 27,000 men.
21 October	Franco-Spanish fleet destroyed at Trafalgar; Nelson killed.
26 October	*Grande armée* marches from Boulogne for the Rhine.
29 October	Archduke Charles checks Massena at Caldiero.
3 November	Prussia signs Treaty of Potsdam with Austria and Russia, effectively committing herself to entering the war.
11 November	10,000 French troops under Gazan defeat 40,000 Russians at Dürrenstein.
12 November	French occupy Vienna.
17 November	British forces begin disembarking in Hanover.

20 November	Anglo-Russian expeditionary force lands at Naples.
21 November	Serbs capture Semendria (Smederevo).
2 December	Austro-Russian forces defeated at Austerlitz (Slavkov).
15 December	Prussia signs Treaty of Schönbrunn with France.
26 December	Austria signs Treaty of Pressburg (Bratislava).

1806
6 January	British expeditionary force disembarks at Capetown.
8 January	Dutch defeated at Blauewberg.
18 January	Dutch surrender Cape Province.
19 January	Anglo-Russian expeditionary force embarks from Naples.
23 January	Death of Pitt.
6 February	Duckworth destroys French fleet off Santo Domingo.
9 February	French invade Naples.
11 February	Ferdinand IV and Maria Carolina flee to Sicily.
13 February	British evacuate Hanover.
16 February	British forces disembark in Sicily.
4 March	French besiege Gaeta.
5 March	Russians seize Cattaro (Kotor); Napoleon opens peace negotiations with Britain, whose new government – the Ministry of All the Talents – is eager for peace.
9 March	Neapolitans defeated at Campo Tenese.
11 March	Joseph Bonaparte proclaimed king of Naples.
15 March	Napoleon creates Grand Duchy of Berg.
22 March	Revolt breaks out in Calabria.
30 March	Marshal Berthier created Prince of Neuchâtel.
26 May	French occupy Ragusa (Dubrovnik).
5 June	Holland becomes a kingdom under Louis Bonaparte.
17 June	Russians and Montenegrins defeat French outside Ragusa (Dubrovnik).
18 June	Russians and Montenegrins besiege Ragusa (Dubrovnik).
25 June	British expeditionary force occupies Buenos Aires.
4 July	British expeditionary force defeats French at Maida in Calabria.

6 July	French relieve Ragusa (Dubrovnik).
17 July	Napoleon establishes Confederation of the Rhine.
18 July	French capture Gaeta.
20 July	D'Oubril signs abortive Russo-French peace treaty.
6 August	Francis II of the Holy Roman Empire takes the title 'Francis I of Austria'.
9 August	Prussian government resolves on war with Napoleon.
12 August	*Criollo* militia recapture Buenos Aires.
13 August	Serbs defeat Turks at Misar.
26 August	Prussia issues ultimatum demanding withdrawal of French forces from Germany.
13 September	With the death of the British foreign secretary, Charles James Fox, all hope of peace between France and Britain collapses.
1 October	Russians repulse French assault at Castelnuovo (Hercegnovi).
10 October	Prussians defeated at Saalfeld.
14 October	Prussians defeated at Jena and Auerstädt.
16 October	Russians invade Danubian provinces after the Turks replace their governors with men of pro-French sympathies.
17 October	Prussians defeated at Halle.
22 October	French besiege Magdeburg.
25 October	*Grande armée* enters Berlin.
28 October	Hohenlohe capitulates with 10,000 men at Prenzlau.
29 October	French capture Stettin (Sczecin).
6 November	Blücher capitulates with 20,000 men at Lübeck.
10 November	Surrender of Magdeburg.
21 November	Continental System inaugurated by Decree of Berlin.
28 November	French enter Warsaw.
24 December	Russians occupy Bucharest.
26 December	Russians fight off French attack at Pultusk, but retreat during the night.
29 December	Serbs capture Belgrade.

1807
6 January	Serbs capture Sabać, and thus eliminate the last Ottoman outpost in Serbia.

7 January	British respond to Decree of Berlin with Orders-in-Council.
15 January	British open siege of Montevideo.
30 January	French besiege Stralsund.
3 February	British capture Montevideo; Bennigsen repulses Napoleon at Jenkendorf (Ionkovo).
7–8 February	Bennigsen holds Napoleon to a draw at Eylau (Bagrationovsk).
19 February	British naval squadron enters the Dardenelles.
1 March	British evacuate Dardanelles.
17 March	British invade Egypt.
18 March	French besiege Danzig (Gdansk).
20 March	French besiege Kolberg (Kolobrszeg); under Gneisenau the defenders hold out until peace is signed in July.
21 March	British capture Alexandria (El Iskandariya).
29 March	British defeated in first battle of Rosetta (Rashid).
21 April	British defeated in second battle of Rosetta (Rashid).
26 April	Prussia and Russia sign Convention of Bartenstein (Bartoszyce), abjuring a separate peace and declaring their aim to be the expulsion of the French from Germany.
27 May	Surrender of Danzig (Gdansk).
28 May	Neapolitan invasion of Calabria defeated at Mileto.
29 May	Selim III deposed and replaced by Mustapha IV.
2 June	After repulsing a series of Russian attempts to cross the Danube, Turks recapture Bucharest.
3 June	Turks defeat Serb offensive at Loznica; Russians defeat Turks at Bazardik (Dobrić).
10 June	French repulsed at Heilsberg (Lidzbark Warminski).
14 June	Napoleon defeats Bennigsen at Friedland (Pravdinsk).
25 June	Napoleon meets Alexander at Tilsit (Sovetsk).
1 July	Russians defeat Turkish navy off Lemnos.
5 July	Whitelocke attacks Buenos Aires, but is forced to capitulate with 2,000 men and to agree to evacuate Montevideo.
7–9 July	Treaties of Tilsit (Sovetsk).

323

16 July	British expeditionary force lands on the island of Rügen off Stralsund.
22 July	Treaty of Dresden formally establishes Grand Duchy of Warsaw.
31 July	Napoleon sends ultimatum to Danes to sign a military alliance or face war.
3 August	French occupy Ionian islands.
4 August	British withdraw from Rügen.
10 August	Swedes surrender Stralsund.
16 August	British forces disembark on Zealand (Denmark).
17 August	Turks besiege Alexandria (El Iskandariya).
29 August	Danes defeated at Koge.
2–7 September	Bombardment of Copenhagen.
7 September	Danish government capitulates and surrenders its fleet to Britain.
14 September	British evacuate Alexandria (El Iskandariya).
19 October	French forces enter Spain en route for Portugal.
20 October	British evacuate Zealand.
27 October	France and Spain agree to partition Portugal (Treaty of Fontainebleau).
30 October	Denmark signs an alliance with France and admits a Franco-Spanish army under Bernadotte.
23 November	Napoleon strengthens Continental System with first Decree of Milan.
27 November	Portuguese royal family take ship for Brazil.
30 November	French forces enter Lisbon.
17 December	Continental System further modified by second Decree of Milan.

1808

2 February	French occupy Rome.
9 February	French troops enter Catalonia.
16 February	French seize Pamplona.
21 February	Russia invades Finland.
29 February	Denmark declares war on Sweden; French seize citadel of Barcelona.
5 March	French troops seize San Sebastián.
13 March	French commence march on Madrid.
15 March	France annexes Tuscany, Parma and Piacenza.
17–19 March	Charles IV deposed in riots at Aranjuez; Godoy imprisoned; crown prince proclaimed Ferdinand VII.

23 March	French occupy Madrid.
24 March	Ferdinand VII enters Madrid in triumph.
24–30 March	Russians occupy Aland islands.
18 April	Swedes defeat Russians at Siikojaki.
20 April	Ferdinand arrives at Bayonne to meet Napoleon.
24 April	Russians occupy Gotland.
27 April	Swedes defeat Russians at Revolax.
2 May	Uprising of the Dos de Mayo in Madrid.
5–6 May	Charles IV and Ferdinand VII agree to renounce their rights to the Spanish throne.
7 May	Sveaborg capitulates after nominal resistance.
10 May	Joseph Bonaparte proclaimed king of Spain; Russian garrison of Aland islands forced to capitulate by Swedish naval landing.
14 May	Swedish expeditionary force lands on Gotland.
16 May	France annexes Rome.
17 May	British expeditionary force arrives at Göteborg under Moore.
18 May	Garrison of Gotland capitulates.
23 May	National uprising breaks out in Spain.
6 June	National uprising breaks out in Portugal.
15 June	French open first siege of Zaragoza.
23 June	After travelling to Stockholm and engaging in a series of stormy discussions, Moore is placed under house arrest by Gustav IV.
27 June	Moore escapes from Stockholm.
28 June	Moncey repulsed from Valencia.
30 June	Moore's expeditionary force sails for England.
14 July	Bessières defeats Cuesta and Blake at Medina de Río Seco; Swedes defeat Russians at Lapua.
19 July	Dupont forced to surrender at Bailén with 20,000 men by Castaños.
20 July	Joseph enters Madrid.
28 July	Mustapha IV deposed and replaced by Mahmud II.
1 August	Joseph evacuates Madrid and retreats to river Ebro; British army disembarks in Portugal.
6 August	Spaniards blockade Barcelona.
7 August	Spanish forces in Denmark revolt and escape by sea.
15 August	Spanish forces invade Santo Domingo from Puerto Rico.
21 August	Wellington defeats Junot at Vimeiro.

25 August	British defeat Russians in naval action off Hango (Hanko).
30 August	Junot capitulates (Convention of Sintra).
1 September	Swedes defeated at Ruona.
6 September	Murat enters Naples as Joachim I.
14 September	Swedes defeated at Oravainen.
25 September	Junta Suprema Central established at Aranjuez.
26 September	Sir John Moore appointed to command the British forces in Portugal.
27 September– 14 October	Napoleon and Alexander confer at Erfurt; in exchange for recognition of Russian gains in eastern Europe, Alexander promises, if necessary, to join France in a war with Austria.
4 October	Murat invades Capri.
18 October	Garrison of Capri capitulates.
25 October	Following the launch of a French counter-offensive, the Spaniards are defeated at Logroño.
29 October	Lefebvre defeats Blake at Zornoza (Amorebieta).
5 November	Napoleon enters Spain.
7 November	Spaniards defeat French garrison of Santo Domingo at Palo Hincado.
10 November	Napoleon defeats Belveder at Gamonal.
10–11 November	Victor defeats Blake at Espinosa de los Monteros.
13 November	British advanced guard reaches Salamanca.
15 November	Swedes sign armistice of Olkioki and agree to evacuate Finland.
23 November	Lannes defeats Castaños at Tudela.
24 November	Napoleon forces Frederick William to dismiss Stein.
30 November	Napoleon defeats Spaniards at Somosierra.
4 December	Madrid surrenders to Napoleon.
16 December	Saint Cyr relieves Barcelona.
20 December	French besiege Zaragoza for a second time.
21 December	Moore attacks French at Sahagún de Campos; Spaniards defeated at Molíns de Rey.
23 December	Moore commences 'Retreat to Corunna'.
26 December	Insurgent leader, Peter Karajordjević, recognised as hereditary ruler of Serbia.

1809

3 January	Napoleon leaves his army in Spain and sets off for Paris.
7 January	British and Portuguese forces seize Cayenne.
13 January	Victor defeats Venegas at Uclés.
16 January	Moore defeats Soult at La Coruña, but is killed in the moment of victory.
17 January	Moore's army is evacuated by the Royal Navy; French now occupy Galicia which promptly rises in revolt.
30 January	British invade Martinique.
19 February	French capture Zaragoza.
24 February	French garrison of Martinique capitulates.
25 February	Saint Cyr defeats Reding at Valls.
2 March	Beresford appointed to command Portuguese army.
9 March	Soult invades Portugal.
13 March	Gustav IV of Sweden overthrown by a military coup; Russians recapture Aland islands.
20 March	Portuguese defeated at Braga.
22 March	Russians seize Umea after marching across the frozen Gulf of Bothnia from Finland.
25 March	Swedes defeated at Kalix after Russians invade northern Sweden.
27 March	Sébastiani defeats Cartaojal at Ciudad Real.
28 March	Spaniards recapture Vigo.
29 March	Victor defeats Cuesta at Medellín.
2–3 April	Friedrich von Katte attempts to instigate a revolt in Stendal.
8 April	Revolt breaks out in the Tyrol.
9 April	Austria declares war on France and invades Bavaria, Tyrol and northern Italy.
12 April	Tyrolean insurgents liberate Innsbruck and capture the garrison; after other French and Bavarian forces are forced to surrender at Wilten, the whole of the Tyrol is freed.
15 April	Austrians invade Grand Duchy of Warsaw under Archduke Ferdinand.
19 April	Ferdinand defeats Poles at Raszyn.
21 April	Austrians occupy Warsaw.
22 April	Napoleon defeats Archduke Charles at Eggmühl; Wilhelm von Dörnberg leads a revolt in

	Westphalia; Wellington takes command of the British army in Portugal.
28 April	Ferdinand von Schill invades Westphalia in an attempt to stir up revolt.
1 May	*Riksdag* opens in Sweden to elaborate new constitution.
5 May	Russia declares war on Austria.
8 May	Eugene defeats Archduke John at Campana.
12 May	Wellington defeats Soult at Oporto, whereupon French commence retreat from Portugal; French occupy Vienna.
14 May	Poniatowski captures Lublin after invading Austrian Galicia.
15 May	Ferdinand repulsed at Thorn (Torun).
16–19 May	Serbs defeated at Nis.
18 May	Poniatowski captures Sandomierz.
19 May	Lefebvre retakes Innsbruck; Turks defeat Serbs at Nis.
20 May	Poniatowski captures Zamosc.
21–22 May	Archduke Charles defeats Napoleon at Aspern-Essling.
22 May	French defeated by Spaniards at Santiago.
23 May	Blake defeats Suchet at Alcañiz.
24 May	French besiege Gerona; Schill captures Stralsund.
29 May	Tyrolean victory at Bergisl forces Bavarians to evacuate first Innsbruck and then the whole of the Tyrol.
31 May	Stralsund stormed; Schill killed in the fighting; Poniatowski captures Lemberg (Lwow).
5 June	Britain and Turkey sign treaty of friendship.
8 June	Spaniards defeat French at Sanpayo.
9 June	Duke of Brunswick invades Saxony at the head of the 'Black Legion of Vengeance' that he had raised to fight for Austria.
11 June	Brunswick seizes Dresden.
14 June	Eugene defeats Austrians at Raab (Gyor).
15 June	Sucet defeats Blake at María.
18 June	Suchet defeats Blake at Belchite; Austrians retake Sandomierz.
19 June	Brunswick seizes Leipzig.
22 June	French commence evacuation of Galicia.
3 July	Wellington enters Spain.

5 July	Pope Pius VII is arrested by French Troops and sent into exile.
5–6 July	Napoleon defeats Archduke Charles at Wagram.
6 July	French garrison of Santo Domingo surrenders.
8 July	British invade Senegal.
12 July	Archduke Charles agrees armistice of Znaim (Znojmo).
13 July	French garrison of Senegal capitulates.
15 July	Poniatowski captures Cracow.
17 July	Poniatowski defeats Austrians at Wieniawka.
29 July	Wellington defeats Victor and Joseph at Talavera de la Reina.
30 July	After being chased from Saxony by Jerome Bonaparte, Brunswick captures Braunschweig; British army disembarks on Walcheren island; Lefebvre retakes Innsbruck.
1 August	Brunswick defeats his pursuers, but decides to flee for the coast, he and his forces later being picked up by British ships.
2 August	British besiege Flushing (Vlissingen).
8 August	Soult defeats Cuesta at Arzobispo.
11 August	Joseph defeats Venegas at Almonacid de Toledo.
13 August	Heavy Tyrolean attacks force Lefebvre to evacuate Innsbruck; the Tyrol is liberated for the third time.
16 August	Flushing (Vlissingen) capitulates to British.
16–21 August	Swedish attempt to attack Russian bridgehead at Umea from the sea is thwarted at Ratan.
17 September	Sweden makes peace with Russia by Treaty of Fredrikshamn (Hamma).
22 September	Turks defeat Russians at Tartarica.
30 September	British commence reconquest of Ionian islands and quickly capture Zante (Zákinthos), Cephalonia (Kefallinía), and Ithaca (Itháki).
9 October	Stein issues Emancipation Edict in Prussia.
14 October	Austrians sign Treaty of Schönbrunn.
18 October	Del Parque defeats French at Tamames.
25 October	Bavarians reoccupy Innsbruck for the third and last time; thereafter Tyrolean revolt collapses.
19 November	Soult defeats Areizaga at Ocaña.
28 November	Kellermann defeats Del Parque at Alba de Tormes.

10 December	Sweden signs peace treaty with Denmark.
11 December	French capture Gerona.
23 December	British evacuate Walcheren.

1810

10 January 1810	Sweden signs peace treaty with France and joins Continental System.
19–21 January	French force passes of the Sierra Morena and invade Andalucía.
24 January	Seville revolts against the Junta Suprema Central.
27 January	British invade Guadeloupe.
29 January	Council of regency installed in Cádiz.
31 January	Soult captures Seville.
3 February	Garrison of Guadeloupe capitulates.
5 February	Soult besieges Cádiz.
8 February	Napoleon creates six military governments in northern Spain, thereby stripping Joseph of much of his authority.
20 February	Andreas Hofer executed in Mantua; Spaniards defeated at Vich.
21 March	French besiege Astorga.
22 March	British invade Santa Maura (Levkás).
29 March	After several times being thwarted by guerrilla raids, French occupy Oviedo.
13 April	French besiege Lérida.
15 April	Spaniards defeated at Zalamea.
16 April	French garrison of Santa Maura (Levkás) capitulates.
19 April	Spanish-American revolution begun by revolt in Venezuela.
22 April	French capture Astorga.
24 April	Spaniards defeated at Margalef.
14 May	French capture Lérida.
15 May	French besiege Mequinenza.
6 June	French besiege Ciudad Rodrigo.
8 June	French capture Mequinenza.
23–24 June	Turks defeat Russians in first battle of Shumla (Sumen).
1 July	With French troops pouring into his country, Louis Bonaparte abdicates as King of Holland.
7 July	British invade Réunion.
9 July	French capture Ciudad Rodrigo.

10 July	French garrison of Réunion capitulates.
13 July	France annexes Holland.
21 July	Massena invades Portugal.
23 July	Turks and Russians fight drawn battle of Kargali Dere.
24 July	British rearguard driven over river Coa.
5 August	Napoleon legitimises import of colonial goods but imposes punitive tariffs.
8 August	Russians defeat Turks at second battle of Shumla (Sumen), and go on to capture fortresses of Rustchuk (Ruse), Nicopolis (Nikopol), and Giurgevo (Giurgiu).
15 August	Massena besieges Almeida.
23 August	French defeat British naval squadron off Mahébourg (Martinique).
27 August	Massena captures Almeida.
7 September	Russians defeat Turks at Batin.
14 September	Spaniards secure minor victory at La Bisbal.
17–18 September	French attempt to invade Sicily is driven off.
24 September	*Cortes* opens in Cádiz.
27 September	Wellington defeats Massena at Busaco, but continues to retreat on Lisbon.
10 October	Wellington retreats within Lines of Torres Vedras.
12 October	Massena invests Lines of Torres Vedras.
18 October	Napoleon imposes savage new laws against smuggling.
20 October	Bernadotte arrives in Sweden as crown prince.
3 November	Spaniards defeated at Baza.
14 November	Massena retreats from Lines of Torres Vedras to Santarem.
29 November	British invade Martinique.
3 December	French garrison of Martinique capitulates.
13 December	France annexes Oldenburg, Hanseatic towns, and parts of Hanover and Berg.
16 December	Suchet besieges Tortosa.
31 December	Alexander I imposes heavy tariff on French imports; France annexes the Valais.
1811	
2 January	Suchet captures Tortosa.
11 January	Soult besieges Olivenza.
15 January	Spaniards secure minor victory at Plá.

23 January	Soult captures Olivenza.
27 January	Soult besieges Badajoz.
19 February	Soult defeats Mendizabal at the river Gebora.
20 February	Chief remaining Calabrian rebel, Parafante, captured and shot; thereafter Calabrian revolt quickly collapses.
4 March	French retreat from Santarem for Spanish frontier.
5 March	Graham defeats Victor at Barosa.
10 March	Soult captures Badajoz.
14 March	Soult besieges Campo Mayor.
21 March	Soult captures Campo Mayor.
25 March	Beresford recaptures Campo Mayor.
3 April	Massena defeated at Sabugal, and is driven across the border into Spain.
7 April	Wellington blockades Almeida.
10 April	Spaniards seize Figueras.
14 April	Beresford recaptures Olivenza.
17 April	French besiege Figueras.
3–5 May	Wellington defeats Massena at Fuentes de Oñoro.
6 May	Wellington besieges Badajoz.
8 May	Suchet besieges Tarragona.
10 May	Garrison of Badajoz breaks out and makes a successful dash for safety.
12 May	British raise siege of Badajoz.
16 May	Beresford defeats Soult at La Albuera.
25 May	Wellington resumes siege of Badajoz.
10 June	Soult and Marmont relieve Badajoz.
17 June	Wellington retreats into Portugal.
23 June	Spaniards defeat French at river Orbigo.
28 June	Suchet captures Tarragona.
25 July	French storm Monserrat.
4 August	British invade Java.
10 August	Spaniards defeated at Las Vertientes.
11 August	Wellington blockades Ciudad Rodrigo.
19 August	French capture Figueras.
17 September	Suchet blockades Peñiscola.
18 September	Garrison of Java capitulates.
23 September	Dorsenne and Marmont relieve Ciudad Rodrigo; Suchet besieges Sagunto.
25 September	Marmont drives back Wellington at El Bodón.

25 October	Suchet defeats Blake at Sagunto.
26 October	French capture Sagunto.
28 October	Hill defeats French at Arroyomolinos de Montánchez.
20 December	French besiege Tarifa.
26 December	Suchet drives Blake into Valencia.

1812

4 January	French abandon siege of Tarifa.
8 January	Wellington besieges Ciudad Rodrigo.
9 January	Suchet captures Valencia.
19 January	Wellington storms Ciudad Rodrigo; Spaniards defeat French at Villaseca.
24 January	Spaniards defeated at Altafulla.
26 January	France annexes Catalonia.
2 February	French capture Peñiscola.
5 March	Spaniards defeat French at Roda.
16 March	Wellington besieges Badajoz.
19 March	Promulgation of Spanish constitution of 1812.
29 March	Arrest of Speransky.
5 April	Russia signs treaty of alliance with Sweden.
6 April	Wellington storms Badajoz.
18 May	After securing further victories at Silistria (Silistra) and Vidin in 1811, Russia makes peace with Turkey by means of Treaty of Bucharest.
18–19 May	Hill captures Almaraz.
24 May	Napoleon takes final decision to invade Russia.
1 June	Spaniards defeated at Bornos.
4 June	United States declares war on Britain.
15 June	French evacuate Oviedo.
17 June	Wellington besieges Salamanca forts.
23 June	*Grande armée* invades Russia.
27 June	Wellington captures Salamanca forts.
28 June	French occupy Vilna (Vilnius).
2 July	Spaniards besiege Astorga.
8 July	French occupy Minsk.
20 July	Sicilian parliament agrees new constitution.
21 July	Spaniards defeated at first battle of Castalla.
22 July	Wellington defeats Marmont at Salamanca.
24 July	Macdonald besieges Riga.
27 July	Russians check Reynier at Kobrin.
28 July	French occupy Vitebsk.

7 August	Anglo-Sicilian force lands at Alicante under Murray.
10 August	Joseph evacuates Madrid.
12 August	Wellington enters Madrid; Austrians defeat Russians at Gorodechna.
13 August	Spaniards capture Bilbao.
16 August	Americans defeated at Detroit.
16–17 August	Russians check French at Smolensk, but nevertheless continue to retreat.
18 August	Oudinot and Saint Cyr defeat Russians at first battle of Polotsk; Spaniards capture Astorga.
19 August	U.S.S. *Constitution* secures first of a series of minor American naval victories.
24 August	Soult raises siege of Cádiz and commences evacuation of Andalucía.
27 August	Spaniards storm Seville.
29 August	Kutusov assumes command of Russian forces facing Napoleon; French recapture Bilbao.
7 September	Napoleon secures marginal victory at Borodino.
14 September	Russians evacuate Moscow.
15 September	French enter Moscow.
19 September	Wellington besieges Burgos.
22 September	Wellington offered command of the Spanish army.
13 October	Americans defeated at Queenston Heights.
18 October	Murat defeated at Vinkovo.
19 October	Napoleon evacuates Moscow.
21 October	Wellington abandons siege of Burgos.
24 October	Napoleon defeats Russians at Maloyaroslavets, but fails to follow up his success; the *grande armée* is therefore condemned to retreat along the same road by which it advanced.
31 October	British evacuate Madrid.
3 November	*Grande armée* attacked at Fyodorovskoy.
9 November	Division of Baraguey d'Hilliers captured outside Smolensk.
14 November	Victor defeats Russians at second battle of Polotsk.
17 November	Napoleon defeats the Russians at Krasnoye.
18 November	Ney cut off at Krasnoye, but succeeds in escaping in an epic three-day march.
22 November	Russians cut the French line of march at the river Berezina.

25–29 November	*Grande armée* breaks through Russian encirclement in battle of the river Berezina.
5 December	Napoleon abandons *grande armée*.
14 December	*Grande armée* retreats across frontier into East Prussia.
18 December	Macdonald raises siege of Riga and retreats for frontier.
25 December	Prussians cut off.
30 December	Yorck signs Convention of Taurroggen (Taurage).

1813

4 January	French evacuate Königsberg (Kaliningrad) and retreat to the line of the Vistula (Wisla); Alexander resolves to continue the war into Poland and Germany.
8 January	Yorck occupies Königsberg.
12 January	Russians cross the river Niemen (Nemen).
16 January	Russians besiege Danzig (Gdansk).
21 January	Americans defeated at Frenchtown.
22 January	Stein arrives at Königsberg (Kaliningrad) and convokes meeting of the estates of East Prussia; Frederick William flees Berlin for Breslau (Wrocław).
24 January	Metternich informs Napoleon that Austria is withdrawing from its alliance with France.
3 February	Frederick William authorises enlistment of volunteer *jäger*.
5–7 February	East Prussian estates decree formation of a *landwehr*.
7 February	Russians occupy Warsaw.
9 February	Frederick William abolishes all exemptions to conscription.
12 February	French abandon the line of the Vistula, leaving garrisons in Thorn (Torun) and Modlin (Nowy Dwor).
26 February	Russia and Prussia sign secret treaty of alliance at Kalisch (Kalisz).
1 March	French abandon the line of the Oder, leaving garrisons in Stettin (Szcecin), Küstrin (Kostryzn), Glogau (Glogow) and Spandau.
4 March	Russians enter Berlin.

12 March	French evacuate Hamburg.
17 March	Prussia declares war on France; French abandon the line of the upper Elbe and fall back towards the Saale.
18 March	Prusso-Russian raiding force seizes Hamburg; Swedish army disembarks at Stralsund under Bernadotte; Frederick William decrees formation of a *landwehr* in the whole of Prussia.
27 March	Prussians occupy Dresden.
2 April	French defeated at Lüneberg.
3–5 April	French defeated at Mockern.
13 April	French defeated at second battle of Castalla.
15 April	Napoleon leaves Paris for the front.
18 April	Russians capture Thorn (Torun).
21 April	Russians capture Spandau; Frederick William orders formation of a *landsturm*.
27 April	Americans capture York (Toronto).
1 May	Napoleon advances into Saxony.
2 May	Napoleon defeats Prussians and Russians at Lützen.
8 May	Napoleon occupies Dresden.
20–21 May	Napoleon defeats Prussians and Russians at Bautzen.
27 May	French evacuate Madrid for the last time; Americans capture Fort George.
31 May	Franco-Danish forces reoccupy Hamburg.
2 June	British launch amphibious operation against Tarragona.
4 June	Napoleon agrees armistice of Pläswitz with Russia and Prussia.
15 June	First Treaty of Reichenbach (Dzierzoniow); Britain, Russia and Prussia agree not to make a separate peace with Napoleon, and to maintain an agreed level of commitment to the struggle.
18 June	British abandon operations against Tarragona.
21 June	Wellington defeats Joseph at Vitoria.
26 June	Napoleon meets Metternich at Dresden.
27 June	Second Treaty of Reichenbach (Dzierzoniow); Austria agrees to enter the war if Napoleon refuses to accept her mediation.
1 July	Spaniards besiege Pamplona.
5 July	Spaniards evacuate Valencia.

7 July	Wellington besieges San Sebastián.
13 July	Compact of Trachenberg (Zmigrod); Frederick William and Alexander force Bernadotte to agree to sending his main forces against Napoleon (rather than Denmark) and agree a common strategy in case hostilities should resume.
25 July	Soult launches counter-offensive in the Pyrenees.
26 July	Wellington raises siege of San Sebastián.
28 July	Wellington defeats Soult at first battle of Sorauren.
30 July	Wellington defeats Soult at second battle of Sorauren; Bentinck besieges Tarragona.
11 August	Austria declares war on France.
15 August	Hostilities resume in Saxony and Silesia; Suchet relieves and evacuates Tarragona.
16 August	Austrians invade Illyrian provinces.
22 August	Wellington resumes siege of San Sebastián.
23 August	Oudinot defeated at Grössbeeren.
26 August	Macdonald defeated at the river Katzbach (Kaczawa).
26–27 August	Napoleon defeats Allies at Dresden.
30 August	Vandamme defeated at Kulm.
31 August	Wellington storms San Sebastián; Spaniards defeat Soult at San Marcial.
6 September	Ney defeated at Dennewitz.
8 September	Citadel of San Sebastián surrenders.
9 September	Americans defeat British in naval action on Lake Erie.
13–14 September	Suchet defeats Bentinck at Ordal and Villafranca.
15 September	Allies besiege Magdeburg; French hold out until peace is signed.
16 September	French defeated at Göhrde.
30 September	Eugene withdraws to line of the river Isonzo and abandons Illyrian provinces.
5 October	Americans defeat British at the river Thames; Indian leader, Tecumseh, killed.
7 October	Wellington invades France; after a sustained Turkish offensive, Karajordjević is decisively defeated, the Turks going on to take Belgrade.
8 October	Bavaria signs Treaty of Ried with Austria,

	agreeing to join Allies in exchange for a guarantee of her continued independence.
14 October	Eugene abandons the river Isonzo and retreats to the Adige.
16–19 October	Napoleon defeated at Leipzig.
31 October	Pamplona surrenders to Spaniards.
2 November	Württemberg and Hesse-Cassel join the Allies.
5 November	Austrians besiege Venice, which holds out till the end of the war.
9 November	Metternich offers Napoleon favourable peace terms (Frankfurt Proposals); Eugene defeats Austrians at Ala.
10 November	Wellington defeats Soult at river Nivelle.
11 November	American attempt to capture Montreal defeated at Chrysler's Farm.
12 November	Allied troops enter Holland; French concentrate their troops at Utrecht.
13 November	Eugene defeats Austrians at Caldiero.
16 November	Revolution breaks out in those areas of Holland left unoccupied by the French.
18 November	Helvetic Confederation declares its neutrality.
21 November	Provisional government formed in The Hague; Brunswick, Hanover and Hesse-Cassel restored as independent states.
29 November	Allies capture Danzig.
30 November	Napoleon defeats Bavarians at Hanau.
1 December	Bernadotte invades Denmark.
4 December	Karajordjević forced to flee into Austrian territory, whereupon the Serbian revolt finally collapses.
6 December	British expeditionary force disembarks in Holland.
9–13 December	Wellington defeats Soult outside Bayonne.
10 December	Napoleon signs Treaty of Valençay with Ferdinand VII.
22 December	Bavarians besiege Hüningen (Huningue).
24 December	Allies besiege Hamburg where Davout holds out until Napoleon abdicates; revolution breaks out in the Helvetic Confederation where the Act of Mediation is overthrown by resentful patricians.
29 December	Allies move across the Rhine in force.

1814

11 January	Murat joins the Allies and renounces his claim to Sicily in exchange for the throne of Naples.
14 January	Denmark makes peace by means of Treaty of Kiel.
18 January	Suchet retreats from Barcelona whose garrison is then blockaded.
22 January	Blücher crosses the Meuse.
24 January	Mortier defeated at Bar-sur-Aube.
28 January	Murat invades Kingdom of Italy.
29 January	Napoleon defeats Blücher at Brienne.
1 February	Napoleon defeated at La Rothière; Eugene withdraws from the Adige to the Mincio.
4 February	*Cortes* declares Treaty of Valençay invalid.
5 February	Peace talks open at Chatillon.
8 February	Eugene defeats the Austrians at the river Mincio.
10 February	Napoleon defeats Russians at Champaubert.
11 February	Napoleon defeats Allies at Montmirail.
14 February	Napoleon defeats Blücher at Vauchamps.
14–18 February	Garrisons of Lérida, Monzón and Mequinenza tricked into surrender by Spaniards.
18 February	Napoleon defeats Allies at Montereau.
27 February	British besiege Bayonne; Wellington defeats Soult at Orthez; Grenier defeats the Austrians at Parma; Schwarzenburg defeats Oudinot at Bar-sur-Aube.
7 March	Blücher holds Napoleon to a draw at Craonne; Murat drives Grenier out of Parma.
8–9 March	British assault on Bergen-op-Zoom repulsed with heavy casualties.
9 March	Conference of Allied leaders agrees to continue the war until Napoleon is finally defeated (Treaty of Chaumont).
10 March	Blücher defeats Napoleon at Laon.
12 March	Bordeaux declares for Louis XVIII.
13 March	Napoleon defeats Russians at Rheims.
14 March	Anglo-Sicilian expeditionary force lands at Livorno under Bentinck.
20 March	Schwarzenburg holds Napoleon to a draw at Arcis-sur-Aube.
21 March	Chatillon discussions break up.

24 March	Ferdinand VII returns to Spain.
25 March	Combined Allied army marches on Paris; French defeated at La Fère-Champenoise.
30 March	Allies assault Paris and storm the heights of Montmartre.
31 March	Marmont surrenders Paris, and leads his troops over to the Allies.
1 April	Allies declare that they will no longer treat with Napoleon or any of his family, and that France's future must be decided by her own people.
2 April	Stage-managed by Talleyrand, the Senate calls for the return of Louis XVIII; Napoleon's marshals refuse to continue the war.
4 April	Napoleon abdicates in favour of his son.
6 April	Napoleon abdicates unconditionally.
10 April	Wellington defeats Soult at Toulouse.
12 April	Murat defeats French at Borgo San Donnino.
14 April	British repulse sortie by garrison of Bayonne.
16 April	Allies ratify Treaty of Fontainebleau giving Elba to Napoleon; Spaniards repulse sortie by garrison of Barcelona; Elió 'pronounces' against constitution of 1812 in Valencia.
17 April	Eugene agrees armistice with Austrians.
18 April	Bentinck captures Genoa.
20 April	Napoleon sails for Elba.
3 May	Louis XVIII enters Paris.
10–11 May	Spanish army restores absolutism.
17 May	Norway declares its independence.
18 May	Fernando VII enters Madrid.
30 May	Peace officially restored by first Treaty of Paris.
5 July	British defeated at Chippewa.
25 July	Americans defeated at Lundy's Lane.
26 July	Bernadotte invades Norway.
1 August	British besiege Fort Erie.
14 August	Norwegians surrender to Bernadotte, but are granted liberal terms of autonomy (Convention of Moss).
24 August	Americans defeated at Bladensberg.
25 August	British burn Washington.
13–14 September	Americans repulse British attack on Baltimore.

15 September	Discussions with regard to the settlement of Europe begin in Vienna.
17 September	Garrison of Fort Erie drives off the besiegers in a successful sortie.
4 December	United States and Britain sign Treaty of Ghent.

1815

8 January	British heavily defeated at New Orleans.
26 February	Napoleon sets sail from Elba.
1 March	Napoleon lands in France.
5 March	Napoleon declared an outlaw by the Congress of Vienna.
17 March	Murat marches north across the Neapolitan frontier.
19 March	Louis XVIII flees Paris.
20 March	Napoleon enters Paris.
25 March	Seventh Coalition formed at Vienna; Allies abjure separate peace and agree to fight on until Napoleon is overthrown.
4 April	Murat defeats Austrians at river Panaro and enters Modena.
1–2 May	Murat defeated at Tolentino.
19 May	Murat sails for France to join Napoleon.
15 June	Napoleon invades Belgium.
16 June	Napoleon defeats Blücher at Ligny and forces Wellington to retreat at Quatre Bras.
18 June	Napoleon attacks Wellington at Waterloo, but is checked; attacked by Grouchy at Wavre, Blücher manages to disengage most of his troops and marches to attack Napoleon's right flank and rear; by nightfall the entire French army is in flight.
19–21 June	Austro German forces invade France on a front stretching from Sedan to Basle and invest Mézières, Montmédy and Strasbourg; meanwhile Wellington and Blücher cross the frontier in pursuit of Napoleon's army.
22 June	Napoleon abdicates in favour of the King of Rome.
27 June	Prussians defeated at Senlis; French defeated at Villers-Cotterets.
28 June	Austrians storm Montbéliard; French defeated at Soissons.

29 June	French defeated at La Souffel.
29 June–3 July	Allies surround Paris.
4 July	Imperial government capitulates.
8 July	Louis XVIII restored to the throne.
9 July	Piedmontese capture Grenoble.
10 July	Napoleon surrenders to British at Rochefort.
11 July	Austrians capture Lyons.
24 July	Strasbourg capitulates.
26 July	H.M.S. *Northumberland* sets sail for Saint Helena with Napoleon.
26 August	Hüningen (Huningue) capitulates.
1 September	Mézières capitulates.
13 September	Montmédy capitulates; the Napoleonic Wars are finally at an end.

ABBREVIATIONS

AHR	American Historical Review
CEH	Central European History
CHJ	Cambridge Historical Journal
CJH	Canadian Journal of History
CREP	Consortium on Revolutionary Europe Proceedings
EcHR	Economic History Review
EEH	Explorations in Economic History
EHQ	European History Quarterly
EHR	English Historical Review
ESR	European Studies Review
FH	French History
FHS	French Historical Studies
HAHR	Hispanic American Historical Review
HJ	The Historical Journal
HT	History Today
IHR	International History Review
IRSH	International Review of Social History
JEH	Journal of Economic History
JHI	Journal of the History of Ideas
JLAS	Journal of Latin American Studies
JMH	Journal of Modern History
JSAHR	Journal of the Society for Army Historical Research
MM	Mariner's Mirror
PP	Past and Present
RP	Review of Politics
RR	Russian Review
SEER	Slavonic and East European Review
SH	Social History
TRHS	Transactions of the Royal Historical Society

BIBLIOGRAPHICAL ESSAY

The bibliography of the Napoleonic Wars is vast but flawed. Biographies and campaign histories abound (though even their coverage is extremely partial), but, at least in the English language, studies of society, politics and economics tend to be lacking. Some improvement could be achieved here by the inclusion of foreign-language works, but the author has nevertheless elected to confine himself to works in English in the regretful but realistic assumption that the average undergraduate student will be resolutely mono-lingual.

REFERENCE AND INTRODUCTORY

Two useful bibliographies have recently been published in English, these being J. A. Meyer, *An Annotated Bibliography of the Napoleonic Era: Recent Publications, 1945–1975* (Westport, Connecticut, 1987), and the rather narrower D. D. Horward (ed.), *Napoleonic Military History: a Bibliography* (New York, 1986). A discussion of bibliographical problems may meanwhile be found in C. J. Esdaile, 'The Napoleonic period: some thoughts on recent historiography', *European History Quarterly* (hereafter *EHQ*), XXIII, No. 3 (July, 1993), 415–32.

Works of reference, by contrast, are rather more numerous. Pride of place here must be given to C. Emsley, *The Longman Companion to Napoleonic Europe* (London, 1993), which is a mine of information of all sorts and an essential addition to any library. Also in existence are three historical dictionaries, namely O. Connelly (ed.), *Historical Dictionary of Napoleonic France, 1799–1815* (Westport, Connecticut, 1985), D. G. Chandler, *Dictionary of the Napoleonic Wars* (London, 1979), and A. Palmer, *An Encyclopaedia of Napoleon's Europe* (London, 1984).

General textbooks covering the period may be divided into those which include it as part of a wider study, and those which

344

adopt it as their chief focus, albeit usually in conjunction with the French Revolution. In the first category, I. Collins, *The Age of Progress: a Survey of European History between 1789 and 1870* (London, 1964), remains a useful general survey written by a specialist in the field. F. L. Ford, *Europe, 1780–1830* (London, 1989), is suggestive, whilst E. J. Hobsbawm, *The Age of Revolution, 1789–1848* (London, 1962) is a classic Marxian account. C. W. Crawley (ed.), *New Cambridge Modern History, IX: War and Peace in an Age of Upheaval, 1793–1815* (Cambridge, 1965) contains a variety of very useful essays, whilst its predecessor – A. W. Ward *et al.* (ed.), *Cambridge Modern History, IX: Napoleon* (Cambridge, 1934) – may still be read with profit. As a guide to the international history of the period, the relevant sections of D. McKay and H. Scott, *The Rise of the Great Powers, 1648–1815* (London, 1983) are a useful primer. Lastly, an introduction to the interrelationship of war, politics, armed forces and society in the period may be found in G. Best, *War and Society in Revolutionary Europe, 1770–1870* (London, 1982). Also relevant here is such coverage as the period is afforded in A. Vagts, *A History of Militarism, Civilian and Military* (London, 1959), M. Howard, *War in European History* (London, 1976), and J. Gooch, *Armies in Europe* (London, 1980). As to the more specific works, G. Rudé, *Revolutionary Europe, 1783–1815* (London, 1964), O. Connelly, *The French Revolution and Napoleon Era* (Fort Worth, Texas, 1991), N. Hampson, *The First European Revolution, 1776–1815* (London, 1969), and G. Brunn, *Europe and the French Imperium* (New York, 1938) are basic introductions, and F. L. Ford, 'The Revolutionary-Napoleonic era: how much of a watershed?', *American Historical Review* (hereafter *AHR*), LXIX, No. 1 (October, 1963), 18–29, and H. Kohn, 'Napoleon and the age of nationalism', *Journal of Modern History* (hereafter *JMH*), XXII, No. 1 (March, 1950), 21–37, suggestive discussions. Meanwhile, two new works specifically examine the relationship between France and the rest of Europe, namely S. Woolf, *Napoleon's Integration of Europe* (London, 1991) and G. Ellis, *The Napoleonic Empire* (London, 1991), both these being extremely valuable in that they not only draw on a wide range of Continental research, but supplement the largely military, political and biographical focus of the hitherto standard O. Connelly, *Napoleon's Satellite Kingdoms* (New York, 1965).

As might be expected, works on the wars and the armies and navies that fought them are legion, but they are also highly regurgitative, with some issues being covered repeatedly and others hardly at all. Works that deal with particular forces and campaigns can be dealt with more appropriately elsewhere, and we shall here mention only those that cover a broad spectrum. For a detailed military history that covers the main campaigns (but not those in which Napoleon played no part), there is no substitute for D. G. Chandler, *The Campaigns of Napoleon: the Mind and Method of History's Greatest Soldier* (London, 1966), though Chandler is often misleading when he strays into the realm of politics. As competition for Chandler, there is the thinner and deliberately provocative O. Connelly, *Blundering to Glory: Napoleon's Military Campaigns* (Wilmington, Delaware, 1987). Rather broader, at least geographically speaking, but otherwise extremely disappointing, is P. Fregosi, *Dreams of Empire: Napoleon and the First World War, 1792–1815* (London, 1989). Turning to tactics, technology and military organisation, G. Rothenberg, *The Art of Warfare in the Age of Napoleon* (London, 1977) is indispensable, though it may be supplemented by M. Glover, *Warfare in the Age of Bonaparte* (London, 1980) and R. Quimby, *The Background to Napoleonic Warfare* (New York, 1957). Also extremely useful here are the relevant chapters of H. Strachan, *European Armies and the Conduct of War* (London, 1983), J. Keegan, *The Face of Battle: a Study of Agincourt, Waterloo and the Somme* (London, 1976), and M. van Creveld, *Supplying War: Logistics from Wallenstein to Patton* (Cambridge, 1977). Detailed information on the organisation and composition of Europe's armies may be found in R. Johnson, *Napoleonic Armies: a Wargamer's Campaign Directory, 1805–1815* (London, 1984) and O. von Pivka, *Armies of the Napoleonic Era* (Newton Abbott, 1979). Moving on to how the armies fought, G. Jeffrey, *Tactics and Grand Tactics of the Napoleonic Wars* (New York, 1982) is an exhaustive study of manoeuvre on the battlefield and B. P. Hughes, *Firepower: Weapons Effectiveness on the Battlefield, 1630–1850* (London, 1974) a helpful study of military technology. For infantry tactics see C. Oman, 'Column and line in the Peninsula', in C. Oman (ed.), *Studies in the Napoleonic Wars* (London, 1929), pp. 82–108, S. Ross, *From Flintlock to Rifle: Infantry Tactics, 1740–1866* (London, 1979), J. R. Arnold, 'A reappraisal of column versus line in the Napoleonic Wars', *Journal of the Society for Army Historical Research* (hereafter *JSAHR*), LX, No. 4 (Winter, 1982), 196–208, and the third chapter of P. Griffith, *Forward into Battle: Tactics from Waterloo to Vietnam* (Chichester, 1981), whilst a rather brief discussion of matters relating to the artillery may be found in B. P. Hughes, *Open Fire! Artillery Tactics from Marlborough to Wellington* (Chichester, 1983). Naval warfare, by contrast, is much less well covered, practically the only source that offers a general overview being O. von Pivka, *Navies of the Napoleonic Era* (Newton Abbott, 1980).

Mention of seapower brings us to the long naval and commercial struggle between Britain and France. Here the obvious starting point remains A. T. Mahan, *The Influence of Seapower upon the French Revolution and Empire, 1793–1812* (London, 1892), though P. Kennedy, *The Rise and Fall of British Naval Mastery* (London, 1976), and D. D. Horward, 'The influence of British seapower upon the Peninsular War, 1808–1814', *Naval War College Review*, XXXI (1978), 54–71, should also be consulted. For the French, see, J. H. Rose, 'Napoleon and seapower', *Cambridge Historical Journal* (hereafter *CHJ*), I, No. 2 (1924), 138–57, P. Crowhurst, *The French War on Trade: Privateering, 1793–1815* (London, 1989), and R. Glover, 'The French fleet, 1807–1814: Britain's problem and Madison's opportunity', *JMH*, XXXIX, No. 3 (September, 1967), 233–52. Having thus charted the causes of Britain's naval supremacy, we come to the Continental blockade that was its result. Here, though old, E. F. Hecksher, *The Continental System: an Economic Interpretation* (Oxford, 1922) is vital, as is F. Crouzet, 'Wars, blockade and economic change in Europe, 1792–1815', *Journal of Economic History* (hereafter *JEH*), XXIV, No. 4 (December, 1964), 567–90. For a more purely strategic view, see F. E. Melvin, *Napoleon's Navigation System: a Study of Trade Control during the Continental Blockade* (London, 1919). Finally, a great deal of useful information may be gleaned from A. Milward and N. Saul, *The Economic Development of Continental Europe, 1780–1870* (London, 1979).

NAPOLEON AND FRANCE

Discussion of the Continental System bringing us to the end of those works that examine the period in overall terms, we must now consider the national and regional historiography, the obvious subject with which to start being Napoleon and the French. The emperor himself, of course, has generated a host of biographies and other studies, the most helpful being R. B. Jones, *Napoleon, Man and Myth* (London, 1977), G. Lefebvre, *Napoleon* (London, 1969), I. Collins, *Napoleon, First Consul and Emperor of the French* (London, 1986), F. Markham, *Napoleon* (New York, 1963), J. M. Thompson, *Napoleon Bonaparte* (Oxford, 1952), J. Tulard,

Napoleon: the Myth of the Saviour (London, 1984), and, most importantly, M. Lyons, *Napoleon Bonaparte and the Legacy of the French Revolution* (London, 1994). Less scholarly, but more provocative is V. Cronin, *Napoleon* (London, 1971). In addition, a number of articles examine Napoleon's personality in some depth, the most useful examples being D. G. Chandler, 'Napoleon as man and leader', *Consortium on Revolutionary Europe Proceedings* (hereafter *CREP*), 1989, I, 581–606, and H. Parker, 'The formation of Napoleon's personality: an exploratory essay', *French Historical Studies* (hereafter *FHS*), VII, No. 1 (Spring, 1971), 6–26. Meanwhile, the proceedings of a most interesting panel discussion on the emperor are contained in 'Napoleon: civil executive and revolutionary', *CREP*, 1972, 18–49. For the state that he ruled, D. M. G. Sutherland, *France, 1789–1815: Revolution and Counter-Revolution* (Fontana, 1985), L. Bergeron, *France under Napoleon* (Princeton, 1981), J. Godechot, 'The sense and importance of the transformation of the institutions of the Revolution in the Napoleonic epoch', in F. A. Kafker and J. M. Laux, *Napoleon and his Times: Selected Interpretations* (Malabar, Florida, 1989), pp. 278–95, and R. Holtman, *The Napoleonic Revolution* (Philadelphia, 1967) are key texts, whilst important aspects of its politics and governance are examined in E. Whitcomb, 'Napoleon's prefects', *AHR*, LXXXIX, No. 4 (October, 1974), 1089–1118, E. A. Arnold, *Fouché, Napoleon and the General Police* (Washington, DC, 1979), C. Church, *Revolution and Red Tape: the French Ministerial Bureaucracy, 1770–1850* (Oxford, 1981), I. Collins, *Napoleon and his Parliaments* (London, 1979), and I. Collins, 'Napoleon's Wars: the parliamentary dimension', in T. Fraser and K. Jeffery (eds.), *Men, Women and War* (Dublin, 1993), pp. 86–9. For the wider empire, Woolf and Ellis are indispensable (see above), but there is also much specific material on the institutions, ideology and personnel that helped bind it together. Taking the pinnacle of the imperial world first of all, D. Seward, *Napoleon's Family* (London, 1986) is the most recent study of Napoleon's family, whilst P. Mansel, *The Eagle in Splendour: Napoleon I and his Court* (London, 1987) is a mine of information on their milieu and its function. On the ideology of the empire, R. Holtman, *Napoleonic Propaganda* (Baton Rouge, 1950), is first-class, and can usefully be supplemented by J. K. Burton, *Napoleon and Clio: Historical Writing, Teaching and Thinking during the First Empire* (Durham, North Carolina, 1979). J. J. Matthews, 'Napoleon's military bulletins', *JMH*, XXII, No. 2 (June, 1950), 137–44, looks at the generation of the empire's legend of military glory, as does D. G. Chandler, '"To lie like a bulletin": an examination of Napoleon's re-writing of the history of the battle of Marengo', *Proceedings of the Annual Meeting of the Western Society for French History*, XVIII (1991), 33–43. Art, music, architecture and even archaeology were all pressed into service for political purposes, of course, and here reference can profitably be made to A. Boime, *A Social History of Modern Art, II: Art in an Age of Bonapartism, 1800–1815* (Chicago, 1993), J. L. Connolly, 'Napoleon as Hercules: a Revolutionary or royal revival?', *CREP*, 1987, 647–66, J. L. Connolly, 'Napoleon on the bridge: a note on the iconography of passage', *CREP*, 1985, 45–64, C. Donakowski, 'Giovanni Paisiello, the emperor's musician', *CREP*, 1986, 424–30, W. Miller, 'Napoleon and Cherubini: a discordant relationship', *CREP*, 1989 (Bicentennial Consortium), 260–69, J. Yorke, 'Percier and Fontaine: propagators of empire-style architecture', *CREP*, 1989 (Bicentennial Consortium), 734–41, and R. Hodges, *The Eagle and the Spade: the Archaeology of Rome during the Napoleonic Era, 1809–1814* (Cambridge, 1992). For another aspect of the same issue, see D. M. Quynn, 'The art confiscations of the Napoleonic Wars', *AHR*, L, No. 1 (October, 1944), 437–60.

Before the Napoleonic empire could be 'socialised' in the approved style, it first had to be conquered, studies of the army therefore forming an important section of the period's historiography. For a mass of technical information of every sort, see the highly idiosyncratic but nonetheless useful J. R. Elting, *Swords around a Throne: Napoleon's Grande Armée* (New York, 1988) and the briefer but less extravagant H. C. B. Rogers, *Napoleon's Army* (London, 1974). Meanwhile, the gradual transformation of the citizens' army of 1793 to the essentially professional *grande armée* may be examined in J. Bertaud, *The Army of the French Revolution: from Citizen Soldiers to Instrument of Power* (Princeton, 1988) and J. Lynn, 'Toward an army of honour: the moral evolution of the French army, 1789–1815', *FHS*, XVI, No. 1 (Spring, 1989), 152–82. On its élites, D. G. Chandler (ed.), *Napoleon's Marshals* (New York, 1987) is the most recent guide to the marshalate, whilst J. Bertaud, 'Napoleon's officers', *Past and Present* (hereafter *PP*), No. 112 (August, 1986), 91–111, looks at the officer corps as a whole. On the rank and file, conscription is examined in I. Woloch, 'Napoleonic conscription: state power and civil society', *PP*, No. 111 (May, 1986), 101–29, whilst large quantities of material may also be found in A. Forrest, *Conscripts and Deserters: the Army and*

French Society during the Revolution and Empire (Oxford, 1989). As Forrest's title implies, the question of conscription is intimately linked with popular resistance to the empire, as witness E. A. Arnold, 'Some observations on the French opposition to Napoleonic conscription, 1804–1806', *FHS*, IV, No. 4 (Autumn, 1966), 453–62 and A. Forrest, 'Conscription and crime in rural France during the Directory and the Consulate', in G. Lewis and C. Lucas (eds.), *Beyond the Terror: Essays in French Regional and Social History, 1794–1815* (Cambridge, 1983), pp. 92–120. Meanwhile, a somewhat broader perspective on popular disorder may be found in G. Lewis, *The Second Vendée: the Continuity of Counter-Revolution in the Department of the Gard, 1789–1815* (Oxford, 1978), R. Cobb, *The Police and the People: French Popular Protest, 1789–1820* (Oxford, 1970), and C. Emsley, 'Policing the streets of early nineteenth-century Paris', *French History* (hereafter *FH*), I, No. 2 (October, 1987), 257–82. Meanwhile, opposition at the level of the élite may be approached via L. de Villefosse and J. Bouissounouse, *The Scourge of the Eagle: Napoleon and the Liberal Opposition* (London, 1972), and G. Artom, *Napoleon is Dead in Russia* (New York, 1970), whose slightly obscure title hides an account of the Malet conspiracy of 1812.

French society under the empire has not received the attention that it deserves, though G. Ellis, 'Rhine and Loire: Napoleonic élites and social order', in Lewis and Lucas, *Beyond the Terror*, pp. 232–67, and R. Forster, 'The survival of the nobility during the French Revolution', *PP*, No. 37 (July, 1967), 71–86, are both helpful on its upper echelons. For the peasantry, A. Moulin, *Peasantry and Society in France since 1789* (Cambridge, 1991) and G. Dupeux, *French Society, 1789–1970* (London, 1976) should both be consulted, though the coverage that they offer is sketchy in the extreme. In contrast, by a curious irony there is considerable material on one of the more marginalised sections of French society, namely the Jews, sources here including Z. Szajkowski, *Agricultural Credit and Napoleon's Anti-Jewish Decrees* (New York, 1953), F. Kobler, *Napoleon and the Jews* (New York, 1976), S. Schwarzfuchs, *Napoleon, the Jews and the Sanhedrin* (London, 1979), and F. Malino, *The Sephardic Jews of Bordeaux: Assimilation and Emancipation in Revolutionary and Napoleonic France* (Birmingham, Alabama, 1978). There is, however, little on women, except for S. Conner, '*Les femmes militaires*: women in the French army, 1792–1815', *CREP*, 1982, 290–302. Turning to the economy, G. Ellis, *Napoleon's Continental Blockade: the Case of Alsace* (Oxford,

1981) is essential, and this may be supplemented by R. Barker, 'The Conseil Général des Manufactures under Napoleon (1810–1814)', *FHS*, VI, No. 2 (1969), 185–213, and R. Barker, 'The Conseil Général des Manufactures: business leaders and the state economic administration during the empire and restoration', *CREP*, 1989, II, 47–66.

Having dealt with the governance, institutions and structure of imperial France, there remains its foreign policy. Here general discussions include P. Paret, 'Napoleon as enemy', *CREP*, 1983, 49–61, O. Murphy, 'Napoleon and French old-régime politics and diplomacy', *CREP*, 1989 (Bicentennial Consortium), 97–103, P. Schroeder, 'Napoleon's foreign policy: a criminal enterprise', *CREP*, 1989 (Bicentennial Consortium), 104–11, R. B. Mowat, *The Diplomacy of Napoleon* (London, 1924), H. Butterfield, *The Peace Tactics of Napoleon* (Cambridge, 1929), and H. C. Deutsch, *The Genesis of Napoleonic Imperialism* (Cambridge, Massachusetts, 1938). More narrowly focused are H. Ragsdale, *Détente in the Napoleonic Era: Bonaparte and the Russians* (Lawrence, Kansas, 1980), V. Puryear, *Napoleon and the Dardanelles* (Cambridge, 1951), A. C. Niven, *Napoleon and Alexander I: a Study in Anglo-Russian Relations, 1807–1812* (Washington, DC, 1978), and H. Parker, 'Why did Napoleon invade Russia? A study in motivation, personality and social structure', *CREP*, 1989 (Bicentennial Consortium), 86–96. Needless to say, the surfeit of works on Talleyrand is also helpful here, the most important being E. Dard, *Napoleon and Talleyrand* (London, 1937), and J. F. Bernard, *Talleyrand: a Biography* (London, 1973). Finally, the agents of French foreign policy may be examined in E. A. Whitcombe, *Napoleon's Diplomatic Service* (Durham, North Carolina, 1979), and E. Whitcomb, 'The duties and functions of Napoleon's external agents', *History*, LVII, No. 190 (June, 1972), 189–204.

GREATER FRANCE AND THE WIDER EMPIRE

Before we proceed to specifics, the student is first referred to the works already cited by Ellis, Woolf and Connelly. However, the position of the Jews may be studied in H. Graetz, *History of the Jews from the Earliest Times to the Present Day* (London, 1892), and, especially, R. Mahler, *A History of Modern Jewry* (London, 1971), whilst there is also a growing literature on the individual regions of the grand empire. Beginning with the Low Countries, Belgium and Holland are considered together in the appropriate section of E. H. Kossmann, *The Low Countries, 1780–1940* (Oxford, 1978). There is little else on Belgium, but Holland is discussed at length in the magisterial S. Schama, *Patriots and Liberators: Revolution in the Netherlands, 1780–1813* (London, 1977), various aspects of Dutch affairs also being covered in S. Schama, 'The exigencies of war and the policies of taxation in the Netherlands, 1795–1810', in J. Winter (ed.), *War and Economic Development: Essays in Memory of David Joslin* (Cambridge, 1975), pp. 103–38, and G. Bond, 'Louis Bonaparte and the collapse of the Kingdom of Holland', *CREP*, 1974, 141–53. Finally, economic matters are dealt with in J. Dhondt, 'The cotton industry at Ghent during the French Revolution' in F. Crouzet, W. Chaloner and W. Stern (ed.), *Essays in European Economic History, 1789–1914* (London, 1969), pp. 15–52, and J. Mokyr, 'The industrial revolution in the Low Countries in the first half of the nineteenth century: a comparative case study', *JEH*, XXXIV, No. 1 (June, 1974), 365–89.

Moving eastwards to Germany, basic introductions to the period which cover not just the annexed territories and the Confederation of the Rhine, but also Prussia, and, in the case of Sheehan, Austria as well, may be found in H. Kohn, *Prelude to Nation States: the French and German Experience, 1789–1815* (Princeton, 1967), M. Hughes, *Nationalism and Society: Germany, 1800–1945* (London, 1988), T. C. W. Blanning, 'The French Revolution and the modernization of Germany', *Central European History* (hereafter *CEH*), XXII, No. 2 (June, 1989), 109–29, J. Breuilly, 'State-building, modernization and liberalism from the late eighteenth century to unification: German peculiarities', *EHQ*, XXII, No. 2 (April, 1992), 257–84, G. P. Gooch, 'Germany's debt to the French Revolution', in G. P. Gooch (ed.), *Studies in German History* (London, 1948), pp. 190–209, and J. J. Sheehan, *German History, 1770–1866* (Oxford, 1989). Meanwhile, the political situation at the beginning of the Napoleonic era may be approached via J. Gagliardo, *Reich and Nation: the Holy Roman Empire as Idea and Reality, 1763–1806* (Bloomington, Indiana, 1980). Turning more specifically to the Napoleonic zone of influence, H.A.L. Fisher, *Studies in Napoleonic Statesmanship – Germany* (Oxford, 1903), though very old, remains a helpful starting point. Other than W. O. Shanahan, 'A neglected source of German nationalism: the Confederation of the Rhine, 1806–13', in M. Palumbo and W. O. Shanahan, *Nationalism: Essays in Honour of Louis L. Snyder* (Westport, Connecticut, 1981), pp. 106–32, and H.

Schmitt, 'Germany without Prussia: a closer look at the Confederation of the Rhine', *German Studies Review*, VI, No. 1 (January, 1983), 9–39, there is no general study of the Rheinbund, but many of its component states have attracted attention. Bavaria is particularly well covered, as witness H. C. Vedeler, 'The genesis of the toleration reforms in Bavaria under Montgelas', *JMH*, X, No. 4 (December, 1938), 473–95, A. Cronenberg, 'Montgelas and the reorganization of Napoleonic Bavaria', *CREP*, 1989 (Bicentennial Consortium), 712–19, and the misleadingly titled D. Klang, 'Bavaria and the war of liberation, 1813–14', *FHS*, IV, No. 1 (Spring, 1965), 22–41 (this is in fact a wide-ranging discussion of the motivation of the Bavarian reformers). Meanwhile, Nassau can be examined in B. C. Anderson, 'State-building and bureaucracy in early nineteenth-century Nassau', *CEH*, XXIV, No. 3 (September, 1991), 222–47, and Baden in L. E. Lee, 'Baden between revolutions: state-building and citizenship, 1800–1848', *CEH*, XXIV, No. 3 (September, 1991), 248–67. For the armies of the Confederation of the Rhine, meanwhile, see J. Gill, *With Eagles to Glory: Napoleon and his German Allies in the 1809 Campaign* (London, 1992). Coverage of social and economic issues is by contrast limited, but some interesting material may nevertheless be found in J. M. Diefendorff, *Businessmen and Politics in the Rhineland, 1789–1834* (Princeton, 1980), J. Whaley, *Religious Toleration and Social Change in Hamburg, 1529–1819* (Cambridge, 1985), and H. Kisch, 'The impact of the French Revolution on the lower-Rhine textile districts', *Economic History Review* (hereafter *EcHR*), XV, No. 2 (December, 1962), 304–27.

If material on the nature and impact of the Napoleonic domination of Germany is limited, the same cannot be said of the response which it evoked. General introductions to the emergence of German nationalism may be found in L. L. Snyder, *Roots of German Nationalism* (Bloomington, Indiana, 1978), R. R. Ergang, *Herder and the Foundations of German Nationalism* (New York, 1931), and H. Schulze, *The Course of German Nationalism: from Fichte to Bismarck, 1763–1867* (Cambridge, 1991), the subject being more specifically related to the Revolutionary and Napoleonic era in H. Segeberg, 'Germany', in O. Dann and J. Dinwiddy, *Nationalism in the Age of the French Revolution* (London, 1988), pp. 137–56, H. Kohn, 'The eve of German nationalism', *Journal of the History of Ideas* (hereafter *JHI*), XII, (April, 1951), 256–84, and H. Kohn, 'Romanticism and the rise of German nationalism', *Review of Politics* (hereafter *RP*), XII, No. 4 (October, 1950),

443–72. Developments in the period 1806–13 are covered by G. A. Craig, 'German intellectuals and politics, 1789–1815: the case of Heinrich von Kleist', *CEH*, II, No. 1 (March, 1969), 3–21, P. R. Sweet, *Friedrich von Gentz: Defender of the Old Order* (Madison, Wisconsin, 1941), G. Mann, *Secretary of Europe: the Life of Friedrich von Gentz, Enemy of Napoleon* (New Haven, Connecticut, 1946), A. G. Pundt, *Arndt and the Nationalist Awakening in Germany*, (New York, 1935), O. Johnston, 'The myth of Andreas Hofer: origins and essence', *CREP*, 1989 (Bicentennial Consortium), 720–28, O. Johnston, 'British pounds and Prussian patriots', *CREP*, 1986, 294–305, H. Kohn, 'Father Jahn's nationalism', *RP*, XI, No. 4 (October, 1949), 419–32, O. Johnston, 'The Spanish guerrilla in German literature during the Peninsular War', in A. D. Berkeley (ed.), *New Lights on the Peninsular War* (Lisbon, 1991), pp. 347–56, and S. Heit, 'German romanticism: an ideological response to Napoleon', *CREP*, 1980, I, 184–97. Disappointingly, little is available on such armed resistance as actually broke out, but T. C. W. Blanning, *The French Revolution in Germany: Occupation and Resistance in the Rhineland, 1792–1802* (Oxford, 1983) has a fascinating discussion of banditry, whilst D. Gray, 'The French invasion of Hanover in 1803 and the origins of the King's German Legion', *CREP*, 1980, I, 198–212, is helpful on military emigration.

Coming now to the easternmost extremity of French control, we reach the Grand Duchy of Warsaw. Here, however, apart from C. Blackburn, 'Prince Poniatowski finds an army: Galician attitudes in 1809', *CREP*, 1992, 215–22, we must perforce rely on general histories of Poland, of which the two of most value are W.F. Reddaway *et al.* (eds.), *The Cambridge History of Poland – From Augustus II to Pilsudski (1697–1935)* (Cambridge, 1951), and P. Wandycz, *The Lands of Partitioned Poland, 1795–1918* (Seattle, 1974).

Linking the two eastern and southern 'horns' of the French empire, we have Switzerland, and here again there is no option but to turn to general works, virtually the only one available being W. Oechsli, *History of Switzerland, 1499–1914* (Cambridge, 1922).

Beyond Switzerland lay Italy and the Illyrian provinces. For the former, an indispensable introduction may be found in S. Woolf, *A History of Italy, 1700–1860: the Social Constraints of Political Change* (London, 1979). This may be supplemented by a number of regional studies. For the north, see M. Broers, 'Revolution as vendetta: Napoleonic Piedmont, 1801–1814', *The Historical Journal* (hereafter *HJ*), XXXIII, No. 4 (December, 1990), 787–810, A. Grab,

'The Kingdom of Italy and Napoleon's Continental Blockade', *CREP*, 1988, 587–604, and L. Macaluso, 'Policing the people: Genoa under the empire', *CREP*, 1989, II, 558–76, whilst the Naples of Joseph and Murat may be examined in E. Noether, 'Change and Continuity in the Kingdom of Naples, 1806–1815', *CREP*, 1988, 605–18, J. A. Davis, 'The impact of French rule on the Kingdom of Naples, 1806–1815', *Ricerche Storiche*, XX, Nos 2–3 (May-December, 1990), 367–405, and the old but still useful R. Johnston, *The Napoleonic Empire in Southern Italy and the Rise of the Secret Societies* (London, 1904). Finally, it is also worth noting that biographies of varying degrees of historical worth exist of most of the Napoleonic potentates who ruled in Italy, viz. O. Connelly, *The Gentle Bonaparte: a Biography of Joseph, Napoleon's Elder Brother* (New York, 1968), M. Ross, *The Reluctant King: Joseph Bonaparte, King of the Two Sicilies and Spain* (London, 1976), J. Bear, *Caroline Murat: a Biography* (London, 1972), H. Cole, *The Betrayers: Joachim and Caroline Murat* (London, 1972), M. Weiner, *The Parvenu Princesses: Elisa, Pauline and Caroline Bonaparte* (London, 1964), Carola Oman, *Napoleon's Viceroy: Eugene de Beauharnais* (London, 1966), and A. H. Atteridge, *Joachim Murat, Marshal of France and King of Naples* (London, 1911).

Military affairs are well covered. Popular resistance is examined in D. Koenig, 'Banditry in Napoleonic Italy', *CREP*, 1975, 72–9, A. Grab, 'Popular risings in Napoleonic Italy', *CREP*, 1989 (Bicentennial Consortium), 112–19, M. Finlay, 'The most monstrous of wars: suppression of Calabrian brigandage, 1806–1811', *CREP*, 1989, II, 251–66, M. Finlay, 'Patriots or brigands? The Calabrian partisans, 1806–1812', *CREP*, 1991, 161–70, and M. Finlay, 'The siege of Amantea', *CREP*, 1992, 256–65. Some suggestive material on Calabria may also be found in W. H. Flayhart, 'The Neapolitan reaction to the Allied invasions of 1805–1806', *CREP*, 1989, II, 235–50, and W. H. Flayhart, *Counterpoint to Trafalgar: the Anglo-Russian Invasion of Naples, 1805–1806* (Columbia, South Carolina, 1992). For the imperial war effort (at least in so far as regards the Kingdom of Italy), see F. della Peruta, 'War and society in Napoleonic Italy: the armies of the Kingdom of Italy at home and abroad', in J. Davis and P. Ginsborg (eds.), *Society and Politics in Italy in the Age of the Risorgimento* (Cambridge, 1991), pp. 26–49.

Turning now to the other area of French rule in southern Europe, we come to the Illyrian provinces. With the exception of H. Bjelović, *The Ragusan Republic: Victim of Napoleon and its own Conservatism* (Leiden, 1970) and the relevant sections of F. W.

Carter, *Dubrovnik (Ragusa): a Classic City-State* (London, 1972), we must here again rely largely on published conference papers. These include P. Adler, 'The Illyrian provinces of France: economic aspects', *CREP*, 1989 (Bicentennial Consortium), 931–8, L. Plut-Pregelj, 'The Illyrian provinces: the South Slavs and the French Revolution', *CREP*, 1989 (Bicentennial Consortium), 600–09, and C. Rogel, 'The Slovenes in the Revolutionary Period', *CREP*, 1980, I, 254–63 (despite their titles, both Plut-Pregelj and Rogel concentrate on the period after 1809.

IBERIA

Never really part of the French empire, the Iberian Peninsula requires separate treatment. Beginning with Spain, the historiography of the period before 1808 has been distorted by an endless fascination with the quarrels that beset the royal family, of which the latest examples are D. Hilt, *The Troubled Trinity: Godoy and the Spanish Monarchs* (Tuscaloosa, Alabama, 1987) and J. Chastenet, *Godoy: Master of Spain, 1792–1808* (London, 1953). Far more useful as an approach to the crisis of the *ancien régime* in Spain are R. Herr, 'Good, evil and Spain's uprising against Napoleon', in R. Herr and H. Parker (eds.), *Ideas in History* (Durham, North Carolina, 1965), pp. 157–81, R. Herr, *The Eighteenth-Century Revolution in Spain* (Princeton, 1958), J. Lynch, *Bourbon Spain, 1700–1808* (Oxford, 1989), and C. Crowley, '*Luces* and *hispanidad*: nationalism and modernization in eighteenth-century Spain', in Palumbo and Shanahan, *Nationalism*, pp. 87–102. Meanwhile, economic questions are examined in B. Hamnett, 'The appropriation of Mexican Church wealth by the Spanish Bourbon government: the consolidation of the *vales reales*, 1805–1809', *Journal of Latin-American Studies* (hereafter *JLAS*), I, No. 2 (November, 1969), 85–113, E. J. Hamilton, 'War and inflation in Spain, 1780–1800', *Quarterly Journal of Economics*, LIX, No. 1 (November, 1944), 36–77, E. J. Hamilton, *War and Prices in Spain, 1651–1800* (Cambridge, Massachusetts, 1947), R. Herr, *Rural Change and Royal Finances in Spain at the End of the Eighteenth Century* (Los Angeles, 1989), and J. Barbier and H. Klein, 'Revolutionary wars and public finances: the Madrid treasury, 1784–1807', *JEH*, XLI, No. 2 (December, 1981), 315–39. For the armed forces, see C. J. Esdaile, *The Spanish Army in the Peninsular War* (Manchester, 1988), M. Espadas Burgos, 'The Spanish army in the crisis of the Old Régime', in R. Bañon Martínez and T. Barker (eds.), *Armed Forces and Society in Spain, Past and Present* (New York, 1988), pp. 81–103, J. de Zulueta, 'Trafalgar: the Spanish view', *Mariner's Mirror* (hereafter *MM*), LXVI, No. 4 (November, 1980), 293–318, J. Harbron, *Trafalgar and the Spanish Navy* (London, 1988) and J. Harbron, 'Spain's forgotten naval renaissance', *History Today* (hereafter *HT*), XL, No. 8 (August, 1990), 29–34. Finally, also helpful are W. Callahan, 'The origins of the conservative Church in Spain, 1789–1823', *European Studies Review* (hereafter *ESR*), X, No. 2 (April, 1980), 199–223, W. Callahan, *Church, Politics and Society in Spain, 1750–1854* (London, 1985), and R. Barahona, 'Basque regionalism and centre-periphery relations, 1759–1833', *ESR*, XIII, No. 3 (July, 1983), 271–96.

In so far as the War of Independence of 1808–14 is concerned, by far the best general introduction is G. Lovett, *Napoleon and the Birth of Modern Spain* (New York, 1965). Meanwhile the most comprehensive guide to its military history remains C. Oman, *A History of the Peninsular War* (Oxford, 1902–1930). More accessible, but less detailed, are D. Gates, *The Spanish Ulcer: a History of the Peninsular War* (London, 1986) and J. Read, *War in the Peninsula* (London, 1977). For more detailed discussion of the Spanish war effort, C. J. Esdaile, *The Spanish Army in the Penisular War* (Manchester, 1988), C. J. Esdaile, *The Duke of Wellington and the Command of the Spanish Army, 1812–14* (London, 1990), C. J. Esdaile, 'War and politics in Spain, 1808–1814', *HJ*, XXXI, No. 2 (June, 1988), 295–317, C. J. Esdaile, 'The duke of Wellington and the military eclipse of Spain, 1808–1814', *International History Review* (hereafter *IHR*), XI, No. 1 (February, 1989), 55–67, and C. J. Esdaile, 'The Duke of Wellington and the command of the Spanish army, 1812–1814', in N. Gash (ed.), *Wellington: Studies in the Military and Political Career of the First Duke of Wellington* (Manchester, 1990), pp. 66–86, will all be found to be helpful. The uprising of 1808 and, in the case of Zaragoza, its aftermath, are dealt with in Herr, 'Good, evil and Spain's uprising against Napoleon' and R. Rudorff, *War to the Death: the Sieges of Saragossa, 1808–1809* (London, 1974). For the guerrillas, G. Lovett, 'The Spanish guerrillas and Napoleon', *CREP*, 1975, 80–90, and D. W. Alexander, 'The impact of guerrilla warfare in Spain on French combat strength', *CREP*, 1975, 91–8, present a favourable view, whilst C. J. Esdaile, 'Heroes or Villains? The Spanish guerrillas and the Peninsular War', *HT*, XXXVIII, No. 4 (April, 1988), 29–35, C. J. Esdaile, 'The problem of the Spanish guerrillas', in Berkeley, *New*

Lights, 191–200, and C. J. Esdaile, 'The duke of Wellington and the Spanish guerrillas: the campaign of 1813', *CREP*, 1991, 298–306, are more sceptical.

Looking at the war from the French point of view, M. Glover, *Legacy of Glory: the Bonaparte Kingdom of Spain, 1808–1813* (New York, 1971) is a campaign history with little to say on the régime of Joseph Bonaparte, whilst its discussion even of the military problems facing the French is far outshone by D. D. Horward, *Napoleon and Iberia: the Twin Sieges of Ciudad Rodrigo and Almeida* (Tallahassee, 1984) and D. W. Alexander, *Rod of Iron: French Counterinsurgency Policy in Aragón during the Peninsular War* (Wilmington, Delaware, 1985). On the political aspects of the French occupation there is almost nothing, however, except R. Barahona, 'The Napoleonic occupation and its political consequences in the Basque provinces (1808–1813)', *CREP*, 1985, 101–16, though the student is also referred to the biographies of Joseph Bonaparte cited above.

Nor have the politics of Patriot Spain merited the attention that they deserve. However, the key figure of Jovellanos is examined in J. Polt, *Gaspar Melchor de Jovellanos* (New York, 1971), whilst C. W. Crawley, 'English and French influences in the *cortes* of Cádiz', *CHJ*, VI, No. 2 (1939), 176–206, B. Hamnett, 'Spanish constitutionalism and the impact of the French Revolution, 1808–1814', in H. T. Mason and W. Doyle (eds.) *The Impact of the French Revolution on European Consciousness* (Gloucester, 1989), pp. 64–80, and B. Hamnett, 'Constitutional theory and political reality: liberalism, traditionalism and the Spanish *cortes*, 1810–1814', *JMH*, XL, No. 1 (March, 1977), on-demand supplement, are all important. Three moments of political crisis are examined in C. J. Esdaile, 'The Marqués de la Romana and the Peninsular War: a case-study in civil-military relations', *CREP*, 1993, 366–74, C. J. Esdaile, 'Wellington and the Spanish army, 1812: the revolt of General Ballesteros', *CREP*, 1987, 79–92, and G. Lovett, 'The fall of the first Spanish liberal régime, 1813–1814', *CREP*, 1974, 176–88. Given the major role played by the Latin-American revolutions in Spanish politics, not to mention Anglo-Spanish relations, it is also worth mentioning J. Lynch, *The Spanish-American Revolutions, 1808–1826* (London, 1973), T. Anna, *Spain and the Loss of America* (Lincoln, Nebraska, 1983), M. P. Costeloe, *Response to Revolution: Imperial Spain and the Latin-American Revolutions* (Cambridge, 1986), W. Robertson, 'The juntas of 1808 and the Spanish colonies', *EHR*, XXXI, No. 124 (October, 1916), 573–85,

M. P. Costeloe, 'Spain and the Spanish-American Wars of Independence: the Comisión de Reemplazos, 1811–1820', *JLAS*, XIII, No. 2 (November, 1981), 223–37, and C.J. Esdaile, 'Latin America and the Anglo-Spanish alliance against Napoleon, 1808–1814', *Bulletin of Hispanic Studies*, LXIX, No. 3 (July, 1992), 55–70. For the part played by other powers, see J. Lynch, 'British policy and Spanish America, 1783–1808', *JLAS*, I, No. 1 (May, 1969), 1–30, C. Mullet, 'British schemes against Spanish America in 1806', *Hispanic American Historical Review* (hereafter *HAHR*), XXVII, No. 2 (May, 1947), 269–78, W. Kaufmann, *British Policy and the Independence of Latin-America, 1804–1828* (London, 1967), J. Rydjord, 'British mediation between Spain and her colonies, 1811–1813', *HAHR*, XXI, No. 1 (February, 1941), 29–50, and W. Robertson, *France and Latin-American Independence* (Baltimore, 1939).

Turning now to Portugal, we once again find that there are no major studies of the French Wars. However, M. Goldstein, 'The Stuart-Vaughan mission of 1808: the genesis of the Peninsular alliance', *CREP*, 1977, 99–104, M. Fryman, 'Charles Stuart and the "common cause": Anglo-Portuguese diplomatic relations, 1810–1814', *CREP*, 1977, 105–15, F. de la Fuente, 'Portuguese resistance to Napoleon: Dom Miguel Forjaz and the mobilization of Portugal', *CREP*, 1983, 141–55, D. D. Horward, 'Wellington and the defence of Portugal', *IHR*, XI, No. 1 (February, 1989), 55–67, and F. O. Cetre, 'Beresford and the Portuguese army, 1809–1814', in Berkeley, *New Lights*, 149–55, all examine various aspects of Britain's attempts to extend her influence over the kingdom, whilst C. MacKay, 'Conflicting goals: Napoleon, Junot and the occupation of Portugal', *CREP*, 1992, 445–55, looks at the brief French occupation of 1807–1808.

BRITAIN

Having passed through the contested area of the Peninsula, we now come to Napoleon's opponents, and, particularly, to Britain. Here a number of general works exist that provide useful starting points, the most important being I. Christie, *Wars and Revolutions: Britain, 1760–1815* (London, 1982), J. S. Watson, *The Reign of George III, 1760–1815* (Oxford, 1960), and A. Briggs, *The Age of Improvement* (London, 1959). More specific coverage of her involvement in the French Wars may be found in the introductory S. Wood, *Britain and the French Wars* (London, 1973), and in A. Bryant's super-patriotic trilogy, *The Years of Endurance, 1793–1802* (London, 1942), *The Years of Victory, 1802–1812* (London, 1944), and *The Age of Elegance, 1812–1822* (London, 1950), whilst there is an innovative and stimulating comparative study in A. Harvey, *Collision of Empire: Britain in Three World Wars* (London, 1992). For the period up till 1805, see P. Mackesy, *War Without Victory: the Downfall of Pitt, 1799–1802* (Oxford, 1984), and J. H. Rose, *William Pitt and the Great War* (London, 1911). Moving more specifically into the realms of strategy and foreign policy, the former is competently examined in C. Hall, *British Strategy in the Napoleonic War, 1803–15* (Manchester, 1992), P. Mackesy, 'Strategic problems of the British war effort', in H. T. Dickinson (ed.), *Britain and the French Revolution, 1789–1815* (London, 1989), pp. 147–64, and C. Fedorak, 'Maritime vs. continental strategy: Britain and the defeat of Napoleon', *CREP*, 1989 (Bicentennial Consortium), 176–83. Foreign policy, meanwhile, is reviewed in J. R. Jones, *Britain and the World, 1649–1815* (London, 1980), C. Bayly, *Imperial Meridian; the British Empire and the World, 1780–1830* (London, 1989), C. Middleton, *The Administration of British Foreign Policy, 1782–1846* (Durham, North Carolina, 1977), A. Ward and G. Gooch (eds.), *The Cambridge History of British Foreign Policy, 1783–1919,* (Cambridge, 1919), M. Chamberlain, *Pax Britannica? British Foreign Policy, 1789–1914* (London, 1988), and J. Clarke, *British Diplomacy and Foreign Policy, 1782–1865: the National Interest* (London, 1989), more specific monographs and articles on this subject including M. Duffy, 'British diplomacy and the French Wars, 1789–1815', in Dickinson, *Britain and the French Revolution,* pp. 127–45, J. Sherwig, *Guineas and Gunpowder: British Foreign Aid in the Wars with France, 1793–1815* (Cambridge, Massachusetts, 1969), C. Webster, *The Foreign Policy of Castlereagh, 1812–1815: Britain and the Reconstruction of Europe* (London, 1931), H. Butterfield, *Charles James Fox and Napoleon* (London, 1962), F. Walker, 'The Grenville-Fox "junction" and the problem of peace', *Canadian Journal of History* (hereafter *CJH*), XII, No. 1 (April, 1977), 51–64, J. K. Severn, *A Wellesley Affair: Richard, Marquess Wellesley, and the Conduct of Anglo-Spanish Diplomacy, 1809–1812* (Tallahassee, 1981), E. Roach, 'Anglo-Russian relations from Austerlitz to Tilsit', *IHR*, V, No. 2 (May, 1983), 181–200, J. H. Rose, 'Canning and the Spanish patriots in 1808', *AHR*, XII, No. 1 (October, 1906), 39–52, A. Ryan, 'An ambassador afloat: Vice-Admiral Saumarez and the Swedish court, 1808–1812', in J. Black and P. Woodfine (eds.), *The*

British Navy and the Use of Naval Power in the Eighteenth Century (Leicester, 1988), pp. 237–58, and H. Barnes, 'Canning and the Danes, 1807', *HT*, XV, No. 8 (August, 1965), 530–8. Finally, an interesting contrast to the slightly sanctimonious tone of much British writing on the subject is provided by A. Harvey, 'European attitudes to Britain during the French Revolutionary and Napoleonic Wars', *History*, LXIII, No. 209 (October, 1978), 356–65.

A further source for British policy in the war against France may be found in the wealth of minutely-researched political biographies that have been written of leading British statesmen. Notable here are P. Ziegler, *Addington: a Life of Henry Addington, First Viscount Sidmouth* (London, 1965), W. Hinde, *George Canning* (London, 1973), P. Rolo, *George Canning: Three Biographical Studies* (London, 1965), P. Dixon, *Canning, Politician and Statesman* (London, 1976), J. Derry, *Charles James Fox* (London, 1972), P. Jupp, *Lord Grenville, 1759–1834* (Oxford, 1985), N. Gash, *Lord Liverpool: the Life and Political Career of Robert Banks Jenkinson, Second Earl of Liverpool, 1770–1828* (London, 1984), C. Bartlett, *Castlereagh* (London, 1966), J. Derry, *Castlereagh* (London, 1976), D. Gray, *Spencer Perceval, 1762–1812: the Evangelical Prime Minister* (Manchester, 1963), and I. Butler, *The Oldest Brother: the Marquess Wellesley, 1760–1842* (London, 1973).

Of course, such biographies are as valuable for the domestic history of Britain as they are for the conduct of war and foreign affairs, the most useful starting point here being A. Harvey, *Britain in the Early Nineteenth Century* (London, 1978). Otherwise, high politics may be studied in B. Hill, *British Parliamentary Parties, 1742–1832* (London, 1985), A. Aspinall, *Politics and the Press, c.1780–1850* (London, 1949), and F. O'Gorman, *The Emergence of the British Two-Party System, 1760–1832* (London, 1982). For the Tories, see F. O'Gorman, 'Pitt and the "Tory" reaction to the French Revolution, 1789–1815', in Dickinson (ed.), *Britain and the French Revolution* (London, 1979), pp. 21–38, J. McQuiston, 'Rose and Canning in opposition, 1806–7', *HJ*, XIV, No. 3 (September, 1971), 503–28, and J. Severn, 'The Peninsular War and the ministerial crisis of 1812', *CREP*, 1992, 80–94. As for their opponents, J. Derry, 'The opposition Whigs and the French Revolution, 1789–1815', in Dickinson (ed.), *Britain and the French Revolution* (London, 1979), pp. 39–60, R. Willis, 'Fox, Grenville and the recovery of the Opposition', *Journal of British Studies*, XI, No. 2 (May, 1972), 24–43, J. Dinwiddy, 'Charles James Fox and the People', *History*, LV, No. 185 (October, 1970), 342–59, J. Sack,

The Grenvillites (Chicago, 1979), A. Harvey, 'The "Ministry of all the Talents": the Whigs in office, February 1806 to March 1807', *HJ*, XV, No. 4 (December, 1972), 619–48, M. Roberts, *The Whig Party, 1807–1812* (London, 1939), and G. Davies, 'The Whigs and the Peninsular War', *Transactions of the Royal Historical Society* (hereafter, *TRHS*), Fourth Series, IV, (1919), 113–31, are all useful. Extra-parliamentary opposition, meanwhile, is covered by J. Cookson, *The Friends of Peace: Anti-War Liberalism in England, 1793–1815* (Cambridge, 1982), and D. Moss, 'Birmingham and the campaign against the Orders-in-Council and the East-India-Company charter, 1812–13', *CJH*, XI, No. 2 (August, 1976), 173–88. Closely connected with opposition to the war is the subject of political radicalism. A brief introduction to this question is provided by H. T. Dickinson, *British Radicalism in the French Revolution, 1789–1815* (Oxford, 1985), whilst more detailed studies include J. Stevenson, 'Popular radicalism and popular protest, 1789–1815', in Dickinson (ed.), *Britain and the French Revolution* (London, 1979), pp. 61–82, J. A. Hone, *For the Cause of Truth: Radicalism in London, 1796–1821* (Oxford, 1982), N. C. Miller, 'John Cartwright and radical parliamentary reform, 1808–1819', *English Historical Review* (hereafter *EHR*), LXXXIII, No. 329 (October, 1968), 705–28, and J. R. Dinwiddy, 'Sir Francis Burdett and Burdettite radicalism', *History*, LXV, No. 213 (February, 1980), 17–31.

Given the heated controversy over whether or not the Napoleonic Wars witnessed the 'making' of the English working class, the subject of political protest leads us to a discussion of British society and popular unrest. Here D. Low, *That Sunny Dome: a Portrait of Regency Britain* (London, 1977) and H. Perkin, *The Origins of Modern English Society* (London, 1969) are helpful introductions, the subject being specifically related to the impact of the struggle with Napoleon by C. Emsley, *British Society and the French Wars, 1793–1815* (London, 1979), and C. Emsley, 'The social impact of the French Wars', in Dickinson (ed.), *Britain and the French Revolution* (London, 1979), pp. 211–28. For the labouring classes and their reactions to the social and economic developments of the war years, see J. and B. Hammond, *The Skilled Labourer, 1760–1832* (London, 1919), E. Hobsbawm, *Labouring Men* (London, 1964), and, above all, E. P. Thompson, *The Making of the English Working Class* (London, 1963). Social and political unrest in general is reviewed in R. Wells, *Insurrection: the British Experience, 1795–1803* (Gloucester, 1983), J. Bohstedt, *Riots and Community Politics in England and Wales, 1790–1810* (Cambridge,

Massachusetts, 1983), J. Stevenson, *Popular Disturbances in England, 1700–1870* (London, 1979), M. Thomis and P. Holt, *Threats of Revolution in Britain, 1789–1848* (London, 1977), A. W. Smith, 'Irish rebels and English radicals, 1798–1820', *PP*, No. 7 (April, 1955), 78–85, J. Baxter and F. Donnelly, 'Sheffield and the English revolutionary tradition, 1791–1820', *International Review of Social History* (hereafter *IRSH*), XX, No. 3 (Autumn, 1975), 398–423, J. Bohstedt, 'Women in English riots, 1790–1810', *PP*, No. 120 (August, 1988), 88–122, and J. Stevenson, 'Food riots in England, 1792–1818', in J. Stevenson and R. Quinault (eds.), *Popular Protest and Public Order: Six Studies in British History, 1790–1820* (London, 1974), pp. 33–74. For the situation at the time of the outbreak of war, see A. J. Randall, 'The shearmen and the Wiltshire outrages of 1802: trade unionism and industrial violence', *Social History* (hereafter *SH*), VII, No. 3 (October, 1982), 283–304, M. Elliott, 'The "Despard Conspiracy" reconsidered', *PP*, No. 75 (May, 1977), 46–61, J. R. Dinwiddy, 'The "Black Lamp" in Yorkshire, 1801–1802', *PP*, No. 64 (August, 1974), 113–23, J. Baxter and F. Donnelly, 'The revolutionary "underground" in the West Riding: myth or reality?', *PP*, No. 64, (August, 1974), 124–32, and A. Booth, 'The United Englishmen and radical politics in the industrial north-west of England, 1795–1803', *IRSH*, XXXI, No. 3 (Autumn, 1986), 271–97. For the Luddites, meanwhile, see F. Darvall, *Popular Disturbances and Public Order in Regency England* (Oxford, 1934), M. Thomis, *The Luddites: Machine-Breaking in Regency England* (Newton Abbot, 1970), M. Thomis, *Luddism in Nottinghamshire* (London, 1972), F. K. Donnelly, 'Ideology and early English working-class history: Edward Thompson and his critics', *SH*, I, No. 2 (May, 1976), 219–38, and J. Dinwiddy, 'Luddism and politics in the northern counties', *SH*, IV, No. 1 (January, 1979), 33–63.

For the forces of order, meanwhile, see K. Fox, *Making Life Possible: a Study of Military Aid to the Civilian Power in Regency England* (Kineton, 1982), A. Babington, *Military Intervention in Britain from the Gordon Riots to the Gibraltar Incident* (London, 1990), and L. Boyd, *The Role of the Military in Civil Disorders in England and Wales, 1780–1811* (Knoxville, Tennessee, 1977). Meanwhile, some less tangible forces for stability are examined in L. Colley, *Britons: Forging the Nation, 1707–1837* (London, 1994), L. Colley, 'The apotheosis of George III: loyalty, royalty and the British nation, 1760–1820', *PP*, No. 102 (February, 1984), 94–129, L. Colley, 'Whose nation? Class and national consciousness in Britain,

1750–1830', *PP*, No. 113 (November, 1986), 97–117, and W. Stafford, 'Religion and the doctrine of nationalism at the time of the French Revolution and the Napoleonic Wars', in S. Mews (ed.), *Religion and National Identity* (Oxford, 1982), pp. 381–95. For an excellent summary of the 'Church and King' movement, see H. Dickinson, 'Popular conservatism and militant loyalism, 1789–1815', in Dickinson (ed.), *Britain and the French Revolution* (London, 1979), pp. 103–26.

Mention of military intervention in support of the civil power brings us neatly to the subject of the armed forces. Starting at the summit of British military administration, A. H. Burne, *The Noble Duke of York: the Military Life of Frederick, Duke of York and Albany* (London, 1949) does something to redress the unfortunate impression created by a certain nursery rhyme, whilst Britain's two most influential military commanders may be studied in Carola Oman, *Sir John Moore* (London, 1953), P. Guedalla, *The Duke* (London, 1946), E. Longford, *Wellington: the Years of the Sword* (London, 1971), A. Bryant, *The Great Duke* (London, 1971), L. James, *The Iron Duke: a Military Biography of Wellington* (London, 1992) and P. Griffith (ed.), *Wellington-Commander: the Iron Duke's Generalship* (Chichester, 1986). For the army in general, R. Glover, *Peninsular Preparation: the Reform of the British Army, 1795–1802* (Cambridge, 1963), C. Oman, *Wellington's Army, 1809–1814* (London, 1913), G. Davies, *Wellington and his Army* (Oxford, 1954), M. Glover, *Wellington's Army in the Peninsula, 1808–1814* (Newton Abbot, 1977), A. Brett-James, *Life in Wellington's Army* (London, 1972), F. Page, *Following the Drum: Women in Wellington's Wars* (London, 1986), T. McGuffie, 'Recruiting the ranks of the regular British army during the French Wars', *JSAHR*, XXXIV, No. 138 (June, 1956), 50–8, and No. 139 (September, 1956), 123–32, and D. Gates, *The British Light-Infantry Arm, c.1790–1815: its Creation, Training and Operational Role* (London, 1987) between them cover the ground very well. Also helpful on the officer-corps is M. Glover, 'Purchase, patronage and promotion in the British army at the time of the Peninsular War', *Army Quarterly and Defence Journal*, CIII, No. 2 (January, 1973), 211–15 and No. 3 (April, 1973), 355–62. For the numerous auxiliary forces raised by the British, see M. Yaple, 'The auxiliaries: foreign and miscellaneous regiments in the British army, 1802–17', *JSAHR*, L, No. 201 (Spring, 1972), 10–28, G. Tylden, 'Sir Richard Church, K.C.H., and the Greek Light Infantry, 1810 to 1816', *JSAHR*, XLI, No. 167 (September, 1963), 159–61, and R. Buckley, *Slaves in Red Coats:*

the British West-India Regiments, 1795–1815 (New Haven, Connecticut, 1979). On home defence, despite their age, C. Sebag-Montefiore, *A History of the Volunteer Forces* (London, 1908), J. Fortescue, *The County Lieutenancies and the Army, 1803–1814* (London, 1909), and H. Wheeler and A. Broadley, *Napoleon and the Invasion of England* (London, 1908) should all still be consulted, more modern studies being afforded by R. Glover, *Britain at Bay: Defence against Napoleon, 1803–1814* (London, 1973), E. Renn, 'England faces invasion: the land forces, 1803–1805', *CREP*, 1974, 129–40, I. Beckett, 'The militia and the King's enemies, 1793–1815' in A. Guy (ed.), *The Road to Waterloo: the British Army and the Struggle against Revolutionary and Napoleonic France, 1793–1815* (London, 1990), pp. 32–9, C. Emsley, 'The volunteer movement', in Guy, *Road to Waterloo*, pp. 40–7, and, especially, J. Cookson, 'The English volunteer movement of the French Wars, 1793–1815: some contexts', *HJ*, XXXII, No. 4 (December, 1989), 867–92. For the navy, of the infinity of Nelsoniana, perhaps the most useful work is D. Howarth, *Trafalgar: the Nelson Touch* (London, 1969), whilst more general works include G. Marcus, *A Naval History of England, II: the Age of Nelson* (New York, 1971), and C. N. Parkinson, *Britannia Rules: the Classic Age of Naval History, 1793–1815* (London, 1977). As for recruitment and composition, C. Lloyd, *The British Seaman, 1200–1860: a Social Survey* (London, 1968), P. Kemp, *The British Sailor: a Social History of the Lower Deck* (London, 1970), and M. Lewis, *England's Sea Officers: the Story of the Naval Profession* (London, 1939), may be supplemented by the more specific M. Lewis, *A Social History of the Navy, 1793–1815* (London, 1960), D. Pope, *Life in Nelson's Navy* (Annapolis, 1991), C. Emsley, 'The recruitment of petty offenders during the French Wars, 1793–1815', *MM*, LXVI, No. 3 (August, 1980), 199–209, and N. McCord, 'The impress service in north-east England during the Napoleonic Wars', *MM*, LIV, No. 2 (May, 1968), 163–80. Finally, various aspects of naval administration are examined in R. Moriss, *The Royal Dockyards during the Revolutionary and Napoleonic Wars* (Leicester, 1983), R. Moriss, 'Labour relations in the royal dockyards, 1801–1805', *MM*, LXII, No. 4 (November, 1976), 337–46, P. Webb, 'Construction, repair and maintenance in the battle fleet of the Royal Navy, 1793–1815', in Black and Woodfine, *British Navy*, 207–20, and P. Crimmin, 'Admiralty relations with the Treasury, 1783–1806: the preparation of naval estimates and the beginnings of Treasury control', *MM*, LIII, No. 1 (February, 1967), 63–74.

Seapower was vital to the well-being of British trade – indeed, the connection is made explicit in A. Ryan, 'The defence of British trade with the Baltic', *EHR*, LXXIV, No. 292 (July, 1959), 443–66, and P. Crimmin, 'The Royal Navy and the Levant trade, *c*.1795–*c*.1805', in Black and Woodfine, *British Navy*, pp. 221–36 – and trade in turn was vital to the British war effort. Here the student should begin with C. N. Parkinson, *The Trade Winds: a Study of British Overseas Trade during the French Wars, 1793–1815* (London, 1948), and then turn to the various specialised monographs in existence on the subject. These include A. Ryan, 'Trade with the enemy in the Scandinavian and Baltic ports during the Napoleonic War: for and against', *TRHS*, Fifth Series, XII (1962), 123–40, D. C. M. Platt, *Latin America and British Trade, 1806–1914* (London, 1972), M. Edwards, *The Growth of the British Cotton Trade, 1780–1815* (Manchester, 1967), D. Goebel, 'British trade to the Spanish colonies, 1796–1823', *AHR*, XLIII, No. 2 (January, 1938), 288–320, J. Frankel, 'The 1807–1809 embargo against Great Britain', *JEH*, XLII, No. 2 (June, 1982), 291–308, and J. H. Rose, 'British West-India commerce as a factor in the Napoleonic Wars', *CHJ*, II, No. 1 (1929), 34–46. For the supply of food, meanwhile, see W. Galpin, *The Grain Supply of England during the Napoleonic Period* (New York, 1925), and M. Olson, *The Economics of Wartime Shortage: a History of British Food Supplies in the Napoleonic Wars and World Wars One and Two* (Durham, North Carolina, 1963).

For the general economic context of the French wars in Britain, the student is referred to C. More, *The Industrial Age: Economy and Society in Britain, 1750–1855* (London, 1989), A. Gayer, W. Rostow and A. Schwartz, *The Growth and Fluctuation of the British Economy, 1790–1850* (Oxford, 1953), W. Court, *A Concise Economic History of Britain from 1750 to Recent Times* (Cambridge, 1962), and N. Crafts, *British Economic Growth during the Industrial Revolution* (Oxford, 1985). More specific studies of the impact of the wars may be found in F. Crouzet, 'The impact of the French Wars on the British economy', in Dickinson, *Britain and the French Revolution*, pp. 189–210, P. Deane, 'War and industrialization', in Winter, *War and Economic Development*, pp. 91–102, and G. Hueckel, 'War and the British economy, 1793–1815: a general equilibrium analysis', *Explorations in Economic History* (hereafter, *EEH*), X, No. 4 (Summer, 1973), 365–96. Finally, agricultural issues are explored in G. Hueckel, 'Relative prices and supply response in English agriculture during the

Napoleonic Wars', *EcHR*, XXXIX, No. 3 (August, 1976), 401–14, G. Hueckel, 'English farming profits during the Napoleonic Wars, 1793–1815', *EEH*, XIII, No. 3 (July, 1976), 331–46, A. John, 'Farming in wartime, 1793–1815', in E. Jones and G. Mingay, (eds.), *Land, Labour and Population in the Industrial Revolution* (London, 1967), pp. 28–47, and D. Thomas, *Agriculture in Wales during the Napoleonic Wars: a Study in the Geographical Interpretation of the Historical Sources* (Cardiff, 1963).

Finally, we come to the vital issue of finance. A good introduction here is P. O'Brien, 'Public finance in the wars with France, 1793–1815', in Dickinson, *Britain and the French Revolution*, pp. 165–88, which should be used to supplement the older A. Cunningham and J. Lasalle, *British Credit in the Last Napoleonic War* (Cambridge, 1910). For greater detail on certain aspects of the subject, see A. Hope Jones, *Income Tax and the Napoleonic Wars* (Cambridge, 1939), and S. Cope, *The Goldsmids and the development of the London money market during the Napoleonic Wars* (London, 1942).

THE EUROPEAN GREAT POWERS

Of Napoleon's Continental opponents, the least studied by far has been Austria, although the period is covered by several general surveys, *viz.* C. A. Macartney, *The Habsburg Empire, 1790–1918* (London, 1969), V. Tapié, *The Rise and Fall of the Habsburg Monarchy* (London, 1971), R. A. Kann, *A History of the Habsburg Empire, 1526–1918* (Los Angeles, 1974), and C. W. Ingrao, *The Habsburg Monarchy, 1618–1815* (Cambridge, 1994). Foreign policy may be approached via K. Roider, *Baron Thugut and Austria's Response to the French Revolution* (Princeton, 1987), E. Kraehe, *Napoleon's German Policy, I: the Contest with Napoleon* (Princeton, 1963), A. Palmer, *Metternich: Councillor of Europe* (London, 1972), C. de Grunwald, *Metternich* (London, 1953), and C. Buckland, *Metternich and the British Government from 1809 to 1813* (London, 1932), matters military being dealt with in G. Rothenberg, *Napoleon's Great Adversaries: the Archduke Charles and the Austrian Army, 1792–1814* (London, 1982), G. Rothenberg, 'The Archduke Charles and the question of popular participation in war', *CREP*, 1982, 214–24, G. Rothenberg, *The Military Border in Croatia: a Study of an Imperial Institution* (Chicago, 1966), and L. Sondhaus, *The Habsburg Empire and the Sea: Austrian Naval Policy, 1797–1866* (West Lafayette, Indiana, 1989). For more general discussions of internal reform, see K. Roider, 'The Habsburg foreign ministry and political reform, 1801–1805', *CEH*, XXII, No. 2 (June, 1989), 160–82, J. A. Vann, 'Habsburg policy and the Austrian war of 1809', *CEH*, VII, No. 4 (December, 1974), 291–310, and W. C. Langsam, *The Napoleonic Wars and German Nationalism in Austria* (New York, 1930), though some of the latter's judgements are clearly dated. For the Tyrolean revolt, see L. Harford, 'Napoleon and the subjugation of the Tyrol', *CREP*, 1989 (Bicentennial Consortium), 704–11, and F. G. Eyck, *Loyal Rebels: Andreas Hofer and the Tyrolean Uprising of 1809* (New York, 1986), whilst more general views of the war of 1809 may be found in J. R. Arnold, *Crisis on the Danube: Napoleon's Austrian Campaign of 1809* (London, 1990), F. L. Petre, *Napoleon and the Archduke Charles: a History of the Franco-Austrian Campaign in the Valley of the Danube in 1809* (London, 1909), and G. Bond, *The Grand Expedition: the British Invasion of Holland in 1809* (Athens, Georgia, 1979). Finally, the impact of French ideas on some of the empire's constituent peoples may be approached via B. Király, 'Napoleon's proclamation of 1809 and its Hungarian echo', in S. Winters and J. Held (eds.), *Intellectual and Social Developments in the Habsburg Empire from Maria Theresa to World War I* (New York, 1975), pp. 31–54, G. Heltai, 'Colonel Lacuée, Lezay-Marnesia and the last Hungarian levée en masse', *CREP*, 1983, 156–67, J. Zacek, 'The French Revolution, Napoleon and the Czechs, *CREP*, 1980, I, 254–63, J. Zacek, 'Contemporary Czech popular sentiment toward the French Revolution and Napoleon', *CREP*, 1989 (Bicentennial Consortium), 592–9, and S. Musulin, *Vienna in the Age of Metternich: from Napoleon to Revolution, 1805–1848* (London, 1975).

On Prussia, by contrast, the literature is extensive, at least with regard to the reform movement. As a starting point, the cataclysm of 1806 is covered by F. L. Petre, *Napoleon's Conquest of Prussia, 1806* (London, 1914). Equally elderly but still useful, if only in the latter case as an introduction to patriotic Prussian myth-making, are J. R. Seeley, *Life and Times of Stein* (Cambridge, 1878) and the first volume of H. von Treitschke, *History of Germany in the Nineteenth Century* (London, 1915). More scholarly analyses of the role of nationalism may be found in W. M. Simon, 'Variations in nationalism during the great reform period in Prussia', *AHR*, LIX, No. 2 (January, 1954), 305–21, and E. N. Anderson, *Nationalism and the Cultural crisis in Prussia, 1806–1815* (New York, 1939), whilst the reforms themselves are examined in G. S. Ford, *Stein and the Era of Reform in Prussia, 1807–1815* (Princeton, 1922), W. M. Simon, *The Failure of the Prussian Reform Movement, 1807–1819* (New York, 1971), M. Gray, *Prussia in Transition: Society and Politics under the Stein Reform Ministry of 1808* (Philadelphia, 1986), M. Gray, 'Schroetter, Schön and society: aristocratic liberalism versus middle-class liberalism in Prussia, 1808', *CEH*, VI, No. 1 (March, 1973), 60–82, and M. Gray, 'Bureaucratic transition and accommodation of the aristocracy in the Prussian reform year of 1808', *CREP*, 1981, 86–92, and the important figure of Humboldt in P. R. Sweet, *Wilhelm von Humboldt, a Biography, II: 1808–1835* (Columbus, Ohio, 1980). Meanwhile, R. Berdahl, *The Politics of the Prussian Nobility: the Development of a Conservative Ideology, 1770–1848* (Princeton, 1988), and F. L. Carsten, *A History of the Prussian Junkers* (Aldershot, 1989), examine the reforms' social context. C. E. White, *The Enlightened Soldier: Scharnhorst and the Militärische Gesellschaft in Berlin, 1801–1805* (New York, 1989), W. Shanahan, *Prussian Military Reforms, 1786–1813* (New York, 1945), P. Paret, *Yorck and the Era of Prussian Reform, 1807–1815* (Princeton, 1966), and P. Paret, *Clausewitz and the State* (Oxford, 1976) all cover the military aspects of the reforms, there also being significant chapters on this subject in G. A. Craig, *The Politics of the Prussian Army, 1640–1945* (Oxford, 1955), G. Ritter, *The Sword and the Sceptre: the Problem of Militarism in Germany* (London, 1972), and J. Ellis, *Armies in Revolution* (London, 1973). Also helpful in this respect are R. Parkinson, *Clausewitz: a Biography* (London, 1971), M. Howard, *Clausewitz* (Oxford, 1983), and P. Paret, 'Education, politics and war in the life of Clausewitz', *JHI*, XXIX, No. 3 (July, 1968), 394–408. More specific in their approach are D. Showalter, 'Manifestation of reform: the rearmament of the Prussian infantry, 1806–1813', *JMH*, XLIV, No. 4 (September, 1972), 364–80 and D. Showalter, 'The Prussian *landwehr* and its critics, 1813–1819, *CEH*, IV, No. 1 (March, 1971), 3–33, the latter picking up on themes which are also revealed by R. C. Raack, *The Fall of Stein* (Cambridge, Massachusetts, 1965), and G. A. Craig, 'The failure of reform: Stein and Marwitz', in G. A. Craig (ed.), *The End of Prussia* (Madison, Wisconsin, 1984), pp. 8–26.

By contrast, Russia has received comparatively little attention. Beginning with narrative histories, H. Seton Watson, *The Russian Empire, 1801–1917* (Oxford, 1967), E. Thaden, *Russia since 1801: the Making of a New Society* (New York, 1971), and D. Saunders, *Russia in the Age of Reaction and Reform, 1801–1881* (London,

1992), all have reasonably full sections on the Napoleonic period. However, A. Palmer, *Russia in War and Peace* (London, 1972) is the only general overview to make it its central focus. Foreign policy is covered in A. Lobanov Rostovsky, *Russia and Europe, 1789–1825* (Durham, North Carolina, 1947), P. K. Grimsted, *The Foreign Ministers of Alexander I: Political Attitudes and the Conduct of Russian Foreign Policy, 1801–1825* (Los Angeles, 1969), N. Saul, *Russia and the Mediterranean, 1797–1807* (Chicago, 1970), H. Ragsdale, 'A continental system in 1801: Paul I and Bonaparte', *JMH*, XLII, No. 1 (March, 1970), 70–89, H. Ragsdale, 'Russian influence at Lunéville', *FHS*, V, No. 3 (Spring, 1968), 274–84, W. H. Zawadzki, 'Prince Adam Czartorysky and Napoleonic France, 1801–1805: a study in political attitudes', *HJ*, XVIII, No. 2 (July, 1975), 245–77, C. Morley, 'Alexander I and Czartorysky: the Polish question from 1801 to 1813', *Slavonic and East European Review* (hereafter, *SEER*), XXV, No. 65 (April, 1947), 405–26, and W. H. Zawadzki, 'Russia and the reopening of the Polish question, 1801–1814', *IHR*, VII, No. 1 (February, 1985), 19–44. There is also much of interest in M. Kukiel, *Czartorysky and European Unity, 1770–1861* (Ithaca, New York, 1955) and W. H. Zawadzki, *A Man of Honour: Adam Czartorysky as a Statesman of Russia and Poland, 1795–1831* (Oxford, 1993). The army, meanwhile, is dealt with by J. Keep, *Soldiers of the Tsar: Army and Society in Russia, 1462–1874* (Oxford, 1985), J. Keep, 'The Russian army's response to the French Revolution', *CREP*, 1980, I, 231–6, and R. Pipes, 'The Russian military colonies, 1810–1831', *JMH*, XXII, No. 3 (1950), 205–19, two key generals being covered by M. Jenkins, *Arakcheev: Grand Vizier of the Russian Empire* (London, 1969), and M. Josselson, *The Commander: a Life of Barclay de Tolly* (Oxford, 1980). Otherwise, with the exception of R. S. Wortman, 'Images of rule and problems of gender in the upbringing of Paul I and Alexander I', in E. Mendelsohn and M. Shatz (eds.), *Imperial Russia, 1700–1917: Essays in Honour of Marc Raeff* (DeKalb, Illinois, 1988), the literature is best divided in terms of reigns. For Paul I, see R. McGrew, *Paul I of Russia, 1754–1801* (Oxford, 1992), H. Ragsdale, 'The case of Paul I of Russia: an approach to psycho-biography', *CREP*, 1989, II, 617–24, and H. Ragsdale (ed.), *Paul I: a Reassessment of his Life and Reign* (Pittsburgh, 1979), and, for Alexander I, J. Hartley, *Alexander I* (London, 1994), M. Dziewanowski, *Alexander I: Russia's Mysterious Tsar* (New York, 1990), A. McConnel, *Alexander I: Paternalistic Reformer* (Arlington Heights, Illinois, 1970), A. Palmer, *Alexander I, Tsar of War and*

Peace (London, 1974), and L. I. Strakhovsky, *Alexander I of Russia: the Man who Defeated Napoleon* (London, 1949). Administrative and political affairs in the period of the Unofficial Committee are covered by E. E. Roach, 'The origins of Alexander I's Unofficial Committee', *Russian Review* (hereafter *RR*), XXVIII, No. 3 (July, 1969), 315–26, D. Christian, 'The senatorial party and the theory of collegial government, 1801–1803', *RR*, XXXVIII, No. 3 (July, 1979), 298–322 (an important piece that significantly revises previous views on this subject), and O. Narkiewicz, 'Alexander I and Senate reform', *SEER*, XLVII, No. 1 (January, 1969), 115–36. For Speransky, by contrast, see M. Raeff, *Michael Speransky, Statesman of Imperial Russia, 1772–1839* (The Hague, 1957), D. Christian, 'The political deals of Michael Speransky', *SEER*, LIV, No. 2 (April, 1976), 192–213, and J. Gooding, 'The liberalism of Michael Speransky', *SEER*, LXIV, No. 3 (July, 1986), 401–24.

THE PERIPHERY: SICILY, SCANDINAVIA AND
SOUTHEASTERN EUROPE

For Sicily, and, indeed, Bourbon Naples, H. Acton, *The Bourbons of Naples* (London, 1956) is an obvious source, but its focus on the personalities of the court is old-fashioned and unhelpful. Much more useful here are D. Mack Smith, *Modern Sicily after 1713* (London, 1968), D. Gregory, *Sicily, the Insecure Base: a History of the British Occupation of Sicily, 1806–1815* (Rutherford, New Jersey, 1988), J. H. Roselli, *Lord William Bentinck: the Making of a Liberal Imperialist, 1774–1839* (London, 1974), and J. H. Roselli, *Lord William Bentinck and the British Occupation of Sicily, 1811–1814* (Cambridge, 1956).

With regard to Scandinavia, such attention as has been paid the region by English-language historians has largely been confined to Sweden, with the exception of T. Derry, *A History of Scandinavia* (London, 1979), T. Derry, *A Short History of Norway* (London, 1957), S. Oakley, *The Story of Denmark* (London, 1972), and R. Ruppenthal, 'Denmark and the Continental System', *JMH*, XV, No. 1 (March, 1943), 7–23. For Sweden, the most useful general histories are F. Scott, *Sweden: the Nation's History* (Minneapolis, 1977) and I. Andersson, *A History of Sweden* (London, 1955), whilst these may usefully be supplemented with H. Barton, 'Late Gustavian autocracy in Sweden: Gustav IV Adolf and his opponents, 1792–1809', *Scandinavian Studies*, XLVI, No. 3 (Summer, 1974), 265–84, H. Barton, 'Sweden and the Atlantic Revolution, 1760–

1815', *CREP*, 1982, 145–58, and R. Carr, 'Gustavus IV and the British government, 1804–9', *EHR*, LX, No. 1 (January, 1945), 36–46. For Marshal Bernadotte as crown prince, see A. Palmer, *Bernadotte: Napoleon's Marshal, Sweden's King* (London, 1990).

Less directly affected by the Napoleonic Wars, but still highly influenced by them, south-eastern Europe is another area which merits further study. For a general overview, B. Jelavich, *History of the Balkans, I: Eighteenth and Nineteenth Centuries* (Cambridge, 1983) is an essential starting point. For the Ottomans, see S. Shaw, *History of the Ottoman Empire and Modern Turkey* (Cambridge, 1976–7), J. Kinross, *The Ottoman Centuries: the Rise and Fall of the Turkish Empire* (London, 1977), S. Shaw, *Between Old and New: the Ottoman Empire under Sultan Selim III, 1789–1807* (Cambridge, Massachusetts, 1971), S. Shaw, 'The origins of Balkan military reform: the Nizam-i-Cedid army of Sultan Selim III', *JMH*, XXXVII, No. 3 (September, 1965), 290–305, and W. Johnson and C. Bell, *The Ottoman Empire and the Napoleonic Wars* (Leeds, 1988). For general treatments of the subject nationalities, R. Seton Watson, *The Rise of Nationality in the Balkans* (London, 1917), L. Stavrianos, 'Antecedents to the Balkan revolutions of the nineteenth century', *JMH*, XXIX, No. 4 (December, 1957), 290–305, D. Djordjevic and S. Fischer Galati, *The Balkan Revolutionary Tradition* (New York, 1981), P. Kitromilides, 'Republican aspirations in south-eastern Europe in the age of the French Revolution', *CREP*, 1980, I, 275–85, and A. Haas, 'The impact of the French Revolution on central and southeastern Europe: some thoughts, comments and comparisons', *CREP*, 1980, I, 286–91, are all helpful. As to the individual peoples, most attention has been paid to the Greeks. Here, R. Clogg, *A Short History of Modern Greece* (Cambridge, 1979), D. Dakin, *The Unification of Greece, 1770–1923* (London, 1972), E. Kefallineou, 'The myth of Napoleon in modern Greek literature and historiography, 1797–1850', *CREP*, 1991, 106–15, and K. Hatzopoulos, 'Greek volunteers from Wallachia in the Chasseurs de l'Orient during the campaign of the French army in Dalmatia (1808–1809)', *Balkan Studies*, XXIV, No. 2 (n.d., 1983), 425–35, together provide a mass of information. Other peoples are less well served, but W. Vucinich (ed.), *The First Serbian Uprising, 1804–1813* (Boulder, Colorado, 1982) is a much needed supplement to the badly dated H. Temperley, *History of Serbia* (London, 1917), whilst R. Forrest, 'The Rumanians and the French Revolution', *CREP*, 1989, I, 486–500, and R. Forrest, 'Rumour into myth: the image of Napoleon among the Rumanians',

CREP, 1991, 98–105, together constitute a useful introduction to the Danubian provinces, and, indeed, to Habsburg Transylvania.

THE DOWNFALL OF NAPOLEON AND THE RESTORATION SETTLEMENT

The disintegration of the Napoleonic empire may clearly be dated from the disastrous campaign of 1812, general studies of this affair including C. Cate, *The War of the Two Emperors: the Duel between Napoleon and Alexander, Russia, 1812* (New York, 1985), C. Duffy, *Borodino and the War of 1812*, (London, 1973), R. Riehn, *1812: Napoleon's Russian Campaign* (New York, 1991), and E. Tarle, *Napoleon's Invasion of Russia, 1812* (London, 1942). Meanwhile, A. Brett James (ed.), *1812: Eyewitness Accounts of Napoleon's Invasion of Russia* (London, 1966) contains much that is helpful, whilst useful comment may be found in I. Collins, 'Variations on the theme of Napoleon's Moscow campaign', *History*, LXXXI, No. 231 (February, 1976), 39–53, P. Henry, 'Clausewitz and the campaign of 1812 in Russia', *CREP*, 1989 (Bicentennial Consortium), 298–307, B. Hollingsworth, 'The Napoleonic invasion of Russia and recent Soviet historical writing', *JMH*, XXXVIII, No. 1 (March, 1966), 38–52, G. Nafziger, 'Logistics in the 1812 campaign: the cause of Napoleon's defeat', *CREP*, 1989 (Bicentennial Consortium), 308–15, and H. Schmitt, '1812: Stein, Alexander I and the campaign against Napoleon', *JMH*, XXXI, No. 4 (December, 1959), 325–8. Far less attention has been paid to the events of 1813 and 1814, but for the former see F. L. Petre, *Napoleon's Last Campaign in Germany, 1813* (London, 1912), A. Dorpalen, 'The German struggle against Napoleon: the East-German view', *JMH*, XLI, No. 4 (December, 1969), 485–516, G. Nafziger, 'Cossack operations in western Germany, spring 1813', *CREP*, 1992, 374–82, and A. Brett-James (ed.), *Europe against Napoleon: the Leipzig Campaign, 1813, from Eyewitness Accounts* (London, 1970). Meanwhile, aspects of the collapse of imperial rule in France are described in F. L. Petre, *Napoleon at Bay, 1814*, (London, 1914), J. Bury, 'The end of the Napoleonic Senate', *CHJ*, IX, No. 2 (1948), 165–89, and P. Mansel, 'How forgotten were the Bourbons in France between 1812 and 1814?', *ESR*, XIII, No. 1 (January, 1983), 13–38, whilst the end of the Kingdom of Italy is addressed by R. Rath, *The Fall of the Napoleonic Kingdom of Italy* (New York, 1941), F. Schneid, 'Eugene and the defence of Italy, 1813', *CREP*, 1991, 171–81, and E. Gum, 'Eugene de Beauharnais and an affair of honour', *CREP*, 1974, 154–62. Finally, E. Gillick, *Europe's Classic Balance of Power: a Case History of the Theory and Practice of One of the Great Concepts of European Statecraft* (Ithaca, New York, 1955) is a general study of European diplomacy in the period 1813–15, narrower foci being provided by G. Renier, *Great Britain and the Establishment of the Kingdom of the Netherlands, 1813–1815* (London, 1930), J. Horgan, 'Restoration of the Bourbon monarchy, 1813–1814: a matter of great-power self-interest', *CREP*, 1991, 43–55, P. Schroeder, 'An unnatural "natural alliance": Castlereagh, Metternich and Aberdeen in 1813', *IHR*, X, No. 4 (November, 1988), 522–40, J. H. Rose, 'Austria and the downfall of Napoleon', in J. H. Rose (ed.), *Napoleonic Studies* (London, 1904), pp. 243–74, and P. Mansel, 'Wellington and the French restoration', *IHR*, XI, No. 1, (London, February, 1989), 76–83 (though the student is, of course, also urged to refer to such already-cited works as Webster, *Foreign Policy of Castlereagh*, and Kraehe, *Metternich's German Policy*). For the activities of two key figures, in particular, see F. D. Scott, *Bernadotte and the Fall of Napoleon* (Cambridge, Massachusetts, 1935), F. D. Scott, 'Bernadotte and the throne of France, 1814', *JMH*, V, No. 4 (December, 1933), 465–78, and M. Chamberlain, *Lord Aberdeen: a Political Biography* (London, 1983).

With Napoleon overthrown, attention shifted to the peace conference at Vienna, of which there are three good studies in English. C. Webster, *The Congress of Vienna* (London, 1919) remains a basic text despite its age and obvious patriotic bias, but it should be supplemented by H. Nicholson, *The Congress of Vienna: a Study in Allied Unity, 1812–1822* (London, 1946), and, especially, E. Kraehe, *Metternich's German Policy, II: the Congress of Vienna, 1814–1815* (Princeton, 1983). Last but not least, the role of the duke of Wellington is discussed in R. Muir, 'From soldier to statesman: Wellington in Paris and Vienna, 1814–15', in Guy, *Road to Waterloo*, pp. 155–63. Whilst Wellington and his counterparts were conducting their discussions in Vienna, Napoleon, of course, was in exile on the island of Elba, his doings there, together with his escape, being covered by N. Mackenzie, *The Escape from Elba: the Fall and Flight of Napoleon, 1814–1815* (Oxford, 1982). Studies of the climactic struggle to which this event gave rise are probably more numerous than that of all the other campaigns of the Napoleonic Wars put together. For developments in France, see H. Kurtz, 'Napoleon in 1815: the second reign', *HT*, XV, No. 10 (October, 1965), 673–87, R. Alexander, *Bonapartism and*

Revolutionary Tradition in France: the Fédérés of 1815 (Cambridge, 1991), R. Alexander, 'The *fédérés* of Dijon in 1815', *HJ*, XXX, No. 2 (June, 1987), 367–90, and, especially, A. Schom, *One Hundred Days: Napoleon's Road to Waterloo* (London, 1993), the response of the Allies being addressed in E. Kraehe, 'Wellington and the reconstruction of the Allied armies during the Hundred Days', *IHR*, XI, No. 1 (February, 1989), 84–97. As for Waterloo itself, modern accounts include A. Brett-James, *The Hundred Days: Napoleon's Last Campaign from Eyewitness Accounts* (London, 1965), C. Hibbert, *Waterloo: Napoleon's Last Campaign* (London, 1967), J. Weller, *Wellington at Waterloo* (London, 1967), D. Howarth, *A Near-Run Thing: the Day of Waterloo* (London, 1968), and A. Chalfont (ed.), *Waterloo: Battle of the Three Armies* (London, 1979). With Waterloo fought, Napoleon was finished, the aftermath of his defeat being detailed in J. Gallaher, 'Marshal Davout and the second Bourbon restoration', *FHS*, VI, No. 3 (Spring, 1970), 350–64, and G. Lewis, 'The white terror of 1815 in the Department of the Gard: counter-revolution, continuity and the individual', *PP*, No. 58 (February, 1973), 108–35. For the emperor himself, of course, no options were left, and it is perhaps fitting that the last item in this essay should be G. Martineau, *Napoleon Surrenders* (London, 1971).

MAPS

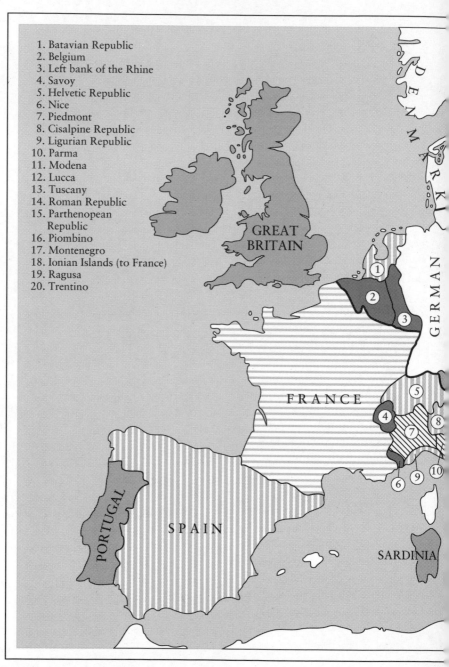

1. Batavian Republic
2. Belgium
3. Left bank of the Rhine
4. Savoy
5. Helvetic Republic
6. Nice
7. Piedmont
8. Cisalpine Republic
9. Ligurian Republic
10. Parma
11. Modena
12. Lucca
13. Tuscany
14. Roman Republic
15. Parthenopean Republic
16. Piombino
17. Montenegro
18. Ionian Islands (to France)
19. Ragusa
20. Trentino

1. Europe, January 1799

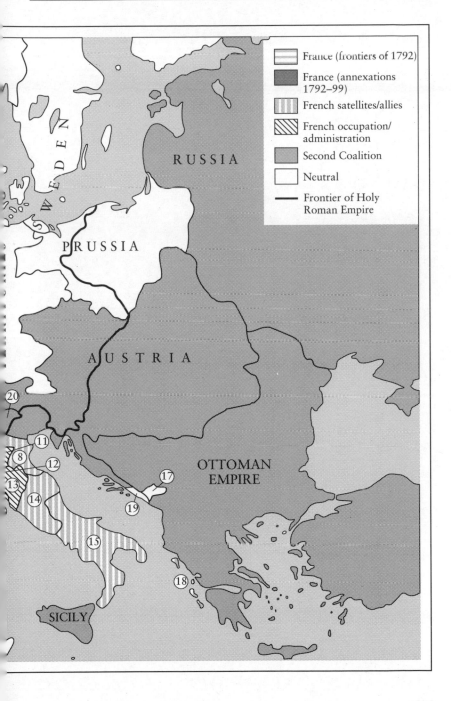

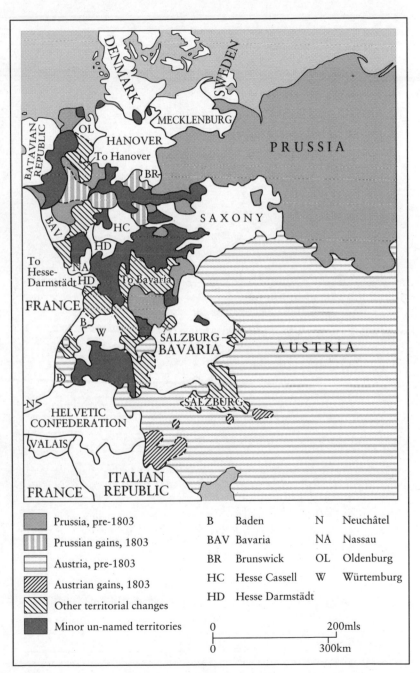

Prussia, pre-1803

Prussian gains, 1803

Austria, pre-1803

Austrian gains, 1803

Other territorial changes

Minor un-named territories

B	Baden	N	Neuchâtel
BAV	Bavaria	NA	Nassau
BR	Brunswick	OL	Oldenburg
HC	Hesse Cassell	W	Würtemburg
HD	Hesse Darmstädt		

0   200mls

0   300km

2. Napoleon's Re-organization of Germany, 1803

1. Hanover/Oldenburg, etc.
2. Batavian Republic
3. Neuchâtel
4. Helvetic Confederation
5. Republic of the Valais
6. Piedmont
7. Ligurian Republic
8. Parma
9. Italian Republic (showing
   territory gained since 1799)
10. Kingdom of Etruria
11. Papal States
12. Montenegro
13. Ionian Islands
14. Piombino
    (French occupied)
15. Lucca
16. Ragusa

3. Europe, July 1803

1. Holland
2. Minor German territories excluded from Confederation of the Rhine
3. Bayreuth
4. Neuchâtel
5. Helvetic Confederation
6. Republic of the Valais
7. Kingdom of Italy
8. Parma
9. Ligurian Republic
10. Lucca
11. Piombino
12. Kingdom of Etruria
13. Papal States
14. Istria/Dalmatia
15. Ragusa
16. Montenegro
17. Tyrol/Vorarlberg (to Bavaria 1805)
18. Venetia (to Kingdom of Italy 1805)
19. Hanover (to Prussia 1806)
20. Hamburg
21. Salzburg (to Austria 1805)

4. Europe, September 1806

France (frontiers of 1803)

France (annexations 1803–6)

French occupation/ administration

French satellites/allies

Fourth Coalition

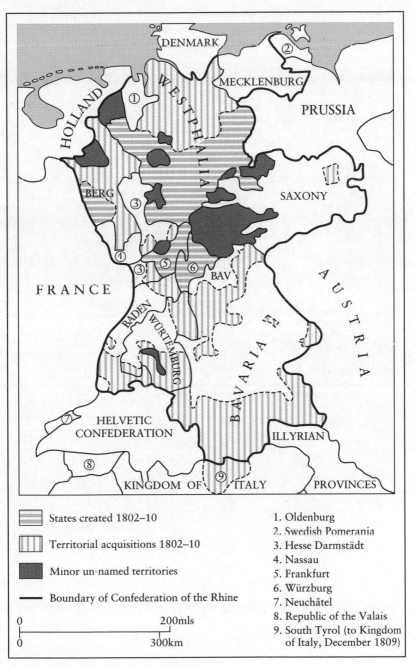

States created 1802–10

Territorial acquisitions 1802–10

Minor un-named territories

Boundary of Confederation of the Rhine

0   200mls
0   300km

1. Oldenburg
2. Swedish Pomerania
3. Hesse Darmstädt
4. Nassau
5. Frankfurt
6. Würzburg
7. Neuchâtel
8. Republic of the Valais
9. South Tyrol (to Kingdom of Italy, December 1809)

5. Central Europe, September 1809

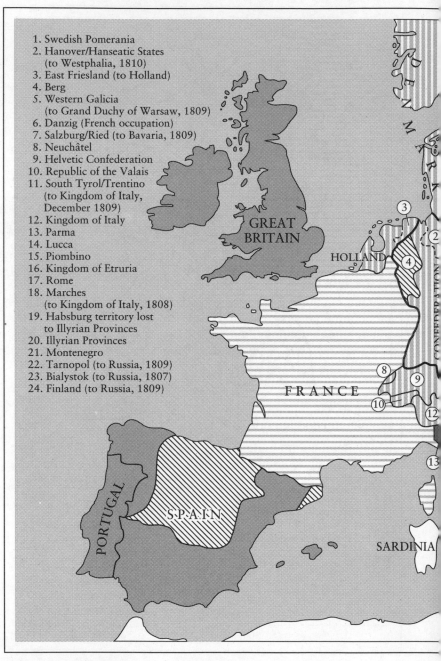

1. Swedish Pomerania
2. Hanover/Hanseatic States
   (to Westphalia, 1810)
3. East Friesland (to Holland)
4. Berg
5. Western Galicia
   (to Grand Duchy of Warsaw, 1809)
6. Danzig (French occupation)
7. Salzburg/Ried (to Bavaria, 1809)
8. Neuchâtel
9. Helvetic Confederation
10. Republic of the Valais
11. South Tyrol/Trentino
    (to Kingdom of Italy,
    December 1809)
12. Kingdom of Italy
13. Parma
14. Lucca
15. Piombino
16. Kingdom of Etruria
17. Rome
18. Marches
    (to Kingdom of Italy, 1808)
19. Habsburg territory lost
    to Illyrian Provinces
20. Illyrian Provinces
21. Montenegro
22. Tarnopol (to Russia, 1809)
23. Bialystok (to Russia, 1807)
24. Finland (to Russia, 1809)

6. Europe, March 1810

1. Holland
2. Berg (part)
3. Oldenburg
4. Hanseatic States and Hanover (part)
5. Danzig (French occupation)
6. Berg
7. Neuchâtel
8. Helvetic Confederation
9. Republic of the Valais
10. Kingdom of Italy
11. Lucca
12. Piombino
13. Illyrian Provinces
14. Montenegro
15. Bessarabia
    (to Russia, 1812)
16. Catalonia

7. Europe, May 1812

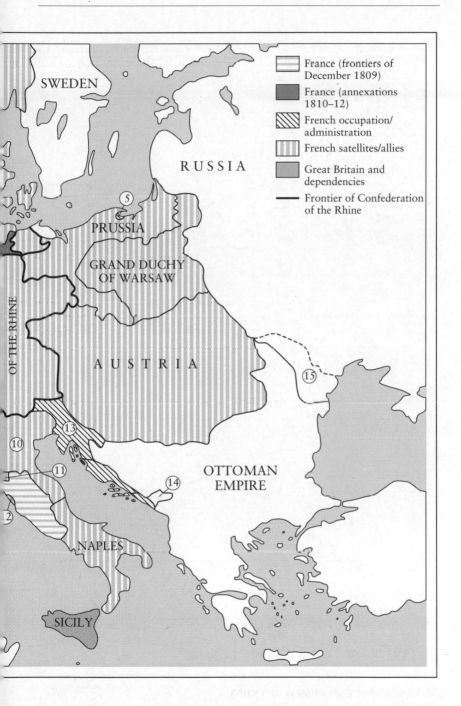

SWEDEN

RUSSIA

PRUSSIA

GRAND DUCHY
OF WARSAW

AUSTRIA

OTTOMAN
EMPIRE

NAPLES

SICILY

OF THE RHINE

France (frontiers of
December 1809)

France (annexations
1810–12)

French occupation/
administration

French satellites/allies

Great Britain and
dependencies

Frontier of Confederation
of the Rhine

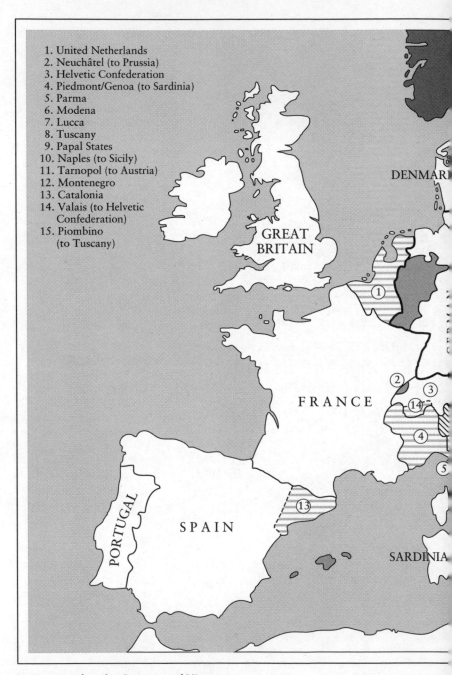

1. United Netherlands
2. Neuchâtel (to Prussia)
3. Helvetic Confederation
4. Piedmont/Genoa (to Sardinia)
5. Parma
6. Modena
7. Lucca
8. Tuscany
9. Papal States
10. Naples (to Sicily)
11. Tarnopol (to Austria)
12. Montenegro
13. Catalonia
14. Valais (to Helvetic
    Confederation)
15. Piombino
    (to Tuscany)

8. Europe after the Congress of Vienna

Territorial restorations
and acquisitions

- ▨ Prussia
- ▨ Austria
- ▨ Russia
- ▨ Sweden
- ▨ Other
- ── Frontier of German
  Confederation

SWEDEN

RUSSIA

PRUSSIA

CONGRESS
POLAND

⑪

AUSTRIA

OTTOMAN
EMPIRE

⑥ ⑦
⑧
⑨
⑮
⑫
⑩

SICILY

Index